MW00875583

SQL Interoperability Joes 2 Pros

SQL 2008 Techniques with XML, C#, and PowerShell
(SQL Exam Prep Series 70-433 Volume 5 of 5)

By
Rick A. Morelan
MCDBA, MCTS, MCITP, MCAD, MOE, MCSE, MCSE+I

ISBN: 1-4515-7950-0
EAN: 978-1451579505

Rick A. Morelan
RMorelan@live.com

Table of Contents

About the Author

In 1994, you could find Rick Morelan braving the frigid waters of the Bering Sea as an Alaska commercial fisherman. His computer skills were non-existent at the time, so you might figure such beginnings seemed unlikely to lead him down the path to SQL Server expertise at Microsoft. However, every computer expert in the world today woke up at some point in their life knowing nothing about computers. They say luck is what happens when preparation meets opportunity. In the case of Rick Morelan, people were a big part of his good luck.

Making the change from fisherman seemed scary and took daily schooling at Catapult Software Training Institute. Rick got his lucky break in August 1995, working his first database job at Microsoft. Since that time, Rick has worked more than 10 years at Microsoft and has attained over 30 Microsoft technical certifications in applications, networking, databases and .NET development.

Acknowledgements

As a book with a supporting web site, illustrations, media content, and software scripts, it takes more than the usual author, illustrator, and editor to put everything together into a great learning experience. Since my publisher has the more traditional contributor list available, I'd like to recognize the core team members:

Editor: Jessica Brown
Cover Illustration: Jungim Jang
Technical Review: Vinay Chopra, Joel Heidal, Pinal Dave
Software Design Testing: Irina Berger, Simon Nicholson
User Acceptance Testing: Michael McLean
Website & Digital Marketing: Gaurav Singhal

This experience has taught me that extraordinary talents are in people everywhere around us. For every need we've encountered, talented and motivated people have come out of the woodwork and showed up at just the right moment to support this effort.

Jessica Brown started out as my student in 2008 and her passion to help put accessible, user-friendly SQL education in the hands of students is a great gift to the *Joes 2 Pros* book series. She sees the good in everyone and every situation, and what I can say in one paragraph would only be a fraction of her value to these books.

Simon Nicholson has done so much for this book to support *Joes 2 Pros*. Perhaps the most important contributor who I have yet to meet in real life. I am so glad to have found Simon early on in the creation of the last two books.

Before this book started, I would have described Irina Berger as a dedicated successful graduate of my SQL class from years ago. She is an MCTS in SQL 2005 and a software designer. Today I can also tell you she uses her great understanding of technology at a project level. She made many suggestions that really raised the level of this book. With the use of a Windows Home Server, even when traveling out of the country, she continued to send her edits and kept things on track.

Joel Heidal and Vinay Chopra were just perfect for doing the technical editing work for this book. They both have a sharp eye and a goal-oriented nature. There is no better technical reviewer than someone who knows technology and wants to get every point made to complete their knowledge set.

Preface

About 4 years ago I was in an advanced training with another SQL expert name Gary who worked for the defense industry. At the time I was a Microsoft employee. With just the two of us taking this Koenig class in Goa, India was covered a lot of ground as we prepared for the SQL 2005 certification. Needless to say we both passed our test with very little worry. Then we prepare for another SQL test to get our MCITP in SQL server. At the end I did not say anything about my scores being about 100 points higher than his as it seemed luck was on my side since he was equally as complete as I was. Gary beat me to the punch and said he thought our SQL skills were about the same but in today's world it matters almost as much was SQL touches in addition to what you can do with SQL itself.

At the time that mostly meant my MCSE experience and a big jump start I had from doing a SQL-XML project. The power of new tools and languages is an opportunity for SQL to become more powerful by interoperating with these technologies. As time goes on these powerful touch points get even more useful and now you need to know this very well if one of your goals is to pass the Microsoft 70-433 certification.

Introduction

When I was a kid I liked listening to the radio before falling asleep. Commercials were a big part of airplay and there is one funny one that comes to mind. In this ad a TV and Newspaper are arguing about what median is better. The TV proudly says "You can't change channels on a newspaper". The newspaper voice came up and said "You can't put a TV set in the bottom of a bird cage". If a funny way of pointing out each mainstream median has its own unique advantages and uses and its own disadvantages.

My friend Fayyaz and I have a running gag with each other. He loves C# and knows SQL and the opposite is true for me. He might hear me say how C# is a good language and SQL is the real langue. His witty comebacks are themed at how C# is way cool and SQL is just OK. One day we were teaching a class tighter and a student wanted to know which was true. Fayyaz said that all kidding aside these two languages do different things and we need both in a good enterprise. For extracting data SQL is king. For complex function and calculations C# does circles around SQL. By interoperating you can use the best of both worlds.

I am not an expert in automotive engineering but still benefit from driving a car. This is not an invitation to be an expert at many other languages. You likely will want to stay specialized in SQL and have just a working knowledge of other languages but benefit from their power in SQL server.

Each lesson and chapter builds sequentially until you know how to use interoperability with XML, C# and PowerShell. The good news is we don't assume you know a single thing about any of these languages. Those basics and the terms will be taught in the first chapter of each language and build from there into how SQL can use them. The labs have been created and delivered by me over several years of teaching SQL. The labs in this book are the end result, and each one consistently elicits "ah-ha" moments in my classes. If you would like to gain the confidence that comes with really knowing how to get things done, this book is your ticket.

Downloadable files help make this book a true learning experience. Answer keys, quiz games, and setup scripts will prepare you and your instance of SQL Server for practices that will hone your skills. The files can be found at www.Joes2Pros.com. After you have run the right code several times, you are ready to write code and help others do the same by spotting errors in code samples. Each chapter's interactive Bug Catcher section highlights common mistakes people make and improves your code literacy.

This book is an essential tool. When used correctly, you can determine how far and fast you can go. It has been polished and tuned for your use and benefit. In fact, this is the book I really wished was in my possession years ago when I was learning about SQL Server. What took me years of struggle to learn can now be yours in only months in the form of efficient, enjoyable, and rewarding study.

Skills Needed for this Book

This book assumes a high level of SQL query and programming knowledge. If you have no SQL coding experience, then you will need to read and cover the following books first.

Volume 1
Beginning SQL Joes 2 Pros: The SQL Hands-On Guide for Beginners
ISBN 1-4392-5317-X

Volume 2
SQL Queries Joes 2 Pros: SQL Query Techniques for Microsoft SQL Server 2008
ISBN 1-4392-5318-8

Volume 3
SQL Architecture Basics Joes 2 Pros: Core Architecture Concepts
ISBN: 1-4515-7946-2

Volume 4
SQL Programming Joes 2 Pros: Programming & Development for Microsoft SQL Server 2008
ISBN: 1-4515-7948-9

The discussion of SQL programming concepts and the index lessons presented in *SQL Programming Joes 2Pros* are the ideal preparation for the interoperability topics contained in this volume. As this series precisely follows my MCTS preparatory course, I have carefully sequenced the chapters and topics to build upon each other. However, intermediates and developers with a good handle on T-SQL and SQL query writing and how programming objects work should be able to approach the programming topics without much difficulty.

About this Book

The *Joes 2 Pros* series began in the summer of 2006. The project started as a few easy-to-view labs to transform the old, dry text reading into easier and fun lessons for the classroom. The labs grew into stories. The stories grew into chapters. In 2008, many people whose lives and careers had been improved through my classes convinced me to write a book to reach out to more people. In 2009 the first book began in full gear until its completion (*Beginning SQL Joes 2 Pros*, ISBN 1-4392-5317-5) and three books later, the adventure continues.

My understanding of how to build an elevator very limited, yet I benefit everyday from its underlying complexity because I know how to operate the buttons. I don't need to be an expert at engineering to use it effectively. Very few people in the company will actually want or need direct access to SQL Server. Rather, their goal will be to have your work benefit them, their people, and their business but without needing to

Data needs to be useful to a business. In the *Beginning SQL Joes 2 Pros* book the very first chapter talked about turning data into information. For the large part we saw how to do that in the *SQL Queries Joes 2 Pros* book. Data has been around for thousands of years but quick business information (reports) from that data has only become instantaneous in the last few decades. Having access to the right information is complex but crucial to business. SQL Programming is your chance to bridge this critical gap of information to the right people.

Most of the exercises in this book are designed introduce to you how the power of other languages can be put inside and harnessed by SQL. I'm often asked about the Points to Ponder feature, which is popular with both beginners and experienced developers. Some have asked why I don't simply call it a "Summary Page." While it's true that the Points to Ponder page generally captures key points from each section, I frequently include options or technical insights not contained in the chapter. Often these are points which I or my students have found helpful and which I believe will enhance your understanding of SQL Server.

How to Use the Downloadable Companion Files

Clear content and high-resolution multimedia videos coupled with code samples will take you on this journey. To give you all this and save printing costs, all supporting files are available with a free download from www.Joes2Pros.com. The breakdown of the offerings from these supporting files is listed below:

Training videos: To get you started, the first three chapters are in video format for free downloading. Videos show labs, demonstrate concepts, and review Points to Ponder along with tips from the appendix. Ranging from 3-15 minutes in length, they use special effects to highlight key points. You can go at your own pace and pause or replay within lessons as needed.

Answer keys: The downloadable files also include an answer key. You can verify your completed work against these keys. Another helpful use is these coding answers are available for peeking if you get really stuck.

Resource files: If you are asked to import a file into SQL Server, you will need that resource file. Located in the resources sub-folder from the download site are your practice lab resource files. These files hold the few non-SQL script files needed for some labs.

Lab setup files: SQL Server is a database engine and we need to practice on a database. The Joes 2 Pros Practice Company database is a fictitious travel booking company whose name is shortened to the database name of JProCo. The scripts to set up the JProCo database can be found here.

Chapter review files: Ready to take your new skills out for a test drive? We have the ever popular Bug Catcher game located here.

What this Book is Not

This book will start you off on the cornerstones of the language behind SQL Server. It will not cover every keyword, as you will get many of them as you work and become a SQL Server expert.

This is not a memorization book. Rather, this is a skills book to make preparing for the certification test a familiarization process. This book prepares you to apply what you've learned to answer SQL questions in the job setting. The highest hopes are that your progress and level of SQL knowledge will soon have business managers seeking your expertise to provide the reporting and information vital to their decision making. It's a good feeling to achieve and to help at the same time. Many students commented that the training method used in *Joes 2 Pros* was what finally helped them achieve their goal of certification.

When you go through the *Joes 2 Pros* series and really know this material, you deserve a fair shot at SQL certification. Use only authentic testing engines drawing on your skill. Show you know it for real. At the time of this writing, MeasureUp® at http://www.measureup.com provides a good test preparation simulator. The company's test pass guarantee makes it a very appealing option.

Chapter 1.   Introduction to XML

XML stands for **Ex**tensible **M**arkup **L**anguage. No matter what your programming level or job experience, if you've had any degree of exposure to the IT world in the last decade, you probably have heard of XML. At its simplest level, it is a file format consumable by nearly all browsers and programs. It is also very readable by humans.

SQL Server 2000 was the first version to include XML support, including streaming XML. Its flexibility rapidly accelerated adoption of the XML standard by the IT world, generally, and by SQL Server, specifically. SQL Server's next version (SQL Server 2005) included a significantly larger degree of XML support and functionality, including SQL Server's launch of the **XML data type**.

The first seven chapters of this volume are an extended review of XML and its interoperability with SQL Server. The goals of this chapter are to introduce you to XML and enable you to begin working hands-on with XML data.

*__READER NOTE:__ Please run the script SQLInteropChapter1.0Setup.sql in order to follow along with the examples in the first section of Chapter 1. (You only need to run this script once for all examples in Chapters 1 through 4.) All scripts mentioned in this chapter may be found at **www.Joes2Pros.com**.*

What is XML?

A common observation by people seeing XML for the first time is that it looks like just a bunch of data inside a text file. XML files are text-based documents, which makes them easy to read. All of the data is literally spelled out in the document and relies on a just a few characters (<, >, =) to convey relationships and structure of the data. XML files can be used by any commonly available **text editor**, such as Notepad and WordPad.

Much like a book's Table of Contents, your first glance at well-written XML will tell you the subject matter of the data and its general structure. Hints appearing within the data help you to quickly identify the main theme (similar to book's subject), its headers (similar to chapter titles or sections of a book), data elements (similar to a book's characters or chief topics), and so forth.

Later in this chapter we'll learn to recognize and use the structural "hints," which are XML's markup components (e.g., XML tags, root elements). Applications and websites scan XML and read these components to understand the organization and structure of the data. Additionally, XML can include instructions for how a program should consume its data. To understand how this works, we first must discuss the concept of data and metadata.

Data

In the opening pages of Volume 1 *(Beginning SQL Joes 2 Pros)*, the first concept distinguishes between "data" and "information." That discussion helps us get clear on the idea of **data** – the raw numbers and most granular components that you store in a database. **Information** is what you find in a report and is the end result when raw data undergoes value-added processing (e.g., aggregations, calculations, data being combined with or compared to other data, etc.) in order for it to appear in a format consumable by decision makers.

List A (on the lefthand side of Figure 1.1, next page) contains raw data in a single list. When we look closely at the data values (i.e., the names of the items in the list), we can see a few words that hint at a possible hierarchy. However, there's no outline or formatting to help impart clues about the hierarchical relationships contained within the data.

Metadata

In short, **metadata** is data about data. A timestamp, a row number, a column name, the name of table, a data type – these are examples of metadata, because they help characterize and describe your data but aren't actually part of the raw data itself. **Metadata** describes your data, including relationships within your data.

Indentation is a simple formatting cue used to show structure, such as subtopics belonging to a topic. (*Examples:* A class outline or a book's Table of Contents.) In Data List B (see Figure 1.1, righthand side), indentation serves as metadata because it helps us understand the relationships between the items in the list. Later we will see the layout of an XML document includes fairly simple cues, like indentation and tags to help distinguish one hierarchical level from another.

Since the heading "Veggies" appears below the title "Food" and is indented once, we know Veggies is a category belonging to Food. "Meat" and "Fruit" appear at the same level as Veggies, so they are a peer of Veggies and also a type of Food. Below each type sits a further indented level, which indicates that these items (Carrots, Chicken, Banana, etc.) are types of Veggies, Meat, and Fruit and are sub-types of Food.

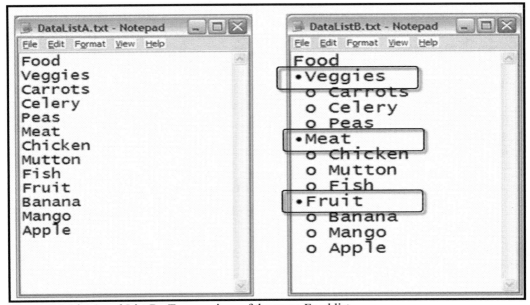

Figure 1.1 List A and List B: Two versions of the same Food list.

XML is comprised of two components:
1) Data
2) Metadata – the description of the data, including relationships and properties of the data

Let's first consider the data component of XML with a look at the following list of countries (see Figure 1.2). When we look at the countries included in the list, we detect countries which we know are related. For example, Spain and Finland are both located in Europe. Let's recognize that nothing appearing in the list or its structure tells us these are two European countries – it's just an observation we can make since we are familiar with the items contained in the list.

Figure 1.2 List of countries.

Let's next look at a list which fewer readers will be familiar with. This is useful because it will better allow us to appreciate the concept of **self-describing data**.

These are the teams of the NFL, the National Football League (see Figure 1.3). This simple list doesn't tell us much about the relationships between these 32 items. Later on, we will see that the XML version of this list will tell us more about the structure of the NFL and how these 32 teams are related.

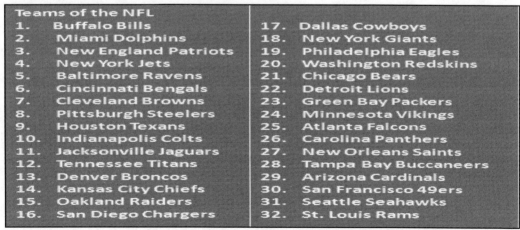

Figure 1.3 The 32 teams of the NFL. Later we will see this data organized in an XML document.

Text Data

Text files are useful for some things. The Notepad program is included with every version of Windows, so it's widely available and requires no additional purchase, installation, or training. You can easily fit lots of data into a text (.txt) file, which you can then pump into a SQL table. You can also take the data from a table and pump it into a text file. We used **BCP** to perform both of these operations in Volume 1 (*Beginning SQL Joes 2 Pros*). When importing data into SQL Server from a text file, you need to take extra care and examine the contents of the file to ensure that the right data goes into the right field. This is because a text file lacks programmatic features to support metadata or to help you recognize the true meaning or intended destination of the data. A little research on your part is necessary to make this work. In short, text data is just data (no metadata).

On occasion, a text file can be a handy way of looking at relatively small quantities of data. Even without the field headers, we would be able to look at many of JProCo's tables in a text file and be able to comfortably recognize data from the Employee or Grant table. Viewing raw table data in a text file is a trick used by data experts to find unexpected spaces or delimiters (e.g., an extra tab or carriage return) hidden in your Excel or Access data. These cause problems when you need to export your table data to another program (e.g., SQL Server).

Figure 1.4 Think of a list of data stored in SQL Server versus the same list stored as a text file.

Relational Data

We know SQL Server is an **RDBMS**, a relational database management system. The power of an RDBMS is its ability to programmatically track, store, and organize your data and metadata. Throughout the *Joes 2 Pros* series, we see that using relational database design (e.g., normalized data to minimize data redundancy, primary and foreign key relationships, lookup tables) to store and maintain data improves the efficiency and scalability of your database systems.

If we use SQL Server's programmatic capabilities to store the NFL list efficiently, our database users will be able to discern quite a bit about the NFL. Just by looking at how the data is stored in tables and lookup tables, users can see how the 32 teams are organized into conferences and regional divisions. However, the same data exported from SQL Server to a text file will simply store a flat version of this list and, therefore, will not be able to tell users about the data or relationships within the data.

Let's consider the same scenario, except with two frequently used tables in the JProCo database. The Employee table has about seven columns and the Location table about five columns. If you wanted to export all of this data from SQL Server into a single text file, you would need some sort of marker for where the Employee data ends and the Location table begins.

The text file can't win in this export scenario: text files can't describe data, because they have no features capable of supporting metadata. They can't describe one table, let alone two. However, this can be accomplished using XML. An XML file can contain many tables, meaning both the raw data and metadata needed to build the tables.

Metadata in XML Data

In a SQL Server database, we know the data is relational and descriptive. Text files are simply flat lists of data, and you have to figure out what the data means. XML is known as **self-describing data**, because you get the data plus metadata.

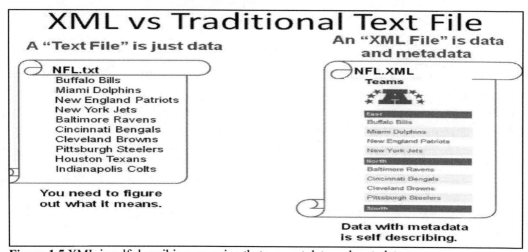

Figure 1.5 XML is self-describing, meaning that you get data and metadata.

An XML file reads more like an outline. Notice how seeing the list of 32 NFL teams in outline form (raw data plus some metadata) helps us understand quite a bit more about the data relationships (see Figure 1.6).

AFC Teams	NFC Teams
East	**East**
Buffalo Bills	Dallas Cowboys
Miami Dolphins	New York Giants
New England Patriots	Philadelphia Eagles
New York Jets	Washington Redskins
North	**North**
Baltimore Ravens	Chicago Bears
Cincinnati Bengals	Detroit Lions
Cleveland Browns	Green Bay Packers
Pittsburgh Steelers	Minnesota Vikings
South	**South**
Houston Texans	Atlanta Falcons
Indianapolis Colts	Carolina Panthers
Jacksonville Jaguars	New Orleans Saints
Tennessee Titans	Tampa Bay Buccaneers
West	**West**
Denver Broncos	Arizona Cardinals
Kansas City Chiefs	San Francisco 49ers
Oakland Raiders	Seattle Seahawks
San Diego Chargers	St. Louis Rams

Figure 1.6 Seeing list data in outline form helps illustrate the relationships between the elements.

XML's capabilities allow it to serve much like a self-describing relational database stored as a file (i.e., an XML document) or a stream (i.e., a tabular view of XML data produced by a program like SQL Server). All data-aware applications can interact with XML.

XML Tags

XML utilizes tags < > to create the data "outline." These tags can also be nested.

Here (see Figure 1.7) the first "NFL" shown is the **beginning tag**. It sits between brackets and contains no slash. The lower "NFL" is the **ending tag**. It appears identical to the beginning tag, except it contains a forward slash. Ending tags must follow the same sequence as the beginning tags.

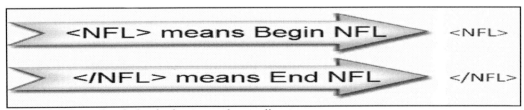

Figure 1.7 Example of a beginning tag and an ending tag.

XML Elements

Elements are actually the tags themselves. Element data is the data which sits between tags. For example, Seahawks is element data. It is data belonging to the element, Team.

<Team>Seahawks</Team>

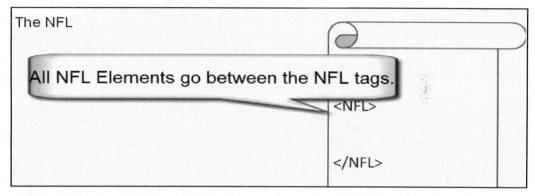

Figure 1.8 Seahawks belongs to the Team element.

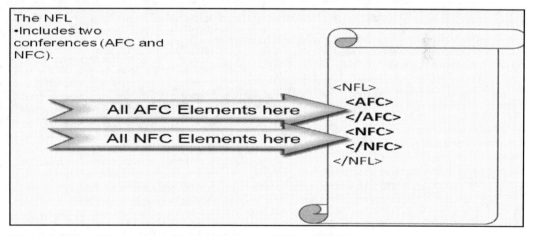

Figure 1.9 The NFL consists of two conferences, AFC and NFC.

Two elements belonging to the NFL element are AFC and NFC (see Figure 1.9). All of the data belong to the AFC and NFC must sit between the respective beginning and ending tags. Each division element (e.g., West, North, South, and East) must also include a beginning and ending tag (see Figure 1.10).

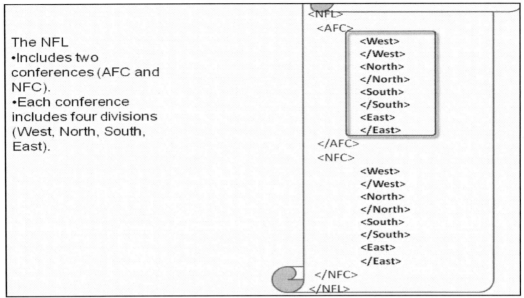

Figure 1.10 All AFC data goes between the AFC tags; the same is true for NFC data, which goes between the NFC tags.

Each of the four divisions belonging to a conference contains multiple teams. The AFC East division consists of four teams: the Buffalo Bills, the Miami Dolphins, the New England Patriots, and the New York Jets (see Figure 1.11).

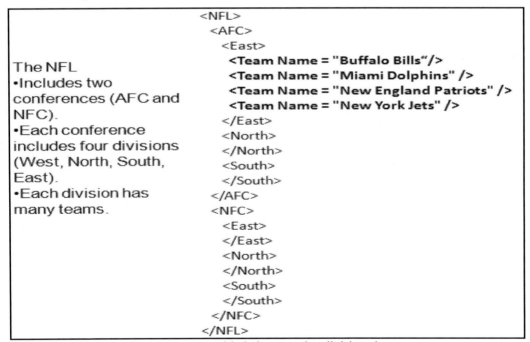

Figure 1.11 The team elements appear with their respective division element.

Notice that if a tag contains no element data, or element children, then the beginning and ending tag may be combined into one tag. For example we don't see a <Team Name> beginning tag and a </Team Name> ending tag. We see <Team Name/> which serves as the single tag. Since <East> has many child elements, it needs an </East> ending element to mark the end.

Suppose hypothetically that the South division contained no teams. In that case, we could choose either to leave it as shown above (in Figure 1.11), or we could show it as <South/>.

An XML file is a lot like a mini-database stored inside a file. The XML file contains data and the accompanying metadata needed to interpret the relationships amongst the data.

If you were to put all 32 teams in their divisions and in proper XML, it would look quite a bit this like (see Figure 1.12).

Notice that three of the AFC teams aren't shown here (due to space considerations). However, this is the way the actual XML document appears – one long column enclosed with an <NFL> opening tag at the top and a closing tag </NFL> at the bottom.

```
  <Team Name = "New York Jets" />
 </East>
 <North>
  <Team Name = "Baltimore Ravens"/>
  <Team Name = "Cincinnati Bengals"/>
  <Team Name = "Cleveland Browns"/>
  <Team Name = "Pittsburgh Steelers"/>
 </North>
 <South>
  <Team Name = "Houston Texans"/>
  <Team Name = "Indianapolis Colts"/>
  <Team Name = "Tennessee Titans"/>
  <Team Name = "Jacksonville Jaguars"/>
 </South>
 <West>
  <Team Name = "Denver Broncos"/>
  <Team Name = "San Diego Chargers"/>
  <Team Name = "Oakland Raiders"/>
  <Team Name = "Kansas City Chiefs"/>
 </West>
 </AFC>
 <NFC>
  <East>
  <Team Name = "Dallas Cowboys"/>
  <Team Name = "New York Giants" />
  <Team Name = "Philadelphia Eagles" />
  <Team Name = "Washington Redskins" />
  </East>
 <North>
  <Team Name = "Chicago Bears"/>
  <Team Name = "Detroit Lions"/>
  <Team Name = "Green Bay Packers"/>
  <Team Name = "Minnesota Vikings"/>
 </North>
 <South>
  <Team Name = "Atlanta Falcons"/>
  <Team Name = "Carolina Panthers"/>
  <Team Name = "New Orleans Saints"/>
  <Team Name = "Tampa Bay Buccaneers"/>
 </South>
 <West>
  <Team Name = "Arizona Cardinals"/>
  <Team Name = "St. Louis Rams"/>
  <Team Name = "San Francisco 49ers"/>
  <Team Name = "Seattle Seahawks"/>
 </West>
 </NFC>
</NFL>
```

Figure 1.12 The NFL teams shown by conference & division.

For illustrative purposes, let's enlarge this list, split it horizontally, and look at it side by side, which makes it a bit easier to read (see Figure 1.13).

```
<NFL>                                          <NFC>
 <AFC>                                           <East>
  <East>                                          <Team Name = "Dallas Cowboys"/>
   <Team Name = "Buffalo Bills"/>                 <Team Name = "New York Giants" />
   <Team Name = "Miami Dolphins" />               <Team Name = "Philadelphia Eagles" />
   <Team Name = "New England Patriots"/ >         <Team Name = "Washington Redskins" />
   <Team Name = "New York Jets" />                <East>
  </East>                                         <North>
  <North>                                          <Team Name = "Chicago Bears"/>
   <Team Name = "Baltimore Ravens"/>              <Team Name = "Detroit Lions"/>
   <Team Name = "Cincinnati Bengals"/>            <Team Name = "Green Bay Packers"/>
   <Team Name = "Cleveland Browns"/>              <Team Name = "Minnesota Vikings"/>
   <Team Name = "Pittsburgh Steelers"/>          </North>
  </North>                                        <South>
  <South>                                          <Team Name = "Atlanta Falcons"/>
   <Team Name = "Houston Texans"/>                <Team Name = "Carolina Panthers"/>
   <Team Name = "Indianapolis Colts"/>           <Team Name = "New Orleans Saints"/>
   <Team Name = "Tennessee Titans"/>             <Team Name = "Tampa Bay Buccaneers"/>
   <Team Name = "Jacksonville Jaguars"/>         </South>
  </South>                                        <West>
  <West>                                          <Team Name = "Arizona Cardinals"/>
   <Team Name = "Denver Broncos"/>               <Team Name = "St. Louis Rams"/>
   <Team Name = "San Diego Chargers"/>           <Team Name = "San Francisco 49ers"/>
   <Team Name = "Oakland Raiders"/>              <Team Name = "Seattle Seahawks"/>
   <Team Name = "Kansas City Chiefs"/>          </West>
  </West>                                        </NFC>
 </AFC>                                         </NFL>
```

Figure 1.13 Our XML data has been split, so we can see the AFC and NFC data side-by-side.

Supposed we are asked a question, such as, "What division are the Denver Broncos in?" We can answer it by looking at the XML document. Even if we don't really know much about football or the NFL, we can easily see they are in the AFC West division (see Figure 1.14).

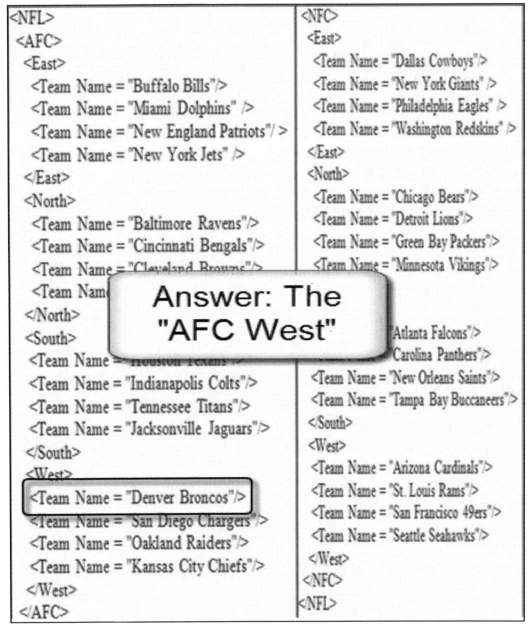

Figure 1.14 An XML file is like a mini-database stored inside of a file. The self-describing nature of XML allows us to answer questions, even when we aren't very familiar with the subject matter.

Here, the NFL is known as the **root element** (also known as the **root node**). The entire list of 32 teams is encompassed within the NFL. In other words, all data in this XML appears beneath the **root element** of NFL.

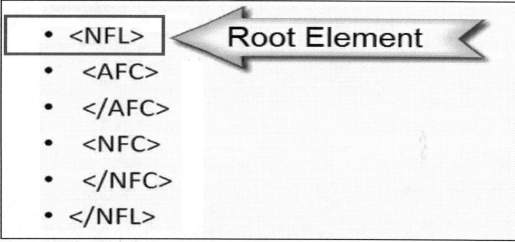

Figure 1.15 The NFL is the root element of our XML data.

The AFC and NFC are known as **top level elements**.

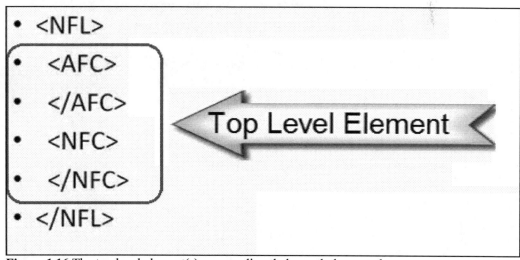

Figure 1.16 The top level element(s) appear directly beneath the root element.

XML Attributes

XML element tags may contain information within the tags providing descriptive information about the element or its properties. These are known as **attributes**.

Attribute data appears with the opening tag name and is enclosed in quotation marks: <Team Name = "Seahawks"></Team>

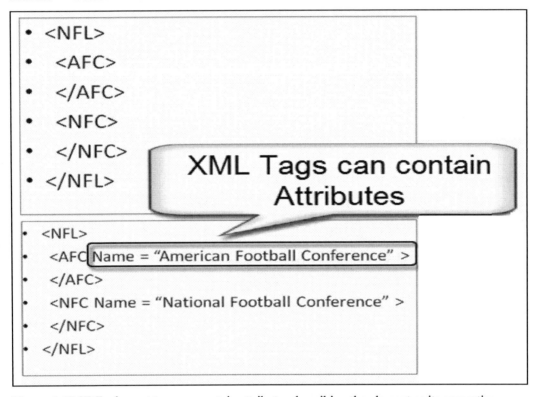

Figure 1.17 XML element tags can contain attributes describing the element or its properties.

Lab 1.1: What is XML

Lab Prep: Before you can begin the lab, you must have SQL Server installed and have run the script SQLInteropChapter1.0Setup.sql. View the lab video instructions in Lab1.1_WhatIsXML.wmv.

Skill Check 1: Based on the XML in the right half of figure below, answer the questions in the left side of the figure.

1.) How many customers are listed in this XML file? _____	```<SalesOrderHistory> <Customer CustomerID="1" CustomerType="S"> <Order InvoiceID="43860" OrderDate="2001-08-01"> <OrderDetail ProductID="761" Quantity="2" /> <OrderDetail ProductID="770" Quantity="1" /> </Order>```
2.) Which customer ordered the greatest quantity of total products? _____	```<Order InvoiceID="43861" OrderDate="2001-08-01"> <OrderDetail ProductID="781" Quantity="4" /> <OrderDetail ProductID="778" Quantity="5" /> </Order>```
3.) Which customer has more than one invoice?_____	```</Customer> <Customer CustomerID="2" CustomerType="S"> <Order InvoiceID="43862" OrderDate="2001-08-02"> <OrderDetail ProductID="761" Quantity="8" /> <OrderDetail ProductID="770" Quantity="9" /> <OrderDetail ProductID="771" Quantity="4" /> </Order>```

1.) How many customers are listed in this XML file? _____

2.) Which customer ordered the greatest quantity of total products? _____

3.) Which customer has more than one invoice?_____

4.) Which Invoice # did not have an order for product 770? _____

5.) What is the name of the root node?

_____

6.) Which invoice number has the most number of distinct products?_____

```
<SalesOrderHistory>
<Customer CustomerID="1" CustomerType="S">
<Order InvoiceID="43860" OrderDate="2001-08-01">
    <OrderDetail ProductID="761" Quantity="2" />
    <OrderDetail ProductID="770" Quantity="1" />
</Order>
<Order InvoiceID="43861" OrderDate="2001-08-01">
    <OrderDetail ProductID="781" Quantity="4" />
    <OrderDetail ProductID="778" Quantity="5" />
</Order>
</Customer>
<Customer CustomerID="2" CustomerType="S">
<Order InvoiceID="43862" OrderDate="2001-08-02">
    <OrderDetail ProductID="761" Quantity="8" />
    <OrderDetail ProductID="770" Quantity="9" />
    <OrderDetail ProductID="771" Quantity="4" />
</Order>
</Customer>
<Customer CustomerID="3" CustomerType="C">
<Order InvoiceID="43863" OrderDate="2001-08-02">
    <OrderDetail ProductID="761" Quantity="20" />
    <OrderDetail ProductID="770" Quantity="11" />
</Order>
</Customer>
</SalesOrderHistory>
```

Figure 1.18 Skill Check 1 consists of six questions regarding the XML document in the right panel.

Skill Check 2: Based on the XML in the right half of figure below, answer the questions in the left side of the figure.

1.) Which song title has only been sung by one band?_____
 	
2.) From question 1 what is the TitleID?
_____
 	
3.) Bands sing songs. Which songs were sung and written by the same person?
 	
_____
 	
4.) Which song(s) was never sung by its writer? _____
 	
5.) What is the name of the root node?
 	
_____
 	
6.) How many different bands sang "Red Red Wine"?_____
	`<Music>`
	  `<Song TitleID="13159">`
	    `<WriterName>Neil Diamond</WriterName>`
	    `<Title>Red Red Wine</Title>`
	    `<Singer OrderID="1">`
	      `<BandName>Neil Diamond</BandName>`
	    `</Singer>`
	    `<Singer OrderID="2">`
	      `<BandName>UB40</BandName>`
	    `</Singer>`
	  `</Song>`
	  `<Song TitleID="13160">`
	    `<WriterName>Prince</WriterName>`
	    `<Title>Manic Monday</Title>`
	    `<Singer OrderID="1">`
	      `<BandName>Bangles</BandName>`
	    `</Singer>`
	  `</Song>`
	  `<Song TitleID="13161">`
	    `<WriterName>Roy Orbison</WriterName>`
	    `<Title>Pretty Woman</Title>`
	    `<Singer OrderID="1">`
	      `<BandName>Roy Orbison</BandName>`
	    `</Singer>`
	    `<Singer OrderID="2">`
	      `<BandName>Van Halen</BandName>`
	    `</Singer>`
	  `</Song>`
	`</Music>`

Figure 1.19 Skill Check2 consists of six questions regarding the XML document in the right panel.

Answer Code: The answers to this lab can be found in the downloadable files in a file named Lab1.1_WhatIsXML.sql.

What is XML - Points to Ponder

1. Metadata is data about your data. Metadata is information which helps to describe the properties and relationships of data.

2. SQL Server is relational and therefore supports data and keeps track of its metadata, too.

3. Text files only contain data (no metadata). It's up to you to understand what the data means.

4. XML is self-describing data, as it contains both data and metadata.

5. XML holds its data and metadata in a hierarchical set of tags.

6. A beginning and ending tag always have the same name. You can tell them apart because the ending tag starts with a forward slash.

7. The ending tag for <Joes2Pros> would be </Joes2Pros>.

8. The data in XML can be in the form of attributes or elements.

9. Element data is stored between the beginning and ending element tag.

10. Attribute data is stored inside of a beginning tag.

11. Any data-aware application can interact with XML.

12. XML is case-sensitive.

13. XML tag names cannot have spaces between them.

Streams

In the IT world, the term **stream** signifies the output of information by a program or process.

Don't feel badly if that definition doesn't immediately register with you. It took me years to understand the "streams" concept. A colleague finally sat me down and explained it. It's understandable if you're picturing a flowing bed of water running past a mountain cabin, but XML streams are really nothing like that. Let me save you years of bewilderment on this funny geek-speak term.

Instead of water, these days I think "result set" when I hear the term **stream**. As we know, the form of a result set can change slightly depending on the context.

In SQL Server terms, a **stream** resembles a table: the gridlike presentation of rows and columns that you get when you run a query. This is because SQL Server prefers to present data in a grid shape. SQL Server even produces spatial data first as a grid, although we humans prefer to view the result shaped as a sphere or map. However, XML does not set things up in rows and columns.

Tabular Stream

Let's look at a simple SELECT statement from JProCo's Location table and notice we get a table-like result set, also known as a tabular result set (see Figure 1.20). As noted above, the tabular stream is SQL Server's preferred mode of streaming output from its data engine to your display.

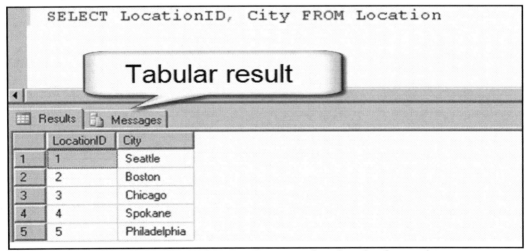

Figure 1.20 Example of a tabular result, SQL Server's preferred mode of streaming output.

XML Streams

Unlike SQL Server, XML actually has many modes of streaming output. You can instruct SQL Server to stream your XML result using the mode you prefer.

Let's look again at the data we queried from the Location table. This time we will have the output appear as an XML stream, rather than a tabular result.

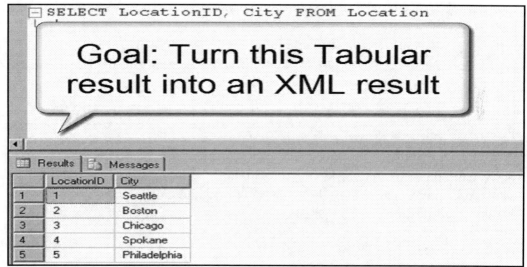

Figure 1.21 Our next goal will be to make this output appear as an XML stream.

XML Raw Mode

To our base query, we need to add the keywords "FOR XML" in order for our results to appear as XML. We also need to specify the mode, which in this case is raw (see Figure 1.22).

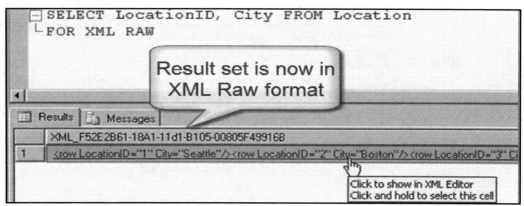

Figure 1.22 Adding keywords FOR XML RAW will make our output appear as an XML stream.

Raw is the easiest type of XML to run. We would say this result set now appears in an XML raw data format. Notice the result is a hyperlink, which you click to view your results. The XML raw mode is the only mode we will explore in this beginning chapter. In subseqent chapters, we will see many other modes.

Notice that the default tag label is "row" for each row of our result set. And the data appear as attributes (see Figure 1.23).

```
<row LocationID="1" City="Seattle" />
<row LocationID="2" City="Boston" />
<row LocationID="3" City="Chicago" />
<row LocationID="4" City="Spokane" />
<row LocationID="5" City="Philadelphia" />
```

Figure 1.23 XML creates a <row> tag for each row.

XML will allow you to override the default name <row> and set it to something more descriptive. The syntax shown here will change the name for each attribute tag to "RowLocation" (see Figure 1.24).

Figure 1.24 We've changed our code to override the default label for each row attribute.

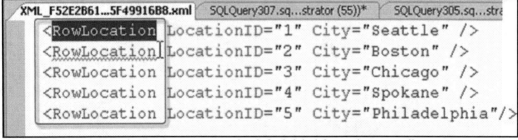

Figure 1.25 "RowLocation" now appears as the default label for each row attribute.

Let's see what happens when we remove the term row and simply rename the tag as "Location" (see Figure 1.26).

Figure 1.26 This syntax will change the name for each row element tag to "Location."

Observe the red IntelliSense underline and mouseover tag appearing in the result figure below ("XML document cannot contain multiple root level elements"). Also notice we have five (5) top level nodes and no root (see Figure 1.27). SQL Server would prefer that we have a root element appearing in our data.

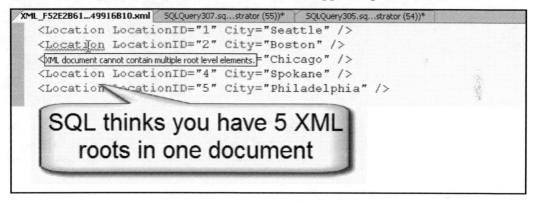

Figure 1.27 SQL Server interprets our XML RAW result as having multiple root level elements.

Raw is the simplest mode where all data is considered to be at the same level with no nesting. The XML RAW command by default does not create a root.

Next, we'll see how we can alter our code to add a root element to our XML.

Root Element Option

XML is considered complete (known as **well-formed XML**) only if it has a root tag which encompasses all other tags. Adding the keyword **ROOT** to our code specifies the ROOT element option (see Figure 1.28).

Adding the ROOT command to our code will add root tags in our XML data.

```
SELECT LocationID, City FROM Location
FOR XML RAW('Location'), ROOT
```

Results	Messages

XML_F52E2B61-18A1-11d1-B105-00805F49916B
1	<root><Location LocationID="1" City="Seattle"/><...

Figure 1.28 Our code now specifies the ROOT element option.

And now instead of just an **XML fragment**, our code produces an entire XML stream. This output is a well-formed XML document.

```
<root>
    <Location LocationID="1" City="Seattle" />
    <Location LocationID="2" City="Boston" />
    <Location LocationID="3" City="Chicago" />
    <Location LocationID="4" City="Spokane" />
    <Location LocationID="5" City="Philadelphia" />
</root>
```

Figure 1.29 Our result is no longer an XML fragment. It is a well-formed XML document.

We will add a name for our root tag to our code. In the code below, you can see we've added the name JProCo (see Figure 1.30).

```
SELECT LocationID, City FROM Location
FOR XML RAW('Location'), ROOT('JProCo')
```

Results	Messages

XML_F52E2B61-18A1-11d1-B105-00805F49916B
1	<JProCo><Location LocationID="1" City="Seattle"/...

Figure 1.30 We've modified our code to provide a name for our root tag.

Our result shows the root is now called JProCo (see Figure 1.31).

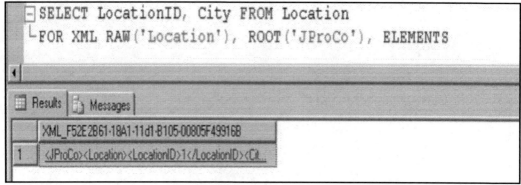

```
XML_F52E2B61...49916B12.xml   SQLQuery307.sq...strator (55))*   SQLQuery305.sq...strator (54)
<JProCo>
    <Location LocationID="1" City="Seattle" />
    <Location LocationID="2" City="Boston" />
    <Location LocationID="3" City="Chicago" />
    <Location LocationID="4" City="Spokane" />
    <Location LocationID="5" City="Philadelphia" />
</JProCo>
```

Figure 1.31 Our XML RAW result now shows one root level element.

Notice the data appears as attributes inside of the tag. Next we will make all this data display as sub-elements of the top element, Location.

Elements Option

The raw mode likes to store all of its data as attributes. You can choose whether data appears as attributes or as elements. If you prefer elements, then you can append the ELEMENTS option to the XML Raw mode (see Figure 1.32).

```
SELECT LocationID, City FROM Location
FOR XML RAW('Location'), ROOT('JProCo'), ELEMENTS
```

| Results | Messages |

XML_F52E2B61-18A1-11d1-B105-00805F499168
1	<JProCo><Location><LocationID>1</LocationID><Cit...

Figure 1.32 Adding the keyword ELEMENTS will make our output display as elements.

Look closely at the XML output, and you'll recognize the values for Records 1, 2, 3, and 4 from the Location table (see Figure 1.33).

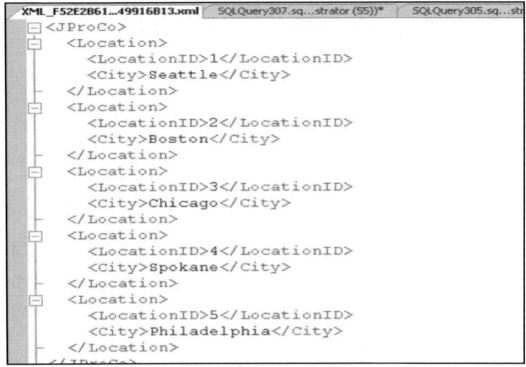

Figure 1.33 Our same data now appears as elements.

Let's look at another example from the Employee table. If you ran the reset script for this chapter, you should see 14 JProCo employees showing in your Employee table (see Figure 1.34).

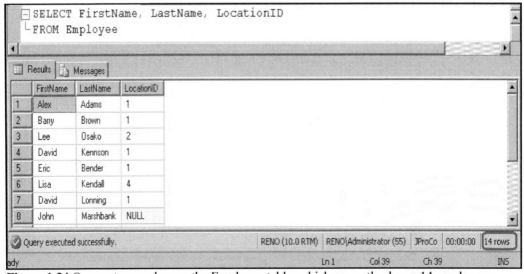

Figure 1.34 Our next example uses the Employee table, which currently shows 14 employees.

Next we will add FOR XML RAW to view the result from the Employee table as an XML output and using the raw mode (see Figure 1.35).

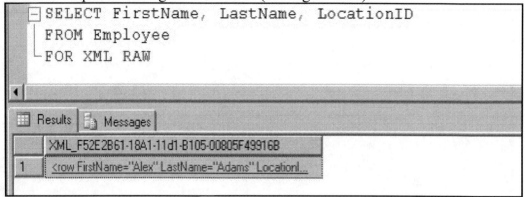

```
SELECT FirstName, LastName, LocationID
FROM Employee
FOR XML RAW
```

Figure 1.35 We have changed our Employee table result to output as XML RAW.

Notice that every row of our XML RAW output is labeled "row" by default.

```
XML_F52E2B61...49916B14.xml   SQLQuery308.sq...strator (55))*   SQLQuery305.sq...strator (54))*
<row FirstName="Alex" LastName="Adams" LocationID="1" />
<row FirstName="Barry" LastName="Brown" LocationID="1" />
<row FirstName="Lee" LastName="Osako" LocationID="2" />
<row FirstName="David" LastName="Kennson" LocationID="1" />
<row FirstName="Eric" LastName="Bender" LocationID="1" />
<row FirstName="Lisa" LastName="Kendall" LocationID="4" />
<row FirstName="David" LastName="Lonning" LocationID="1" />
<row FirstName="John" LastName="Marshbank" />
<row FirstName="James" LastName="Newton" LocationID="2" />
<row FirstName="Terry" LastName="O'Haire" LocationID="2" />
<row FirstName="Sally" LastName="Smith" LocationID="1" />
<row FirstName="Barbara" LastName="O'Neil" LocationID="4" />
<row FirstName="Phil" LastName="Wilconkinski" LocationID="1" />
<row FirstName="Janis" LastName="Smith" LocationID="1" />
```

Figure 1.36 Each row of an XML RAW output is labeled "row" by default.

We next will add a root to our output. We will add the keyword ROOT to our existing code (see Figure 1.37) and then look at our revised output (Figure 1.38).

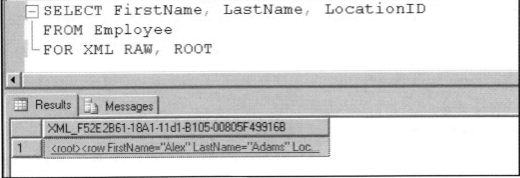

Figure 1.37 We are adding the keyword ROOT in order to see a root node in our XML output.

We now see the **root node** (a.k.a., the root element). Not only is our output more readable and organized, but this is considered "well-formed XML" (Figure 1.38).

```
XML_F52E2B61...49916B15.xml    SQLQuery308.sq...strator (55))*    SQLQuery305.sq...strator (54))*
<root>
    <row FirstName="Alex" LastName="Adams" LocationID="1" />
    <row FirstName="Barry" LastName="Brown" LocationID="1" />
    <row FirstName="Lee" LastName="Osako" LocationID="2" />
    <row FirstName="David" LastName="Kennson" LocationID="1" />
    <row FirstName="Eric" LastName="Bender" LocationID="1" />
    <row FirstName="Lisa" LastName="Kendall" LocationID="4" />
    <row FirstName="David" LastName="Lonning" LocationID="1" />
    <row FirstName="John" LastName="Marshbank" />
    <row FirstName="James" LastName="Newton" LocationID="2" />
    <row FirstName="Terry" LastName="O'Haire" LocationID="2" />
    <row FirstName="Sally" LastName="Smith" LocationID="1" />
    <row FirstName="Barbara" LastName="O'Neil" LocationID="4" />
    <row FirstName="Phil" LastName="Wilconkinski" LocationID="1" />
    <row FirstName="Janis" LastName="Smith" LocationID="1" />
</root>
```

Figure 1.38 Adding the root node makes our XML output well-formed XML.

Now let's put the data into elements (see Figure 1.39).

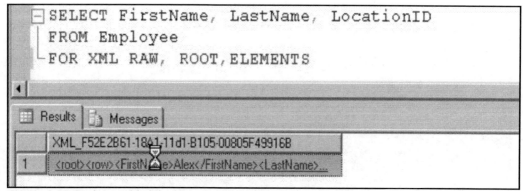

Figure 1.39 We have added the keyword ELEMENTS in order to see our data as elements.

We can see each employee now has three sub-elements under the top element, which is "row" (see Figure 1.40).

Figure 1.40 Each employee now has three sub-elements beneath the top element, "row."

The exception is John Marshbank, who only has two elements (see Figure 1.41).

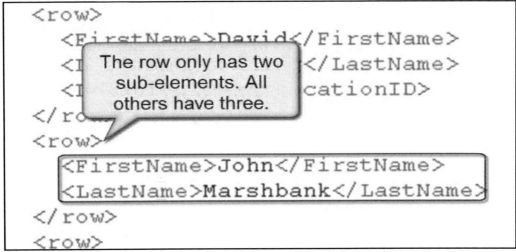

Figure 1.41 John Marshbank has just two sub-elements beneath the top element, "row".

If we query the Employee table, we quickly see the reason for this is that John Marshbank is the only one with a NULL LocationID (see Figure 1.42).

	FirstName	LastName	LocationID
7	David	Lonning	1
8	John	Marshbank	NULL
9	James	Newton	2
10	Terry	O'Haire	2
11	Sally	Smith	1
12	Barbara	O'Neil	4
13	Phil	Wilconki...	1
14	Janis	Smith	1

Figure 1.42 Recall that John Marshbank is the only employee with a NULL LocationID.

Our mystery is solved – we understand John Marshbank's having just two data sub-elements is caused by his LocationID value being a NULL. Suppose the program which needs to consume our result requires three data sub-elements. Or suppose company policy specifies that each employee record must contain three data sub-elements. John Marshbank's record doesn't meet the criteria and would thus be in violation of the policy.

XSINIL

The **XSINIL** option allows you to force a tag(s) to be present, even if the underlying data is NULL. Our next example will show us how to make a LocationID tag appear for John Marshbank.

For fields in SQL Server which include a null value for some records but are populated with regular values in the other records, you will seem to have missing tags for the null record. Often this is alright, as missing tags are presumed to be null. However, if you require all tags to be present (even if they have no data), then you can specify the XSINIL option for your XML stream. The XSINIL option will force tags to be present for all records, including those which contain null values. Let's rerun our prior code and add the XSINIL option (Figure 1.43).

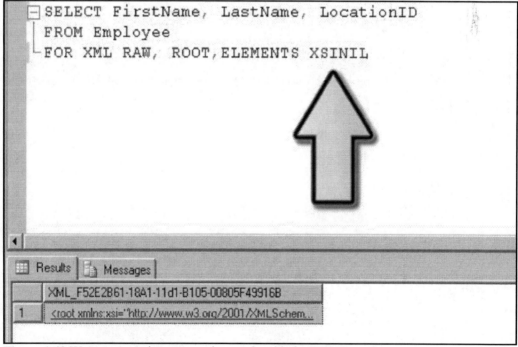

```
SELECT FirstName, LastName, LocationID
FROM Employee
FOR XML RAW, ROOT, ELEMENTS XSINIL
```

	XML_F52E2B61-18A1-11d1-B105-00805F49916B
1	<root xmlns:xsi="http://www.w3.org/2001/XMLSchem...

Figure 1.43 We are re-running our previous code with the XSINIL option.

We now see a third sub-element for John Marshbank. The LocationID tag is no longer missing. It is present and shows the value "xsi:nil="true" in place of a LocationID (see Figure 1.44).

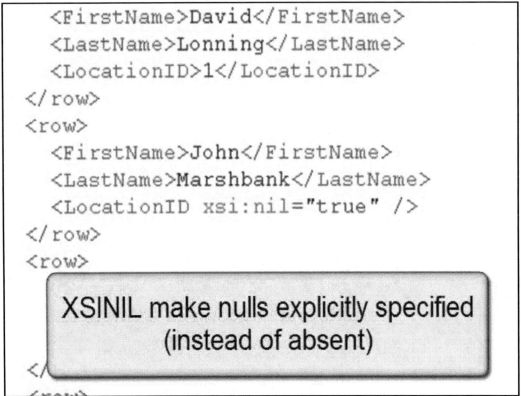

```
    <FirstName>David</FirstName>
    <LastName>Lonning</LastName>
    <LocationID>1</LocationID>
</ row>
<row>
    <FirstName>John</FirstName>
    <LastName>Marshbank</LastName>
    <LocationID xsi:nil="true" />
</ row>
<row>
```

XSINIL make nulls explicitly specified (instead of absent)

Figure 1.44 Our objective has been met: John Marshbank's record now includes three data elements thanks to XSINIL.

Lab 1.2: XML Streams

Lab Prep: Before you can begin the lab, you must have SQL Server installed and have run the script SQLInteropChapter1.0Setup.sql. View the lab video instructions in Lab1.2_SQL_XMLStreams.wmv

Skill Check 1: Create an XML stream using the RAW option to get the ClassID and ClassName fields from the MgmtTraining table. Each top level element should be named after the table. When you're done, your screen should resemble the figure below (see Figure 1.45).

```
XML_F52E2B61...49916B18.xml   SQLQuery308.sq...strator (55))*   SQLQuery305.sq...strator (54))*
  <MgmtTraining ClassID="1" ClassName="Embracing Diversity" />
  <MgmtTraining ClassID="2" ClassName="Interviewing" />
  <MgmtTraining ClassID="3" ClassName="Difficult Negotiations" />
  <MgmtTraining ClassID="4" ClassName="Empowering Others" />
```

Figure 1.45 Skill Check 1 result.

Skill Check 2: Create an XML stream using the RAW option to get the GrantName and Amount fields from the [Grant] table. Make sure you have a root element named <root> and each top level element should be named after the table. All the data should be in Attributes inside the top level element. When you are done, your result should resemble Figure 1.46 below.

```
<root>
  <Grant GrantName="92 Purr_Scents %% team" Amount="4750.0000" />
  <Grant GrantName="K-Land fund trust" Amount="15750.0000" />
  <Grant GrantName="Robert@BigStarBank.com" Amount="18100.0000" />
  <Grant GrantName="BIG 6's Foundation%" Amount="21000.0000" />
  <Grant GrantName="TALTA_Kishan International" Amount="18100.0000" />
  <Grant GrantName="Ben@MoreTechnology.com" Amount="41000.0000" />
  <Grant GrantName="www.@-Last-U-Can-Help.com" Amount="25000.0000" />
  <Grant GrantName="Thank you @.com" Amount="21500.0000" />
  <Grant GrantName="Just Mom" Amount="9900.0000" />
  <Grant GrantName="Big Giver Tom" Amount="95900.0000" />
  <Grant GrantName="Mega Mercy" Amount="55000.0000" />
</root>
```

Figure 1.46 Skill Check 2 result.

Skill Check 3: Create an XML stream using the RAW option to get all fields from the contractor table. Make sure you have a root element named <root> and each top level element should be named after the table. The data should be contained in sub elements of the top element. When you are done, your result should resemble Figure 1.47 below.

```
<root>
  <Contractor>
    <ctrID>1</ctrID>
    <lastname>Barker</lastname>
    <firstname>Bill</firstname>
    <hiredate>2006-01-07T00:00:00</hiredate>
    <LocationID>1</LocationID>
  </Contractor>
  <Contractor>
    <ctrID>2</ctrID>
    <lastname>Ogburn</lastname>
    <firstname>Maurice</firstname>
    <hiredate>2006-10-27T00:00:00</hiredate>
    <LocationID>1</LocationID>
  </Contractor>
</root>
```

Figure 1.47 Skill Check 3 result.

Skill Check 4: Create an XML stream using the RAW option to get all fields from the PayRates table. Make sure you have a root element named <root> and each top level element should be named <PR>. The data should be contained in sub elements of the top element. Elements must be present even if their value is null. When you are done, your result should resemble Figure 1.48.

```
<root xmlns:xsi="http://www.w3.org/2001/XMLSchema-instance">
  <PR>
    <EmpID>1</EmpID>
    <YearlySalary>99000.0000</YearlySalary>
    <MonthlySalary xsi:nil="true" />
    <HourlyRate xsi:nil="true" />
  </PR>
  <PR>
    <EmpID>2</EmpID>
    <YearlySalary>87000.0000</YearlySalary>
    <MonthlySalary xsi:nil="true" />
    <HourlyRate xsi:nil="true" />
  </PR>
```

Figure 1.48 Skill Check 4 result.

Answer Code: The T-SQL code to this lab can be found in the downloadable files in a file named Lab1.2_SQL_XML_Streams.sql.

XML Streams - Points to Ponder

1. The FOR XML clause instructs SQL Server to return data as an XML stream rather than a rowset.

2. The FOR XML clause is appended at the end of your SELECT statement.

3. Two common reasons why you might want to retrieve data as XML instead of a SQLServer table could be:

- o Publishing data to a website.

- o Retrieving data to exchange with a trading partner who should not have direct access to your SQL Server.

4. FOR XML has four mode options and RAW is just one of them.

5. The RAW option can be used with the ROOT or ELEMENTS keywords or both to customize your expected XML stream.

6. The ROOT and ELEMENTS keywords are optional.

7. FOR XML RAW defaults to making a <row> tag. You can change this to anything you like by using the optional parentheses ( ) after the word RAW.

- o FOR XML RAW – – Results in <row…>

- o FOR XML RAW('Emp') – – Results in <Emp…>

Chapter Glossary

Attributes: data stored inside of a beginning tag.

BCP (bulk copy program)**:** a utility used to export data into/out of a SQL Server table.

Beginning tag: this sits between brackets and contains no slash.

Data: the raw numbers and most granular components that you store in a database.

Elements: XML node storing data between the beginning and ending element tags.

ELEMENTS: optional keyword used to customize the XML stream.

Ending tag: this appears identical to the beginning tag, except it contains a forward slash. Ending tags must follow the same sequence as the beginning tags.

FOR XML: clause which instructs SQL to return data as an XML stream rather than a rowset. The FOR XML clause is appended at the end of the SELECT statement.

Information: the end result after data undergoes value-added processing (e.g., aggregations, calculations, data combined with or compared to other data).

Metadata: data about data; describes your data, including relationships within your data.

Raw: the simplest mode where data is all considered to be at the same level with no nesting. The FOR XML RAW command by default does not create a root. The raw mode likes to store all of its data as attributes.

RDBMS: a relational database management system, such as SQL Server.

ROOT: optional keyword which specifies the ROOT element option.

Root element: also known as the **root node**;

Self-describing data: data and metadata presented together.

Stream: the forming of the data in the way which a program or process prefers to output information. In SQL Server terms, a stream resembles a table: the gridlike presentation of rows and columns that you get when you run a query.

Text editor: text-based program often used to write code (e.g., for use by HTML); Notepad and WordPad are examples of simple text editors.

Top level element: appears directly beneath the root element.

Well-formed XML: XML is considered complete (known as well-formed XML) only if it has a root tag which encompasses all other tags.

XML: Extensible Markup Language.

XML fragment: any XML document, or partial document, that doesn't meet the criteria of well-formed XML.

XSNIL: option which allows you to force a tag(s) to be present even if the underlying data is NULL.

Chapter One - Review Quiz

1.) What do text files, XML streams, and SQL databases all have in common?

O a. They all run only on Windows servers.
O b. They all contain data.
O c. They all contain metadata.

2.) Your root tag is named <Joes2Pros> in your well-formed XML stream. How should the ending root tag be named?

O a. </Joes2Pros>
O b. <\Joes2Pros>
O c. <--Joes2Pros>
O d. <Joes2Pros/>
O e. <Joes2Pros\>

3.) What do you call data inside of a tag like the example seen in below?

<Team Name = "Vikings">

O a. Data fragment
O b. XML fragment
O c. Element
O d. Attribute

4.) RAW is the only XML mode. (Choose True/False.)

O a. True
O b. False

5.) RAW automatically adds the root element tag in SQL Server. (Choose T/F.)

O a. True
O b. False

6.) If you don't specify any option, then XML RAW will have your data streamed in…

O a. Element text.
O b. Attributes.

49

7.) Without XSINIL, what happens to null values from your result set?

    O a. They error out since XSINIL does not allow nulls.

    O b. They appear as empty tags.

    O c. No tags are present for null values.

8.) You are using FOR XML RAW to get your relational data. After testing this, you notice that not all items from the query appear in the XML stream. You notice that this is happening when fields have a NULL value. Only those employees who have values for all elements appear. You need to modify your T-SQL statement so that all employees' tags appear in the XML document. What should you do?

    O a. Add a HAVING clause to the query.

    O b. Remove the RAW option and let SQL pick the default.

    O c. Add the XSINIL argument to the ELEMENTS option in the query.

    O d. Add the replace value to the clause of the query.

Answer Key

1.) b   2.) a   3.) d   4.) b   5.) b   6.) b   7.) c   8.) c

Bug Catcher Game

To play the Bug Catcher game run the SQLInteropBugCatcherCh1.pps from the BugCatcher folder of the companion files. You can obtain these files from www.Joes2Pros.com or by ordering the Companion CD.

Chapter 2.   XML Modes

In the last chapter, we covered creating the XML RAW stream. This chapter will introduce additional XML modes, including XML AUTO and XML PATH. These modes are more commonly used than RAW. We will also explore some additional options to further customize your XML stream.

READER NOTE: *Please run the script SQLInteropChapter1.0Setup.sql in order to follow along with the examples in the first section of Chapter 2. (You only need to run this script once for all examples in Chapters 1 through 4.) All scripts mentioned in this chapter may be found at **www.Joes2Pros.com**.*

XML Auto Mode

By way of contrast, let's first review some features of the Raw mode before we look at Auto. We then will compare the output streams produced by these two XML modes.

In the last chapter, we used the following code to create an XML stream using the Raw mode (see code in Figure 2.1, result stream in Figure 2.2). This code generates one element for each record which appears in the tabular result set. The data appear as attributes, and the default tag is named <row>.

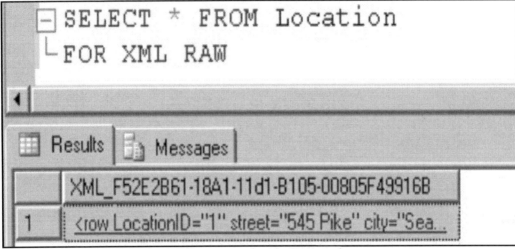

Figure 2.1 This code creates an XML stream using the Raw mode.

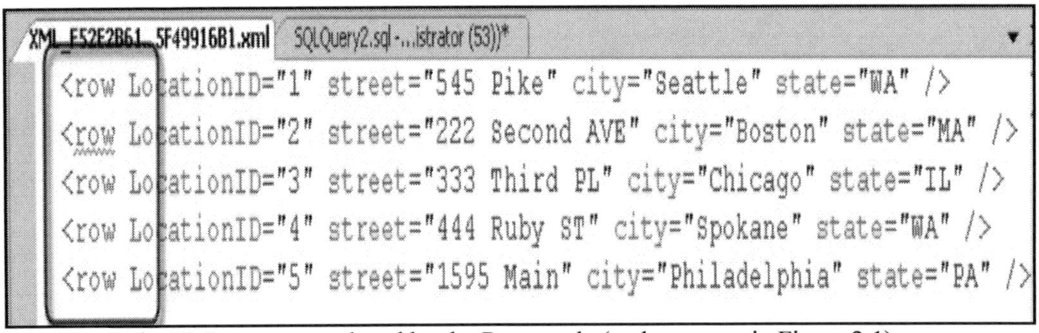

Figure 2.2 The XML stream produced by the Raw mode (code appears in Figure 2.1).

When selecting from a single table, the Auto mode resembles the Raw mode with one exception. Whereas the Raw mode defaults each tag to <row>, the Auto mode names each tag according to the table name (or table alias) listed in the FROM clause of the query.

The code for the Auto mode is similar to the code for Raw.

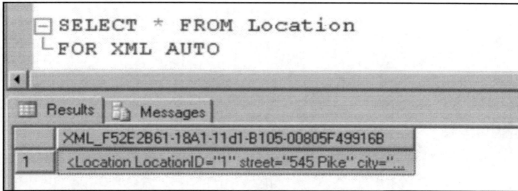

Figure 2.3 This code creates an XML stream using the Auto mode.

The resulting XML is also quite similar to the Raw mode. The data appear as attributes, and by default there is no root element. However, note that the Auto mode has defaulted the row tags to the table name as it appears in the FROM clause. The tag <Location> is named for the Location table.

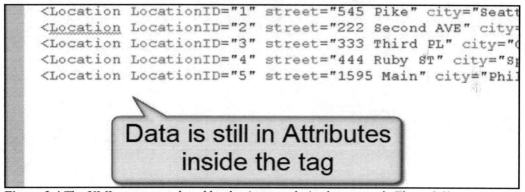

Figure 2.4 The XML stream produced by the Auto mode (code appears in Figure 2.3).

If we specify "Location" in our XML Raw code, then the stream resulting from our Raw query would be identical to our Auto query (see code in Figure 2.5, result stream in Figure 2.6).

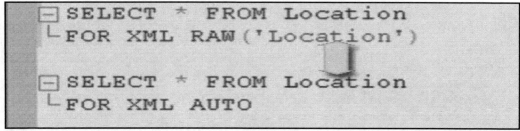

Figure 2.5 These queries will produce an identical result.

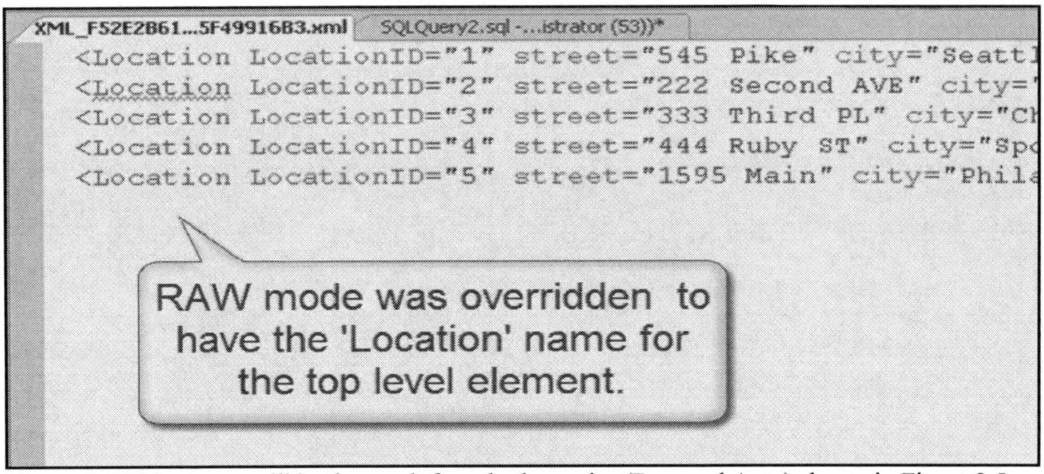

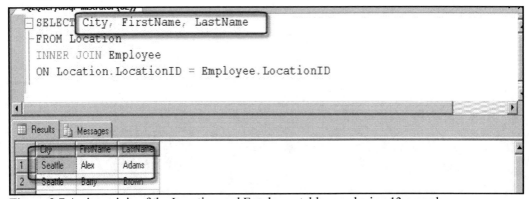

Figure 2.6 This stream will be the result from both queries (Raw and Auto) shown in Figure 2.5.

Our Raw query overrode the default top level element name <row> with <Location>. Because we added this tag name specification to our Raw code, both the Raw and Auto queries produced the same result. This will always be the case, so long as you are selecting from a single table.

MultipleTable XML Queries

Next we will query multiple tables and see that the Raw and Auto modes will again produce similar results.

The query in this example will be an inner join of the Location and Employee tables on the LocationID field (see Figure 2.7). Note that we have 13 records in our result set. Since we've chosen an inner join, John Marshbank's record does not appear in our result.

Figure 2.7 An inner join of the Location and Employee tables producing 13 records.

Now let's view the query above and its result using the XML Raw mode (see code in Figure 2.8, result stream in Figure 2.9). The result is straightforward and consistent with the other streams we've seen thus far in this chapter – the data are contained in attributes, there is no root element, and each record has the default tag name of <row>.

```
SELECT City, FirstName, LastName
FROM Location
INNER JOIN Employee
ON Location.LocationID = Employee.LocationID
FOR XML RAW
```

Results	Messages

XML_F52E2B61-18A1-11d1-B105-00805F49916B

1   <row City="Seattle" FirstName="Alex" LastName="A...

Figure 2.8 Our same inner join query, now adding the XML Raw mode.

```
XML_F52E2B61...5F49916B4.xml    SQLQuery3.sql -...istrator (52))*
<row City="Seattle" FirstName="Alex" LastName="Adams" />
<row City="Seattle" FirstName="Barry" LastName="Brown" />
<row City="Boston" FirstName="Lee" LastName="Osako" />
<row City="Seattle" FirstName="David" LastName="Kennson" />
<row City="Seattle" FirstName="Eric" LastName="Bender" />
<row City="Spokane" FirstName="Lisa" LastName="Kendall" />
<row City="Seattle" FirstName="David" LastName="Lonning" />
<row City="Boston" FirstName="James" LastName="Newton" />
<row City="Boston" FirstName="Terry" LastName="O'Haire" />
```

Figure 2.9 The XML stream produced by the Raw mode (code appears in Figure 2.8).

Add Location to specify that we want the row tag to be named <Location>.

```
SELECT City, FirstName, LastName
FROM Location
INNER JOIN Employee
ON Location.LocationID = Employee.LocationID
FOR XML RAW('Location')
```

Results	Messages

XML_F52E2B61-18A1-11d1-B105-00805F49916B

1   <Location City="Seattle" FirstName="Alex" LastNa...

Figure 2.10 This code specifies that each row tag should be named <Location>.

```
<Location City="Seattle" FirstName="Alex" LastName="Adams" />
<Location City="Seattle" FirstName="Barry" LastName="Brown" />
<Location City="Boston" FirstName="Lee" LastName="Osako" />
<Location City="Seattle" FirstName="David" LastName="Kennson" />
<Location City="Seattle" FirstName="Eric" LastName="Bender" />
<Location City="Spokane" FirstName="Lisa" LastName="Kendall" />
<Location City="Seattle" FirstName="David" LastName="Lonning" />
<Location City="Boston" FirstName="James" LastName="Newton" />
<Location City="Boston" FirstName="Terry" LastName="O'Haire" />
<Location City="Seattle" FirstName="Sally" LastName="Smith" />
<Location City="Spokane" FirstName="Barbara" LastName="O'Neil" />
<Location City="Seattle" FirstName="Phil" LastName="Wilconkinski" />
<Location City="Seattle" FirstName="Janis" LastName="Smith" />
```

We picked the name 'Location' with the Raw option.

Figure 2.11 The XML stream produced by the Raw mode (code appears in Figure 2.10).

Now let's turn our attention to the Auto mode. Since the Auto mode names the tag after the table, how would you expect the result to appear in a multi-table query? Will the tag be named after the Location table or after the Employee table?

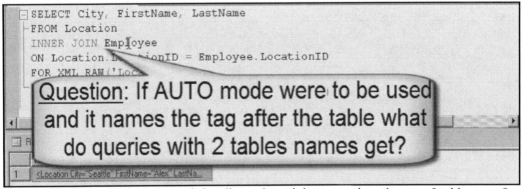

```
SELECT City, FirstName, LastName
FROM Location
INNER JOIN Employee
ON Location.LocationID = Employee.LocationID
FOR XML RAW ('Loc
```

Question: If AUTO mode were to be used and it names the tag after the table what do queries with 2 tables names get?

Figure 2.12 How will the Auto mode handle our inner join query, since there are 2 table names?

Let's test this out by changing our query to include the Auto mode.

```
SELECT City, FirstName, LastName
FROM Location
INNER JOIN Employee
ON Location.LocationID = Employee.LocationID
FOR XML AUTO
```

Results | Messages

XML_F52E2B61-18A1-11d1-B105-00805F49916B

1 | <Location City="Seattle"><Employee FirstName="Al...

Figure 2.13 Our same inner join query, now adding the XML Auto mode.

The answer is "both." The Auto mode generates a tag for each table: the Location data attribute (City) is contained in the <Location> tag, and the Employee data attributes (FirstName, LastName) are contained in the <Employee> tag (see Figure 2.14).

```
XML_F52E2B61...5F49916B6.xml    SQLQuery3.sql -...istrator (52))*

<Location City="Seattle">
    <Employee FirstName="Alex" LastName="Adams" />
    <Employee FirstName="Barry" LastName="Brown" />
</Location>
<Location City="Boston">
    <Employee FirstName="Lee" LastName="Osako" />
</Location>
<Location City="Seattle">
    <Employee FirstName="David" LastName="Kennson" />
    <Employee FirstName="Eric" LastName="Bender" />
</Location>
<Location City="Spokane">
    <Employee FirstName="Lisa" LastName="Kendall" />
</Location>
<Location City="Seattle">
    <Employee FirstName="David" LastName="Lonning" />
</Location>
<Location City="Boston">
    <Employee FirstName="James" LastName="Newton" />
    <Employee FirstName="Terry" LastName="O'Haire" />
</Location>
<Location City="Seattle">
    <Employee FirstName="Sally" LastName="Smith" />
</Location>
```

Figure 2.14 The Auto mode produces a tag for each table in our join query.

So this demonstrates a difference between the Auto mode and the Raw mode. The Auto mode will nest the results, but the Raw mode will not.

Look back to our query (Figure 2.13) and note that the Auto mode placed the tags in the order in which the tables appeared in our query. In this example, the Location table becomes the top level element tag because the first field in the select list is City which is from the Location table (Figure 2.13). The second (nested) table is Employee which appears beneath as a child element.

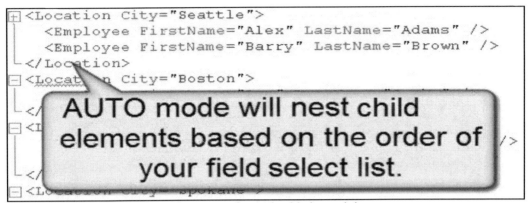

Figure 2.15 The Auto mode produces a tag for each table in our join query.

If you were to list any field from the Employee table first, rather than a field from the Location table, then the Employee element would have the Location element nested inside of it (see Figure 2.16).

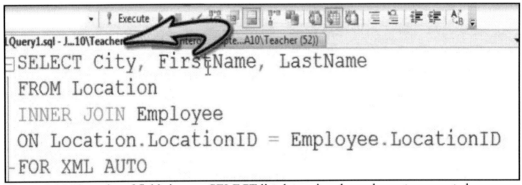

Figure 2.16 The order of fields in your SELECT list determines how elements are nested.

If you switch the field select list and have FirstName appear before City (Figure 2.17) this will cause your XML stream to have Employee as the parent element even though the Location table is listed before the Employee table in the join.

```
SELECT FirstName, City,   LastName
 FROM Location
 INNER JOIN Employee
 ON Location.LocationID = Employee.LocationID
 FOR XML AUTO


<Employee FirstName="Alex" LastName="Adams">
   <Location City="Seattle" />
</Employee>
<Employee FirstName="Barry" LastName="Brown">
   <Location City="Seattle" />
</Employee>
<Employee FirstName="Lee" LastName="Osako">
   <Location City="Boston" />
```

Figure 2.17 The Employee table is the parent element shown here.

Using Root With Auto

Next we'll add a root element (also called *root node*), so that our stream will be well-formed XML.

Using the ROOT keyword in combination with the Auto mode produces the same result as it does with the Raw mode: your XML stream will contain a root (named <root> by default). To specify a name for the root, put this name in the parentheses inside single quotes right after the ROOT keyword in your code (shown in Figure 2.20).

Now let's add a ROOT to our code, because we want to have well-formed XML.

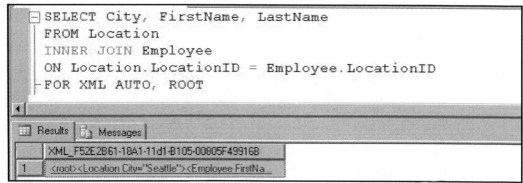

Figure 2.18 We are adding a root element, in order to achieve well-formed XML.

Our XML result appears the same as in the prior result, except that now all of our data is enclosed within the opening and closing tags named <root>.

```
XML-F52E2061...5F49916B7.xml   SQLQuery3.sql -...istrator (52))*                    ▼
<root>
  <Location City="Seattle">
    <Employee FirstName="Alex" LastName="Adams" />
    <Employee FirstName="Barry" LastName="Brown" />
  </Location>
  <Location City="Boston">
    <Employee FirstName="Lee" LastName="Osako" />
  </Location>
  <Location City="Seattle">
    <Employee FirstName="David" LastName="Kennson" />
    <Employee FirstName="Eric" LastName="Bender" />
  </Location>
  <Location City="Spokane">
    <Employee FirstName="Lisa" LastName="Kendall" />
  </Location>
  <Location City="Seattle">
    <Employee FirstName="David" LastName="Lonning" />
  </Location>
  <Location City="Boston">
    <Employee FirstName="James" LastName="Newton" />
    <Employee FirstName="Terry" LastName="O'Haire" />
  </Location>
  <Location City="Seattle">
    <Employee FirstName="Sally" LastName="Smith" />
  </Location>
  <Location City="Spokane">
    <Employee FirstName="Barbara" LastName="O'Neil" />
  </Location>
  <Location City="Seattle">
    <Employee FirstName="Phil" LastName="Wilconkinski" />
    <Employee FirstName="Janis" LastName="Smith" />
  </Location>
</root>
```

Figure 2.19 Our result is the same as previous (Figure 2.14) with the addition of a root element.

Let's take our same code and give the root a more meaningful name. To specify a name for the root, put the name inside single quotes, within parentheses, right after the ROOT keyword in your code. We'll name it <JProCo> after the database which both of our tables come from (please see the code in Figure 2.20 and the result stream in Figure 2.21).

```
SELECT City, FirstName, LastName
FROM Location
INNER JOIN Employee
ON Location.LocationID = Employee.LocationID
FOR XML AUTO, ROOT('JproCo')
```

Results	**Messages**

	XML_F52E2B61-18A1-11d1-B105-00805F49916B
1	<JproCo><Location City="Seattle"><Employee First...

Figure 2.20 We are specifying JProCo as the name of our root element.

```
XML_F52E2B61...5F499168B.xml    SQLQuery3.sql -...istrator (52))*
  <JproCo>
    <Location City="Seattle">
      <Employee FirstName="Alex" LastName="Adams" />
      <Employee FirstName="Barry" LastName="Brown" />
    </Location>
    <Location City="Boston">
      <Employee FirstName="Lee" LastName="Osako" />
    </Location>
    <Location City="Seattle">
      <Employee FirstName="David" LastName="Kennson" />
      <Employee FirstName="Eric" LastName="Bender" />
    </Location>
    <Location City="Spokane">
      <Employee FirstName="Lisa" LastName="Kendall" />
    </Location>
    <Location City="Seattle">
      <Employee FirstName="David" LastName="Lonning" />
    </Location>
    <Location City="Boston">
      <Employee FirstName="James" LastName="Newton" />
      <Employee FirstName="Terry" LastName="O'Haire" />
    </Location>
    <Location City="Seattle">
      <Employee FirstName="Sally" LastName="Smith" />
    </Location>
    <Location City="Spokane">
      <Employee FirstName="Barbara" LastName="O'Neil" />
    </Location>
    <Location City="Seattle">
      <Employee FirstName="Phil" LastName="Wilconkinski" />
      <Employee FirstName="Janis" LastName="Smith" />
    </Location>
  </JproCo>
```

Figure 2.21 The root element of our well-formed XML has been re-named <JProCo>.

Sorting Nested Elements

XML offers a great deal of flexibility in how you can choose to organize your result output. For example, since nine JProCo employees are listed under Seattle, then there is really no need to see Seattle listed multiple times. By sorting on the higher level element, you can put all related child elements under the same parent. This way you don't have to repeatedly list the parent element.

Let's combine our results together in a more efficient and readable manner by grouping the Seattle employees together.

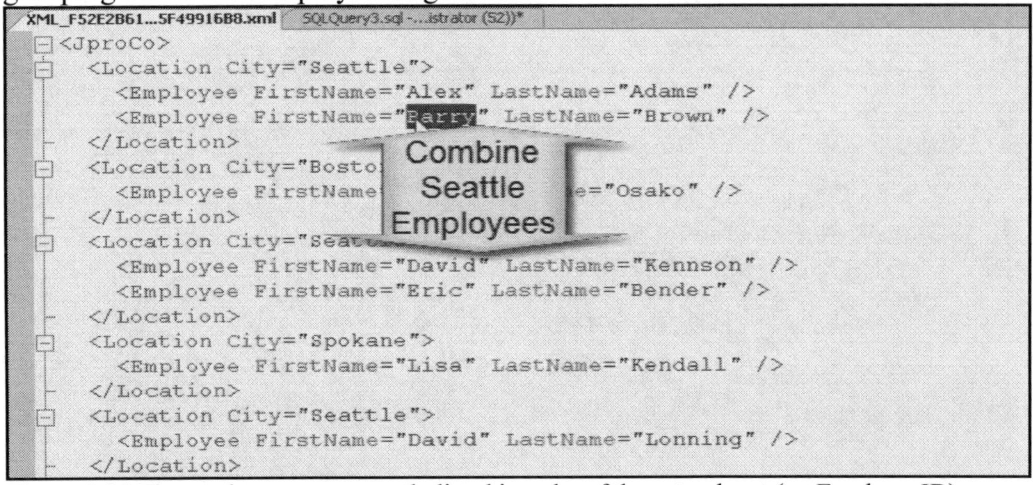
XML_F52E2B61...5F49916B8.xml
SQLQuery3.sql -...istrator (52))*
<JproCo>
<Location City="Seattle">
<Employee FirstName="Alex" LastName="Adams" />
<Employee FirstName="Barry" LastName="Brown" />
</Location>
<Location City="Bosto
<Employee FirstName
e="Osako" />
</Location>
<Location City="Sea
<Employee FirstName="David" LastName="Kennson" />
<Employee FirstName="Eric" LastName="Bender" />
</Location>
<Location City="Spokane">
<Employee FirstName="Lisa" LastName="Kendall" />
</Location>
<Location City="Seattle">
<Employee FirstName="David" LastName="Lonning" />
</Location>
Combine
Seattle
Employees

Figure 2.22 The employees are currently listed in order of the natural sort (on EmployeeID).

Instead of grouping the results by the natural sort of the table (i.e., by EmployeeID), we would prefer to have the the results grouped by city. An ORDER BY clause will help achieve our goal.

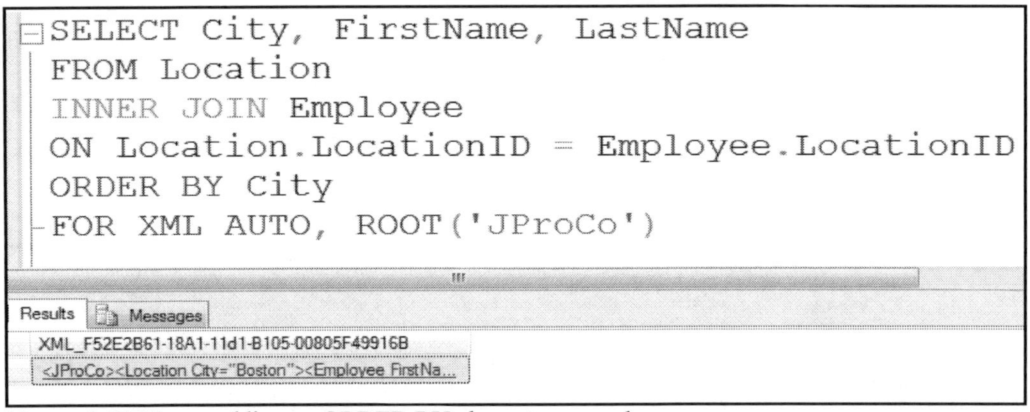
SELECT City, FirstName, LastName
FROM Location
INNER JOIN Employee
ON Location.LocationID = Employee.LocationID
ORDER BY City
FOR XML AUTO, ROOT('JProCo')
Results
Messages
XML_F52E2B61-18A1-11d1-B105-00805F49916B
<JProCo><Location City="Boston"><Employee FirstNa...

Figure 2.23 We are adding an ORDER BY clause to our code.

This result is very readable. We now see each city (Boston, Seattle, and Spokane) listed once along with the employees working in each one.

```
<JProCo>
  <Location City="Boston">
    <Employee FirstName="Lee" LastName="Osako" />
    <Employee FirstName="James" LastName="Newton" />
    <Employee FirstName="Terry" LastName="O'Haire" />
  </Location>
  <Location City="Seattle">
    <Employee FirstName="Alex" LastName="Adams" />
    <Employee FirstName="Barry" LastName="Brown" />
    <Employee FirstName="David" LastName="Kennson" />
    <Employee FirstName="Eric" LastName="Bender" />
    <Employee FirstName="David" LastName="Lonning" />
    <Employee FirstName="Sally" LastName="Smith" />
    <Employee FirstName="Phil" LastName="Wilconkinski" />
    <Employee FirstName="Janis" LastName="Smith" />
  </Location>
  <Location City="Spokane">
    <Employee FirstName="Lisa" LastName="Kendall" />
    <Employee FirstName="Barbara" LastName="O'Neil" />
  </Location>
</JProCo>
```

Figure 2.24 The ORDER BY clause has reorganized and tidied up our XML stream.

Each of the JProCo employees from Boston is listed as a child element below the top level element <Location> which has a City attribute with a value of "Boston". We similarly see the Seattle employees nested beneath the Location with a City attribute of "Seattle".

Lab 2.1: XML Auto Mode

Lab Prep: Before you can begin the lab, you must run the SQLInteropChapter1.0Setup.sql script. It is recommended that you view the lab video instructions found in Lab2.1_XML_AUTO.wmv, available at *www.Joe2Pros.com.*

Skill Check 1: Write a query from the Employee table and join it to the Grant table. Your field select list should include the Employee LastName, FirstName, GrantName, and Amount. Use the correct FOR XML AUTO option and ORDER BY clause to achieve the following output (see Figure 2.25).

```xml
<Charity>
  <Employee LastName="Bender" FirstName="Eric">
    <Grant GrantName="Just Mom" Amount="9900.0000" />
  </Employee>
  <Employee LastName="Brown" FirstName="Barry">
    <Grant GrantName="K-Land fund trust" Amount="15750.0000" />
  </Employee>
  <Employee LastName="Kennson" FirstName="David">
    <Grant GrantName="BIG 6's Foundation%" Amount="21000.0000" />
  </Employee>
  <Employee LastName="Lonning" FirstName="David">
    <Grant GrantName="Robert@BigStarBank.com" Amount="18100.0000" />
    <Grant GrantName="92 Purr_Scents %% team" Amount="4750.0000" />
    <Grant GrantName="www.@-Last-U-Can-Help.com" Amount="25000.0000" />
    <Grant GrantName="Big Giver Tom" Amount="95900.0000" />
  </Employee>
  <Employee LastName="Newton" FirstName="James">
    <Grant GrantName="Mega Mercy" Amount="55000.0000" />
  </Employee>
  <Employee LastName="O'Haire" FirstName="Terry">
    <Grant GrantName="Ben@MoreTechnology.com" Amount="41000.0000" />
  </Employee>
```

Figure 2.25 The result produced by Skill Check 1.

Skill Check 2: Write a query from the Location table and join it to the Employee table. Your field select list should include [State], FirstName, and LastName. Make sure the results cluster the employees by state. Also make sure each employee within each state is listed alphabetically by last name. Use the FOR XML AUTO option and ORDER BY clause. The XML stream should be well formed and include the root called <EmpLocReport>. Your result should resemble Figure 2.26.

```
<EmpLocReport>
  <Location State="MA">
    <Employee FirstName="James" LastName="Newton" />
    <Employee FirstName="Terry" LastName="O'Haire" />
    <Employee FirstName="Lee" LastName="Osako" />
  </Location>
  <Location State="WA">
    <Employee FirstName="Alex" LastName="Adams" />
    <Employee FirstName="Eric" LastName="Bender" />
    <Employee FirstName="Barry" LastName="Brown" />
    <Employee FirstName="Lisa" LastName="Kendall" />
    <Employee FirstName="David" LastName="Kennson" />
    <Employee FirstName="David" LastName="Lonning" />
    <Employee FirstName="Barbara" LastName="O'Neil" />
    <Employee FirstName="Janis" LastName="Smith" />
    <Employee FirstName="Sally" LastName="Smith" />
    <Employee FirstName="Phil" LastName="Wilconkinski" />
  </Location>
</EmpLocReport>
```

Figure 2.26 The result produced by Skill Check 2.

XML Auto Mode - Points to Ponder

1. The FOR XML clause instructs SQL Server to return data as an XML stream rather than a rowset.

2. Each row in XML Auto is named after the table (or the table alias).

3. Raw does not nest the result of multi-table queries, whereas Auto does.

4. When you use Auto mode with a JOIN query, SQL Server nests the resulting values in the order in which the tables appear in the SELECT list.

5. Auto mode also enables you to specify whether columns are mapped as elements or attributes within the XML stream:

   o If you specify the ELEMENTS option, then your Auto data will appear as elements.

   o If you leave the ELEMENTS option off, then Auto will default to showing your data as attributes.

6. You can use Auto to organize your data into either elements or attributes, but you cannot mix them. Your XML result must contain either all elements or all attributes.

XML Path Mode

The XML Raw and Auto modes are great for displaying data as all attributes or all elements – but not both at once. If you want your XML stream to have some of its data shown in attributes and some shown as elements, then you can use the XML Path mode.

The following Select statement shows us all locations and the employees who work in each location. There are 13 matching records in this inner join between the Location and Employee tables. The Location table is aliased "Loc", and the Employee table is aliased "Emp." Recall that in SQL the AS keyword is recommended when aliasing tables, but it is optional (see Figure 2.27).

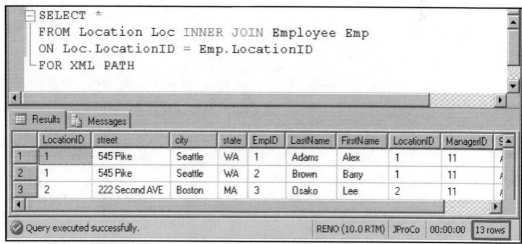

Figure 2.27 An inner join query between the Location and Employee tables.

Let's stream this query in an XML mode, called Path.

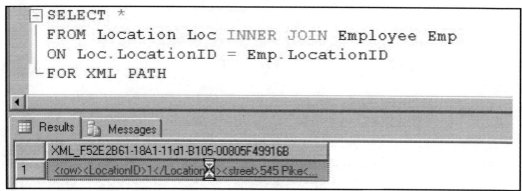

Figure 2.28 We will stream our query in the XML Path mode.

Much like Raw and Auto, each top level element has tag named "row" and by default there is no root element. However, unlike the previous modes we've seen, the Path mode defaults to putting all its data in elements.

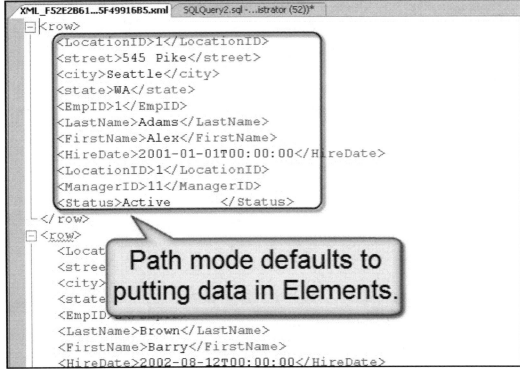

Figure 2.29 Our inner join query streamed as an XML Path output.

Now we'll itemize the fields in our query.

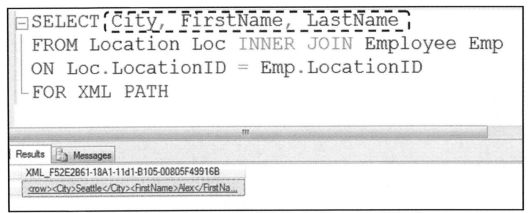

Figure 2.30 We've itemized our field list and will look at the revised XML Path stream.

The result appears much the same. We see "row" as the default name of the opening and closing tags. We also see nested within each "row", elements for each of the three fields we itemized in our query (City, FirstName, LastName).

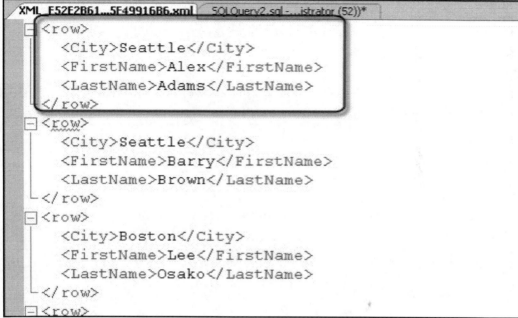

Figure 2.31 Our itemized query (code appears in Figure 2.30) streamed as an XML Path output.

Our next goal is to modify our SQL query, so that our XML result will include an <Employees> root tag.

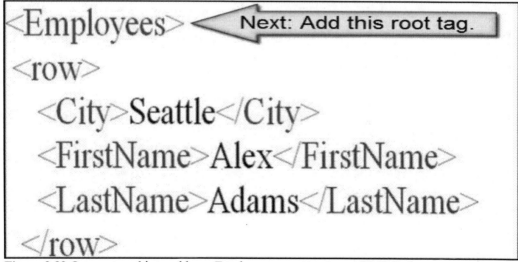

Figure 2.32 Our next goal is to add an <Employees> root tag to our XML Path output.

As we've seen in previous examples, we simply need to modify our FOR XML Path clause to include ROOT('Employees').

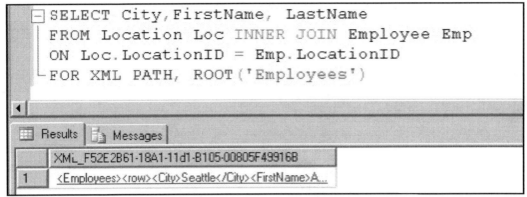

Figure 2.33 Our code now includes the root element <Employees>.

In the result, we see that we now have our root, which is called "Employees" (see Figure 2.34).

Figure 2.34 The root element <Employees> is now visible in our XML Path stream.

Let's change our current stream (code in Figure 2.33, output shown in Figure 2.34) to have each top level element tagged as <Employee> instead of <row>.

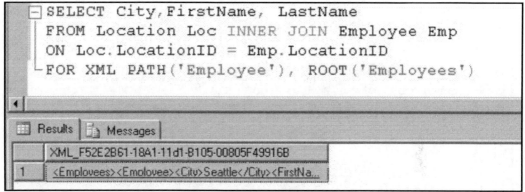

```
SELECT City, FirstName, LastName
FROM Location Loc INNER JOIN Employee Emp
ON Loc.LocationID = Emp.LocationID
FOR XML PATH('Employee'), ROOT('Employees')
```

	XML_F52E2B61-18A1-11d1-B105-00805F49916B
1	<Employees><Employee><City>Seattle</City><FirstNa...

Figure 2.35 Our code will tag each top level element as <Employee> instead of <row>.

Our stream is looking much more readable and organized. Each top level element is now called <Employee> instead of <row> (see Figure 2.36).

Figure 2.36 The top level element <Employee> is now visible in our XML Path stream.

Custom Attributes

If you are using an XML Path stream, then by default all of the values will be shown as elements. However, you can pick one or more of your elements to instead be shown as an attribute(s). Use the [@Fieldname] syntax to do this.

Our next goal is to move City inside the <Employee> tag as an attribute. The [@Fieldname] construct will help us accomplish this.

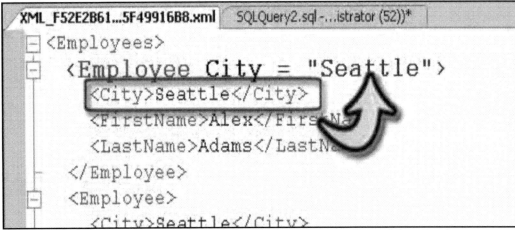

Figure 2.37 A mockup of our next goal: make City become an attribute of the <Employee> tag.

To make our code reflect this change, all we need to do is alias the City field as @City. (For illustrative purposes, we will alias the attribute as "CityName" instead of "City." Just as when we have previously aliased fields and tables in our SQL queries, with our XML queries we also have the freedom to alias the field City using any name we choose.) One easy way to think of this code syntax is to remember that @ (a.k.a., the "at" sign) goes with "**AT**tributes".

```
SELECT City AS [@CityName], FirstName, LastName
FROM Location Loc INNER JOIN Employee Emp
ON Loc.LocationID = Emp.LocationID
FOR XML PATH('Employee'), ROOT('Employees')
```

Results | Messages

XML_F52E2B61-18A1-11d1-B105-00805F49916B

1 | <Employees><Employee CityName="Seattle"><FirstNa...

Figure 2.38 We have aliased the City field to become an attribute of the top-level element.

City is now an attribute of Employee, instead of a separate element.

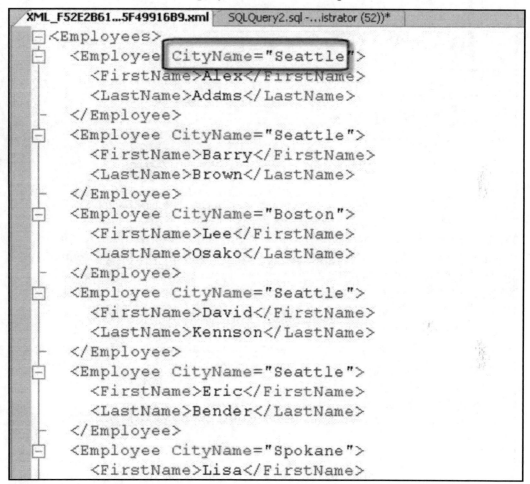

Figure 2.39 Our XML Path output shows CityName as an attribute of the Employee element.

Custom Elements

The element's name does not need to be named after the field from the table. You can set it to anything you want by specifying a field alias.

For our next goal, we want the FirstName element to instead be called <First> and the LastName element to instead be called <Last>. In other words, we will rename (or alias) these two XML elements.

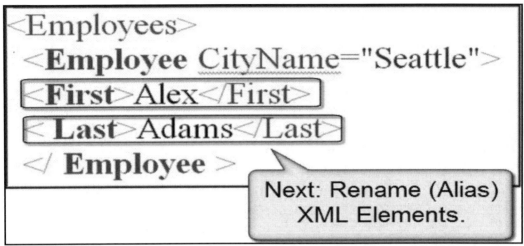

Figure 2.40 A mockup of our next goal: rename two elements (FirstName and LastName).

When we changed the <City> element into the attribute CityName, recall we needed to prefix the alias with the @ symbol (our mnemonic device reminds us we need an "at" sign when turning an element into an "**AT**tribute"). However, the XML Path mode defaults to representing data as elements (as shown earlier in Figure 2.29). So all we need to do here is alias the fields using the AS [ElementName] syntax.

```
SELECT City AS [@CityName], FirstName [First], LastName [Last]
FROM Location Loc INNER JOIN Employee Emp
ON Loc.LocationID = Emp.LocationID
FOR XML PATH('Employee'), ROOT('Employees')
```

Results | Messages
XML_F52E2B61-18A1-11d1-B105-00805F499168
<Employees><Employee CityName="Seattle"><First>A...

Figure 2.41 We have aliased (renamed) the FirstName and LastName elements.

Our result (see Figure 2.42) is similar to our previous stream (shown in Figure 2.39). Data previously shown as attributes are still attributes, and all the elements are still elements. The only change is that the original element names (FirstName and LastName) have changed (to First and Last, respectively).

```
XML_F52E2B61...49916B11.xml    SQLQuery2.sql -...istrator (52))*
<Employees>
   <Employee CityName="Seattle">
      <First>Alex</First>
      <Last>Adams</Last>
   </Employee>
   <Employee CityName="Seattle">
      <First>Barry</First>
      <Last>Brown</Last>
   </Employee>
   <Employee CityName="Boston">
      <First>Lee</First>
      <Last>Osako</Last>
   </Employee>
```

Figure 2.42 The elements originally called FirstName and LastName are now First and Last.

Custom Level and Nesting

The Path mode also nests elements within other elements. The nesting order is based on the order of fields in your SELECT list.

Our final Path example will introduce a custom element <Name> just beneath the top level element <Employee>. We will nest this element above the elements <First> and <Last>.

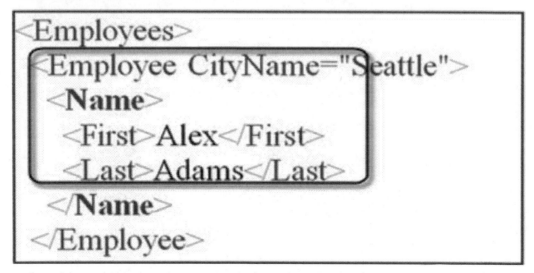

Figure 2.43 A mockup of our next goal: add and nest the custom element <Name>.

Specify a custom level by adding a / (forward slash) before each element that you want nested immediately below the new level. The name of the custom level precedes the forward slash.

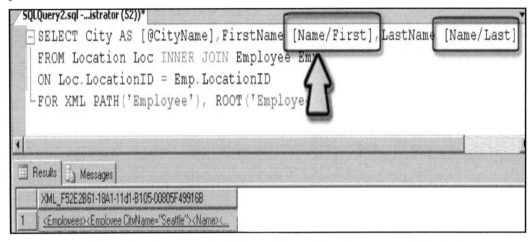

Figure 2.44 We have added a custom level "Name" nested just above the child-level elements, <First> and <Last>.

Our goal has been achieved. A new child level element <Name> appears beneath <Employee> and includes our aliased elements, <First> and <Last>.

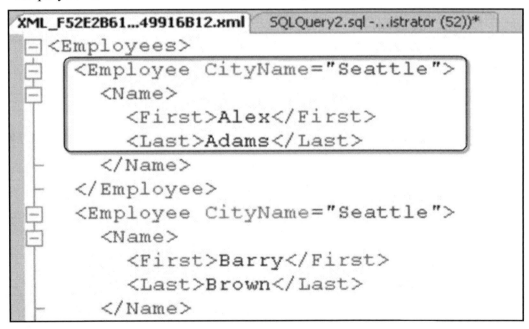

Figure 2.45 Our final Path stream includes a custom level nested beneath the top-level element and above our custom elements, <First> and <Last>.

Lab 2.2: XML Path Mode

Lab Prep: Before you can begin the lab you must run the SQLInteropChapter1.0Setup.sql script. It is recommended that you view the lab video instructions found in Lab2.2_XML_Path_Mode.wmv, available at *www.Joe2Pros.com*.

Skill Check 1: Create an XML stream by selecting the EmpID, FirstName, and LastName fields from the Employee table. Call your root <HR> and your top level element <Employee>. The EmpID field and its value should be an attribute of the <Employee> element. The tags should be <FNmae> for the FirstName field and <LName> for LastName. Your result will match Figure 2.46.

```
<HR>
  <Employee EmpID="1">
    <FName>Alex</FName>
    <LName>Adams</LName>
  </Employee>
  <Employee EmpID="2">
    <FName>Barry</FName>
    <LName>Brown</LName>
  </Employee>
  <Employee EmpID="3">
    <FName>Lee</FName>
    <LName>Osaka</LName>
```

Figure 2.46 XML Stream, Skill Check 1.

Skill Check 2: Create an XML stream by selecting the GrantID, GrantName, and Amount fields from the [Grant] table. Make sure your root is called <Charity> and your top level element is called <Grants>. The GrantID and GrantName fields and their values should be attributes of the Grants element. The value of the Amount field should be an element under the <Grants> element. When done, your result should resemble the figure below (see Figure 2.47).

```
<Charity>
  <Grants GrantID="001" GrantName="92 Purr_Scents %% team">
    <Amount>4750.0000</Amount>
  </Grants>
  <Grants GrantID="002" GrantName="K-Land fund trust">
    <Amount>15750.0000</Amount>
  </Grants>
  <Grants GrantID="003" GrantName="Robert@BigStarBank.com">
    <Amount>18100.0000</Amount>
  </Grants>
  <Grants GrantID="005" GrantName="BIG 6's Foundation%">
    <Amount>21000.0000</Amount>
  </Grants>
  <Grants GrantID="006" GrantName="TALTA_Kishan International">
    <Amount>18100.0000</Amount>
  </Grants>
```

Figure 2.47 XML Stream, Skill Check 2 result.

Skill Check 3: Create an XML stream using the CurrentProducts table's fields ProductID, ProductName, Category, and RetailPrice. Call your root <Products> and your top level element <Product>. The ProductID and Price fields' values should be inside the <Product> element as two attributes. The value for the ProductName field should be an element under the <Product> element and named PName. The value for the ProductCategory field should be an element under the <Product> element and named PCat. When you're done, your result will resemble this figure (see Figure 2.48).

```
<Products>
   <Product ID="1" Price="61.4830">
      <PName>Underwater Tour 1 Day West Coast</PName>
      <PCat>No-Stay</PCat>
   </Product>
   <Product ID="2" Price="110.6694">
      <PName>Underwater Tour 2 Days West Coast</PName>
      <PCat>Overnight-Stay</PCat>
   </Product>
   <Product ID="3" Price="184.4490">
      <PName>Underwater Tour 3 Days West Coast</PName>
      <PCat>Medium-Stay</PCat>
   </Product>
   <Product ID="4" Price="245.9320">
      <PName>Underwater Tour 5 Days West Coast</PName>
      <PCat>Medium-Stay</PCat>
   </Product>
```

Figure 2.48 XML Stream, Skill Check 3 result.

Skill Check 4: Create an XML stream by selecting the EmpID, ManagerID, FirstName and LastName fields from the Employee table. The root should be called JProCo and the top level element called Employee. Set the EmpID as an attribute called ID in the top level element. The ManagerID should appear below the top level element and be called BossID. FirstName and LastName should appear under a custom element named Name. Your result should resemble Figure 2.49.

```
<JProCo>
   <Employee ID="1">
      <BossID>11</BossID>
      <Name>
         <Last>Adams</Last>
         <First>Alex</First>
      </Name>
   </Employee>
   <Employee ID="2">
      <BossID>11</BossID>
      <Name>
         <Last>Brown</Last>
         <First>Barry</First>
      </Name>
   </Employee>
```

Figure 2.49 XML Stream, Skill Check 4.

Answer Code: The T-SQL code to this lab can be found in the downloadable files in a file named Lab2.2_XML_Path_Mode.sql.

XML Path Mode - Points to Ponder

1. Raw and Auto modes both can use the ELEMENTS option. If ELEMENTS is not used, then both Raw and Auto will display your XML stream in attributes.

2. Path mode queries can produce customized XML layouts of mixed attributes and elements which can't be achieved by AUTO or RAW.

3. Path mode queries recognize a syntax called XPath to easily customize the layout.

4. Using @ ("at symbol") at the beginning of your XPath statement tells SQL to make this data part of an attribute.

5. Leaving off @ ("at symbol") means you want the data in an element.

6. The XPath command allows syntax (like EmployeeID "@EmpID", FirstName "EmpName/First") to put data in both elements and attributes.

7. In XPath you can delimit the field names with ' ' or [ ].

8. The FOR XML Path clause supports the addition of a root element by appending a ROOT clause at the end of your statement.

9. If you don't specify the ROOT keyword then there won't be a root tag set.

10. If you don't specify a top level element name after the Path clause then each record's element will have the <row> tag.

XML Nameless Fields

A nameless field belongs to no tag in your XML file. This can be useful for manipulating your XML stream for readability. In the examples we will see, an element tag will be rendered "nameless" by using a wildcard to alias the tag in our XML.

Begin with this simple query which returns two fields from all 14 records of the Employee table.

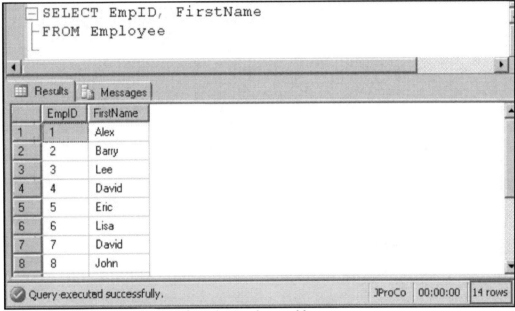

Figure 2.50 Begin with this query from the Employee table.

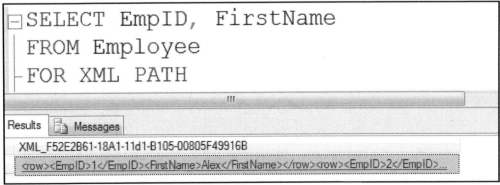

Figure 2.51 Stream this query as an XML Path output.

Since we know XML Path doesn't include a root by default, and we haven't specified a root, this is not well-formed XML.

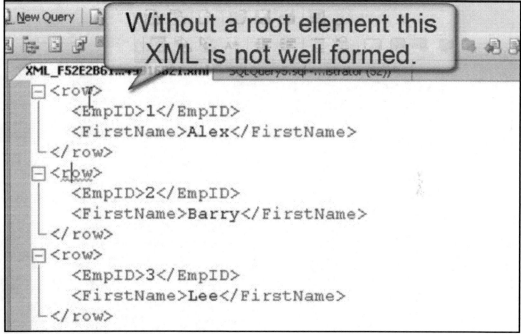

Figure 2.52 This is not well-formed XML.

Add a root and name each top level element <Employee>.

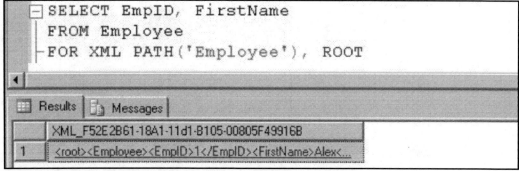

Figure 2.53 This code will produce well-formed XML.

Our code has produced a well-formed XML document.

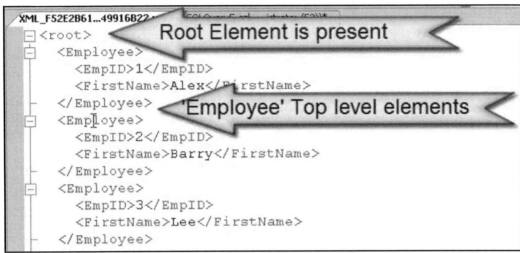

Figure 2.54 This is well-formed XML which now includes a root element.

Our goal will be to move each employee's name up to appear right after the ending tag for </EmpID>. We do not wish to see the element tag <FirstName>.

Figure 2.55 The mockup of our next goal.

If we use a wildcard to accomplish this goal, then our XML stream will appear just like the right hand panel shown here.

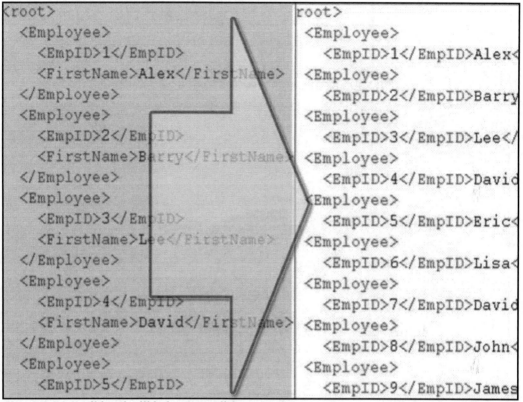

Figure 2.56 A wildcard will help accomplish our goal.

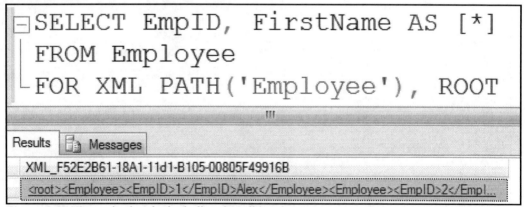

Figure 2.57 The revised code, including the wildcard.

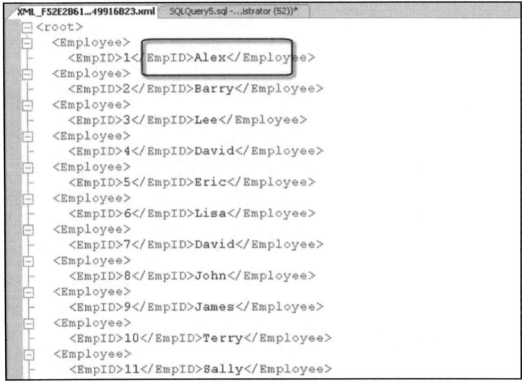

```
XML_F52E2B61...49916823.xml    SQLQuery5.sql -...istrator (52))*
<root>
   <Employee>
      <EmpID>1</EmpID>Alex</Employee>
   <Employee>
      <EmpID>2</EmpID>Barry</Employee>
   <Employee>
      <EmpID>3</EmpID>Lee</Employee>
   <Employee>
      <EmpID>4</EmpID>David</Employee>
   <Employee>
      <EmpID>5</EmpID>Eric</Employee>
   <Employee>
      <EmpID>6</EmpID>Lisa</Employee>
   <Employee>
      <EmpID>7</EmpID>David</Employee>
   <Employee>
      <EmpID>8</EmpID>John</Employee>
   <Employee>
      <EmpID>9</EmpID>James</Employee>
   <Employee>
      <EmpID>10</EmpID>Terry</Employee>
   <Employee>
      <EmpID>11</EmpID>Sally</Employee>
```

Figure 2.58 Our XML Path query, including the wildcard, has accomplished our desired output.

Let's see that step again, this time with two fields from the Location table.

```
SELECT city, Street
FROM Location
```

	city	Street
1	Seattle	545 Pike
2	Boston	222 Second AVE
3	Chicago	333 Third PL
4	Spokane	444 Ruby ST
5	Philadelphia	1595 Main

Figure 2.59 Begin with this query from the Location table.

Figure 2.60 Stream the query as an XML Path output.

Here is our output thus far. There is no root, each record has the default <row> tag, and City and Street are nested elements.

```
<row>
    <city>Seattle</city>
    <Street>545 Pike</Street>
</row>
<row>
    <city>Boston</city>
    <Street>222 Second AVE</Street>
</row>
<row>
    <city>Chicago</city>
    <Street>333 Third PL</Street>
</row>
```

Figure 2.61 The preliminary output produced by our query.

We will name our top level element <Location> and add a root element named <Geography>.

```
SELECT city, Street
FROM Location
FOR XML PATH('Location'), ROOT('Geography')
```

Results   Messages

XML_F52E2B61-18A1-11d1-B105-00805F49916B
1	<Geography><Location><city>Seattle</city><Street

Figure 2.62 Name the top level element <Location> and add a root element named <Geography>.

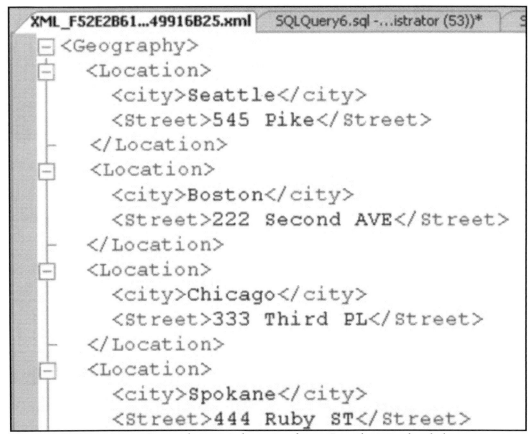

Figure 2.63 We see our <Geography> root element and our <Location> top level element.

Similar to our previous example, our next goal will move the second element <Street> up and have it appear next to the first element, <city>.

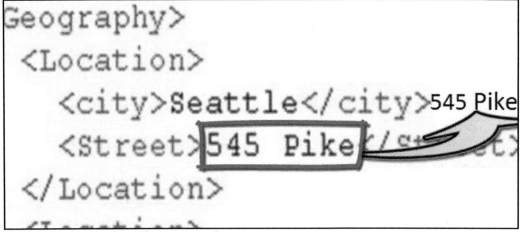

Figure 2.64 The mockup of our next goal.

As we saw previously, the use of an asterisk wildcard [*] will help accomplish our goal.

Figure 2.65 Our revised code, including the wildcard.

Since the wildcard character makes the field "nameless" in the XML stream, the element tag <Street> will not appear in our output (see Figure 2.66).

Figure 2.66 The "nameless" Street field value is now to the right of the <city> element.

Lab 2.3: XML Nameless Fields

Lab Prep: Before you can begin the lab you must run the SQLInteropChapter1.0Setup.sql script. It is recommended that you view the lab video instructions found in Lab2.3_XML_NamelessXMLFields.wmv, available at *www.Joe2Pros.com.*

Skill Check 1: Write a query that shows the CustomerID and CustomerType fields from the Customer Table. Turn this query into an XML Path stream. Name the root SalesData and the top level element Cust. The CustomerID field should be an element. The CustomerType field should be nameless and be placed directly after the ending CustomerID tag.

```
<SalesData>
  <Cust>
    <CustomerID>1</CustomerID>Consumer</Cust>
  <Cust>
    <CustomerID>2</CustomerID>Consumer</Cust>
  <Cust>
    <CustomerID>3</CustomerID>Consumer</Cust>
  <Cust>
    <CustomerID>4</CustomerID>Consumer</Cust>
  <Cust>
    <CustomerID>5</CustomerID>Business</Cust>
  <Cust>
    <CustomerID>6</CustomerID>Consumer</Cust>
  <Cust>
```

Figure 2.67 Skill Check 1 XML stream .

Skill Check 2: Write a query that shows the ProductName and RetailPrice fields from the CurrentProducts Table. Turn this query into an XML Path stream. Name the root ProductFeed and the top level element Product. The RetailPrice field should be named Price and should appear as an attribute of the top level element. The ProductName field should be nameless.

```
<ProductFeed>
  <Product Price="61.4830">Underwater Tour 1 Day West Coast</Product>
  <Product Price="110.6694">Underwater Tour 2 Days West Coast</Product>
  <Product Price="184.4490">Underwater Tour 3 Days West Coast</Product>
  <Product Price="245.9320">Underwater Tour 5 Days West Coast</Product>
  <Product Price="307.4150">Underwater Tour 1 Week West Coast</Product>
  <Product Price="553.3470">Underwater Tour 2 Weeks West Coast</Product>
  <Product Price="80.8590">Underwater Tour 1 Day East Coast</Product>
  <Product Price="145.5462">Underwater Tour 2 Days East Coast</Product>
  <Product Price="242.5770">Underwater Tour 3 Days East Coast</Product>
  <Product Price="323.4360">Underwater Tour 5 Days East Coast</Product>
  <Product Price="404.2950">Underwater Tour 1 Week East Coast</Product>
  <Product Price="727.7310">Underwater Tour 2 Weeks East Coast</Product>
  <Product Price="105.0590">Underwater Tour 1 Day Mexico</Product>
  <Product Price="189.1062">Underwater Tour 2 Days Mexico</Product>
  <Product Price="315.1770">Underwater Tour 3 Days Mexico</Product>
  <Product Price="420.2360">Underwater Tour 5 Days Mexico</Product>
  <Product Price="525.2950">Underwater Tour 1 Week Mexico</Product>
```

Figure 2.68 Skill Check 2 XML stream.

Answer Code: The T-SQL code to this lab can be found in the downloadable files in a file named Lab2.3_NamelessFields.sql

XML Nameless Fields - Points to Ponder

1.   If the column name is aliased with the wildcard character [*], then the content will have no named XML element or attribute.

2.   The wildcard character * should be surrounded by square brackets.

3.   The wildcard character makes the field nameless in your XML stream.

4.   If you have multiple columns with the wildcard [*] then they will be concatenated together in the same nameless field.

Chapter Glossary

Auto mode: XML Auto mode; defaults to display data as attributes.

Nameless fields: aliasing a field within the SELECT list "AS [*]" ensures that the field will have no named XML attribute or element; the wildcard character makes the field nameless in the XML stream.

Path mode: XML Path mode; defaults to display data as elements; Path mode queries can produce customized XML layouts of mixed attributes and elements which cannot be achieved by using AUTO or RAW.

Chapter Two - Review Quiz

1.) What is the only XML mode that will not nest elements of multi-table queries according to the order of fields in the select list?

O a.   XML RAW
O b.   XML AUTO
O c.   XML PATH

2.) What is the only XML mode which defaults to element without using the Elements option?

O a.   XML RAW
O b.   XML AUTO
O c.   XML PATH

3.) What alias will cause the EmpID field to become an attribute?

O a.   EmpID as [@EmpID]
O b.   EmpID as @EmpID
O c.   EmpID as [Employee/EmpID]
O d.   EmpID @ [EmpID]

4.) What XML wildcard can make a field nameless in the XML?

O a.   [null]
O b.   [xsinull]
O c.   [xsinil]
O d.   [*]
O e.   [@]

5.) You want to create an XML stream which is attribute-based and has each row called <row>. Which code do you append to the FOR XML?

O a.   AUTO
O b.   RAW

6.) You want to create an XML stream from a query that uses two tables in an INNER JOIN. You do NOT want any nesting in your XML in the result set. Which code do you append in the FOR XML clause?

O a.   AUTO
O b.   RAW

7.) If you don't put ROOT after the XML AUTO clause, then what happens?

O a.   You get well formed XML.
O b.   You don't get well formed XML.

8.) You have a query which joins tables. You want to create a well-formed XML stream, which is attribute-based and nests the results in the table from the first field of the select list. Which code do you append to the SQL statement?

O a.   FOR XML AUTO
O b.   FOR XML RAW
O c.   FOR XML AUTO, ROOT
O d.   FOR XML RAW, ROOT

9.) You have a table named Location and want to produce the following XML stream.

```
<JProCo>
  <Site LocationID="1"><CityName>Seattle</CityName ></ Site >
  <Site LocationID="2"><CityName >Boston</CityName ></ Site >
  <Site LocationID="3"><CityName >Chicago</CityName ></ Site >
  <Site LocationID="4"><CityName >Spokane</CityName ></ Site>
</JProCo>
```

Which query will achieve this result?

O a.   SELECT LocID AS [@LocationID] , City AS [CityName]
       FROM Location
       FOR XML PATH('Site'), ROOT('JProCo')

O b.   SELECT LocID AS [LocationID] , City AS [@CityName]
       FROM Location
       FOR XML PATH('Site'), ROOT('JProCo')

O c.   SELECT LocID AS [@LocationID] , City AS [@CityName]
       FROM Location
       FOR XML PATH('Site'), ROOT('JProCo')

10.) You are selecting the LocationID, City, and [State] fields from the Location table. Your XML output is seen below.

```
<JProCo>
  <Site LocationID="1"><City>Seattle</CityName >WA</ Site >
  <Site LocationID="2"><City >Boston</CityName >MA</ Site >
  <Site LocationID="3"><City >Chicago</CityName >IL</ Site >
  <Site LocationID="4"><City >Spokane</CityName >WA</ Site>
</JProCo>
```

Which field is using the [*] wildcard?

  O a.   LocationID
  O b.   City
  O c.   State

11.) You have a table named Location and want to produce the following XML stream:

```
<JProCo>
  <Site LocationID="1">
        <Area>
                <City>Seattle</City>
                <State>WA</State>
        </Area>
  </ Site >
  <Site LocationID="2">
        <Area>
                <City>Boston</City>
                <State>MA</State>
        </Area>
  </ Site >
</JProCo>
```

Which query will achieve this result?

O a. SELECT LocationID [@LocationID] ,City [Area], [City], State [State]
       FROM Location
       FOR XML PATH('Site'), ROOT('JProCo')

O b. SELECT LocationID [@LocationID] , City [Area/City], State [Area/State]
       FROM Location
       FOR XML PATH('Site'), ROOT('JProCo')

O c. SELECT LocationID [@LocationID] , City [City/Area], State [State/Area]
       FROM Location
       FOR XML PATH('Site'), ROOT('JProCo')

Answer Key

1.) a   2.) c   3.) a   4.) d   5.) b   6.) b   7.) b   8.) c   9.) a   10.) c   11.) b

Bug Catcher Game

To play the Bug Catcher game run the SQLInteropBugCatcherCh2.pps from the BugCatcher folder of the companion files. You can obtain these files from www.Joes2Pros.com or by ordering the Companion CD.

Chapter 3.   Shredding XML

At the opening of this book, we mentioned the rapid adoption and popularity of the XML standard. Within just a few years of its debut, its flexibility and ability to work between a variety of platforms quickly made XML a "go-to" method for sharing data between programs, as well as with web applications. While SQL Server has provided XML support since its 2000 version, each subsequent version has consistently stepped up SQL Server's capabilities and options for utilizing and interacting with XML. It should be no surprise that your preparation for SQL certification includes XML. No matter what your intended role (Analyst, Developer, or DBA), any serious work in the database world will invariably include XML data.

Our introduction to XML thus far has focused on seeing tabular data taken from SQL Server and streamed into well-formed XML instead of the rowset data we typically work with. The next two chapters will focus on the reverse process. Our starting point will be data which is already in XML and which we will turn into table data, or which we will query in order to answer questions.

Operations which parse and consume XML data are known collectively by the term **shredding XML**. This chapter will focus on the steps to prepare an XML stream so you can turn it into a table or some other tabular result set.

READER NOTE: *Please run the script SQLInteropChapter1.0Setup.sql in order to follow along with the examples in the first section of Chapter 3. (You only need to run this script once for all examples in Chapters 1 through 4.) All scripts mentioned in this chapter may be found at **www.Joes2Pros.com**.*

Consuming XML

Anytime you turn XML into another data format (e.g., into a SQL Server table) that process is called **shredding XML**. Before you can shred your XML, you must first prepare it. **Preparing XML** for SQL means storing the XML in a memory space where a query can retrieve and make use of the data.

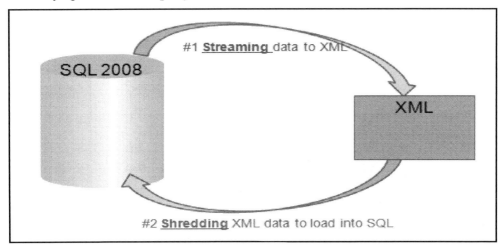

Figure 3.1 SQL Server 2008 provides native XML support to make streaming and shredding XML more robust.

Notice we need to devote an entire chapter to the preparation steps necessary before SQL Server can consume XML. This chapter is being written at the approach of the North American Thanksgiving holidays, which may provide us with a helpful analogy: *think of XML as a big meal for SQL.* While we essentially added just one line of code to our Select query to turn tabular data into an XML document, going the other direction is more complex. Behind the scenes, SQL Server uses additional memory when consuming XML. Our preparation will include a step to parse and store the XML document in memory. And the same way a big feast requires additional cleanup, we must include a step to remove the XML document from the memory cache once it is no longer needed.

In earlier chapters, we produced XML using the modes Raw, Auto, and Path. We used familiar data from the JProCo database (Employee, Location, Grant, and Customer data). We refined and manipulated our XML queries in order for the XML result to appear according to our precise specifications (see example shown in Figure 3.2).

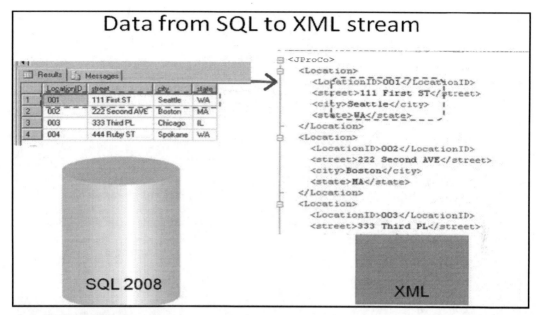

Figure 3.2 Our initial work focused on streaming data into XML.

Now that we understand the essential rules and components of well-formed XML documents, we will turn our attention toward consuming XML data (as shown in Figure 3.3). In Chapter 7 we will see an advanced method (nodes) for shredding XML.

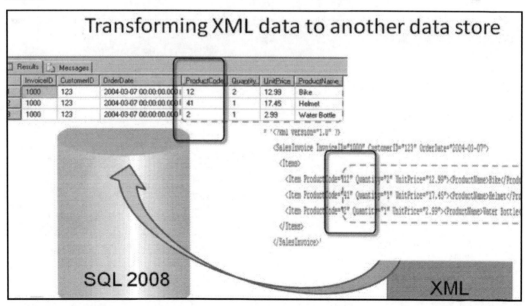

Figure 3.3 Next we will examine the processes for sending data the other direction: from XML into data consumable by SQL Server.

Lab 3.1: Consuming XML

Lab Prep: Before you can begin the lab you must run the SQLInteropChapter1.0Setup.sql script. It is recommended that you view the lab video instructions found in Lab3.1_ConsumingXML.wmv, available at *www.Joe2Pros.com*.

Skill Check 1: Suppose you want to take the XML document shown here and send just the ProductID and Quantity into a result set in SQL server. What type of operation would this be? (Streaming | Parsing | Shredding)

```
<cust CustomerID="2" CustomerType="Consumer">
  <Order InvoiceID="943" OrderDate="2008-02-07T02:45:03.840">
    <OrderDetail ProductID="72" Quantity="4" />
  </Order>
</cust>
```

	ProductID	Quantity
1	72	4

Figure 3.4 Decide whether the action shown is streaming, parsing, or shredding. (Skill Check 1)

Skill Check 2: Which arrow represents Shredding XML?

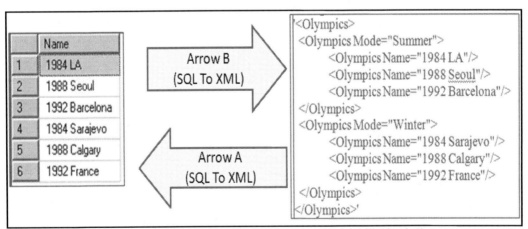

Figure 3.5 Select the Arrow which depicts XML being shredded (Skill Check 2).

Consuming XML - Points to Ponder

1. SQL Server can turn table data into XML data.

2. SQL Server can turn XML data into tabular data.

3. XML shredding is the process of extracting data from XML streams and turning them into a tabular stream (e.g., a table).

Preparing XML in Memory

If you want to take XML data and create a result set in SQL Server, you must first store the XML in memory. The process of preparing XML in SQL includes storing the XML in memory and processing the XML so that all the data and metadata is ready and available for you to query.

Preparing XML for SQL Server is similar to how you prepare anything. If you were preparing a Thanksgiving dinner, you would take the necessary ingredients and follow a process to assemble and present them as a meal – that is, in a way your guests can readily identify and consume them. The internal cache prepares your XML and all the data and metadata so you can consume just the records or fields you want.

We will begin by creating an XML document for use in our example. Begin with this SELECT query before adding the FOR XML Auto clause (Figures 3.6 & 3.7).

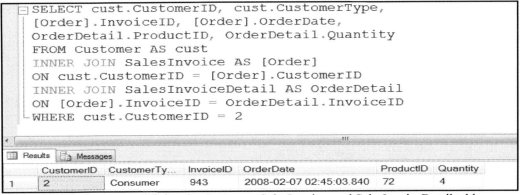

Figure 3.6 The base query joining the Customer, SalesInvoice, and SalesInvoiceDetail tables.

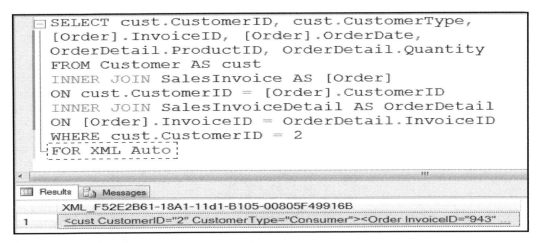

Figure 3.7 The base query with the FOR XML Auto clause.

Recall that element levels in your XML document appear in the same order that tables appear in your SELECT list and are named according to any aliases you may have chosen (e.g., cust, Order, OrderDetail).

```
XML_F52E2B61-1...805F49916B1.xml   Fig 3-6.sql - (loc...chA6\Student (52))*
<cust CustomerID="2" CustomerType="Consumer">
  <Order InvoiceID="943" OrderDate="2008-02-07T02:45:03.840">
    <OrderDetail ProductID="72" Quantity="4" />
  </Order>
</cust>
```

Levels are named after your table aliases

Figure 3.8 The XML stream resulting from running the code in Figure 3.7.

A related query (showing the purchases for CustomerID 1, see Figure 3.9) helps to illustrate our root element (cust) having a top-level element (Order) and a child-level element (OrderDetail). There is a 1:Many (One-to-Many) relationship between the root node and the lower elements.

```
<cust CustomerID="1" CustomerType="Consumer">          Root Level
  <Order InvoiceID="...." OrderDate="2007-11-09T11:23:51.043">
    <OrderDetail ProductID="61" Quantity="4" />
  </Order>          Top Level
  <Order InvoiceID="1027" OrderDate="2008-04-17T16:13:59.480">
    <OrderDetail ProductID="49" Quantity="4" />
  </Order>
  <Order InvoiceID="1401" OrderDate="2009-01-31T07:21:03.997">
    <OrderDetail ProductID="69" Quantity="1" />
    <OrderDetail ProductID="60" Quantity="5" />
    <OrderDetail ProductID="15" Quantity="2" />
    <OrderDetail ProductID="53" Quantity="4" />
    <OrderDetail ProductID="63" Quantity="4" />
    <OrderDetail ProductID="70" Quantity="5" />
    <OrderDetail ProductID="55" Quantity="4" />
    <OrderDetail ProductID="65" Quantity="4" />
```

Figure 3.9 There is a 1:Many relationship between the root node and the lower elements.

Copy your XML result (shown in Figure 3.8 and produced by our query shown in Figure 3.7) into a brand new query window and enclose it in single quotes (see Figure 3.10 below).

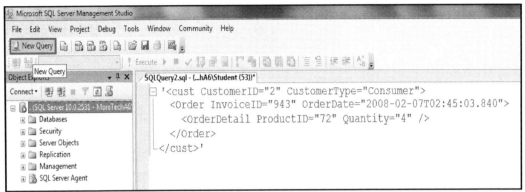

Figure 3.10 Copy the XML into a brand new query window.

Let's briefly digress for another comparison which may be helpful for our next step. Preparing to have your XML document shredded by SQL Server is a bit like the steps you take when having your tailor create a custom garment for you. One of my students recently underwent this process. Her favorite tailor, Kim, had the design for a poncho she liked. The tailor sent my student to the fabric store to select the particular fabric and trim she wanted for her poncho.

When she brought the fabric and trim to Kim's shop, Kim took the fabric, wrote up an order slip, and then gave my student a claim ticket and said her poncho would be done in a week. This tailor runs a small neighborhood shop but is always very busy due to the high quality of her work. While Kim could eventually have located the order without the benefit of the claim ticket, my conscientious student made very sure to bring her ticket when she returned the following week. She submitted her claim ticket and in exchange she was handed her lovely new hand-made garment.

Much the same way, when you send an XML document into memory, SQL Server gives you a number (called a handle) which you need later when referring to that document. In Figure 3.14, we will see the "claim ticket" created: we will send our XML document into memory and in exchange we will get back the handle in the form of an integer.

```
'<cust CustomerID="2" CustomerType="Consumer">
  <Order InvoiceID="943" OrderDate="2008-02-07">
    <OrderDetail ProductID="72" Quantity="4" />
  </Order>
</cust>'
```

You will declare two variables:
1.) An XML variable for SQL
2.) An integer variable for you

Figure 3.11 Two variables are needed when sending our XML document into memory.

To send our document into memory, we first need to declare an XML variable. In order for this variable to contain our XML document, we will set it equal to our XML (see Figure 3.12).

```
DECLARE @Doc xml

SET @Doc = '<cust CustomerID="2" CustomerType="Consumer">
  <Order InvoiceID="943" OrderDate="2008-02-07T02:45:03.840">
    <OrderDetail ProductID="72" Quantity="4" />
  </Order>
</cust>'
```

Figure 3.12 The @Doc variable's data type is XML.

Next we will declare the variable @hDoc, which we know will be an integer because it is the variable which will act as our document handle (i.e., our "claim ticket"). We will also use sp_XML_PrepareDocument, a system-supplied stored procedure which reads our XML document (@Doc), parses it, and makes it available for SQL's use (see Figure 3.13).

```
DECLARE @hDoc int
EXEC SP_xml_prepareDocument @hDoc OUTPUT, @Doc
```

Figure 3.13 The syntax to declare our handle variable and execute sp_XML_PrepareDocument.

When we send our XML to SQL Server's internal cache, we will receive a number which functions as our "claim ticket." Run all of the code together, including a SELECT statement to display the document handle (i.e., our "claim ticket" which SQL Server provides in exchange for the XML document (see Figure 3.14)).

```
DECLARE @Doc xml

SET @Doc = '<cust CustomerID="2" CustomerType="Consumer">
    <Order InvoiceID="943" OrderDate="2008-02-07">
      <OrderDetail ProductID="72" Quantity="4" />
    </Order>
  </cust>'

DECLARE @hDoc int
EXEC SP_xml_prepareDocument @hDoc OUTPUT, @Doc

SELECT @hDoc
```

Results | Messages

	(No column name)
1	1

You get handle #1

Figure 3.14 Run all of the code together and make note of the handle number, which is 1.

Be sure to run this code only once, otherwise you will create multiple handles and instances of your XML document.

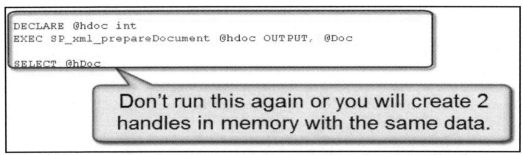

Figure 3.15 Avoid accidentally creating unneeded instances of your document and handle.

Using the OpenXML Function

We just sent our prepared XML into the SQL Server's internal cache so that we may pull out the data we want. The OpenXML function provides a rowset view of your XML data. It works with the in-memory copy of the XML document you've stored and provides a view of the data, no longer formatted as XML but with all its parts separated into a large grid. This allows you to query just the data that you need.

We know the key to accessing the stored XML document is the document handle or "claim ticket." The first argument needed by the OpenXML function is this value expressed as an integer. The second argument is the *rowpattern* hint for the data we wish to see.

After declaring an integer variable and setting it equal to 1 (i.e., the value of our document handle, see Figure 3.14), we can use a SELECT statement to query the result set of the OpenXML function. The variable @iNum is the first parameter. The second parameter '/cust/Order/OrderDetail' specifies that we wish to see data for the OrderDetail element level (see Figure 3.16).

```
--
DECLARE @iNum int
SET @iNum=1
SELECT *
FROM Openxml (@iNum,'/cust/Order/OrderDetail')
```

Results   Messages

id	parentid	nodetype	localname	prefix	namespaceuri	datatype	prev	text
7	4	1	OrderDetail	NULL	NULL	NULL	NULL	NULL
8	7	2	ProductID	NULL	NULL	NULL	NULL	NULL
10	8	3	#text	NULL	NULL	NULL	NULL	72
9	7	2	Quantity	NULL	NULL	NULL	NULL	NULL
11	9	3	#text	NULL	NULL	NULL	NULL	4

Figure 3.16 The OpenXML function works with the XML document we stored in memory. Compare this data with our XML document shown in Figure 3.11.

Rowpattern

Since XML can have root tags, top level tags, and many levels of child tags, *rowpatterns* are needed to figure out which level represent your row data. A *rowpattern* is an XPath pattern telling your query where to look for the data that you want to see in your result.

In our current example, the *rowpattern* hint ('/cust/Order/OrderDetail') narrows our query to the attributes found at the OrderDetail element level (see Figure 3.16). While the surrounding data isn't immediately interpretable, we can see the text for the ProductID attribute shows a 72, and the text for the Quantity attribute shows a 4.

Shredding One Level

Adding the WITH clause to our existing query allows us to pick just the values we wish to see. Our query specifies that we are still interested in data from the OrderDetail element level (see Figure 3.17). Our WITH clause lists the field names we want (ProductID, Quantity) from this element level and that these values should be expressed as integer data. In other words, ProductID and Quantity are both integers.

```
DECLARE @iNum int
SET @iNum=1
SELECT *
FROM Openxml(@iNum,'/cust/Order/OrderDetail')
WITH (ProductID int, Quantity int)
```

ProductID	Quantity
72	4

Figure 3.17 The WITH clause allows us to shred data at a single element level.

Basic Shredding Recap

Let's perform an additional start-to-finish example of shredding a single level of XML. We will prepare the XML document, choose a row pattern, and shred some fields from the XML Stream shown below (Figure 3.18). For this example, you will need the Lab3.2Olympics.sql file found in the Resource Files folder located in the companion files located on ***www.Joes2Pros.com***.

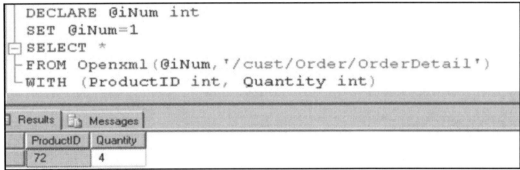

```
'<Olympics>
   <Olympics Mode="Summer">
     <Olympics Name="1984 LA"/>
     <Olympics Name="1988 Seoul"/>
     <Olympics Name="1992 Barcelona"/>
   </Olympics>
   <Olympics Mode="Winter">
     <Olympics Name="1984 Sarajevo"/>
     <Olympics Name="1988 Calgary"/>
     <Olympics Name="1992 France"/>
   </Olympics>
</Olympics>'
```

Figure 3.18 Locate and open the Lab3.2Olympics.sql file.

Add the variable declaration and SET statement, then run the statement to confirm your XML completes without errors (see Figure 3.19).

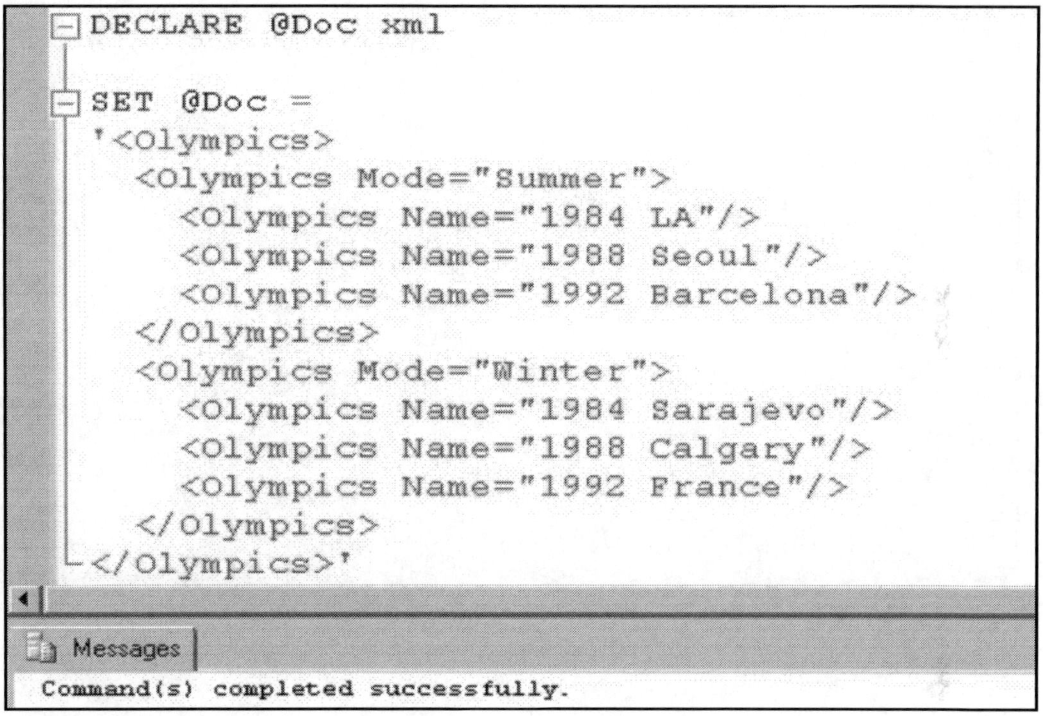

```
DECLARE @Doc xml

SET @Doc =
'<Olympics>
  <Olympics Mode="Summer">
    <Olympics Name="1984 LA"/>
    <Olympics Name="1988 Seoul"/>
    <Olympics Name="1992 Barcelona"/>
  </Olympics>
  <Olympics Mode="Winter">
    <Olympics Name="1984 Sarajevo"/>
    <Olympics Name="1988 Calgary"/>
    <Olympics Name="1992 France"/>
  </Olympics>
</Olympics>'
```

Messages

Command(s) completed successfully.

Figure 3.19 Add the code shown here and execute to confirm that it runs successfully.

Add the code to store the XML document, declare the document handle variable, execute sp_XML_PrepareDocument, and receive the "claim ticket" handle value for our stored document (see Figure 3.20).

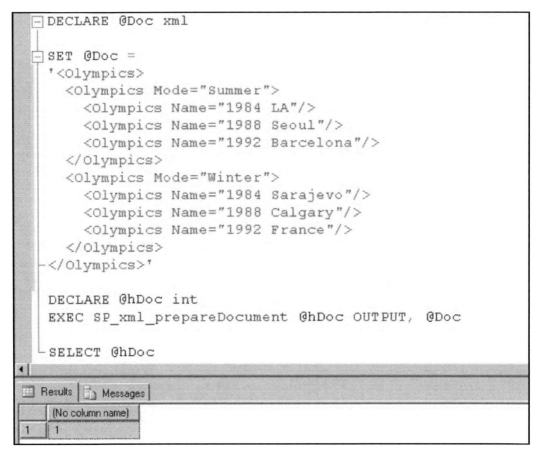

```
DECLARE @Doc xml

SET @Doc =
 '<Olympics>
   <Olympics Mode="Summer">
     <Olympics Name="1984 LA"/>
     <Olympics Name="1988 Seoul"/>
     <Olympics Name="1992 Barcelona"/>
   </Olympics>
   <Olympics Mode="Winter">
     <Olympics Name="1984 Sarajevo"/>
     <Olympics Name="1988 Calgary"/>
     <Olympics Name="1992 France"/>
   </Olympics>
</Olympics>'

 DECLARE @hDoc int
 EXEC SP_xml_prepareDocument @hDoc OUTPUT, @Doc

 SELECT @hDoc
```

Results	Messages

	(No column name)
1	1

Figure 3.20 Run all of this code and make note of the "claim ticket" for our XML document. *Note:* The document handle returned by sp_XML_PrepareDocument is 1 the first time the sproc is executed in a Query Editor Window. If you run the sproc again within the same session, each subsequent run will return another handle incremented by 2 (i.e., 3, 5, 7, 9, etc.).

We want to pull out all the Olympic names (e.g., "1984 LA") so we need to identify the needed level. The level we need is two levels below the root. In other words, our data is at the /Olympics/Olympics/Olympics level. As you can see, it's possible to have lower levels use the same name as parent levels.

```
DECLARE @iDoc int
SET @iDoc = 1
SELECT * FROM
OPENXML (@iDoc,'/Olympics/Olympics/Olympics')
```

	id	parentid	nodetype	localname	prefix	namespaceuri	datatype	prev	text
1	4	2	1	Olympics	NULL	NULL	NULL	NULL	NULL
2	5	4	2	Name	NULL	NULL	NULL	NULL	NULL
3	1..	5	3	#text	NULL	NULL	NULL	NULL	198...
4	6	2	1	Olympics	NULL	NULL	NULL	4	NULL
5	7	6	2	Name	NULL	NULL	NULL	NULL	NULL
6	1..	7	3	#text	NULL	NULL	NULL	NULL	198...
7	8	2	1	Olympics	NULL	NULL	NULL	6	NULL
8	9	8	2	Name	NULL	NULL	NULL	NULL	NULL

Figure 3.21 Query the OpenXML function for the third element level details.

Again, we can use a SELECT statement to query the OpenXML function. The first argument in Figures 3.21-3.22 is the handle and is needed by the OpenXML. The second argument is the *rowpattern* hint for the data we wish to see.

```
DECLARE @iDoc int
SET @iDoc = 1
SELECT * FROM
OPENXML (@iDoc,'/Olympics/Olympics/Olympics')
WITH([Name] varchar(max))
```

	Name
1	1984 LA
2	1988 Seoul
3	1992 Barcelona
4	1984 Sarajevo
5	1988 Calgary
6	1992 France

Figure 3.22 Add a WITH clause to pull just the data belonging to the Name attribute.

We've successfully pulled the data we wanted. As a final step, we want to alias the column as GameName. To accomplish this, we will use the code below (see Figure 3.23). As you can see, we simply replace the column name with our intended alias ("GameName"). Since the name of our XML source field @Name

109

does not match what we want to display, we need to specify how they map. The addition of the columnpattern '@Name' specifies that the data should come from the Name attribute of our XML document. We have chosen to label this column GameName in our tabular (shredded) result.

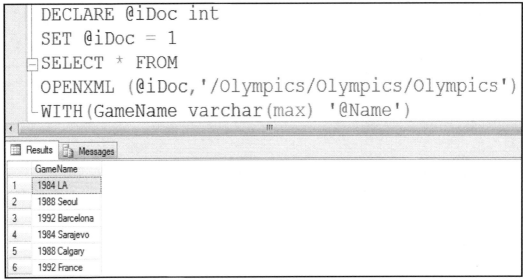

Figure 3.23 Add code to replace the column name with "GameName."

Lab 3.2: Preparing XML

Lab Prep: Before you can begin the lab you must run the SQLInteropChapter1.0Setup.sql script. It is recommended that you view the lab video instructions found in Lab3.2_PreparingXML.wmv, available at *www.Joe2Pros.com.*

Skill Check 1: Change the output from the Olympics resource file (Lab3.2Olympics.sql) to have a different field header of GameName as you see in Figure 3.24.

Figure 3.24 Result produced by Skill Check 1.

Skill Check 2:
Create the XML you see here. Take this XML and prepare it using the correct row pattern to shred just the two fields you see in Figure 3.25.

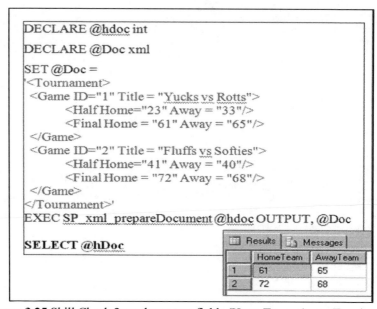

```
DECLARE @hdoc int
DECLARE @Doc xml
SET @Doc =
'<Tournament>
 <Game ID="1" Title = "Yucks vs Rotts">
        <Half Home="23" Away = "33"/>
        <Final Home = "61" Away = "65"/>
 </Game>
 <Game ID="2" Title = "Fluffs vs Softies">
        <Half Home="41" Away = "40"/>
        <Final Home = "72" Away = "68"/>
 </Game>
</Tournament>'
EXEC SP_xml_prepareDocument @hdoc OUTPUT, @Doc

SELECT @hDoc
```

	HomeTeam	AwayTeam
1	61	65
2	72	68

Figure 3.25 Skill Check 2 produces two fields (HomeTeam, Away Team).

111

Skill Check 3: Create the XML you see below and shred it into the result set at the bottom of this figure (see Figure 3.26).

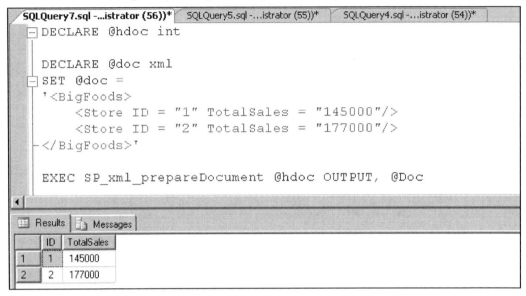

Figure 3.26 Skill Check 3 result.

Answer Code: The T-SQL code to this lab can be found in the downloadable files in a file named Lab3.2_PreparingXML.sql

Shredding XML - Points to Ponder

1. Before you can process an XML document with T-SQL, you must parse the XML into a tree representation of the various nodes and store it within SQL Server's internal cache using the sp_XML_PrepareDocument stored procedure.

2. The sp_XML_PrepareDocument sproc has two required parameters:
   - o handle – an integer handle representing the XML document in memory. Think of this as a label on, or pointer to, the XML data in memory.
   - o xml – the XML doc to be processed.

3. After you have parsed XML using sp_xml_PrepareDocument, SELECT from the OpenXML function result to retrieve a rowset from the parsed tree.

4. The OpenXML function has two required input parameters:
   - o idoc – an integer representing a pointer to the XML document in memory.
   - o rowpattern – an XPath pattern identifying the nodes in the XML to be processed as a rowset.

5. The SELECT statement's WITH clause is used to format the rowset and provide any required mapping information (e.g., mapping a field alias to an attribute).

6. The complete process of transforming XML data into a rowset is called shredding.

7. Each time sp_XML_PrepareDocument is executed within the same Query Editor Window session, the document handle is returned as an integer will increment by 2 (i.e., 1, 3, 5, 7, 9, etc.).

OpenXML Options

The last section introduced us to the OpenXML function. We learned the two required parameters for this function are the handle (which must be in the form of an integer) and the rowpattern.

The OpenXML function offers some helpful options for querying. This section will explore the two main syntaxes for rowpattern recursion (searching lower levels) and column pattern options (searching one level higher).

Rowpattern Recursion

Suppose you are a manager at a company. You work for a supervisor and likely also have people who report to you. Even at the largest company, every person who works there is an employee, from the CEO on down to managers and individual contributors at all levels. Our recursion example will include an XML document having many element levels named "Emp."

It's common to see elements inside of elements with the same name. Sometimes the name of the element is more important than its exact level. In other words, you could see one employee level nested beneath another employee level, and so forth. In our example, we will see how level recursion can help us locate the data we need within XML tags having the same name.

Let's create a simple XML document showing a small organization having one boss, Tom. Tom will have two employees, Dick and Harry.

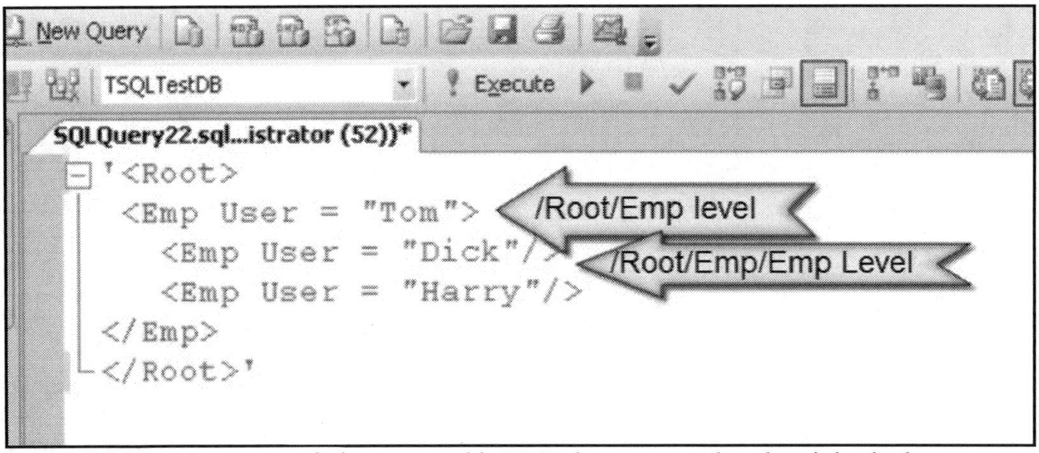

Figure 3.27 In a new query window, create this XML document, and enclose it in single quotes.

Add the code to declare the two variables (the integer to give us the document handle and the xml variable to store our XML document), store the XML document into the variable @Doc, prepare the document, and display the handle.

```
DECLARE @hDoc int
DECLARE @Doc xml

SET @Doc=
'<Root>
 <Emp User = "Tom">
     <Emp User = "Dick"/>
     <Emp User = "Harry"/>
</Emp>
</Root>'

EXEC sp_xml_PrepareDocument @hDoc OUTPUT, @Doc

SELECT @hDoc
---
```

Results | Messages

	(No column name)
1	1

Figure 3.28 Our document handle is 1.

Declare the variable to access our XML document and set it equal to our document handle (which is our "claim ticket" number, 1). Then add the Select statement to query the result set of the OpenXML function. Our rowpattern parameter ('/Root/Emp') specifies that we want only the the top-level element.

```
---
DECLARE @iDoc int
SET @iDoc = 1
SELECT *
FROM OpenXML (@iDoc, '/Root/Emp')
WITH (EmployeeName varchar(max) '@User')
```

Results | Messages

	EmployeeName
1	Tom

Figure 3.29 We only want to see the highest employee level, which is the boss (Tom).

Now let's modify our code to see the next level down. The child-level element (rowpattern '/Root/Emp/Emp') contains Dick and Harry (see Figure 3.30).

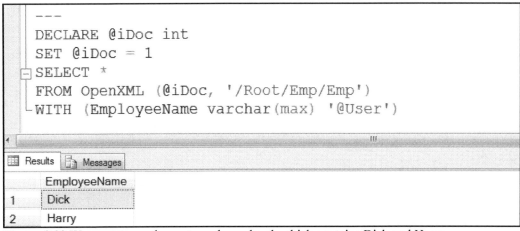

Figure 3.30 We want to see the next employee level, which contains Dick and Harry.

A slight modification to our rowpattern parameter specifies that we want to pull data from every level, at or beneath the Root, and having an XML tag named Emp (see Figure 3.31). This is an example of using rowpattern's *relative* navigation capability. Thus far our row level specifications have been absolute – our OpenXML queries have explicitly named each level and instructed SQL Server to pull data from that level. In our next section, we will see some of the tools SQL Server makes available for *relative* navigation of our XML data.

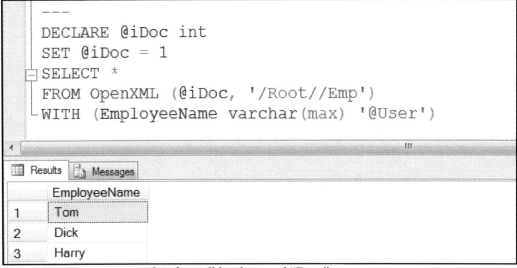

Figure 3.31 We want to see data from all levels named "Emp."

Relative Level

We are already familiar with the concept of defining entities or positions in a relative way – that is, as they relate to other entities or positions rather than explicitly calling them by their unique names or fixed positions. In conversation, my dad often refers to his "two younger sons," rather than explicitly using the names "Jeff" and "Rick." At work I sometimes get visitors who come to my door when they are actually looking for the fellow who occupied my office up until a month ago. Rather than giving them his new office number, it is easier to direct them to take the elevator up to the next floor and then to look for the first door on the right. (I've found when I told them, "He's moved to room 401", I've always needed to give them the friendly directions anyway. So after the first day, I just skipped the **explicit name** 401 and gave them the **relative location**.)

Throughout the *Joes 2 Pros* series, we have seen the importance of variables to make our T-SQL code more flexible and reusable instead of explicitly hardcoding each value. The OpenXML function similarly offers us the option of pulling data in a relative fashion. In other words, instead of explicitly naming the element levels where we want SQL Server to navigate and pull data, our code can provide rowpattern or column pattern instructions relative to a specified context.

In our next example, the rowpattern option will help us pull data from another level relative to our current position. Recall our example of a large organization with many employee levels. You can use rowpattern's ability to query relatively and find the managers who are two levels above a certain manager. Perhaps you've been asked to compile a list of all the employees who are three levels beneath your manager.

We now will modify our current code (refer back to Figure 3.31) to include a column specifying each employee's boss. Our goal (shown in Figure 3.32) is to see the boss' name listed alongside each employee (original XML document appears in Figure 3.28.) *Note that the name of Tom's boss will appear as NULL, since Tom is the highest level boss in the organization.*

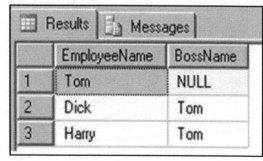

Figure 3.32 We want a boss name for each person.

Recall in Lab 3.2 we added a column to our OpenXML query by simply defining it inside our WITH clause. The new trick here will be to add '.../' to the front of the column pattern (colpattern) parameter, e.g. '../@User' (see Figure 3.33), which tells SQL Server to search the level above. In other words, we want SQL Server to go up one level from the current context and retrieve the User attribute from that level. The syntax '../../@User' would tell SQL Server to go up two levels and retrieve the User attribute.

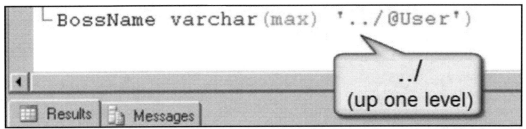

Figure 3.33 This code tells SQL Server to go up one level from the current rowpattern level.

Since our rowpattern itself '/Root//Emp' is relative, it will search for data at the root level and every child level below. If the '/Root//Emp' rowpattern finds an employee at the fifth level, then the '../@User' colpattern specifier will go up one level (i.e., up to the fourth level) to search for corresponding data. For example, when the rowpattern instruction '/Root//Emp' locates an Emp level, the colpattern '@User' will find the first User attribute (Dick) at the Emp level. The colpattern '../@User' instructs SQL Server to retrieve the User attribute (Tom) from the level above Dick's level (Figure 3.34).

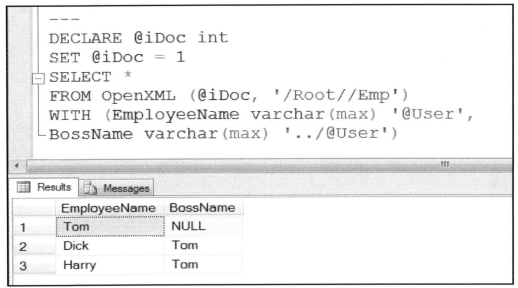

Figure 3.34 Our result shows us the BossName for each employee.

Removing Prepared XML Data

The sproc sp_XML_RemoveDocument will remove an XML document and its handle from memory. If you accidentally create an additional handle during your session or wish to back track and repeat a step, this code will accomplish that for you (see Figure 3.35). In older versions of SQL Server, you needed to perform this step to remove your XML document from the internal cache. However, beginning in SQL Server 2005, this is automatically done for you.

```
</Root>'

EXEC sp_xml_PrepareDocument @hDoc OUTPUT, @Doc

SELECT @hDoc
---
DECLARE @iDoc int
SET @iDoc = 1  ⇐
SELECT *
FROM OpenXML (@iDoc, '/Root//Emp')
WITH (EmployeeName varchar(max) '@User',
BossName varchar(max) '../../@User')

EXEC sp_xml_RemoveDocument 1
```

Messages
Command(s) completed successfully.

Figure 3.35 This code removes our XML document and its handle from the memory cache.

Lab 3.3: OpenXML Options

Lab Prep: Before you can begin the lab you must run the SQLInteropChapter1.0Setup.sql script. It is recommended that you view the lab video instructions found in Lab3.3_OpenXML_Options.wmv, available at *www.Joe2Pros.com*.

Skill Check 1: Open the Lab3.3SK1.sql file from the resources folder. The root element and all child elements are named URI. Get all URI entities from the Doc as seen in the figure to the right.

```
DECLARE @Handle INT
DECLARE @Doc XML
SET @Doc =
  '<URI Name="Joes2Pros.com">
     <URI Name="Books.Joes2Pros.com">
       <URI Name="T-SQL.Books.Joes2Pros.com"/>
       <URI Name="Queries.Books.Joes2Pros.com"/>
       <URI Name="Dev.Books.Joes2Pros.com"/>
     </URI>
     <URI Name="Classes.Joes2Pros.com">
       <URI Name="Seattle.Classes.Joes2Pros.com"/>
       <URI Name="Portland.Classes.Joes2Pros.com"/>
       <URI Name="Spokane.Classes.Joes2Pros.com"/>
     </URI>
  </URI>'
```

	URI
1	Joes2Pros.com
2	Books.Joes2Pros.com
3	T-SQL.Books.Joes2Pros.com
4	Queries.Books.Joes2Pros.com
5	Dev.Books.Joes2Pros.com
6	Classes.Joes2Pros.com
7	Seattle.Classes.Joes2Pros.com
8	Portland.Classes.Joes2Pros.c...
9	Spokane.Classes.Joes2Pros....

Figure 3.36 The XML document and result for Skill Check 1.

Skill Check 2: Open the Lab3.3SK2.sql file from the resources folder. Get all URI entities from the Doc as seen in the figure to the right.

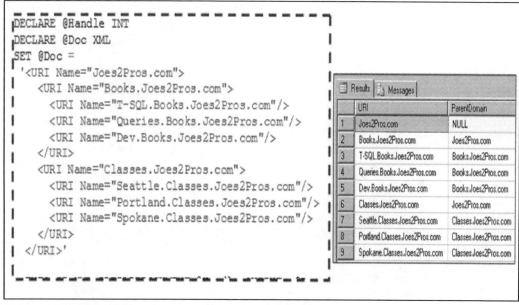

Figure 3.37 The XML document and result for Skill Check 2.

Skill Check 3: Remove the document handle from memory that you used to parse this XML from Skill Check 2.

```
DECLARE @Handle INT
DECLARE @Doc XML
SET @Doc =
  '<URI Name="Joes2Pros.com">
     <URI Name="Books.Joes2Pros.com">
        <URI Name="T-SQL.Books.Joes2Pros.com"/>
        <URI Name="Queries.Books.Joes2Pros.com"/>
        <URI Name="Dev.Books.Joes2Pros.com"/>
     </URI>
     <URI Name="Classes.Joes2Pros.com">
        <URI Name="Seattle.Classes.Joes2Pros.com"/>
        <URI Name="Portland.Classes.Joes2Pros.com"/>
        <URI Name="Spokane.Classes.Joes2Pros.com"/>
     </URI>
  </URI>'
```

Figure 3.38 Skill Check 3 removes a document handle from memory.

Skill Check 4: Open the Lab3.3SK4.sql file from the resources folder. Get all Unit entities from the XML document as seen in the figure to the right.

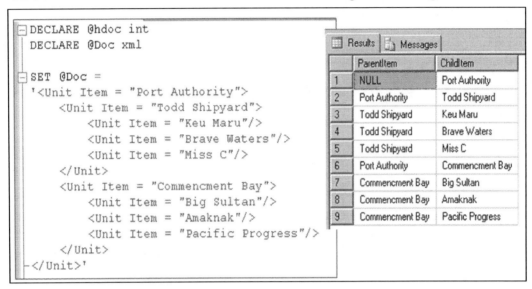

Figure 3.39 The XML document and result for Skill Check 3.

Answer Code: The T-SQL code to this lab can be found in the downloadable files in a file named Lab3.3_OpenXMLOptions.sql

OpenXML Options - Points to Ponder

1. If you have several levels of elements with the same name, you can specify all of the levels in your rowpattern by using a double forward slash before the element name
   - o /Root/Employee – Gets the top-level Element Employee
   - o /Root//Employee – Gets the Employee elements at all levels

2. If you want to get data one level above the current level then you specify two dots and a forward slash. The XPath syntax to go up 1 level is '../' before the colpattern (column pattern).

3. You can have multiple XML trees inside the SQL cache at the same time.

4. Once an XML tree is no longer needed, use sp_XML_RemoveDocument to remove it from the internal cache.

5. In SQL Server 2005, once your query window is closed and your session is done, the internal cache will be cleared. In such cases, you will not need to use the sp_XML_RemoveDocument procedure.

6. Because @hDoc is a local variable, the sp_XML_RemoveDocument must be in the same query session as the sp_XML_RemoveDocument.

7. In SQL Server 2000, the memory used by the internal cache was not cleared by closing your session. You had to use the sp_XML_RemoveDocument procedure or face serious memory leaks.

Chapter Glossary

Column pattern: sometimes shortened to "colpattern"; used in conjunction with the OpenXML function; the colpattern option helps you pull data from another column relative to your current position.

OpenXML: a function used to pull data in a relative fashion; in other words, instead of explicitly naming (i.e., hardcoding) the element levels where we want SQL Server to navigate and pull data, our code can provide rowpattern or column pattern instructions relative to a specified context.

Preparing XML (for SQL): this process includes storing the XML in memory and processing the XML so that all the data and metadata is ready and available for you access via a SQL query.

Rowpattern: used in conjunction with the OpenXML function; the rowpattern option helps you pull data from another level relative to your current position.

Shredding XML: the complete process of transforming XML data into a rowset.

sp_XML_PrepareDocument: a system stored procedure which parses an XML document into a tree representation of the various nodes and stores it within SQL Server's internal cache; the two required parameters are the handle (an integer handle representing the XML document in memory) and the xml document (i.e., the XML document which you wish to process).

sp_XML_RemoveDocument: a system stored procedure which removes an XML document and its handle from memory.

Chapter Three - Review Quiz

1.) What process will transform XML data to a rowset?

O a.   Shredding
O b.   Retrieving

2.) Where does sp_XML_PrepareDocument prepare its data?

O a.   In the MDF file
O b.   In the LDF file
O c.   In the internal cache
O d.   In the messages window

3.) The sp_XML_PrepareDocument stored procedure requires a parameter that is an XML data type. What is the output parameter for?

O a.   The handle as an INT
O b.   The handle as an XML
O c.   The handle as a Varchar

4.) What function is used to take your prepared XML data into a tabular shredded format?

O a.   OpenXML
O b.   GetXML
O c.   RetrieveXML
O d.   ShredXML

5.) Which clause is used to specify the fields you want to use from the OpenXML function?

O a.   FROM
O b.   WITH
O c.   HAVING
O d.   FOR
O e.   WHEN
O f.   LET
O g.   ORDER BY

6.) You have the following XML depicting the employee hierarchy of the two employees working for Tom:

```
'<Root>
 <Emp User = "Tom">
  <Emp User = "Dick"/>
  <Emp User = "Harry"/>
</Emp>
<Root>'
```

You want to query the employees in the XML using the OpenXML function. The results will show the User Name of all Employees in the hierarchy. You have already declared an XML handle named @iDoc. Which query would you use?

O a. DECLARE @iDoc int
    SET @iDoc=1
    SELECT *
    FROM Openxml(@iDoc,'/Root/Emp/Emp')
    WITH (EmployeeName varchar(max) '@User')

O b. DECLARE @iDoc int
    SET @iDoc=1
    SELECT *
    FROM Openxml(@iDoc,'/Root/Emp')
    WITH (EmployeeName varchar(max) '@Emp')

O c. DECLARE @iDoc int
    SET @iDoc=1
    SELECT *
    FROM Openxml(@iDoc,'/Root//Emp')
    WITH (EmployeeName varchar(max) '@User')

O d. DECLARE @iDoc int
    SET @iDoc=1
    SELECT *
    FROM Openxml(@iDoc,'/Root//Emp')
    WITH (EmployeeName varchar(max) '@Emp')

7.) You want your rowpattern to only grab the data from the top-level Employee element. Which rowpattern will do this?

O a.   /Root/Employee
O b.   /Root//Employee
O c.   //Root//Employee

8.) You have an application which is calling on T-SQL code which in turn is preparing XML documents and turning the data into a tabular stream. The code is creating new prepared XML without flushing the old XML from the SQL Server memory. You need to run a system stored procedure which will flush the prepared XML from the system's memory. Which T-SQL statement do you use?

O a.   sp_XML_RemoveDocument
O b.   sp_XML_PrepareDocument
O c.   sp_XML_FlushDocument
O d.   sp_XML_FlushNamespace

Answer Key

1.) a   2.) c   3.) a   4.) a   5.) b   6.) c   7.) a   8.) a

Bug Catcher Game

To play the Bug Catcher game run the SQLInteropBugCatcherCh3.pps from the BugCatcher folder of the companion files. You can obtain these files from www.Joes2Pros.com or by ordering the Companion CD.

Chapter 4.　Shredding Attributes, Elements, and Levels

As SQL Server professionals, we are tasked with bringing data into SQL Server databases so that it can become useful information we can aggregate and then output in the form of reporting or a stream of data made available to another program. XML is one of the many types of inputs and outputs available for use in combination with databases.

From the first three chapters, we understand that XML is an important vehicle for transmitting data between programs and datasources. The near ubiquitousness of XML in IT means we will encounter it on the job and we need to be prepared to handle XML files in our database work. As solution providers, we also need to be familiar with how XML works so we know when to utilize it in accomplishing a development goal.

The last chapter explained and helped us master the steps necessary to prepare our XML document for SQL Server's consumption. We understand the basic flow of shredding XML and are now ready to increase our knowledge by delving into more complex shredding examples. In order to harvest data from XML and bring it into our homebase (i.e., a SQL Server database), we must increase our fluency with XML's methods for storing and organizing data so that we can easily navigate and retrieve our needed data from all levels and types.

READER NOTE: *Please run the script SQLInteropChapter1.0Setup.sql in order to follow along with the examples in the first section of Chapter 4. (You only need to run this script once for all examples in Chapters 1 through 4.) All scripts mentioned in this chapter may be found at* ***www.Joes2Pros.com****.*

Note: The script Lab4.1Starter.sql contains the XML document shown in this section's examples and is available at ***www.Joes2Pros.com.***

OpenXML Column Patterns

We learned in the last chapter that a **rowpattern** is useful for targeting the level where you want to get your data. But what if seven out of eight of the values are at one element level and one important value is at another level? Whenever your levels or names don't match, you need a way to specify how that field will get its data. The use of a **column pattern** allows you to expand beyond the level specified by the rowpattern.

While a rowpattern only lets you pick one level, a column pattern (sometimes called **colpattern**) allows you to specify a level for each column in your data.

Open the starter script Lab4.1Starter.sql in a new query window (it will contain the data you see below in Figure 4.1). Choose any database context you wish except the Master db. (I've chosen TSQLTestDB.) Notice that the data we want is located across three different levels: cust, Order, and OrderDetail.

```
DECLARE @hDoc int
DECLARE @Doc xml

SET @Doc = '<cust CustomerID="2" CustomerType="Consumer">
  <Order InvoiceID="943" OrderDate="2008-02-07">
    <OrderDetail ProductID="72" Quantity="4" />
  </Order>
</cust>'
```

Figure 4.1 The base code available in the Lab4.1Starter.sql script.

Our next step will be to execute **SP_XML_PrepareDocument** in order to pass in our XML document and receive back the document handle (see Figure 4.2).

```
DECLARE @hDoc int
DECLARE @Doc xml

SET @Doc = '<cust CustomerID="2" CustomerType="Consumer">
   <Order InvoiceID="943" OrderDate="2008-02-07">
      <OrderDetail ProductID="72" Quantity="4" />
   </Order>
</cust>'

EXEC SP_xml_prepareDocument @hDoc OUTPUT, @Doc
SELECT @hDoc
```

Results	Messages

	(No column name)
1	1

Figure 4.2 Run all of this code together to store & prepare the XML document as @Doc.

Our handle of 1 (our "claim ticket" result received in Figure 4.2) is used in the following code which pulls the data from the OpenXML function using a Select statement. Our rowpattern specifies we want data from the OrderDetail level.

(Please note that the code shown in Figures 4.2-4.6 has been run from within one window. In order to conserve space, the Figure 4.3 through Figure 4.6 results are shown with just the code which pulled the data from the OpenXML function.)

```
DECLARE @iDoc int
SET @iDoc = 1

SELECT *
FROM OpenXML (@idoc, '/cust/Order/OrderDetail')
```

Results	Messages

	id	parentid	nodetype	localname	prefix	namespaceuri	datatype	prev	text
1	7	4	1	OrderDetail	NULL	NULL	NULL	NULL	NULL
2	8	7	2	ProductID	NULL	NULL	NULL	NULL	NULL
3	10	8	3	#text	NULL	NULL	NULL	NULL	72
4	9	7	2	Quantity	NULL	NULL	NULL	NULL	NULL
5	11	9	3	#text	NULL	NULL	NULL	NULL	4

Figure 4.3 Our initial OpenXML query pulls from just one level, /cust/Order/OrderDetail.

Going Up One Level

Suppose we want to see InvoiceID in our result set, but that data is not at our current rowpattern level (/cust/Order/OrderDetail). This data is one level above our rowpattern at the /cust/Order level.

We can add a colpattern hint (../) to specify that we want data pulled from a parent level of our current rowpattern. To go up one level, use the XPath syntax *../@AttributeSpecification* in the column pattern.

Now we will narrow down our result by specifying the three columns OrderDate, ProductID, and Quantity. In Figure 4.3, we can see the latter two values are already being retrieved by our query (ProductID 72 and Quantity 4) because the rowpattern specifies the OrderDetail level. However to get OrderDate, we need our query to also pull from the Order level, which is one level higher than our other data.

The column pattern hints (@OrderDate, @ProductID, @Quantity) specify that we want the values of the attributes (denoted by the @ symbol) pulled from each of these three columns. The additional ../ hint used with @OrderDate ('../@OrderDate') instructs SQL Server to retrieve the data from one level higher than the rowpattern (see Figure 4.4).

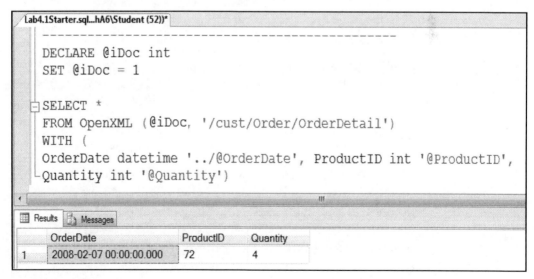

Figure 4.4 The colpattern ('../@OrderDate') retrieves data from one level higher than the rowpattern.

Renaming a Field

The WITH clause allows you to customize the field headers in your result. Specify your preferred naming, as shown in Figure 4.5 with ProdID and Qty.

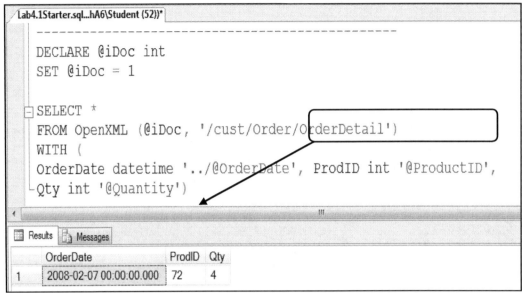

Figure 4.5 The WITH clause allows you to customize and alias your field headers.

Attributes Versus Elements

When pulling data which is contained in attributes, prefix the field name with the @ symbol and enclose it in single quotation marks (e.g., '@Quantity' as shown in Figures 4.4 through 4.6).

To pull the values for data which is contained in elements, simply list the field name in your WITH clause and enclose the name in single quotes.

If the <Quantity> data were contained in elements instead of in attributes, the field reference would have appeared in our WITH clause as 'Quantity', instead of '@Quantity'. This is illustrated in the following comparison:

```
--'@Quantity' in the Column Pattern:  Quantity is an attribute
'<cust CustomerID="2" CustomerType="Consumer">
  <Order InvoiceID="943" OrderDate="2008-02-07">
    <OrderDetail ProductID="72" Quantity="4" />
  </Order>
</cust>'
```

```
--'Quantity' in the Column Pattern:  Quantity is element text
'<cust CustomerID="2" CustomerType="Consumer">
  <Order InvoiceID="943" OrderDate="2008-02-07">
   <OrderDetail ProductID="72">
            <Quantity>4<Quantity>
   </OrderDetail>
  </Order>
</cust>'
```

Note: In both cases, Quantity is a child of OrderDetail. In the first example, Quantity is an attribute child, and in the second example it's an element child.

Going Up Multiple Levels

We know the hint ../ instructs SQL Server to search for data one level above the current rowpattern. To specify multiple levels higher than the rowpattern, add another instance of the parent hint (..) to your rowpattern. *Examples:*

The code ../ in your colpattern will search one level above the rowpattern.
The code ../../ in your colpattern will search two levels above the rowpattern. The code ../../../ will search three levels above the rowpattern, and so forth.

Using these colpattern hints allows us to pull all the values from every level of our current XML document (see Figure 4.6 for results based on the original XML document shown in Figure 4.1). Observe that the InvoiceID and OrderDate column patterns are going up one level, while the Customer and CustomerType column patterns are going up two levels.

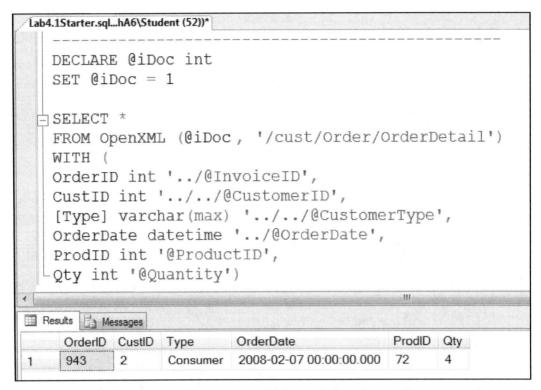

Figure 4.6 We have specified column patterns which search for columnar data at one and two levels (Order level and cust level, respectively) above the rowpattern (the OrderDetail level).

Lab 4.1: OpenXML Column Patterns

Lab Prep: Before you can begin the lab you must run the SQLInteropChapter1.0Setup.sql script. It is recommended that you view the lab video instructions found in Lab4.1_OpenXMLColumnPatterns.wmv, available at *www.Joe2Pros.com*.

Skill Check 1: Open the resource file Lab4.1SK1.sql and shred it as follows.

```
DECLARE @hdoc int
DECLARE @doc xml
SET @doc =
'<BigFoods>
    <Store ID = "1"><TotalSales>145000</TotalSales>
    </Store>
    <Store ID = "2"><TotalSales>177000</TotalSales>
    </Store>
</BigFoods>'
```

	ID	Sales
1	1	145000
2	2	177000

Figure 4.7 The result of Skill Check 1.

Skill Check 2: Open the resource file Lab4.1SK2.sql and shred it so you get all values from all levels as fields in your result set

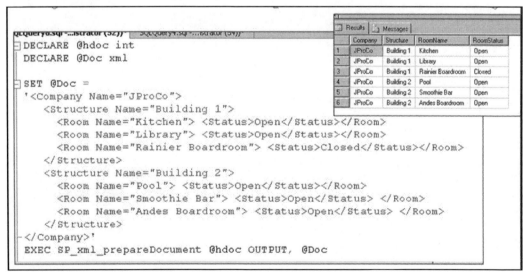

Figure 4.8 The result of Skill Check 2.

OpenXML Column Patterns - Points to Ponder

1. The OpenXML function takes an integer handle parameter which represents your XML and a rowpattern to specify at what level you want to extract your data.

2. The WITH clause contains column patterns which combine the OpenXML function's rowpattern with the XPATH instructions for each field.

3. If you are retrieving attribute data at the same level as the rowpattern specified in the OpenXML function, and the field headers are named the same as the fields, then you can omit the XPATH for that field.

Note: The script Lab4.2Starter.sql contains the XML document shown in this section's examples and is available at ***www.Joes2Pros.com***.

OpenXML Parameters

We are now familiar with the two required parameters of the OpenXML table-valued function: 1) the document handle which identifies the in-memory location of the XML document, and 2) the rowpattern. There is one more optional parameter which can make your life easier when your data is stored in a mixture of attributes and elements.

OpenXML Flag (Optional)

The third parameter of the OpenXML function is the flag. The flag is optional – if you do not specify a flag, your query will search only for values mapped as attributes. Key values for this flag are 1, 2, or 3:

1 = searches for attributes (if no flag specified, your query will bring in the values which are mapped as attributes)

2 = searches for elements

3 = searches for attributes and elements

Begin by opening the starter script Lab4.2Starter.sql in a new query window (it will contain the data you see below in Figure 4.9). Choose any database context you wish except the Master db. (Here we have chosen TSQLTestDB.)

```
DECLARE @doc xml
SET @doc =
'<SalesInvoice InvoiceID="1000" CustomerID="123" OrderDate="2004-03-07">
        <Items>
            <Item ProductCode="12" Quantity="2" UnitPrice="12.99"><ProductName>Bike</ProductName></Item>
            <Item ProductCode="41" Quantity="1" UnitPrice="17.45"><ProductName>Helmet</ProductName></Item>
            <Item ProductCode="2" Quantity="1" UnitPrice="2.99"><ProductName>Water Bottle</ProductName></Item>
        </Items>
        </SalesInvoice>'
```

Figure 4.9 The base code available in the Lab4.2Starter.sql script.

Our next step will be to execute SP_XML_PrepareDocument in order to pass our XML document into the memory cache and receive back the document handle of 1 (our "claim ticket" shown in Figure 4.10).

```
DECLARE @Doc xml
SET @Doc =
'<SalesInvoice InvoiceID="1000" CustomerID="123" OrderDate="2004-03-07">
        <Items>
            <Item ProductCode="12" Quantity="2" UnitPrice="12.99"><ProductName>Bike</Pro
            <Item ProductCode="41" Quantity="1" UnitPrice="17.45"><ProductName>Helmet</P
            <Item ProductCode="2" Quantity="1" UnitPrice="2.99"><ProductName>Water Bottl
        </Items>
    </SalesInvoice>'

DECLARE @HandleDoc int
EXEC SP_xml_prepareDocument @HandleDoc OUTPUT, @Doc
SELECT @HandleDoc AS HandleDoc
```

Results | Messages

	HandleDoc
1	1

Figure 4.10 Run all of this code to store & prepare the XML document at @Doc.

No flag parameter included in the code below indicates that we only want to see attribute data. Values are present for all fields except the element (ProductName), which shows all null values in our tabular result (see Figure 4.11).

```
    SELECT @HandleDoc AS HandleDoc

    DECLARE @INum INT
    SET @INum = 1

    SELECT * FROM
    OPENXML (@INum, 'SalesInvoice/Items/Item')
    WITH
    (
    ProductCode int,
    Quantity int,
    UnitPrice money,
    ProductName varchar(50)
    )
```

Results | Messages

	ProductCode	Quantity	UnitPrice	ProductName
1	12	2	12.99	NULL
2	41	1	17.45	NULL
3	2	1	2.99	NULL

Figure 4.11 We have omitted a flag parameter. Our result includes data for attribute values only.

This is because when you use OpenXML and you're matching on an exact field name, SQL Server looks for *attributes* by default. ProductName is the precise field name to search for this element. However, our code isn't searching for an element – it's searching for attribute data only (see Figure 4.12).

```
Lab4.2Starter    ...chA6\Student (51))*

DECLARE @INum INT
SET @INum = 1

SELECT * FROM
OPENXML (@INum, 'SalesInvoice/Items/Item', 1) --1 shows attribute data
WITH                                          --(when no flag is specified,
(                                             --the OpenXML function searches
ProductCode int,                              --for attribute data)
Quantity int,
UnitPrice money,
ProductName varchar(50)
)
```

	ProductCode	Quantity	UnitPrice	ProductName
1	12	2	12.99	NULL
2	41	1	17.45	NULL
3	2	1	2.99	NULL

Figure 4.12 A flag parameter of 1 yields the same result – we see only attribute data.

Now we see element data because our flag is set to 2 (see Figure 4.13). Notice it found a ProductName as a child element of the rowpattern. There are no values for ProductCode, Quantity, or UnitPrice, as those are all attributes (Figure 4.10).

```
Lab4.2Starter    ...chA6\Student (51))*

DECLARE @INum INT
SET @INum = 1

SELECT * FROM
OPENXML (@INum, 'SalesInvoice/Items/Item', 2) --2 means "show elements"
WITH
(
ProductCode int,
Quantity int,
UnitPrice money,
ProductName varchar(50)
)
```

	ProductCode	Quantity	UnitPrice	ProductName
1	NULL	NULL	NULL	Bike
2	NULL	NULL	NULL	Helmet
3	NULL	NULL	NULL	Water Bottle

Figure 4.13 A flag parameter value of 2 searches for element data only.

139

With our flag set to 3, we finally get all of the datapoints we want to see. The parameter value of 3 instructs our code to look for both attribute and element data (see Figure 4.14).

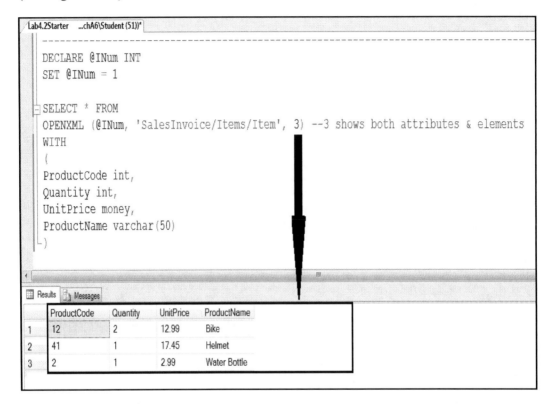

Figure 4.14 A flag parameter value of 3 searches for data from both attributes and elements.

This optional flag is very handy for bringing in all of the attribute and element data we want. Notice that we are able to accomplish this without needing to specify any custom column patterns in any of our examples (see Figures 4.11-4.14). Again, this is due to the fact that our code specifies field names which match the field names as they appear in the XML document.

For any fields which are aliased (i.e., whose names do not match the field names in the XML document), we would need to specify a column pattern in order for our attribute and/or element values to appear in our tabular result (see Figure 4.15).

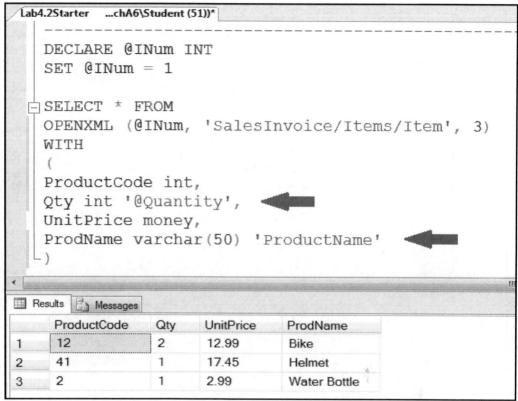

Figure 4.15 Attribute and/or element fields whose names do not match their field names in the XML document must include column patterns.

(Please note that the code shown in Figures 4.9-4.15 has been run from within the same window. In order to conserve space, the Figure 4.10 through Figure 4.15 results are shown with just the code which pulled the data from the OpenXML function.)

Lab 4.2: OpenXML Parameters

Lab Prep: Before you can begin the lab you must run the SQLInteropChapter1.0Setup.sql script. It is recommended that you view the lab video instructions found in Lab4.2_OpenXmlParameters.wmv, available at *www.Joe2Pros.com*.

Skill Check 1: Open the Lab4.2SK1.sql file and use the correct flag parameter value in your OpenXML function to grab the ID and Total Sales from the /BigFoods/Store row pattern. You should not be using any custom colpatterns to get this result.

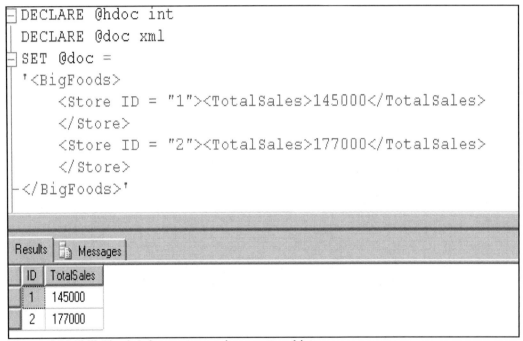

Figure 4.16 Skill Check 1 does not use column pattern hints.

Skill Check 2: Open the Lab4.2SK2.sql file and use the correct flag parameter value in your OpenXML function to grab the [Name] and [Status] from the /Company/Structure/Room rowpattern. You should not be using any custom colpatterns to get this result.

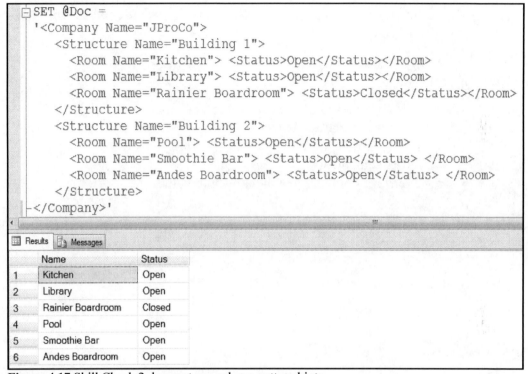

Figure 4.17 Skill Check 2 does not use column pattern hints.

Answer Code: The T-SQL code to this lab can be found in the downloadable files in a file named Lab4.2_OpenXmlParameters.sql

OpenXML Parameters - Points to Ponder

1.   The first parameter of the OpenXML function is the document handle (a.k.a., your "claim ticket"). This parameter is required.

2.   The second parameter of the OpenXML function is the rowpattern. This parameter is required.

3.   The third parameter of the OpenXML function is the flag. This parameter is optional.

4.   The OpenXML Flags determine attribute or element centricity:
   o   0 use mapping (attributes)
   o   1 use attribute values
   o   2 use element values
   o   3 retrieve both element and attribute values

Chapter Glossary

Column pattern: sometimes shortened to "colpattern"; used in conjunction with the OpenXML function; the colpattern option helps you pull data from another column relative to your current position.

Document handle: an integer used to identify the in-memory location of the XML document. The document handle (a.k.a., your "claim ticket") is the first parameter of the OpenXML function. This parameter is required. Typically represented by the

OpenXML: a function used to pull data in a relative fashion; in other words, instead of explicitly naming (i.e., hardcoding) the element levels where we want SQL Server to navigate and pull data, our code can provide rowpattern or column pattern instructions relative to a specified context.

OpenXML flags: these instruct the OpenXML function whether to use attribute and/or element centricity. The flag is the optional third parameter of the OpenXML function. Possible values are 0, 1, 2, 3, or 4.

Preparing XML (for SQL): this process includes storing the XML in memory and processing the XML so that all the data and metadata is ready and available for you access via a SQL query.

Rowpattern: used in conjunction with the OpenXML function; the rowpattern option helps you pull data from another level relative to your current position.

Shredding XML: the complete process of transforming XML data into a rowset.

sp_XML_PrepareDocument: a system stored procedure which parses an XML document into a tree representation of the various nodes and stores it within SQL Server's internal cache; the two required parameters are the handle (an integer handle representing the XML document in memory) and the xml document (i.e., the XML document which you wish to process).

sp_XML_RemoveDocument: a system stored procedure which removes an XML document and its handle from memory.

WITH clause: when used with the OpenXML function, allows you to customize and alias your field headers.

Chapter Four - Review Quiz

1.) You want your column pattern to capture the value of the <Color> element. You are not allowed to change any of the OpenXML parameters. The rowpattern is set to the correct level but you are getting no data. Your WITH statement looks like this:

WITH (MyColor varchar(15) '@Color')

What should your column pattern say to get the value?

O a.   'MyColor'
O b.   'Color'
O c.   '../Color@'
O d.   '../Color'
O e.   './/Color'

2.) You want your column pattern to capture the value of the <Color> element. You are not allowed to change any of the OpenXml Parameters. The rowpattern is set one row below the <Color> element. Your WITH statement looks like this.

WITH (MyColor varchar(15) '@Color')

What should your column pattern say to get the value?

O a.   'MyColor'
O b.   'Color@'
O c.   'Color'
O d.   '../Color'
O e.   './/Color'

3.) All your data is in child elements below the /Root/Data level. Some of your data is in elements and some is in attributes. You want to capture all the fields based on their default names. Which OpenXML flag value do you use?

O a.   OPENXML (@HandleDoc,'Root/Data',0)
O b.   OPENXML (@HandleDoc,'Root/Data',1)
O c.   OPENXML (@HandleDoc,'Root/Data',2)
O d.   OPENXML (@HandleDoc,'Root/Data',3)

Answer Key

1.) b   2.) d   3.) d

Bug Catcher Game

To play the Bug Catcher game run the SQLInteropBugCatcherCh4.pps from the BugCatcher folder of the companion files. You can obtain these files from www.Joes2Pros.com or by ordering the Companion CD.

Chapter 5.   XML Queries

In Chapter 2, we used T-SQL code to stream tabular data and queries from SQL Server into an XML output. Since we took a SQL Server datasource and viewed it in XML format, you may think we have already run some XML queries. We later took an XML datasource, sent it into SQL Server, and saw the data in a tabular format.

Despite these steps we've taken to become familiar with XML, we still haven't performed any substantial XML querying. We haven't yet taken an XML datasource and queried it for just a fragment of the information we want. XML queries get the data you want from an XML source and display the results as XML.

Since this chapter leads us into XQuery, we first need to discuss the XML data type. XQuery works only with the XML data type and its methods.

READER NOTE: *Please run the script SQLInteropChapter5.0Setup.sql in order to follow along with the examples in the first section of Chapter 5. All scripts mentioned in this chapter may be found at **www.Joes2Pros.com**.*

XML Data Type

Integers hold numbers with no decimal points, varchars hold strings of varying length, and the Geography data type holds a position on the earth. Introduced in SQL Server 2005, the XML data type holds and understands valid XML strings.

If an XML document is essentially one long character string, then why should there be a separate XML data type? Like the Geography data type, XML has some built-in functions and methods to help with searching and querying the data inside. For example, the XML data type can detect the difference between valid XML strings (either a valid XML fragment or a well-formed XML document) versus strings which aren't valid XML.

XML as a Field

You can declare a field as an XML data type at the time you create a table in SQL Server, or you can add an XML field later. This would potentially give each record in your table its own well-formed XML data.

How might this capability be a benefit? Suppose you need to store credit history data for each customer. Some customers have one credit reference, some have many, and a few have none at all. These one-to-many relationships could be defined with a new table called dbo.CreditHistory, since a single field does not implement multiple relationships very well. However, XML would allow for this through a series of related tags and without the need to create a separate table.

Our first example will add an XML field to an existing table. The CurrentProducts table (JProCo.dbo.CurrentProducts) has 7 fields and 485 records (see Figure 5.1).

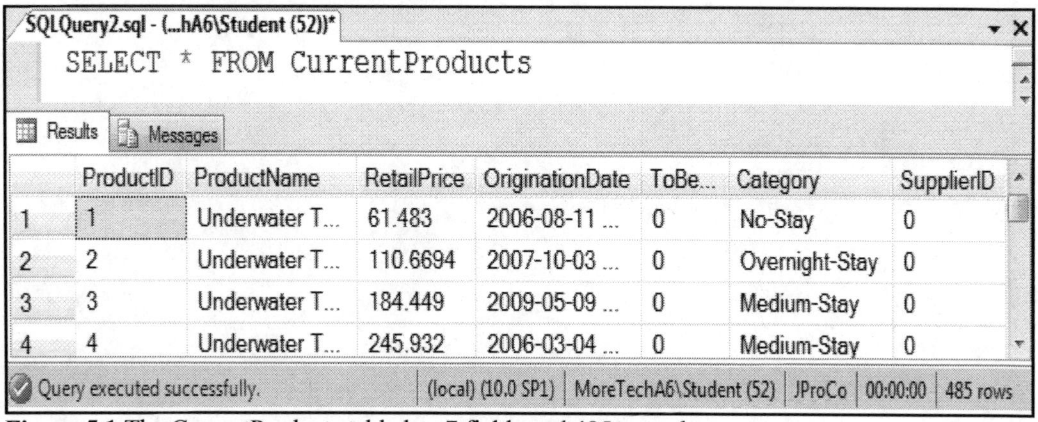

Figure 5.1 The CurrentProducts table has 7 fields and 485 records.

This ALTER TABLE statement code adds a nullable XML field named CategoryCodes to the CurrentProducts table (see Figure 5.2).

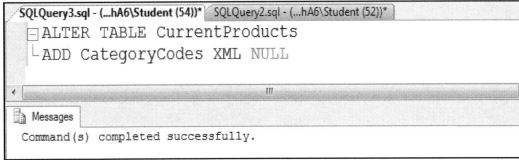

```
SQLQuery3.sql - (...hA6\Student (54))*   SQLQuery2.sql - (...hA6\Student (52))*
ALTER TABLE CurrentProducts
ADD CategoryCodes XML NULL
```

Messages

Command(s) completed successfully.

Figure 5.2 This code adds an XML field, CategoryCodes, to the CurrentProducts table.

If we re-run our Select statement, we can see the new field showing in the table.

```
Fig 5-2.sql - (loc...chA6\Student (54))   SQLQuery2.sql - (...hA6\Student (52))*
SELECT * FROM CurrentProducts
```

Results | Messages

	ProductID	ProductName	RetailPrice	OriginationDate	To...	Category	SupplierID	CategoryCodes
1	1	Underwater To...	61.483	2006-08-11 ...	0	No-Stay	0	NULL
2	2	Underwater To...	110.6694	2007-10-03 ...	0	Overnight-Stay	0	NULL
3	3	Underwater To...	184.449	2009-05-09 ...	0	Medium-Stay	0	NULL
4	4	Underwater To...	245.932	2006-03-04 ...	0	Medium-Stay	0	NULL

Query executed successfully.   (local) (10.0 SP1) | MoreTechA6\Student (52) | JProCo | 00:00:00 | 485 rows

Figure 5.3 The CategoryCodes field now shows in the table.

We want to add some data to the new column. Run this code to populate the CategoryCodes field for Product 1 with a well-formed XML (see Figure 5.4).

```
SQLQuery4.sql - (...hA6\Student (55))*   Fig 5-2.sql - (loc...chA6\Student (54))   SQLQuery2.sql - (...hA6\Studen
UPDATE CurrentProducts
SET CategoryCodes =
'<Root>
  <Category ID = "1"/>
  <Category ID = "4"/>
</Root>'
WHERE ProductID = 1
```

Messages

(1 row(s) affected)

Figure 5.4 This code populates the Product 1 CategoryCodes field with this well-formed XML.

By again running the Select statement, we see the newly populated record in the CategoryCodes field. An XML hyperlink shows for Product 1 (see Figure 5.5).

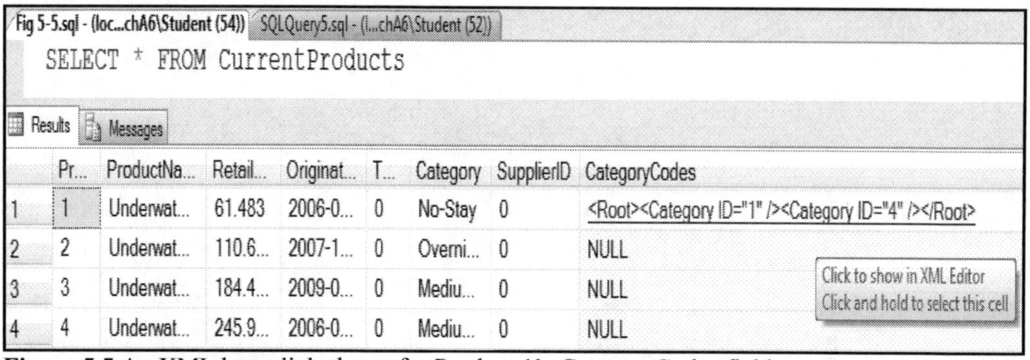

```
Fig 5-5.sql - (loc...chA6\Student (54))   SQLQuery5.sql - (l...chA6\Student (52))
     SELECT * FROM CurrentProducts
```

	Pr...	ProductNa...	Retail...	Originat...	T...	Category	SupplierID	CategoryCodes
1	1	Underwat...	61.483	2006-0...	0	No-Stay	0	<Root><Category ID="1" /><Category ID="4" /></Root>
2	2	Underwat...	110.6...	2007-1...	0	Overni...	0	NULL
3	3	Underwat...	184.4...	2009-0...	0	Mediu...	0	NULL
4	4	Underwat...	245.9...	2006-0...	0	Mediu...	0	NULL

> Click to show in XML Editor
> Click and hold to select this cell

Figure 5.5 An XML hyperlink shows for Product 1's CategoryCodes field.

If we click the XML hyperlink in Figure 5.5, we see the table entity contains this XML result (see Figure 5.6).

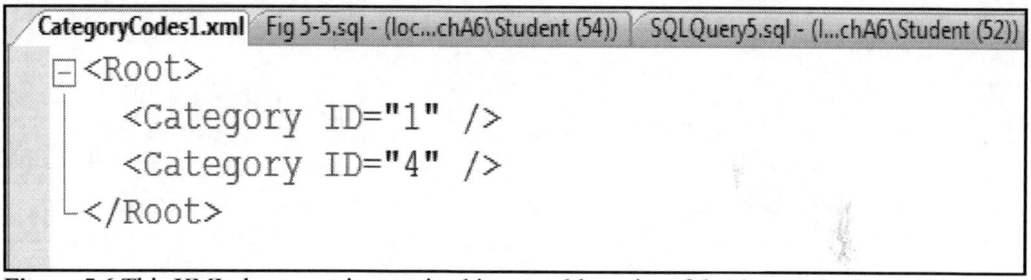

```
CategoryCodes1.xml   Fig 5-5.sql - (loc...chA6\Student (54))   SQLQuery5.sql - (l...chA6\Student (52))
 <Root>
     <Category ID="1" />
     <Category ID="4" />
 </Root>
```

Figure 5.6 This XML document is contained in one table entity of the CurrentProducts table.

Recall the situation we described earlier where a credit history could be stored as one field within a customer's record. Our results here in Figures 5.5 and 5.6 show how this data could appear and how adding an XML field to an existing table would save us from having to create a separate table to contain each customer's credit history data.

XML Variables

SQL Server can declare variables of the XML data type just as easily as it can declare XML fields.

In our next example, we will set an XML variable @Item equal to another well-formed XML (see Figures 5.7 through 5.11).

This code will declare our variable @Item as an XML data type. We then will set this variable equal to our well-formed XML document (see Figure 5.7). This XML document is short, and we can easily see that it is well-formed. (It has a root tag, a top-level element containing attributes, and each beginning tag has a corresponding ending tag.)

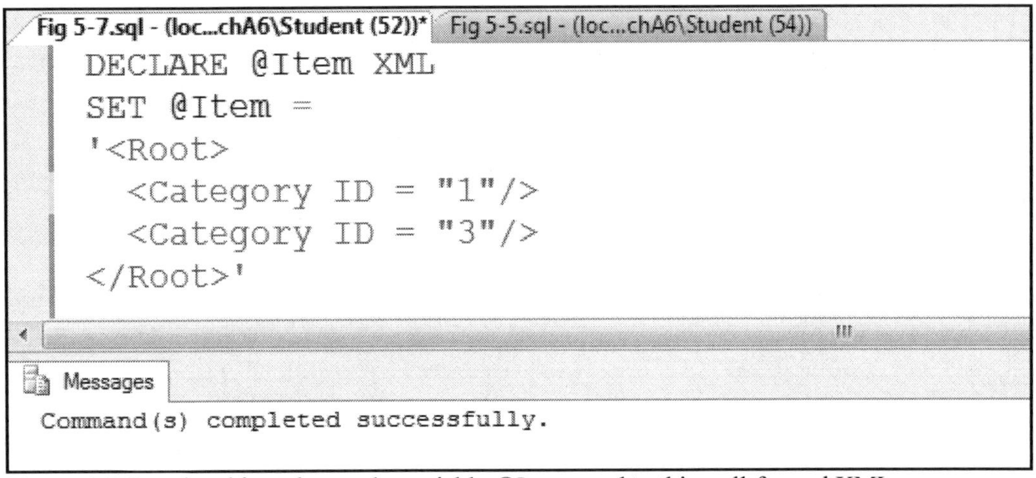
Fig 5-7.sql - (loc...chA6\Student (52))*
Fig 5-5.sql - (loc...chA6\Student (54))
DECLARE @Item XML
SET @Item =
'<Root>
<Category ID = "1"/>
<Category ID = "3"/>
</Root>'
Messages
Command(s) completed successfully.

Figure 5.7 Running this code sets the variable @Item equal to this well-formed XML.

The XML data type detects whether an XML is valid (i.e., either a valid XML fragment or a well-formed XML document). Thus, when our code ran successfully (Figure 5.7), it provided additional confirmation that our XML document is well-formed. For illustrative purposes, we will momentarily remove a necessary character. Notice the forward slash in the ending tag of the first Category element has been removed. Since the document is no longer well-formed, the code will not run (see Figure 5.8).

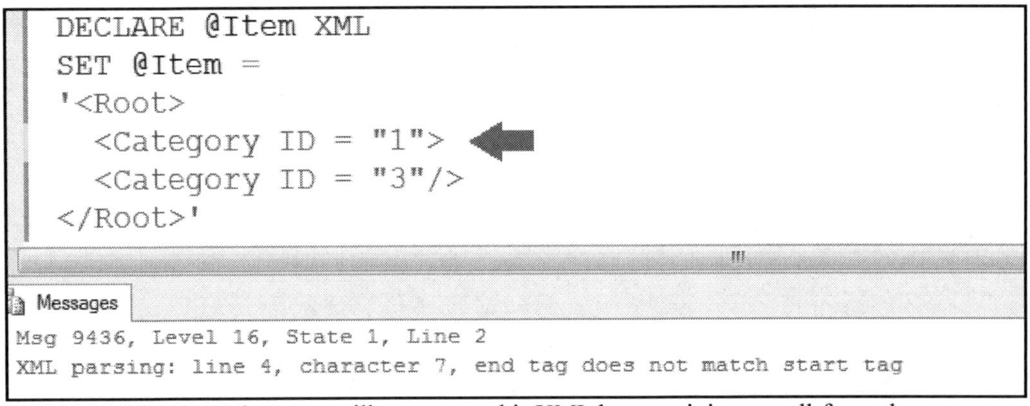
DECLARE @Item XML
SET @Item =
'<Root>
<Category ID = "1">
<Category ID = "3"/>
</Root>'
Messages
Msg 9436, Level 16, State 1, Line 2
XML parsing: line 4, character 7, end tag does not match start tag

Figure 5.8 The XML data type will not accept this XML because it is not well-formed.

Of course, we want to add back the missing character so that our XML once again is well-formed.

Our next step will be to set an entity in CurrentProducts equal to our variable @Item. We don't want every value in the CategoryCodes column to be affected, just Product 2. Be sure to run all of the code shown here (Figure 5.9) together. The scope of the variable @Item makes it available only during runtime. Therefore, in order for your Update statement to use the variable @Item, the code declaring this variable must be included in the same transaction.

```
DECLARE @Item XML
SET @Item =
'<Root>
  <Category ID = "1"/>
  <Category ID = "3"/>
</Root>'

UPDATE CurrentProducts
SET CategoryCodes = @Item
WHERE ProductID = 2
```

Messages

(1 row(s) affected)

Figure 5.9 This value of the XML variable will populate the second CategoryCodes record.

Our Select statement shows us the newly updated CategoryCodes value for Product 2 (see Figure 5.10).

```
SELECT * FROM CurrentProducts
```

Results | Messages

	Product...	ProductName	Reta...	OriginationDate	To...	Category	Supp...	CategoryCodes
1	1	Underwater ...	61.4...	2006-08-11 ...	0	No-Stay	0	<Root><Category ID="1" /><Category ID="4" /></Root>
2	2	Underwater ...	110....	2007-10-03 ...	0			<Root><Category ID="1" /><Category ID="3" /></Root>
3	3	Underwater ...	184....	2009-05-09 ...	0	Medium-...	0	NULL Click to show in XML Editor

Figure 5.10 Run the Select statement again to see the updated field for Product 2.

By clicking through the result hyperlink, we see the XML document contained in the variable @Item (see Figure 5.11).

```
<Root>
    <Category ID="1" />
    <Category ID="3" />
</Root>
```

Figure 5.11 This XML document is contained in the second CategoryCodes record.

Implicit Casting

If you have a varchar which is full of tags and happens to be designed just like a valid XML, then are those essentially the same thing? Yes, they are. If you tell SQL Server to treat this varchar as an XML, you will gain the ability to query this data for fragments which you need to pull from it. In fact, it's so easy that if the varchar is well-formed, you can feed it directly into an XML without even any type of conversion. Just a simple equal sign does the trick.

SET @MyXML = @MyVarchar

This is no different than taking a small int and assigning it to an integer.

SET @ MyInt = @MySmallInt

Any time you are allowed to assign values from one data type to another without needing to use CONVERT or CAST, this is called **implicit casting.**

Now let's repeat this process and observe what is special about the XML data type (i.e., versus a varchar).

Begin by declaring a varchar(max) variable called @sItem and setting it equal to the string of characters shown in Figure 5.12. (*Be sure to type the characters precisely as you see them in Figure 5.12.* While the XML data type is able to check and confirm that your XML is valid, the varchar data type does not have this capability. For example, if you omit an element tag or incorrectly punctuate an attribute, the variable will accept and load whatever you include between the two single quote marks.)

```
DECLARE @sItem varchar(max)
SET @sItem = '<Root>
<Category ID = "1"/>
<Category ID = "5"/>
</Root>'
```

Messages

```
Command(s) completed successfully.
```

Figure 5.12 This code declares a varchar(max) variable and sets it equal to a string.

Our next step will be to insert this variable into the XML field (CategoryCodes) of the CurrentProducts table (see Figure 5.13). The code appears to have run successfully and updated one record.

```
DECLARE @sItem varchar(max)
SET @sItem = '<Root>
<Category ID = "1"/>
<Category ID = "5"/>
</Root>'

UPDATE CurrentProducts
SET CategoryCodes = @sItem
WHERE ProductID = 3
```

Messages

(1 row(s) affected)

Figure 5.13 This code sends our varchar(max) value into the XML field, CategoryCodes.

```
SELECT * FROM CurrentProducts
```

esults   Messages

Pro...	Product...	Reta...	OriginationD...	To...	Categ...	S..	CategoryCodes
1	Underw...	61.4...	2006-08-11 ...	0	No-St...	0	<Root><Category ID="1" /><Category ID="4" /></Root>
2	Underw...	110....	2007-10-03 ...	0	Over...	0	<Root><Category ID="1" /><Category ID="3" /></Root>
3	Underw...	184....	2009-05-09 ...				<Root><Category ID="1" /><Category ID="5" /></Root>
4	Underw...	245....	2006-03-04 ...	0	Mediu...	0	NULL

Figure 5.14 The CategoryCodes value for Product 3 appears to be an XML hyperlink.

By again running our Select statement, we see an XML hyperlink appearing for Product 3's CategoryCodes (see Figure 5.14). And when we click the hyperlink, we see the data we loaded into it from the varchar variable (see Figure 5.15).

```
<Root>
    <Category ID="1" />
    <Category ID="5" />
</Root>
```

Figure 5.15 By clicking Product 3's hyperlink, we see the XML data from our varchar variable.

Implicit casting allowed us to populate an XML field with data from a varchar variable in this case because our varchar data happened to fulfill the requirements of valid XML. Thus far our examples have included well-formed XML documents. We also know that valid XML fragments will work equally well, as we will see later.

Lab 5.1: XML Data Type

Lab Prep: Before you can begin the lab you must run the SQLInteropChapter5.1Setup.sql script. It is recommended that you view the lab video instructions found in Lab5.1_XMLDataType.wmv, available at *www.Joe2Pros.com*.

Skill Check 1: Declare a variable named @item as an XML Data type and populate it with Category 2, 4, and 10. Feed this into the CategoryCodes field for ProductID 5.

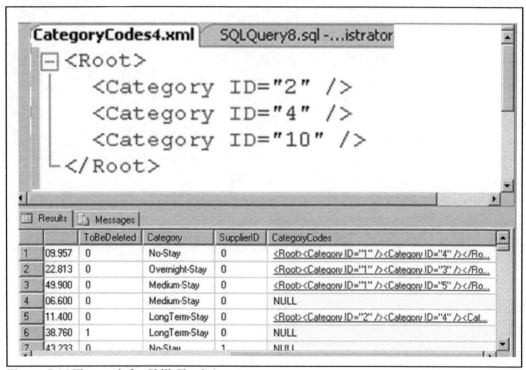

Figure 5.16 The result for Skill Check 1.

Answer Code: The T-SQL code to this lab can be found in the downloadable files in a file named Lab5.1_XML_DataType.sql.

XML Data Type - Points to Ponder

1. SQL Server 2005 and newer versions offer a new data type called XML.

2. The XML data type can be cast from any character data type as long as the character data represents a valid XML fragment or well-formed XML document.

3. When SQL Server implicitly casts XML from character data it might make some alignment modifications to the data (e.g., truncating leading or trailing spaces) but the data and tags remain the same.

4. The XML data type is a LOB (large object type) and may contain up to 2 GB.

Note: Some data elements in this section are misspelled for illustrative purposes. The "corrections" of these values serve as examples in the next chapter when we explore the methods for updating values using XQuery.

XQuery

XQuery is the shorthand term for the **XML Query Language**, the programming language used to handle and query XML data. SQL Server supports most features available in XQuery. XML is layered with elements inside of elements much like your computer's hard drive contains folders inside of folders. XPath is a subset of XQuery, but XPath has no processing capabilities. Like a navigator with a map, XPath can only help point you to the desired level or place within an XML document – it can't process or manipulate your data. Prior to the availability of XQuery, developers could use XPath to navigate within an XML document, but they then needed to export the information to a custom app (e.g., a C# app) in order to perform the actual querying or processing work.

Imagine that you have some XML data which contains the past 10 years' worth of information for your business. The root is called <root> and each top-level node is called <year>. This means you have 10 <year> elements to look through. What if you wanted only the most recent year returned as its own XML? You can use the XQuery langluge to query XML data the same way you use T-SQL code to retrieve just the records you need from tabular data.

The XML data type has a built in method called query( ) which allows you to query the XML for the parts you need. The basics of XQuery are really as simple as specifying the level (like /root/year/) that you want and then optionally picking the value from the level that you want.

XQuery Levels

How deep into the XML is the data which you want to extract? The level (or Path) which your XQuery uses is called the XPath expression. To get the first listed year from the top level your XPath might be expressed as (/root/year[1]). To get the second year listed you would write (/root/year[2]). Let's explore some XPath examples using our music data to get a feel for how this works.

Let's look at the MusicHistory table in the JProCo database. This table has one field (MusicDetails) which is an XML data type (see Figure 5.17).

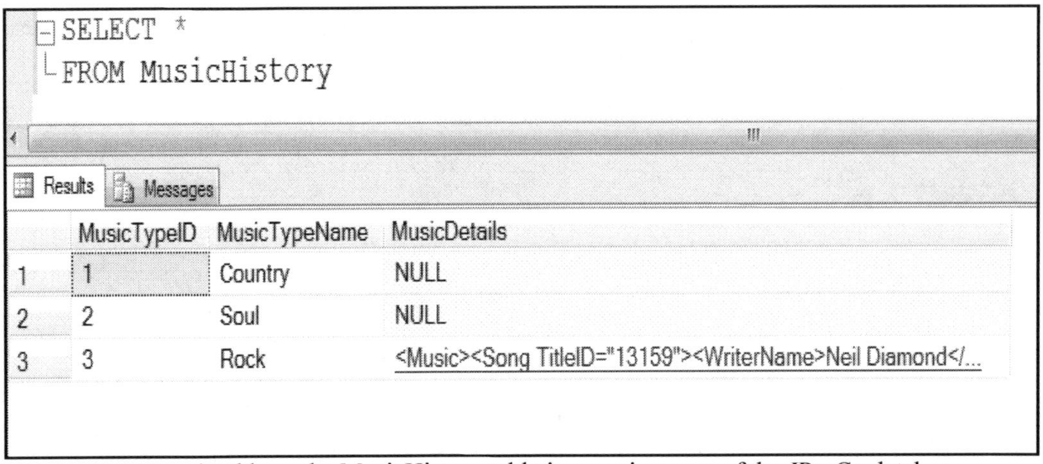

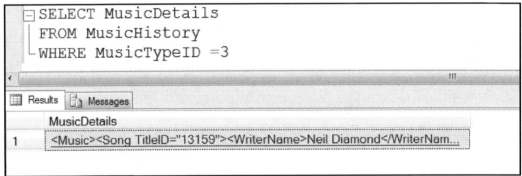

Figure 5.17 You should see the MusicHistory table in your instance of the JProCo database.

We will itemize our Select list to include just the MusicDetails field. We will further narrow our query, so we can take a closer look at the XML value in the third record (see Figure 5.18).

Figure 5.18 We've narrowed down our query to focus on the XML field in Record 3.

When we click through the XML hyperlink, we see the contents of the field. The root element is Music. However, we are interested in Song level. We want to pull out just the XML fragment containing all of the data at or below the Song level (see Figure 5.19).

```
MusicDetails1.xml   SQLQuery1.sql - (...hA6\Student (52))*
  <Music>
    <Song TitleID="13159">
       <WriterName>Neil Diamond</WriterName>
       <Title>Red Red Wine</Title>
       <Singer OrderID="1">
          <BandName>Neil Diamond</BandName>
       </Singer>
       <Singer OrderID="2">
          <BandName>UB40</BandName>
       </Singer>
    </Song>
    <Song TitleID="13160">
       <WriterName>Prince</WriterName>
       <Title>Manic Monday</Title>
       <Singer OrderID="1">
          <BandName>Bangels</BandName>
       </Singer>
    </Song>
  </Music>
```

Figure 5.19 The XML contained in Record 3 of the MusicHistory table.

We will use the *query( ) method* to specify that we want to go beyond the Music level to the Song level (see Figure 5.20). Note that the XQuery syntax requires methods and functions to be lowercase – if you attempt to run this code with a capital Q, you will get an error message.

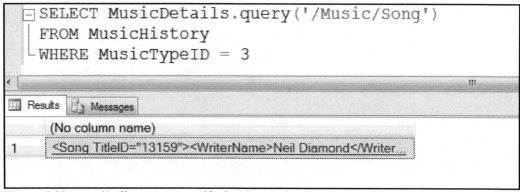

Figure 5.20 query( ) allows us to specify the element level we want.

When we click through the hyperlink produced by our query (see Figure 5.20), we see this XML result (see Figure 5.21). We see the two songs appearing at the top-level <Song> element. We do not see the <Music> element.

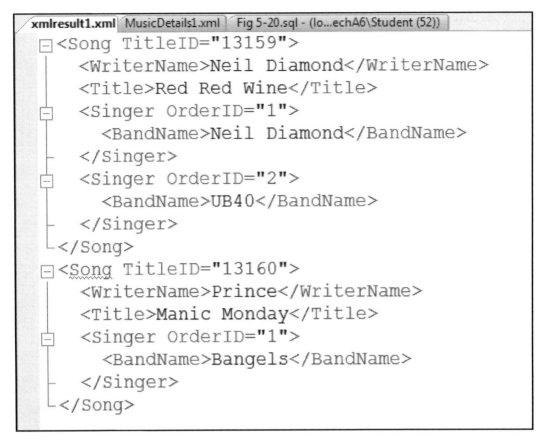

Figure 5.21 Our query produces this XML result and shows the two songs from the <Song> level.

Relative Element Path

Our next goal will be to modify our existing code in order to retrieve just the second song (Song TitleID 13160). Our current code returns all data from the Song level. Adding a [2] to the XPath will return just the second song.

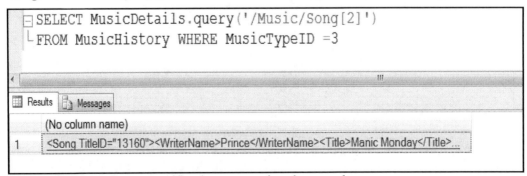

Figure 5.22 Our code now specifies that we want just the second song.

Our code was successful. The XML result now contains just the second song (TitleID 13160, Manic Monday) (see Figure 5.23).

```
<Song TitleID="13160">
    <WriterName>Prince</WriterName>
    <Title>Manic Monday</Title>
    <Singer OrderID="1">
        <BandName>Bangels</BandName>
    </Singer>
</Song>
```

Figure 5.23 We now see just the second song.

This [2] we added to our code forms what's known as a **relative element path**. (Later we will see a related concept known as an **absolute element path**.)

While our code achieved the desired result, a more properly formatted way would have been to put parentheses around the level before specifying the item.

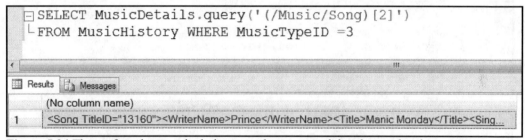

Figure 5.24 The preferred syntax includes parentheses around the element level.

We next will modify our query to return just the first song (Song TitleID 13159). Given the previous example, we would expect this code (see Figure 5.25) to pull out the first song.

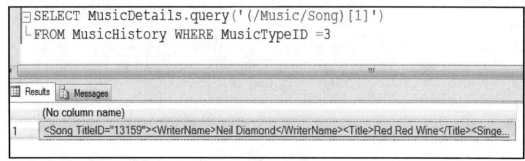

Figure 5.25 We've modified our code to return just the first song.

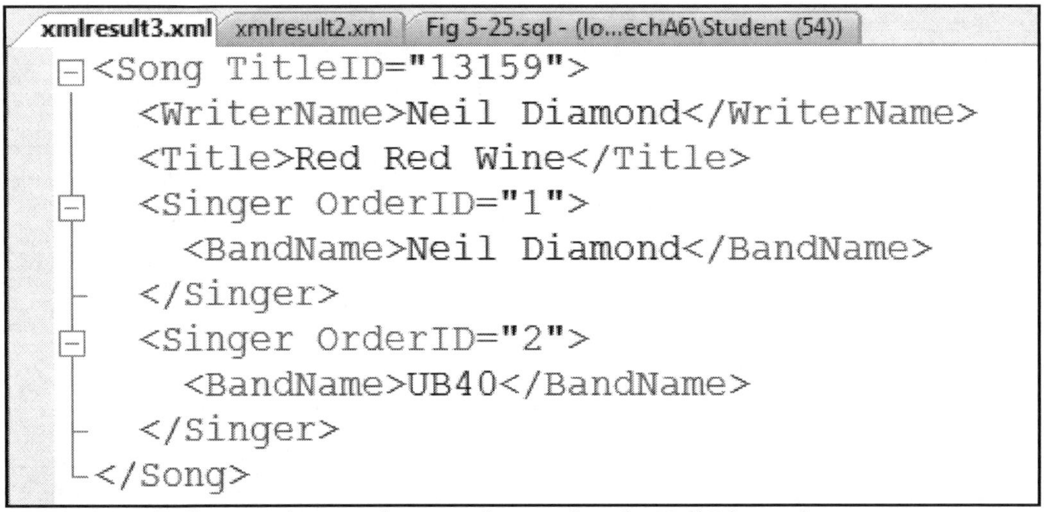

Figure 5.26 The first song has two singers and was written by Neil Diamond.

Now let's adjust our code to return just the XML fragment showing the name of the song writer, Neil Diamond.

Figure 5.27 Our next goal is to return just the XML fragment highlighted here.

To accomplish our goal, we need to add /WriterName to the XPath specified by our existing code. We previously were at the /Music/Song level. We want to go one level deeper to the <WriterName> element.

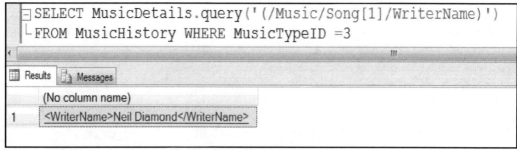

Figure 5.28 Our code now specifies the WriterName level.

By clicking through the XML hyperlink, we see our code successfully pulled out an XML fragment containing just the data we asked for (see Figure 5.29).

```
xmlresult4.xml   Fig 5-28.sql - (lo...echA6\Student (52))

    <WriterName>Neil Diamond</WriterName>
```

Figure 5.29 Our code successfully retrieved just the data we specified.

text( ) Function

The text( ) function is one of XQuery's data accessor functions.

Next we will want to pull out just the writer's name (Neil Diamond). The WriterName element consists of a beginning tag, an ending tag, and the text between the tags. The portion we wish to isolate is known as the *element text.* The *text( )* function retrieves element text without the element tags.

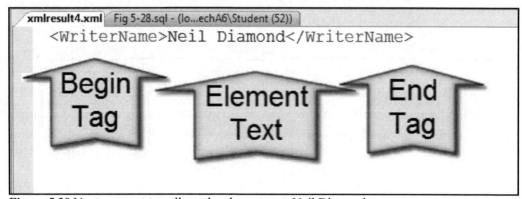

Figure 5.30 Next we want to pull out the element text, Neil Diamond.

To accomplish this, we simply need to add the text function to our current code (see Figure 5.31). Again, observe that the function must be in lowercase letters – it will error if you attempt this code with a capital T (/text( )').

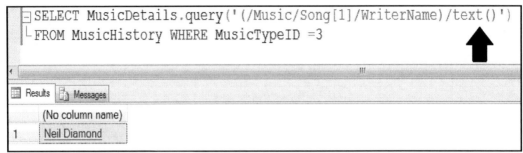

Figure 5.31 We are adding the text( ) function to our current code.

By clicking the XML hyperlink, we see our code successfully pulled out an XML fragment containing just the text between the element tags (Figure 5.32).

```
xmlresult5.xml   Fig 5-31.sql - (lo...echA6\Student (54))
    Neil Diamond
```

Figure 5.32 Our code successfully pulled out just the element text, Neil Diamond.

Next we will switch gears and revert back to the code we used earlier (see Figure 5.25). For our next example, we need to pull data from a higher level.

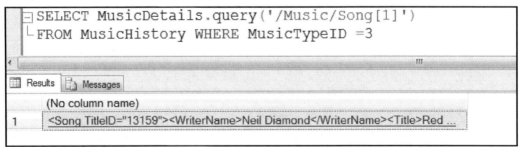

Figure 5.33 We've reverted back to our previous code which returns just the first song.

Our XML hyperlink is the same as we saw previously (in Figure 5.26). We see all the data for just the first song. Notice that this song has two singers, Neil Diamond and UB40 (see Figure 5.34). Our next example will pull out the more recent singer, UB40.

```
<Song TitleID="13159">
    <WriterName>Neil Diamond</WriterName>
    <Title>Red Red Wine</Title>
    <Singer OrderID="1">
        <BandName>Neil Diamond</BandName>
    </Singer>
    <Singer OrderID="2">
        <BandName>UB40</BandName>
    </Singer>
</Song>
```

Figure 5.34 The first song has two singers. We will pull out data for UB40.

We've modified our code to show us only the second singer, UB40 (Figure 5.35).

```
SELECT MusicDetails.query('/Music/Song[1]/Singer[2]')
FROM MusicHistory WHERE MusicTypeID =3
```

	Results	Messages
	(No column name)
1	<Singer OrderID="2"><BandName>UB40</BandName></Singer>

Figure 5.35 Our code now retrieves only the second singer (UB40).

As expected, the XML hyperlink shows us data for just the second singer, UB40 (see Figure 5.36).

```
<Singer OrderID="2">
    <BandName>UB40</BandName>
</Singer>
```

Figure 5.36 Our XML result also shows just the second singer (UB40).

Next we will modify our code to retrieve an XML fragment containing only the BandName element (see Figures 5.37 and 5.38).

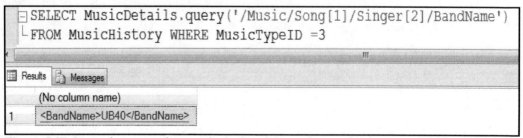

```
SELECT MusicDetails.query('/Music/Song[1]/Singer[2]/BandName')
FROM MusicHistory WHERE MusicTypeID =3
```

	Results	Messages
	(No column name)
1	<BandName>UB40</BandName>

Figure 5.37 Our code now retrieves only the BandName element for the second singer, UB40.

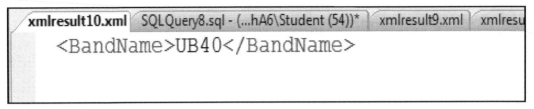

Figure 5.38 Our XML result also shows just the BandName element.

And finally, we'll use the text( ) function to pull out just the band name, which is the text between the element tags:

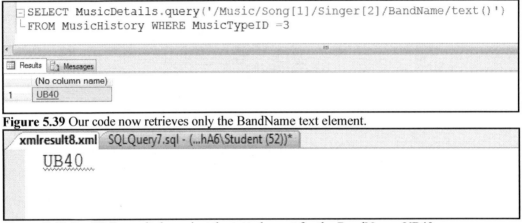

Figure 5.39 Our code now retrieves only the BandName text element.

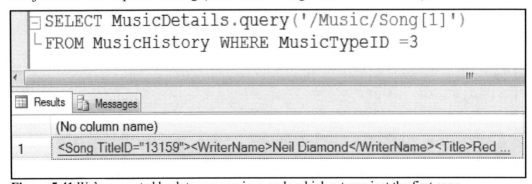

Figure 5.40 Our XML result shows just the text element for the BandName, UB40.

Absolute Element Path

For our final examples, let's again revert back to our previous code which pulls out just the first top-level song (as shown in Figures 5.25 and 5.33).

```
SELECT MusicDetails.query('/Music/Song[1]')
FROM MusicHistory WHERE MusicTypeID =3
```

	(No column name)
1	<Song TitleID="13159"><WriterName>Neil Diamond</WriterName><Title>Red ...

Figure 5.41 We've reverted back to our previous code which returns just the first song.

Our XML hyperlink shows the same data we saw previously (in Figures 5.26 and 5.34). We see all the data for just the first song, TitleID 13159.

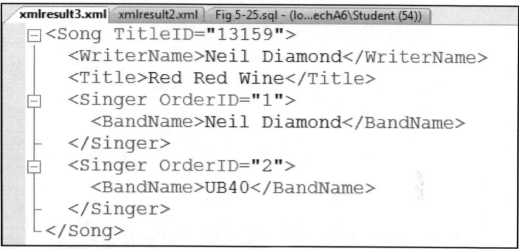

Figure 5.42 This XML contains all the data for the first song, TitleID 13159.

Notice that our current code uses the *relative element path* in order to pull out this song (TitleID 13159). But suppose a Song 13158 were added to the catalog. In that case, the current query wouldn't pull your intended song – the path specified by the current query ('/Music/Song[1]') will always pull whichever song appears first in the top-level tag.

We should be prepared for this possibility and learn how to pull out the top level element by its attribute ID and not simply by its position. This is known as the *absolute element path* (see Figure 5.43).

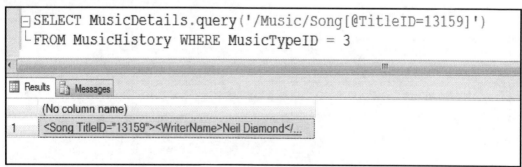

Figure 5.43 This code pulls the data for the song for TitleID 13159.

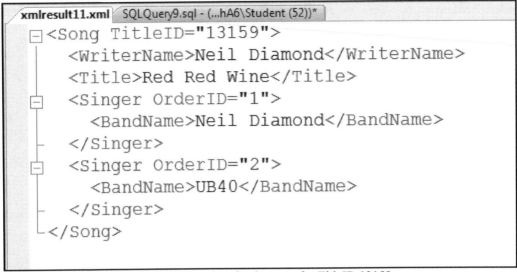

Figure 5.44 This XML contains all the data for the song for TitleID 13159.

Now let's test this technique once again by pulling out the data for song ID 13160 (see Figure 5.45).

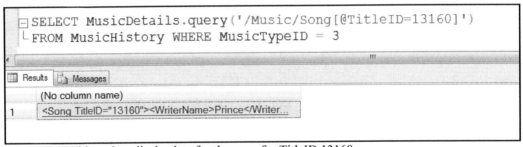

Figure 5.45 This code pulls the data for the song for TitleID 13160.

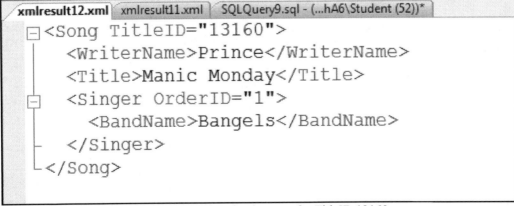

Figure 5.46 This XML contains all the data for the song for TitleID 13160.

Lab 5.2: XQuery

Lab Prep: Before you can begin the lab you must run the SQLInteropChapter5.2Setup.sql script. It is recommended that you view the lab video instructions found in Lab5.2_XQuery.wmv, available at *www.Joe2Pros.com*.

Skill Check 1: Pull out TitleID=13159 from the /Music/Song level regardless of the order it appears in the XML field. Pull out the second singer for this song.

```
<Singer OrderID="2">
   <BandName>UB40</BandName>
</Singer>
```

Figure 5.47 The result for Skill Check 1.

Skill Check 2: Pull out the second record from the Olympics table and show the XML from the Odetails field.

```
<Olympics>
   <Event ID="001" Name="Javelin">
     <Gold>DArto Harkönenn</Gold>
     <Silver>David Ottley</Silver>
     <Bronze>Kenth Eldebrink</Bronze>
   </Event>
   <Event ID="002" Name="Boxing 178.5lbs">
     <Gold>Santon Josipovic</Gold>
     <Silver>Kevin Barry</Silver>
     <Bronze>Mustapha Moussa</Bronze>
     <Bronze>Evander Holyfield</Bronze>
   </Event>
</Olympics>
```

Figure 5.48 The result for Skill Check 1.

Skill Check 3: Pull out the second record from the Olympics table and show the XML from the Odetails field. Show the XML fragment from the first top-level <Event> in the XML data.

```
<Event ID="001" Name="Javelin">
    <Gold>DArto Harkönenn</Gold>
    <Silver>David Ottley</Silver>
    <Bronze>Kenth Eldebrink</Bronze>
</Event>
```

Figure 5.49 The result for Skill Check 3.

Skill Check 4: Pull out the second record from the Olympics table and show the XML from the Odetails field. Show the XML fragment from the gold medal element under the first top-level <Event> in the XML data.

```
<Gold>DArto Harkönenn</Gold>
```

Figure 5.50 The result for Skill Check 4.

Skill Check 5: Use the text( ) function to pull out just the text from Skill Check 4.

```
DArto Harkönenn
```

Figure 5.51 The result for Skill Check 5.

Skill Check 6: Pull out the second record from the Olympics table and show the XML from the Odetails field. Show the XML fragment from the Bronze medal element under the <Event> with Event ID=002.

```
<Bronze>Mustapha Moussa</Bronze>
<Bronze>Evander Holyfield</Bronze>
```

Figure 5.52 The result for Skill Check 6.

Answer Code: The T-SQL code to this lab can be found in the downloadable files in a file named Lab5.2_XQuery.sql

XQuery - Points to Ponder

1. The XML data type has a built-in method called query( ) which allows you to query for the parts of the XML you need.

2. XQuery was created primarily as a query language for getting data stored in an XML form.

3. XQuery is a query and functional programming language that is designed to query collections of XML data

4. The main purpose of XQuery is to get information out of XML databases.

5. XQuery uses a valid XPath expression like /Music/Song/ as a parameter.

6. / slashes are used for traversing element names in a downward direction.

7. [@..] is used to extract attributes.

8. [1] is used to select the first element of your XPath parameter.

9. /Music/Song[1]/Singer[@OrderID=1] would get the <Singer> element having an 'OrderID' attribute value of 1, all for the first song.

10. XQuery is a flexible query language which extracts data from an XML stream.

11. XQuery is also capable of manipulating XML data by updating, inserting, and deleting data or elements.

12. XQuery uses the XPath expression syntax to address specific parts of an XML document.

13. An XPath expression provides the path to a level or location based on a tree-structure of the information contained in an XML stream.

14. XPath is a subset of XQuery.

15. XPath is a query language for selecting nodes from an XML stream.

16. An XPath expression is often called "an XPath."

17. XPath offers a "for" expression which is a mini-version of the XQuery FLWOR expression.

Chapter Glossary

FLWOR: the XPath expressions For, Let, Where, Order By, Return. Often referred to as the "flower statements." The Let clause is new to SQL Server 2008; the other clauses were also available in SQL Server 2005.

Implicit casting: definition.

next( ): these instruct the OpenXML function whether to use attribute and/or element centricity. The flag is the optional third parameter of the OpenXML function. Possible values are 0, 1, 2, 3, or 4.

query( ): a built-in method of the XML data type; allows you to query for just the needed parts of an XML.

text( ): one of XQuery's data accessor functions.

XML data type: holds and understands valid XML strings; introduced in SQL Server 2005.

XQuery: works only with the XML data type and its methods.

Chapter Five - Review Quiz

1.) What is the name of the root node in the code below?

`<TV> <Show>Bob on the job </Show></TV>`

O a. TV

O b. Show

O c. Bob on the Job

2.) You have the following XML stream.

```
<TV>
  <Show Name="Bob on the Job">
   <Starring>
        <Actor>Bob</Actor>
        <Actor>Patrick</Actor>
   </Starring>
  </Show>
  <Show Name="Way Kendall">
   <Starring>
        <Actor>Lisa</Actor>
        <Actor>Peter</Actor>
   </Starring>
  </Show>
</TV>
```

You need to enter the query parameter to get All Actors from the first TV show element, as seen here:

```
<Starring>
    <Actor>Bob</Actor>
    <Actor>Patrick</Actor>
</Starring>
```


Which XPath will get you this Fragment?

O a. 'TV/Show[1]/Starring'

O b. 'TV/Show[2]/Starring'

O c. 'TV/Show[1]/Starring/Actor'

O d. 'TV/Show[2]/Starring/Actor'

O e. 'TV/Show[1]

3.) You have the following XML stream.

```
<TV>
   <Show Name="Bob on the Job">
     <Starring>
         <Actor>Bob</Actor>
         <Actor>Patrick</Actor>
     </Starring>
   </Show>
   <Show Name="Way Kendall">
     <Starring>
         <Actor>Lisa</Actor>
         <Actor>Peter</Actor>
     </ Starring >
   </Show>
</TV>
```

You need to enter the query parameter to get the second actor from the first TV show element, as seen here:

• `<Actor>Patrick</Actor>`

What XPath will get you this Fragment?

O a. 'TV/Show[1]/Starring/Actor[1]'

O b. 'TV/Show[1]/Starring/Actor[2]'

O c. 'TV/Show[2]/Starring/Actor[1]'

O d. 'TV/Show[2]/Starring/Actor[2]'

4.) The XML and varchar(max) data types will both store XML data. What are two key differences between these two types?

□ a. The XML data type does not allow root tags.

□ b. The Varchar(max) does not allow root tags.

□ c. The XML data type will only accept well formed XML

□ d. The Varchar(max) data type will only accept well formed XML

□ e. The XML data type will not truncate leading or trailing spaces.

□ f. The Varchar(max) data type will not truncate leading or trailing spaces.

5.) You have the following XML stream.

```
<TV>
   <Show Name="Bob on the Job">
     <Starring>
         <Actor>Bob</Actor>
         <Actor>Patrick</Actor>
     </Starring>
   </Show>
   <Show Name="Way Kendall">
     <Starring>
         <Actor>Lisa</Actor>
         <Actor>Peter</Actor>
     </Starring>
   </Show>
</TV>
```

You need to enter the query parameter to get All Actors from the first TV show's Starring element, as seen here:

```
<Actor>Bob</Actor>
<Actor>Patrick</Actor>
```

Which XPath will get you this Fragment?

O a. 'TV/Show[1]/Starring'

O b. 'TV/Show[2]/Starring'

O c. 'TV/Show[1]/Starring/Actor'

O d. 'TV/Show[2]/Starring/Actor'

O e. 'TV/Show[1]'

O f. 'TV/Show[2]'

Answer Key

1.) a   2.) a   3.) b   4.) c, f   5.) c

Bug Catcher Game

To play the Bug Catcher game run the SQLInteropBugCatcherCh5.pps from the BugCatcher folder of the companion files. You can obtain these files from www.Joes2Pros.com or by ordering the Companion CD.

Chapter 6.   XQuery Extensions

We know the XML data type was first introduced in SQL Server 2005. This data type continues in SQL Server 2008 where expanded XML features are available. Along with the XML data type comes the power of the XQuery language to analyze and query the values contained in your XML instance.

We will continue to build our expertise using XQuery to query, analyze, and manipulate our XML data. Our code will leverage XPath expressions to "navigate" to the levels and nodes where we want the XML data type methods to perform their work. The methods we will explore are query, value, exist, and modify (all lowercase, since everything in XQuery is case-sensitive). You may occasionally hear developers refer to these as "XQuery methods."

This chapter will demonstrate these built-in methods (also called functions), as well as show you some keyword extensions (FOR, LET, WHERE, ORDER BY, and RETURN).

READER NOTE: *Please run the script SQLInteropChapter6.0Setup.sql in order to follow along with the examples in the first section of Chapter 6. All scripts mentioned in this chapter may be found at **www.Joes2Pros.com**.*

XML Data Type Method Basics

Functions versus Methods. Until this point in each volume of the *Joes 2 Pros* series, we have used the term "functions" to refer to commands which require a set of parentheses in order to perform their work (e.g., MAX( ), COUNT( )). SQL programmers also call these functions. However, XML and object-oriented (OOP) programmers refer to these command items as "methods." Since this book focuses on SQL Server's interaction and interoperability with other programming languages, we will be good guests and speak their language.

In the last chapter, we became proficient at using the most common method of the XML data type. The query( ) method allowed us to take an entire XML stream and query just a specific piece of it. We passed in an XPath and got back an XML fragment.

All XML data type methods require an XPath expression as one of the (or the only) XQuery parameter(s), but not all of the methods return data. Some of these methods simply analyze the data at that level and return a status to you. The remainder of this section breaks down four of these methods: query( ), value( ), exist( ), and modify( ). (The nodes( ) method will be covered in Chapter 7.)

```xml
<Music>
  <Song TitleID="13159">
    <WriterName>Neil Diamond</WriterName>
    <Title>Red Red Wine</Title>
    <Singer OrderID="1">
      <BandName>Neil Diamond</BandName>
    </Singer>
    <Singer OrderID="2">
      <BandName>UB40</BandName>
    </Singer>
  </Song>
  <Song TitleID="13160">
    <WriterName>Prince</WriterName>
    <Title>Manic Monday</Title>
    <Singer OrderID="1">
      <BandName>The Bangles</BandName>
    </Singer>
  </Song>
  <Song TitleID="13161">
    <WriterName>Roy Orbison</WriterName>
    <Title>Pretty Woman</Title>
    <Singer OrderID="1">
      <BandName>Roy Orbison</BandName>
    </Singer>
    <Singer OrderID="2">
      <BandName>Van Halen</BandName>
    </Singer>
  </Song>
</Music>
```

Figure 6.1 In this chapter, we will expand on the XML document containing the Music dataset.

The query( ) Method

As we saw in the last chapter, this method basically needs an XPath expression in the XQuery parameter and returns an XML data type.

Here is a recap of the code we used to retrieve an XML fragment containing only the BandName element (shown in Chapter 5 as Figures 5.37 and 5.38).

The XPath expression ('/Music/Song[1]/Singer[2]/BandName') specifies that we want to navigate to the BandName element of the second Singer of the first Song (Red Red Wine). The query( ) method retrieves the data and returns to SQL Server the XML fragment containing the beginning and ending element tags, along with the element text for the current BandName value, UB40 (Figure 6.2).

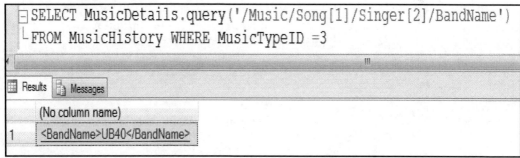

Figure 6.2 query( ) retrieves the BandName element for the second Singer of the first Song.

When we click through the hyperlink result, it launches an XML query window within SQL Server Management Studio (see Figure 6.3).

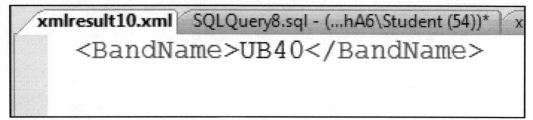

Figure 6.3 Our XML result also shows just the element tags and text for the BandName, UB40.

We also used the text( ) function in conjunction with query( ) to return element text (i.e., an XML fragment without element tags). Essentially the query( ) method only returns XML data -- if you need a single name or value, then you must add the text( ) to your query( ) code.

Here text( ) pulls out just the BandName value, which is the text between the element tags (see Figure 6.4).

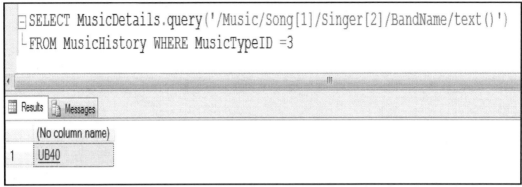

Figure 6.4 We have added text( ) to our existing code in order to retrieve just the BandName.

When we click through the hyperlink result, we see only the element text, UB40. We have used XQuery to query our XML document and returned to SQL Server just the data we wanted (see Figure 6.5).

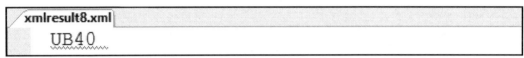

Figure 6.5 Our XML result also shows just the text element for the BandName, UB40.

Let's switch gears and go back up to the Song level for our next query( ) example. This code will return all items found at the Song level (see Figure 6.6).

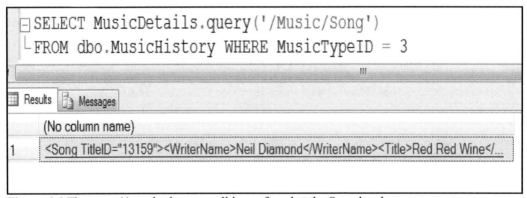

Figure 6.6 The query( ) method returns all items found at the Song level.

When we click through the result hyperlink, we see the XML fragments for all three songs: Red Red Wine, Manic Monday, and Pretty Woman (see Figure 6.7).

```
<Song TitleID="13159">
   <WriterName>Neil Diamond</WriterName>
   <Title>Red Red Wine</Title>
   <Singer OrderID="1">
     <BandName>Neil Diamond</BandName>
   </Singer>
   <Singer OrderID="2">
     <BandName>UB40</BandName>
   </Singer>
</Song>
<Song TitleID="13160">
   <WriterName>Prince</WriterName>
   <Title>Manic Monday</Title>
   <Singer OrderID="1">
     <BandName>Bangels</BandName>
   </Singer>
</Song>
<Song TitleID="13161">
   <WriterName>Roy Orbison</WriterName>
   <Title>Pretty Woman</Title>
   <Singer OrderID="1">
     <BandName>Roy Orbison</BandName>
   </Singer>
   <Singer OrderID="2">
     <BandName>Van Halen</BandName>
   </Singer>
</Song>
```

Figure 6.7 The query( ) method returns all items found at the Song level.

Next we will specify just the first Song, Red Red Wine (see Figures 6.8 and 6.9).

Figure 6.8 We want to see just the first song.

```
<Song TitleID="13159">
   <WriterName>Neil Diamond</WriterName>
   <Title>Red Red Wine</Title>
   <Singer OrderID="1">
     <BandName>Neil Diamond</BandName>
   </Singer>
   <Singer OrderID="2">
     <BandName>UB40</BandName>
   </Singer>
</Song>
```

Figure 6.9 Our result is an XML fragment containing just the first song.

This code specifies that we want data for all Singer-elements found for the first Song (see Figures 6.10 and 6.11).

```
SELECT MusicDetails.query('/Music/Song[1]/Singer')
 FROM dbo.MusicHistory WHERE MusicTypeID = 3
```

| Results | Messages |

(No column name)

| 1 | `<Singer OrderID="1"><BandName>Neil Diamond</BandName></Singer><Singer OrderID="2"><Band...` |

Figure 6.10 Our code now specifies our search should begin at the Singer level.

```
<Singer OrderID="1">
    <BandName>Neil Diamond</BandName>
</Singer>
<Singer OrderID="2">
    <BandName>UB40</BandName>
</Singer>
```

Figure 6.11 Our result is an XML fragment containing all singers of the first song.

This code specifies that we want query( ) to return data for just the first Singer found for the first Song (see Figures 6.12 and 6.13).

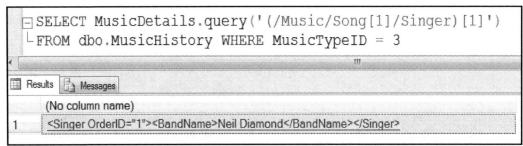

```
SELECT MusicDetails.query('(/Music/Song[1]/Singer)[1]')
 FROM dbo.MusicHistory WHERE MusicTypeID = 3
```

| Results | Messages |

(No column name)

| 1 | `<Singer OrderID="1"><BandName>Neil Diamond</BandName></Singer>` |

Figure 6.12 This code will return data for just the first Singer of the first Song (Red Red Wine).

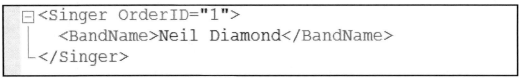

```
<Singer OrderID="1">
    <BandName>Neil Diamond</BandName>
</Singer>
```

Figure 6.13 This XML fragment contains data for Neil Diamond, the first Singer of the first Song.

The value( ) Method

The next method we will explore is value( ). Earlier we used the query( ) method in combination with the text( ) function to pull out just the element text for a single value (as shown earlier in Figure 6.4). Recall that it pulled out our data converted to text (not to XML). When pulling out numerical data, it also formats this data as text.

The value( ) method achieves the same goal as query( ) and text( ) do together, except it allows you to specify the data type you want for your result. It returns just your data (without the metadata – no element tags) and gives you the freedom to specify any data type you would like (i.e., not just XML or text). In other words, if you are pulling from a <Price> element, then you might want the result returned as a Money or a Decimal data type. If you are pulling from the <Singer> element, you might specify that the returning data should be a Varchar.

This method provides an efficient way to retrieve data directly from an XML file and return it to SQL Server.

The query syntax is very similar to our current code (see Figure 6.12). We will use value( ) to return the same data (first singer of the first song). Substitute "value" in place of "query" and run the code. The resulting error message prompts us to supply a data type (see Figures 6.14). *The value( ) method requires two parameters.*

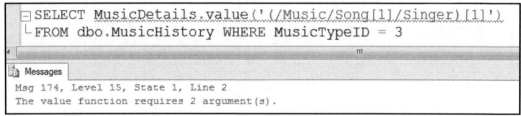

Figure 6.14 The value( ) method requires two parameters, an XPath expression and a data type.

Observe that XQuery gives us the freedom to specify data types which are compatible with character data (e.g., char(20), varchar(max)).

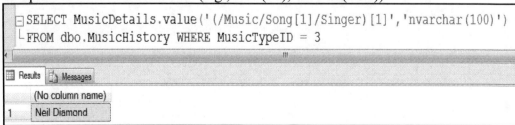

Figure 6.15 When we supply a data type, value( ) returns just the data we specified.

185

The exist( ) Method

In this method you don't want any data returned from the XML stream. You just want to check to know whether it is there. The exist( ) method will check for the existence and even the value of the XPath expression you specify.

Let's return to our code which shows us all the top-level nodes (as seen in Figures 6.6 and 6.7). When we click through the result hyperlink, we see the XML fragments for all three songs: Red Red Wine, Manic Monday, and Pretty Woman.

Figure 6.16 For our next example, we are returning to our code showing all three songs

Now let's drill in and find the fragment which contains data for the Song with title 13161, regardless of whether it is at, or below, the top-level element (Song).

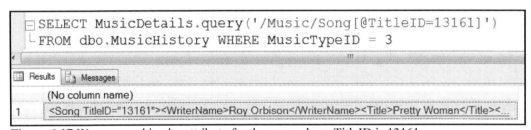

Figure 6.17 We are searching by attribute for the song whose TitleID is 13161.

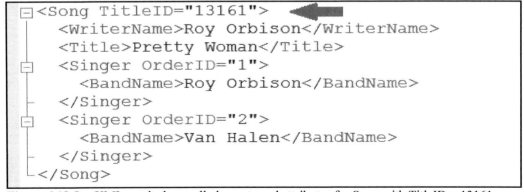

Figure 6.18 Our XML result shows all elements and attributes for Song with TitleID = 13161.

Let's observe what happens when we try to query for a TitleID which doesn't exist. Our XML document contains the TitleIDs 13159, 13160, and 13161 (as we saw earlier in Figure 6.7). Let's modify our code to specify the non-existent TitleID 13162 (see Figure 6.19). XQuery doesn't give us an error message – it simply returns an empty string.

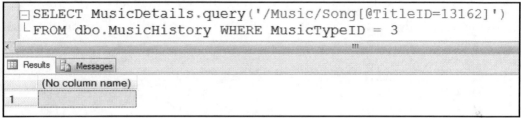

Figure 6.19 TitleID 13162 doesn't exist, so query( ) returns an empty string.

Next we will modify our current code to include the exist( ) method. The syntax and functionality is nearly identical to the syntax we used to search for TitleIDs 13161 and 13162, except that the exist( ) method doesn't return the element data from your XML document. Instead, it returns a "0" if the data doesn't exist or a "1" if the data does exist.

Now let's simply find out whether 13162 exists. Rather than returning a piece of the XML, it will return a 1 (for Yes) or a 0 (for No).

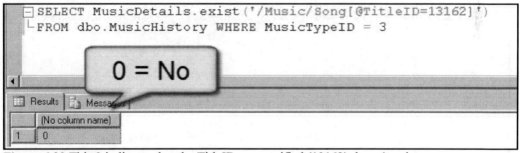

Figure 6.20 This 0 indicates that the TitleID we specified (13162) doesn't exist.

Let's repeat the step for TitleID 13161, an item that we know exists.

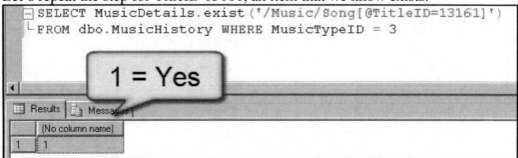

Figure 6.21 This 1 indicates that yes, the TitleID we specified (13161) does exist.

The modify( ) Method

The modify( ) method allows you to change values directly in your XML stream. Like all other XML data type methods, it needs an XPath parameter to know which value to change. However, unlike the other methods, modify( ) works with an UPDATE statement – it won't work with a SELECT statement.

Also, modify( ) can only work with one data value at a time (a mathematical and programming concept known as a *singleton*).

We will use TitleID 13160 (Manic Monday) to explore the modify( ) method.

```
SELECT MusicDetails.query('/Music/Song[@TitleID=13160]')
FROM dbo.MusicHistory WHERE MusicTypeID = 3
```

Results | Messages

(No column name)
1	`<Song TitleID="13160"><WriterName>Prince</WriterName><Title>Manic Monday</Title><Sing...`

Figure 6.22 Our code retrieves all data for the Song with the TitleID of 13160.

```
<Song TitleID="13160">
   <WriterName>Prince</WriterName>
   <Title>Manic Monday</Title>
   <Singer OrderID="1">
      <BandName>Bangels</BandName>
   </Singer>
</Song>
```

Figure 6.23 The XML fragment containing all data for the Song with the TitleID of 13160.

Next, we would like our code to pull out an XML fragment for the Title element.

```
SELECT MusicDetails.query('/Music/Song[@TitleID=13160]/Title')
FROM dbo.MusicHistory WHERE MusicTypeID = 3
```

Results | Messages

(No column name)
1	`<Title>Manic Monday</Title>`

Figure 6.24 We have narrowed our code to retrieve the XML fragment for just the Title element.

```
<Title>Manic Monday</Title>
```

Figure 6.25 The XML fragment containing the Title element for Manic Monday.

Let's modify our code to retrieve only the element text "Manic Monday."

```
SELECT MusicDetails.query('/Music/Song[@TitleID=13160]/Title/text()')
FROM dbo.MusicHistory WHERE MusicTypeID = 3
```

Results	Messages

	(No column name)
1	Manic Monday

Figure 6.26 Our code uses text( ) to retrieve only the element text for "Manic Monday."

```
Manic Monday
```

Figure 6.27 Our code has successfully retrieved just the element text, "Manic Monday."

As we've done with each new method in this chapter, we have used our familiar tools query( ) and text( ) to scaffold and bring our code to a good juncture to introduce the new method. We need to first add one refinement to our current code before we can bring in the modify( ) method.

Earlier we mentioned the modify( ) method can only work with one data value at a time. While it won't alter the result of our current code, we need to add a "[1]" to specify that we only want a single item retrieved (see Figure 6.28).

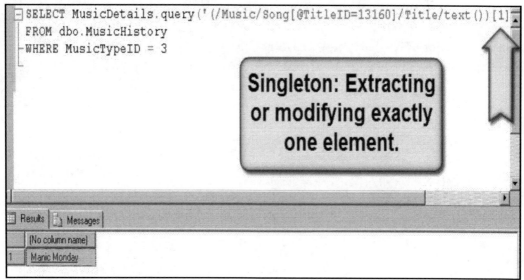

Figure 6.28 Adding the 1 to our code ensures that only one value will be retrieved.

Since there is no limit to the number of elements which can be under another element, any given XPath may have many children. For example, the XPath of /week/day would have three elements below and, therefore, isn't a singleton:

<week>
  <day>Monday<day/>
  <day>Tuesday<day/>
  <day>Wednesday<day/>
<week>

However, if you changed your PATH to be (/week/day)[1], then you would just get Monday. Again, since a song can only have one title, rhen specifying the singelton of [1] doesn't change the appearance of our current result but it helps prepare us for the next method we will explore, which is modify( ).

Let's review our goal for this demonstration. The modify( ) method allows us to change a value in our XML file, which is a helpful capability. Suppose we've brought our XML document into SQL Server and found a typo or need to update just one value. We don't need to rerun the step to bring in the XML document in order to make that change – we can use the modify( ) method and write the change directly to the XML file contained in our SQL Server instance.

'Our scenario is that the title "Manic Monday" needs to be changed to "Walk Like an Egyptian" (see Figure 6.29). Since modify( ) is going to replace the current title, Manic Monday, with the new title, we need to add some code to handle the change. For readability, we will move our existing XPath parameter for Manic Monday **(/Music/Song[@TitleID=13160]/Title/text( ))[1]** down one line to make room for two additional clauses. The syntax essentially does this:

Replace value of *(XPath expression for current item)[1]* with *["new title"]*

```
SELECT MusicDetails.modify('replace value of
 (/Music/Song[@TitleID=13160]/Title/text())[1]     Manic Monday
with "Walk Like an Egyptian"')                      Walk Like an Egyptian
FROM dbo.MusicHistory WHERE MusicTypeID = 3
```

Figure 6.29 We have added code to handle replacing the old value with the new value.

Let's run our code and see whether it works (see Figure 6.30). Recall that earlier we said that the modify( ) method only works with an UPDATE statement. This messaging confirms that we've done something unforeseen by XQuery.

```
SELECT MusicDetails.modify('replace value of
(/Music/Song[@TitleID=13160]/Title/text())[1]
with "Walk Like an Egyptian"')
FROM dbo.MusicHistory WHERE MusicTypeID = 3
```

Messages

```
Msg 8137, Level 16, State 1, Line 2
Incorrect use of the XML data type method 'modify'. A non-mutator method is expected in this context.
```

Figure 6.30 XQuery is prompting us to use an UPDATE statement, instead of a SELECT.

XQuery is reminding us that we must use modify( ) in the SET clause of an UPDATE statement. *The modify( ) method will not work with a SELECT statement.*

We need to add an UPDATE Table statement and change "SELECT MusicDetails.modify" to "SET MusicDetails.modify" (see Figure 6.31). Perfect – our revised code runs, and we see the confirmation (1 row(s) affected).

```
UPDATE dbo.MusicHistory
 SET  MusicDetails.modify ('replace value of
 (/Music/Song[@TitleID=13160]/Title/text())[1]
 with "Walk Like an Egyptian"')
 FROM dbo.MusicHistory WHERE MusicTypeID = 3
```

Messages

```
(1 row(s) affected)
```

Figure 6.31 Our UPDATE statement appears to run and confirm that 1 row was updated.

Now return to our original query (shown in Figure 6.22) and run a SELECT statement to confirm that the title was updated correctly (see Figure 6.32).

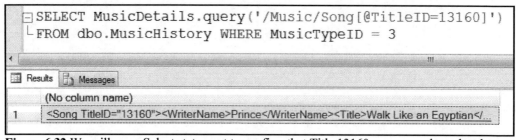

```
SELECT MusicDetails.query('/Music/Song[@TitleID=13160]')
 FROM dbo.MusicHistory WHERE MusicTypeID = 3
```

Results Messages

	(No column name)
1	<Song TitleID="13160"><WriterName>Prince</WriterName><Title>Walk Like an Egyptian</...

Figure 6.32 We will run a Select statement to confirm that Title 13160 was properly updated.

191

```
<Song TitleID="13160">
   <WriterName>Prince</WriterName>
   <Title>Walk Like an Egyptian</Title>◀━
   <Singer OrderID="1">
     <BandName>Bangels</BandName>
   </Singer>
</Song>
```

Figure 6.33 Our Select statement confirms that the Title is now "Walk Like an Egyptian."

Lab 6.1: XML Data Type Methods

Lab Prep: Before you can begin the lab you must run the SQLInteropChapter6.1Setup.sql script. It is recommended that you view the lab video instructions found in Lab6.1_XQueryMethods.wmv, available at *www.Joe2Pros.com*.

Skill Check 1: Prince did not write "Walk Like an Egyptian." Using what you've learned, change the writer name to "Liam Sternberg" for Song 13160.

```
<Song TitleID="13160">
    <WriterName>Liam Sternberg</WriterName>
    <Title>Walk Like an Egyptian</Title>
    <Singer OrderID="1">
       <BandName>Bengals</BandName>
    </Singer>
</Song>
```

Figure 6.34 The result for Skill Check 1.

Skill Check 2: A <BandName> was misspelled. It should be The Bangles, (not Bengals). Make this change to correct the name.

```
<Song TitleID="13160">
    <WriterName>Liam Sternberg</WriterName>
    <Title>Walk Like an Egyptian</Title>
    <Singer OrderID="1">
       <BandName>The Bangles</BandName>
    </Singer>
</Song>
```

Figure 6.35 The result for Skill Check 2.

Skill Check 3: Use the exist( ) method on the Olympics table to see if there is an event named "Boxing 178.5 lbs".

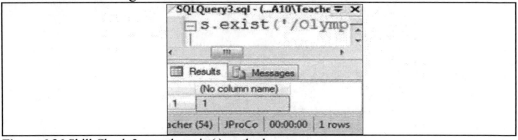

Figure 6.36 Skill Check 3 uses the exist( ) method.

Skill Check 4: Using what you've learned, change the name of TitleID=13159 to add a hyphen to make the song name "Red-Red Wine."

```
<Song TitleID="13159">
   <WriterName>Neil Diamond</WriterName>
   <Title>Red-Red Wine</Title>
   <Singer OrderID="1">
     <BandName>Neil Diamond</BandName>
   </Singer>
   <Singer OrderID="2">
     <BandName>UB40</BandName>
   </Singer>
</Song>
```

Figure 6.37 The result for Skill Check 4.

Skill Check 5: Using what you've learned, change the name of Writer and the first BandName from "Niel Diamond" to "Neil Diamond." Note: you will need to write two update statements.

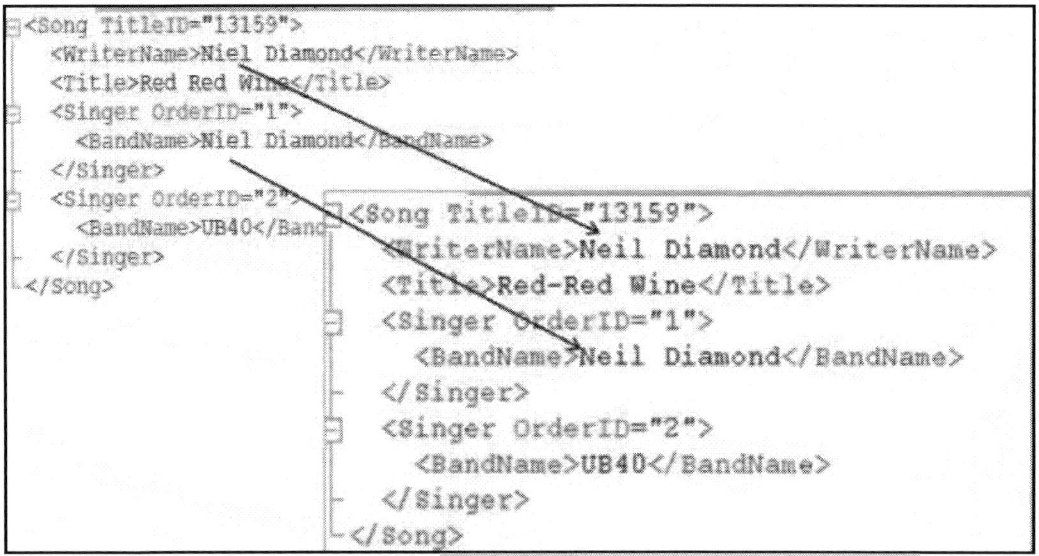

Figure 6.38 The result for Skill Check 5. **[JB TODO** – recapture this image for clarity]

Answer Code: The T-SQL code to this lab can be found in the downloadable files in a file named Lab6.1_XQueryMethods.sql

XML Data Type Methods - Points to Ponder

1. In SQL Server 2005 & 2008, the XML data type provides five methods.
   o query( ) – used to extract XML from an XML data type.
   o value( ) – used to extract a single value from an XML document.
   o exist( ) – used to determine if a specified node exists. Returns 1 if it does, returns 0 if it doesn't exist.
   o modify( ) – updates XML data in an XML data type.
   o nodes( ) – shreds XML data into multiple rows *(this method will be covered in Chapter 7).*

2. The value( ) method requires two parameters, one for the XQuery and the other for the data type you wish to capture.

XPath FLWOR Extensions

Most developers I've encountered whose work includes XML generally consider the FLWOR extensions to be the real power of XQuery. While I tend to agree with them, unfortunately the real power of these extensions is best showcased in larger scale, data-intensive environments, or in data warehousing scenarios requiring frequent iterations and complex queries against massive stores of XML data.

For those planning to work extensively with XML, I highly recommend additional study of the many resources available in this area. As this book's focus is XML's interoperability with SQL Server, you won't become an expert on a topic as vast as FLWOR from this chapter alone. Due to the success and rapid market adoption of Microsoft SQL Server in the Enterprise and BI markets, it is increasingly important for SQL developers and DBAs to be familiar with other programming languages (e.g., C#, .NET CLR, XQuery) which interoperate with SQL Server. The aim of this book is to expose SQL developers, analysts, and DBAs to these other languages they will encounter in their SQL-centric work and to be somewhat of a "survival guide" in this area.

With that said, there is still plenty we can do to understand the mechanics of the XPath FLWOR extensions and observe their application in smaller-scale demonstrations. These keywords are part of the XPath standard, which was formulated by an international consortium (the World Wide Web Consortium or W3C) and not invented by Microsoft. In fact, SQL Server 2005 supported only some of the FLWOR statements. With SQL Server 2008, all of the FLWOR statements are now supported.

Overview

We have seen that it's possible (although rare) for one Olympic event to result in a tie (e.g., two Silver or two Bronze medal winners). However, it's not uncommon for a song to be re-recorded and sung by more than one singer. We have encountered this in our Music dataset (contained in JProCo.dbo.MusicHistory).

One way to find these one-to-many relationship instances is to search for cases where an element, such as <Title>, has two child elements of exactly the same name, such as <Singer> or <Bandname>. A quick glance at the <Music> XML document (see Figure 6.39) shows us two titles with multiple singers (Red Red Wine and Pretty Woman).

Now suppose that our MusicHistory table contains millions of titles. You could search manually for the <Title> or <Song> elements having multiple <Singer> elements, but that would not be a fun or efficient use of time. Instead, it would be preferable to have a robust query run through our giant XML file and give us options to specify our desired criteria.

We know that SQL Server uses criteria with words like WHERE, HAVING, NOT, and IN (among others). XPath also has its own set of words to use. These XPath extensions are the focus of this section.

```xml
<Music>
  <Song TitleID="13159">
    <WriterName>Neil Diamond</WriterName>
    <Title>Red Red Wine</Title>
    <Singer OrderID="1">
      <BandName>Neil Diamond</BandName>
    </Singer>
    <Singer OrderID="2">
      <BandName>UB40</BandName>
    </Singer>
  </Song>
  <Song TitleID="13160">
    <WriterName>Liam Sternberg</WriterName>
    <Title>Walk Like an Egyption</Title>
    <Singer OrderID="1">
      <BandName>Bangles</BandName>
    </Singer>
  </Song>
  <Song TitleID="13161">
    <WriterName>Roy Orbison</WriterName>
    <Title>Pretty Woman</Title>
    <Singer OrderID="1">
      <BandName>Roy Orbison</BandName>
    </Singer>
    <Singer OrderID="2">
      <BandName>Van Halen</BandName>
    </Singer>
  </Song>
</Music>
```

Figure 6.39 The Music dataset contained in JProCo.dbo.MusicHistory table.

First we will explore piece-by-piece how to accomplish the goal of finding all elements at the Song level with two or more Singers below them.

To explore how we might tackle this, let's first look at one of those songs which we know was performed by multiple singers (see Figure 6.40).

```
SELECT MusicDetails.query('/Music/Song[3]')
FROM dbo.MusicHistory WHERE MusicTypeID = 3
```

	Results	Messages
	(No column name)	
1	<Song TitleID="13161"><WriterName>Roy Orbison</WriterName><Title>Pretty Woman</Ti...	

Figure 6.40 We'll begin by looking at the third song, which was performed by multiple singers.

The first singer of "Pretty Woman" was Roy Orbison. The second singer was Van Halen (see Figure 6.41).

```
<Song TitleID="13161">
    <WriterName>Roy Orbison</WriterName>
    <Title>Pretty Woman</Title>
    <Singer OrderID="1">
      <BandName>Roy Orbison</BandName>
    </Singer>
    <Singer OrderID="2">
      <BandName>Van Halen</BandName>
    </Singer>
</Song>
```

Figure 6.41 This song was sung by two singers (Roy Orbison and Van Halen).

XPath Alias

Let's revise our code, beginning by removing the level 3 indicator, because we want to query all the songs (i.e., not just the third one).

Instead we'll use this code syntax (see Figure 6.42). Observe that our code is aliasing the level **/Music/Song** as **$ManyHits**. Therefore returning **$ManyHits** is the same as returning **/Music/Song** (see Figure 6.42).

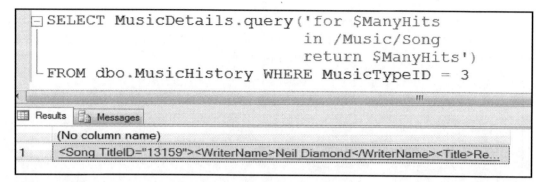

```
SELECT MusicDetails.query('for $ManyHits
                           in /Music/Song
                           return $ManyHits')
FROM dbo.MusicHistory WHERE MusicTypeID = 3
```

Results | Messages

	(No column name)
1	<Song TitleID="13159"><WriterName>Neil Diamond</WriterName><Title>Re...

Figure 6.42 Our code aliases the level /Music/Song as $ManyHits and essentially returns all songs in the catalog.

Our query appears to be returning all songs in the catalog because we haven't yet specified any criteria (see Figure 6.43).

```
<Song TitleID="13159">
   <WriterName>Neil Diamond</WriterName>
   <Title>Red-Red Wine</Title>
   <Singer OrderID="1">
      <BandName>Neil Diamond</BandName>
   </Singer>
   <Singer OrderID="2">
      <BandName>UB40</BandName>
   </Singer>
</Song>
<Song TitleID="13160">
   <WriterName>Liam Sternberg</WriterName>
   <Title>Walk Like an Egyption</Title>
   <Singer OrderID="1">
      <BandName>Bangles</BandName>
   </Singer>
</Song>
<Song TitleID="13161">
   <WriterName>Roy Orbison</WriterName>
   <Title>Pretty Woman</Title>
   <Singer OrderID="1">
      <BandName>Roy Orbison</BandName>
   </Singer>
   <Singer OrderID="2">
      <BandName>Van Halen</BandName>
   </Singer>
</Song>
```

Figure 6.43 Our current code returns all the songs in the catalog.

When we add some filtering criteria, our code will get us closer to the desired result. The criteria we've added here specifies: "Where the count of $ManyHits at the Singer level is greater than 1" (see Figure 6.44).

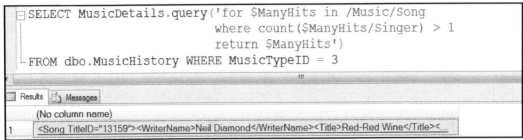

Figure 6.44 Our criteria specifies: "Where the count of $ManyHits at the Singer level is greater than 1".

Figure 6.45 The **/Music/Song** level will look to see how many elements are present.

And our result is precisely what we wanted to see: each song returned has more than one singer (see Figure 6.46).

```
<Song TitleID="13159">
    <WriterName>Neil Diamond</WriterName>
    <Title>Red-Red Wine</Title>
    <Singer OrderID="1">
       <BandName>Neil Diamond</BandName>
    </Singer>
    <Singer OrderID="2">
       <BandName>UB40</BandName>
    </Singer>
</Song>
<Song TitleID="13161">
    <WriterName>Roy Orbison</WriterName>
    <Title>Pretty Woman</Title>
    <Singer OrderID="1">
       <BandName>Roy Orbison</BandName>
    </Singer>
    <Singer OrderID="2">
       <BandName>Van Halen</BandName>
    </Singer>
</Song>
```

Figure 6.46 Each song returned has more than one singer. Notice that The Bangles' song doesn't appear in this XML fragment.

XPath For and Return Extension Words

Notice we used the extension word **for** to establish an alias for a level.

```
QLQuery29.sql...istrator (56))*    SQLQuery28.sql...istrator (54))*    SQLQuery27.sql...istrator (53))*
SELECT MusicDetails.query('for $ManyHits in /Music/Song
    where count($ManyHits/Singer) > 1
    return $ManyHits')
FROM dbo.MusicHistory WHERE MusicTypeID = 3
```

Figure 6.47 The **for** extension helped us to establish an alias for the /Music/Song level.

And we used **return** to show us the results found by our code.

```
SELECT MusicDetails.query('for $ManyHits in /Music/Song
    where count($ManyHits/Singer) > 1
    return $ManyHits')
FROM dbo.MusicHistory WHERE MusicTypeID = 3
```

Figure 6.48 The **return** extension showed us the results found by our code.

XPath Where

The **where** extension in XPath is somewhat similar to our use of the WHERE clause in T-SQL.

We used "where" to find the criteria we needed:

```
SELECT MusicDetails.query('for $ManyHits in /Music/Song
    where count($ManyHits/Singer) > 1
    return $ManyHits')
FROM dbo.MusicHistory WHERE MusicTypeID = 3
```

Figure 6.49 Criteria: *"**where** the count of $ManyHits at the Singer level is greater than 1"*.

We used three of the four XPath statements known by the acronym F-L-W-O-R *(pronounced "flower")*. While you will always see FLWOR in caps, you must use lowercase lettering in order for your code to run.

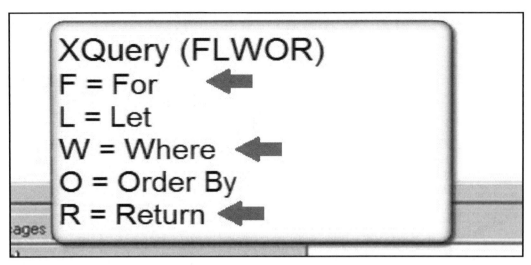

Figure 6.50 Our example utilized three of the four XPath extensions.

Lab 6.2: XPathFLWORExtensions

Lab Prep: Before you can begin the lab you must run the SQLInteropChapter6.2Setup.sql script. It is recommended that you view the lab video instructions found in Lab6.2_FLWOR.wmv, available at *www.Joe2Pros.com.*

Skill Check 1: Using the dbo.Olympics table, find all the events from the Odetails field that have multiple Bronze medal winners. If an event has multiple <Bronze> elements, then show that entire event.

```
<Event ID="002" Name="Boxing 178.5lbs">
   <Gold>Santon Josipovic</Gold>
   <Silver>Kevin Barry</Silver>
   <Bronze>Mustapha Moussa</Bronze>
   <Bronze>Evander Holyfield</Bronze>
</Event>
```

Figure 6.51 The result for Skill Check 1.

Answer Code: The T-SQL code to this lab can be found in the downloadable files in a file named Lab6.2_XPathFlworExtensions.sql

XPath FLWOR Extensions - Points to Ponder

1. The query( ) method uses XPath expression syntax to address specific parts of an XML document. It assists with a SQL-like "FLWOR expression" for performing joins.

2. A FLWOR expression is made of one or more of the five clauses after which it is named: **F**OR, **L**ET, **W**HERE, **O**RDER BY, **R**ETURN.

3. XQuery defines the FLWOR iteration syntax. FLWOR is the acronym based on the following keywords: for, let, where, order by, and return.

4. SQL Server 2005 supported most of the FLWOR iteration syntax while SQL Server 2008 supports all of them.

5. LET was not supported in SQL Server 2005 but is supported in the 2008 version of SQL Server.

Chapter Glossary

FLWOR extension: definition.
exist( ): definition.
modify( ): definition.
query( ): a built-in method of the XML data type; allows you to query for just the needed parts of an XML.
value( ): definition.

Chapter Six - Review Quiz

1.) What is another name for a Method?
- O a. Operator
- O b. Function
- O c. System

2.) Which XML data type method requires more than one parameter?
- O a. query( )
- O b. value( )
- O c. exist( )
- O d. modify( )
- O e. All of them
- O f. Only query( ) and value( )

3.) Which method requires an XPath parameter as the first parameter?
- O a. query( )
- O b. value( )
- O c. exist( )
- O d. modify( )
- O e. All of them
- O f. Only Xquery( ) and Value ( )

4.) Which method returns an XML from the source XML?
- O a. query( )
- O b. value( )
- O c. exist( )
- O d. modify( )
- O e. All of them
- O f. Only query( ) and value( )

5.) Which XML data type method returns a "1" if found and "0" if the specified XPath is not found from the source XML?
- O a. query( )
- O b. value( )
- O c. exist( )
- O d. modify( )
- O e. All of them
- O f. Only query( ) and value( )

6.) Which XML data type method allows you to pick the data type of the value that is returned from the source XML?

O a. query( )
O b. value( )
O c. exist( )
O d. modify( )
O e. All of them
O f. Only query( ) and value( )

7.) Which method will not work with a SQL SELECT statement?

O a. query( )
O b. value( )
O c. exist( )
O d. modify( )
O e. All of them
O f. Only query( ) and value( )

8.) Which of the following is not a FLWOR statement?

O a. For
O b. Let
O c. Where
O d. Or
O e. Return

9.) Which statement will alias the /Olympics/Summer path as $AllSummer?

O a. $AllSummer as /Olympics/Summer
O b. /Olympics/Summer as $AllSummer
O c. for $AllSummer in /Olympics/Summer
O d. for /Olympics/Summer in $AllSummer

Answer Key

1.) b   2.) b   3.) e   4.) a   5.) c   6.) b   7.) d   8.) d   9.) c

Bug Catcher Game

To play the Bug Catcher game run the SQLInteropBugCatcherCh6.pps from the BugCatcher folder of the companion files. You can obtain these files from www.Joes2Pros.com or by ordering the Companion CD.

Chapter 7.   XML Data Binding

An action we frequently perform is joining two or more related tables into a single tabular result set which essentially looks like a new table that contains more fields. SQL Server allows us to perform these logical joins dynamically at query execution time. In Volume 2 (*SQL Queries Joes 2 Pros*) we even saw how a table could be joined to a function to produce a new tabular result set.

The robust capabilities of the XML data type allow us to *bind* (another term for joining) a SQL Server table to an XML document and make a new tabular result set. Similarly, we can bind related SQL Server data and XML data to create an expanded XML datasource.

In this chapter, we will learn how to bind XML to SQL Server data and *vice versa*. We also will see the nodes method, which is the one remaining XML data type method we haven't yet utilized.

READER NOTE: *Please run the script SQLInteropChapter7.0Setup.sql in order to follow along with the examples in the first section of Chapter 7. All scripts mentioned in this chapter may be found at **www.Joes2Pros.com**.*

Binding XML Data to SQL Server Data

A SQL Server table and an XML document may contain many records of related data which you need to combine into one report. Perhaps you need to send this report to a data partner as a new, more elaborate XML stream. Or perhaps you need to store the results as a new table in SQL Server for an ADO (**A**ctiveX **D**ata **O**bject) to render a report.

If your final output for the combined data will come from SQL Server, then you need to bind the XML data to your SQL Server data. This section of the chapter details that process.

CROSS APPLY

If you studied *SQL Queries Joes 2 Pros*, you may remember we used CROSS APPLY so each row in the table could find a value from a function. The data from the table and the function were combined to give you more fields. For example, if you have a table called Customer and a function called fn_GetCustomerOrders( ), you could have a result set showing all Customers and how many orders they have accumulated, even though orders are not contained in the Customer table. By binding the function to the table with a CROSS APPLY, you get an enhanced result set on the corresponding records from both sources.

We will use a similar process with CROSS APPLY in this chapter. In this case we will CROSS APPLY the table to an XQuery statement, which will bind the XML data to our table.

Let's begin by looking at the MusicHistory table. If you successfully ran the first reset script for this chapter (SQLInteropChapter7.0Setup.sql), then you should see all fields of the three records populated, including each record of the XML data type field (MusicDetails) now containing an XML file (see Figure 7.1).

```
SELECT * FROM MusicHistory
```

Results | Messages

	MusicTypeID	MusicTypeName	MusicDetails
1	1	Country	<Music><Song TitleID="11109"><WriterName>The ...
2	2	Soul	<Music><Song TitleID="12151"><WriterName>Bob ...
3	3	Rock	<Music><Song TitleID="13159"><WriterName>Neil ...

Figure 7.1 The current Music catalog contained in the MusicHistory table.

By clicking through the first result hyperlink, we see two country songs below (see Figure 7.2). If we click through all the hyperlinks, we will see the catalog now contains six songs: two Country songs (Titles 11109 and 11110), one Soul song (title 12151), and the three Rock songs we worked with in Chapter 6 (Titles 13159, 13160, 13161).

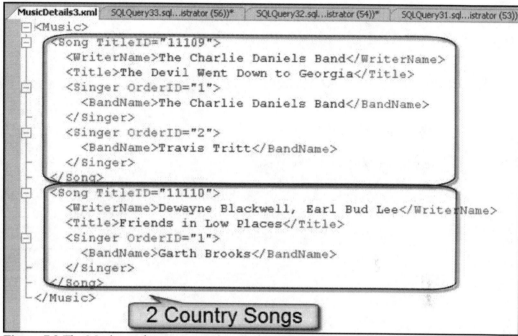

Figure 7.2 The Music catalog now contains six songs, including two Country songs.

Let's look ahead to our goal, which will be to pull out multiple nodes (a.k.a., elements) from the XML data in the MusicDetails field and see those appear alongside the data from the MusicHistory table in a SQL Server query.

MusicTypeID	MusicTypeName	MusicDetails	TitleID	WriterName
1	Country	<Music><Song TitleID="11109"><WriterName>The Charlie...	11109	The Charlie Daniels Band
1	Country	<Music><Song TitleID="11109"><WriterName>The Charlie...	11110	Dewayne Blackwell, Earl Bud Lee
2	Soul	<Music><Song TitleID="12151"><WriterName>Bob West, ...	12151	Bob West, Berry Gordy, Willie Hutch, Hal Davis
3	Rock	<Music><Song TitleID="13159"><WriterName>Neil Diamo...	13159	Neil Diamond
3	Rock	<Music><Song TitleID="13159"><WriterName>Neil Diamo...	13160	Liam Sternberg
3	Rock	<Music><Song TitleID="13159"><WriterName>Neil Diamo...	13161	Roy Orbison

Figure 7.3 Our goal will be to see nodes from the XML data appear as fields in our SQL query.

Let's begin the process of building our query by filtering in just Music Type 3, the Rock music record (see Figure 7.4). This doesn't impact our main query, but it will narrow the dataset we see during most of our demo to the same Rock data we've studied during the last two chapters.

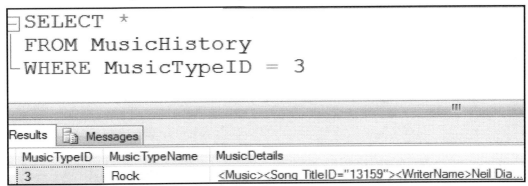

Figure 7.4 Narrow the query to just Music Type 3.

There are three songs contained in the XML document for Music Type 3 (Rock). We know that TitleID is of one of the nodes we want to be able to query as if it were a field in the MusicHistory table (see Figure 7.5).

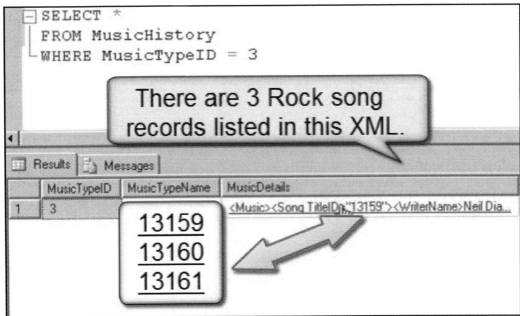

Figure 7.5 There are three Rock songs contained in this XML document, each having a TitleID.

Before we add CROSS APPLY to our code, we need to review the *nodes* and *value* methods of the XML data type.

The nodes( ) Method

As mentioned in an earlier chapter, the *nodes( )* method can be used to shred XML into a tabular result set. The *nodes( )* method accepts an XPath parameter and binds XML data to your table as though it were a join.

Just like binding a table-valued function to a SQL table, there can be be many values contained in one XPath level (e.g., /Music/Song has TitleID and WriterName). CROSS APPLY only lets you choose one name to represent the XML column containing the nodes which will become the applied fields. (In our example, we will call the column **SongTbl(SongDetails)**). SongDetails is the materialized collection of fields which will contain the many values we want.

How can we isolate just the value we want? This is why we must use the value( ) method in combination with the nodes( ) method. Think of the nodes( ) method the way you would think of a rowpattern. It picks the level and gets you rows. From there you get to pick the column. That is where the value( ) method comes in. Think if the value() method the way you think of a colpattern. You specify the column that you want from the row.

The value( ) Method

The value( ) method works with the field returned by the nodes( ) method and pulls out the value you need. If you want many values pulled from the node, use the value( ) method many times in your field Select list (as we will see later in Figures 7.12 and 7.13). Each expression can be aliased and is separated by a comma, as with any field Select list pulling from a regular table.

Combining SQL and XML Fields in Your Tabular Result

Now we are ready to write the rest of the code needed to accomplish our goal of binding the MusicHistory table to our XML data and to be able to query both in a tabular result. Our next step appears in Figure 7.6.

We know CROSS APPLY will bind the XML data in the MusicDetails field to the MusicHistory table. After the FROM clause, we will add CROSS APPLY MusicDetails. We know the *nodes( )* method is needed to shred the XML data in the MusicDetails field.

The nodes( ) method requires an XPath expression as a parameter. The Song level (/Music/Song) contains the TitleID, which is one datapoint we know our result will contain.

The next piece of our code is the alias **SongTbl(SongDetails)** for the fragment shred at the /Music/Song level. We must alias the rowset returned by the nodes( ) method, and the name must be in a *Table(Column)* format. SongTbl(SongDetails) will essentially act as a table whose fields we can combine with the MusicHistory table. Recall that CROSS APPLY only allows us to choose a single name to represent the XML column containing the nodes which will become our applied fields (see Figure 7.6).

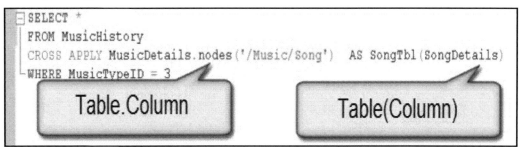

Figure 7.6 Add the CROSS APPLY clause with the nodes( ) method and alias the rowset.

Let's take a moment to review what the new column implies. If we ran the query in the left panel, the result would be the well-formed XML document with the root <Music> and containing the three Rock songs (see Figure 7.7). Earlier we saw that this query produces one record (refer to Figure 7.4).

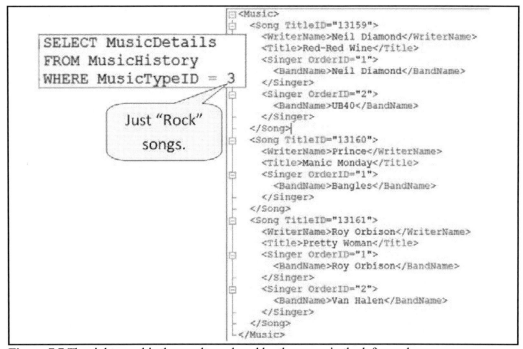

Figure 7.7 The right panel is the result produced by the query in the left panel.

By contrast, notice that when we modify the code and add the query( ) method pulling from the /Music/Song level, a different result is produced. This XQuery statement produces three distinct XML fragments, each representing a song (13159, 13160, and 13161) and each supplying a record to the calling code. Each song record will have the columns TitleID, WriterName, Title, and Singer, since these are the direct children level elements of the /Music/Song level.

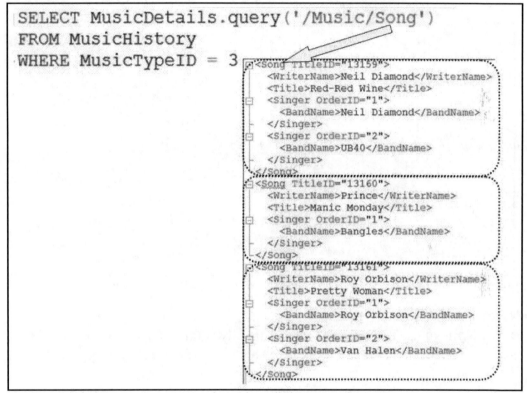

```
SELECT MusicDetails.query('/Music/Song')
FROM MusicHistory
WHERE MusicTypeID = 3
```

```xml
<Song TitleID="13159">
    <WriterName>Neil Diamond</WriterName>
    <Title>Red-Red Wine</Title>
    <Singer OrderID="1">
        <BandName>Neil Diamond</BandName>
    </Singer>
    <Singer OrderID="2">
        <BandName>UB40</BandName>
    </Singer>
</Song>
<Song TitleID="13160">
    <WriterName>Prince</WriterName>
    <Title>Manic Monday</Title>
    <Singer OrderID="1">
        <BandName>Bangles</BandName>
    </Singer>
</Song>
<Song TitleID="13161">
    <WriterName>Roy Orbison</WriterName>
    <Title>Pretty Woman</Title>
    <Singer OrderID="1">
        <BandName>Roy Orbison</BandName>
    </Singer>
    <Singer OrderID="2">
        <BandName>Van Halen</BandName>
    </Singer>
</Song>
```

Figure 7.8 This XQuery statement produces three distinct XML fragments.

Our CROSS APPLY statement works similarly (see Figure 7.9). The XPath parameter (i.e., the /Music/Song level) gets applied to **SongTbl(SongDetails)**, which means that this level supplies three records to **SongTbl(SongDetails)**.

Later we will see that **SongTbl(SongDetails)** is able to pull data from any of the four "fields" (TitleID, WriterName, Title, Singer). (Since only three of these fields contain data, we will focus on those.) only The value( ) method will retrieve one field at a time for our Select list (we will see this in our final steps, Figures 7.11 through 7.13).

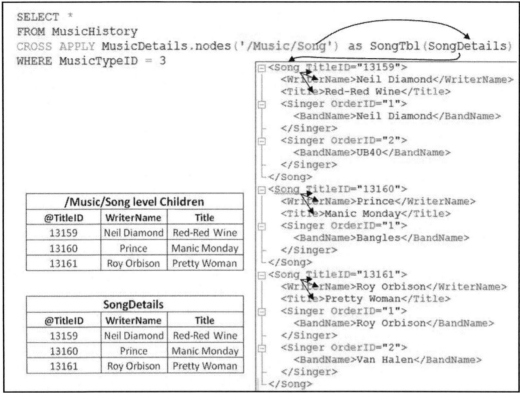

Figure 7.9 This XQuery statement provides 3 Rock records with 4 fields to the CROSS APPLY.

If we attempt to run this code now, we will get an error message that reminds us that we cannot use the nodes( ) method directly (Figure 7.10) – we will need to use the value( ) method to pull out the values we want from the SongDetails column.

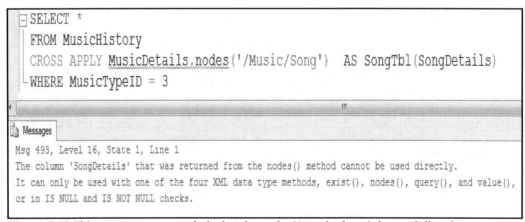

Figure 7.10 This error message reminds that the nodes( ) method can't be used directly.

Next we will use the value( ) method to pull out the TitleID attribute. We will have TitleID returned as an integer data type (see Figure 7.11).

```
SELECT SongDetails.value('@TitleID','int')
FROM MusicHistory
CROSS APPLY MusicDetails.nodes('/Music/Song')  AS SongTbl(SongDetails)
WHERE MusicTypeID = 3
```

	(No column name)
1	13159
2	13160
3	13161

Figure 7.11 Have the value( ) method pull out TitleID and return it as an integer.

We will also pull out the first WriterName as a varchar. Notice that our column header is empty ("No column name"), since it hasn't been aliased (see Figure 7.11). As a best practice, we will alias both fields coming from our XML data, so that we don't have any empty column names (see Figure 7.12).

```
SELECT MusicTypeID, SongDetails.value('@TitleID','int') as TitleID,
SongDetails.value('WriterName[1]','varchar(max)') as WriterName
FROM MusicHistory
CROSS APPLY MusicDetails.nodes('/Music/Song')  AS SongTable(SongDetails)
WHERE MusicTypeID = 3
```

	MusicTypeID	TitleID	WriterName
1	3	13159	Neil Diamond
2	3	13160	Prince
3	3	13161	Roy Orbison

Figure 7.12 Pull out the first WriterName and alias both fields.

Finally, we will add the field Music TypeID from the MusicHistory table. Remove the WHERE clause, so that our result contains data from all three Music Types (Country, Soul, and Rock) (see Figure 7.13).

Our final result achieves our goal. It contains data from the SQL Server table (MusicHistory) and the cross-applied XML data (see Figure 7.13).

```
SELECT MusicTypeID, SongDetails.value('@TitleID','int') as TitleID,
SongDetails.value('WriterName[1]','varchar(max)') as WriterName
FROM MusicHistory
CROSS APPLY MusicDetails.nodes('/Music/Song') AS SongTable(SongDetails)
```

	MusicTypeID	TitleID	WriterName
1	1	11109	The Charlie Daniels Band
2	1	11110	Dewayne Blackwell, Earl Bud Lee
3	2	12151	Bob West, Berry Gordy, Willie Hutch, Hal Davis
4	3	13159	Neil Diamond
5	3	13160	Prince
6	3	13161	Roy Orbison

Figure 7.13 Our final result contains data from the SQL Server table and the XML data contained in each of the MusicDetails records. [JB TODO: replace with clearer figure]

Let's take a closer look at how CROSS APPLY is accomplishing our goal. We know that CROSS APPLY allows us to combine two dissimilar data streams into a single result.

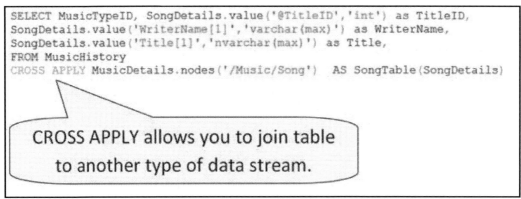

Figure 7.14 CROSS APPLY allows you to join a table to another type of data stream.

In our previous work with the CROSS APPLY operator, we saw it combine a table with a table-valued function and behave similarly to an inner join. In this sample query (from Book 2, *SQL Queries Joes 2 Pros*, p. 275) we see CROSS APPLY matching each CustomerID from the Customer table with each CustomerID in the function dbo.fn_GetCustomerOrders (see Figure 7.15).

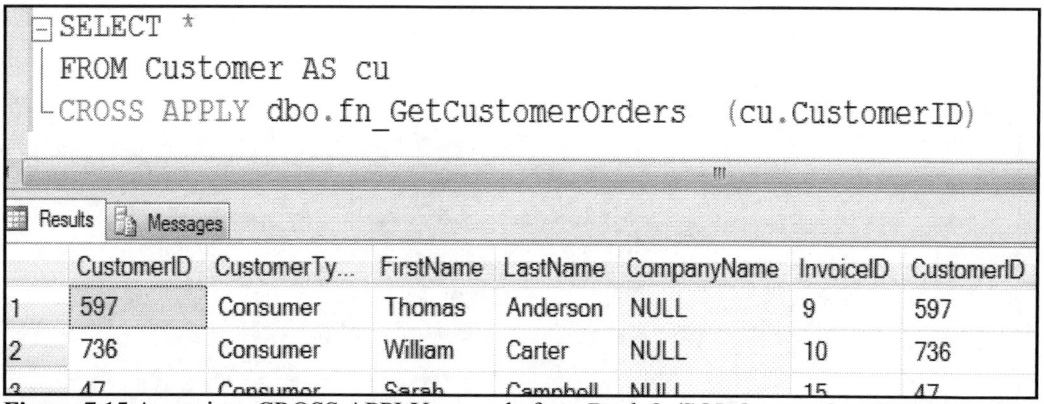

```
SELECT *
FROM Customer AS cu
CROSS APPLY dbo.fn_GetCustomerOrders  (cu.CustomerID)
```

	CustomerID	CustomerTy...	FirstName	LastName	CompanyName	InvoiceID	CustomerID
1	597	Consumer	Thomas	Anderson	NULL	9	597
2	736	Consumer	William	Carter	NULL	10	736
3	47	Consumer	Sarah	Campbell	NULL	15	47

Figure 7.15 A previous CROSS APPLY example from Book 2 *(SQL Queries Joes 2 Pros)*.

You may be wondering how CROSS APPLY is working in our current example, since there is no ON clause or single field serving to correlate our SQL Server table (MusicHistory) with our XML data contained in the MusicDetails field.

Each record in the XML field (MusicDetails) is acting like its own table. The nodes( ) method returns each song as a separate record to the new rowset SongTbl(SongDetails), as we saw earlier in Figure 7.9. It also keeps track of each XML field's original rowset in the parent table (MusicHistory) and knows that the two songs 11109 and 11110 are related to MusicTypeID 1 and MusicTypeName Country (see Figure 7.16).

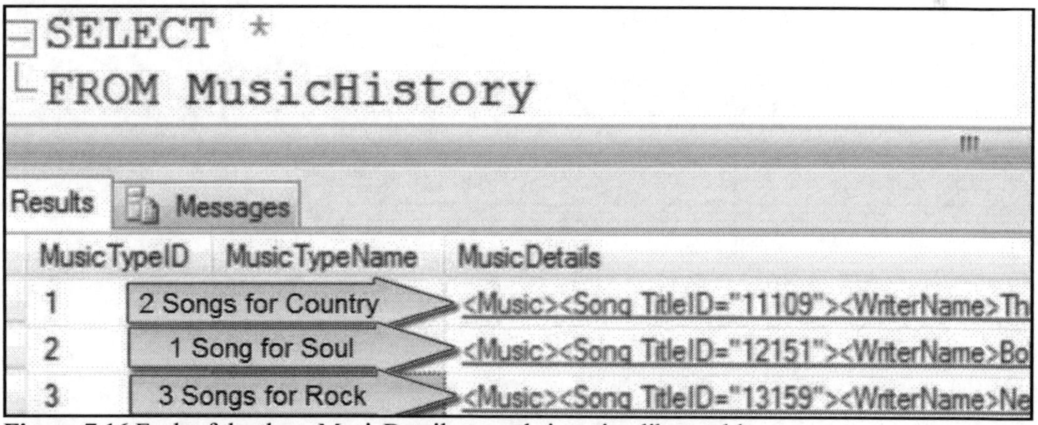

```
SELECT *
FROM MusicHistory
```

MusicTypeID	MusicTypeName	MusicDetails
1	2 Songs for Country	<Music><Song TitleID="11109"><WriterName>Th
2	1 Song for Soul	<Music><Song TitleID="12151"><WriterName>Bo
3	3 Songs for Rock	<Music><Song TitleID="13159"><WriterName>Ne

Figure 7.16 Each of the three MusicDetails records is acting like a table.

In other words, the XML data was turned into a tabular result set (see Figure 7.17).

```
SELECT MusicTypeID, SongDetails.value('@TitleID','int') as TitleID,
SongDetails.value('WriterName[1]','varchar(max)') as WriterName,
SongDetails.value('Title[1]','nvarchar(max)') as Title,
FROM MusicHistory
CROSS APPLY MusicDetails.nodes('/Music/Song') AS SongTable(SongDetails)
```

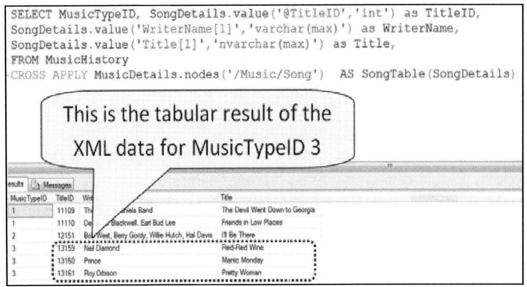

Figure 7.17 The XML data was turned into a tabular result set.

Lab 7.1: Binding XML to SQL

Lab Prep: Before you can begin the lab you must run the SQLInteropChapter7.1Setup.sql script. It is recommended that you view the lab video instructions found in Lab7.1_BindingXMLtoSQL.wmv, available at *www.Joe2Pros.com*.

Skill Check 1: Continue building on your code from the last section and expand it to pull in the Title field. Make sure all fields are aliased as you see below (see Figure 7.18).

	MusicTypeID	TitleID	WriterName	Title
1	1	11109	The Charlie Daniels Band	The Devil Went Down to Georgia
2	1	11110	Dewayne Blackwell, Earl Bud Lee	Friends in Low Places
3	2	12151	Bob West, Berry Gordy, Willie Hutch, Hal Davis	I'll Be There
4	3	13159	Neil Diamond	Red, Red Wine
5	3	13160	Prince	Manic Monday
6	3	13161	Roy Orbison	Pretty Woman

Figure 7.18 Skill Check 1 result.

Answer Code: The T-SQL code to this lab can be found in the downloadable files in a file named Lab7.1_BindingXMLtoSQL.sql

Binding XML to SQL - Points to Ponder

1. SQL Server 2005 & 2008 provide Microsoft specific extensions that enhance XQuery and allow you to reference relational columns or variables.

2. Referencing relational columns in your XML field is known as "binding" the relational column.

Binding SQL to XML

In the last section we stepped through an example of binding XML data to a SQL Server table. In this section, we will do the reverse. Our main focus will be an XML file, and we will bring data from a SQL Server table into our XML file.

Let's look at a new JProCo table which contains XML data, the DeliverySchedule table. Currently it shows two delivery drivers, Sally (Driver 1) and Johnny (Driver 2) (see Figure 7.19).

```
SELECT *
FROM DeliverySchedule
```

	ScheduleID	ScheduleDate	DeliveryRoute	DeliveryDriver	DeliveryList
1	1	2011-02-05 19:57:10.880	3	Silly Sally	<DeliveryList><Delivery SalesOrderID="43659"><Cu...
2	2	2011-02-05 19:57:10.880	7	Big Johnny	<DeliveryList><Delivery SalesOrderID="43661"><Cu...

Figure 7.19 The DeliverySchedule table.

We will narrow our query to show just DeliveryList, which is an XML field containing their delivery routes (see Figure 7.20).

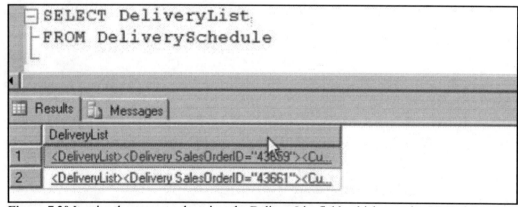

Figure 7.20 Itemize the query to show just the DeliveryList field, which contains XML data.

Click through the result hyperlink and see that Sally's delivery schedule includes the addresses for the two deliveries she will be making (see Figure 7.21).

```
<DeliveryList>
   <Delivery SalesOrderID="43659">
      <CustomerName>Steve Schmidt</CustomerName>
      <Address>6126 North Sixth Street, Rockhampton</Address>
      <PrePaid>Credit</PrePaid>
   </Delivery>
   <Delivery SalesOrderID="43660">
      <CustomerName>Tony Lopez</CustomerName>
      <Address>6445 Cashew Street, Rockhampton</Address>
      <PrePaid>Credit</PrePaid>
   </Delivery>
</DeliveryList>
```

Figure 7.21 Sally's delivery schedule (from result link shown in Figure 7.20).

Johnny's delivery schedule includes the addresses for the three stops he will be making (see Figure 7.22).

```
<DeliveryList>
   <Delivery SalesOrderID="43661">
      <CustomerName>Lenny Lewis</CustomerName>
      <Address>444 North N Street, Rockhampton</Address>
      <PrePaid>Credit</PrePaid>
   </Delivery>
   <Delivery SalesOrderID="43662">
      <CustomerName>Mandy Meyers</CustomerName>
      <Address>555 North M Street, Rockhampton</Address>
      <PrePaid>Credit</PrePaid>
   </Delivery>
   <Delivery SalesOrderID="43663">
      <CustomerName>Nick Nordlund</CustomerName>
      <Address>665 North N street, Rockhampton</Address>
      <PrePaid>COD</PrePaid>
   </Delivery>
</DeliveryList>
```

Figure 7.22 Johnny's delivery schedule (from result link shown in Figure 7.20).

XPath and FLWOR Recap

We will again need to combine our knowledge of XPath with the power of the FLWOR statements from the last chapter. Let's begin with a quick recap.

XPath

Let's use an XQuery statement to pull out of the DeliveryList the data from the Delivery level ('/DeliveryList/Delivery') (see Figure 7.23). Specifying our XPath at this level, we get each Delivery listed for each of our drivers.

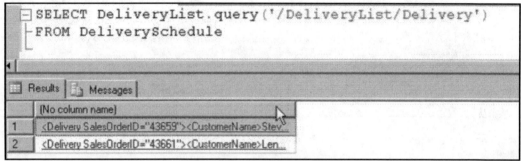

Figure 7.23 This XQuery statement pulls data from the Delivery level.

```
<Delivery SalesOrderID="43659">
   <CustomerName>Steve Schmidt</CustomerName>
   <Address>6126 North Sixth Street, Rockhampton</Address>
   <PrePaid>Credit</PrePaid>
</Delivery>
<Delivery SalesOrderID="43660">
   <CustomerName>Tony Lopez</CustomerName>
   <Address>6445 Cashew Street, Rockhampton</Address>
   <PrePaid>Credit</PrePaid>
</Delivery>
```

Figure 7.24 This XML fragment comes from the first record in Figure 7.23.

FLWOR

In the last chapter, we learned about the XPath extensions known by the FLWOR acronym ("for", "let", "where", "order by", "return").

We will use **for** and **return** statements to alias the Delivery level (/DeliveryList/Delivery). Observe that the query in Figure 7.25 returns the same result as the query in Figure 7.23. (Results shown in Figures 7.26 and 7.24, respectively.)

```
SELECT DeliveryList.query ('for $d
                                in /DeliveryList/Delivery
                                return $d')
FROM DeliverySchedule
```

	(No column name)
1	`<Delivery SalesOrderID="43659"><CustomerName>Steve Schmidt</CustomerName><Addr...`
2	`<Delivery SalesOrderID="43661"><CustomerName>Lenny Lewis</CustomerName><Addre...`

Figure 7.25 This query aliases the Delivery level (/DeliveryList/Delivery) as $d.

```
<Delivery SalesOrderID="43659">
   <CustomerName>Steve Schmidt</CustomerName>
   <Address>6126 North Sixth Street, Rockhampton</Address>
   <PrePaid>Credit</PrePaid>
</Delivery>
<Delivery SalesOrderID="43660">
   <CustomerName>Tony Lopez</CustomerName>
   <Address>6445 Cashew Street, Rockhampton</Address>
   <PrePaid>Credit</PrePaid>
</Delivery>
```

Figure 7.26 Observe that this XML fragment is identical to that in Figure 7.24.

Modify your query to pull from the Address level. The XML for the first driver contains two addresses. The XML for the second driver contains three addresses (Figures 7.27 through 7.29).

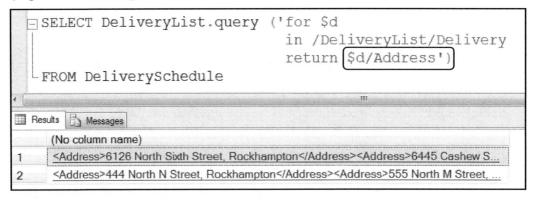

Figure 7.27 Our XQuery statement now pulls from the Address level.

```
<Address>6126 North Sixth Street, Rockhampton</Address>
<Address>6445 Cashew Street, Rockhampton</Address>
```

Figure 7.28 The XML fragment containing the two addresses on Sally's delivery route.

```
<Address>444 North N Street, Rockhampton</Address>
<Address>555 North M Street, Rockhampton</Address>
<Address>665 North N street, Rockhampton</Address>
```

Figure 7.29 The XML fragment containing the three addresses on Johnny's delivery route.

At this deep a level, we no longer have well-formed XML. Most of the examples we've seen in this section have been fragments with a number of nodes sitting side by side and no root. In the next topic discussion, we will see that we can impose our own level in order to make this well-formed XML.

Adding XML Tags

You can use any or all of the XML tags from your XML data. What if you wanted to add a new tag of your own that does not exist in your table or XML data? You can add your own custom tags as part of your XPath statement.

Use {} {for $d in /DeliveryList/Delivery return $d/Address}

The query('**<DeliveryRoute>**
{for $d in /DeliveryList/Delivery return $d/Address}
</DeliveryRoute>')

Change the parentheses enclosing your current XQuery statement to curly braces. Instead of ( ), these will become { }.

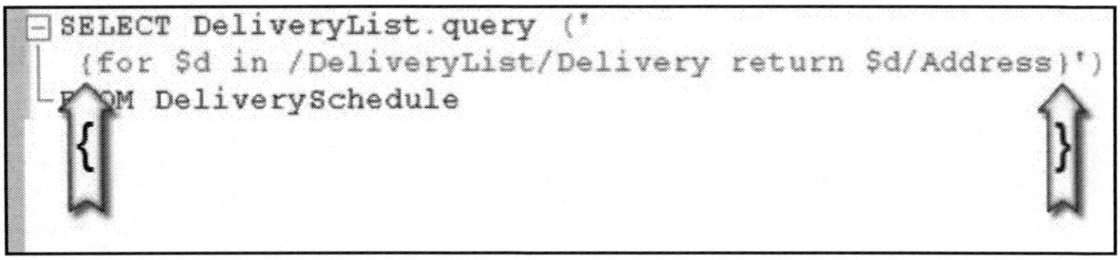

```
SELECT DeliveryList.query ('
   {for $d in /DeliveryList/Delivery return $d/Address}')
FROM DeliverySchedule
   {                                                    }
```

Figure 7.30 Change the parentheses ( ) to curly braces { }.

Within the single quotes, add a beginning tag <DeliveryRoute> and an ending tag </DeliveryRoute> before and after our existing XQuery statement (i.e., which we enclosed in curly braces { }).

Run this code and notice that we have added our own <DeliveryRoute> level (see Figures 7.31 and 7.32).

```
SELECT DeliveryList.query ('<DeliveryRoute>
                           {for $d
                           in /DeliveryList/Delivery
                           return $d/Address}
                           </DeliveryRoute>')
FROM DeliverySchedule
```

	(No column name)
1	<DeliveryRoute><Address>6126 North Sixth Street, Rockhampton</Address><Address>...
2	<DeliveryRoute><Address>444 North N Street, Rockhampton</Address><Address>555 ...

Figure 7.31 This code imposes our own level <DeliveryRoute>.

We have added a the root tag <DeliveryRoute>, which wasn't contained in the original XML document.

```
<DeliveryRoute>
   <Address>6126 North Sixth Street, Rockhampton</Address>
   <Address>6445 Cashew Street, Rockhampton</Address>
</DeliveryRoute>
```

Figure 7.32 We have added a root tag that wasn't contained in the original XML file.

Add a top level tag indicating which driver is responsible. First use a placeholder "Me" in place of the driver's name.

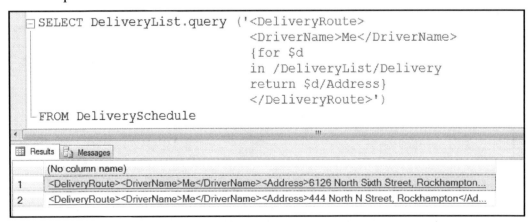

```
SELECT DeliveryList.query ('<DeliveryRoute>
                           <DriverName>Me</DriverName>
                           {for $d
                           in /DeliveryList/Delivery
                           return $d/Address}
                           </DeliveryRoute>')
FROM DeliverySchedule
```

	(No column name)
1	<DeliveryRoute><DriverName>Me</DriverName><Address>6126 North Sixth Street, Rockhampton...
2	<DeliveryRoute><DriverName>Me</DriverName><Address>444 North N Street, Rockhampton</Ad...

Figure 7.33 Add a top level tag <DriverName> with the element tag "Me" as a placeholder.

226

Despite the placeholder "Me" temporarily serving as the element tag for <DriverName>, we know this is actually Sally's and Johnny's route data (Figures 7.34 and 7.35, respectively). [JB TODO

```
<DeliveryRoute>
   <DriverName>Me</DriverName>
   <Address>6126 North Sixth Street, Rockhampton</Address>
   <Address>6445 Cashew Street, Rockhampton</Address>
</DeliveryRoute>
```

Figure 7.34 This is Sally's delivery route data. Our next step will be to add her name dynamically.

```
<DeliveryRoute>
   <DriverName>Me</DriverName>
   <Address>444 North N Street, Rockhampton</Address>
   <Address>555 North M Street, Rockhampton</Address>
   <Address>665 North N street, Rockhampton</Address>
</DeliveryRoute>
```

Figure 7.35 This is Johnny's delivery route data. Our next step will be to add his name.

The sql:column( ) Function

This is one of XQuery's SQL Server extension functions. To get values from a column in a SQL Server table, you use the **sql:column** function.

In our current query (last shown in Figure 7.33), replace the word "Me" with the following expression:

> {sql:column("DeliveryDriver")}

```
liveryList.query ('<DeliveryRoute>
me>{sql:column("DeliveryDriver")}</Dri
in /DeliveryList/Delivery return $d/Ad
yRoute>')
```

Figure 7.36 Replace the "Me" placeholder with a sql:column statement enclosed in curly braces.

Our XQuery statement will dynamically pull the driver name from the DeliveryDriver field of the DeliverySchedule table. In this way, we are *binding* the SQL Server table to the XML data (see Figure 7.37).

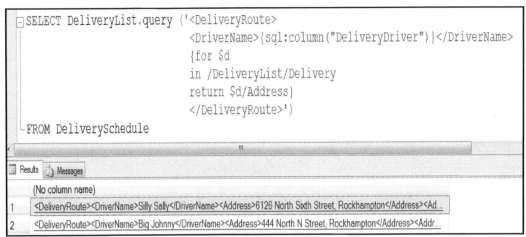

```
SELECT DeliveryList.query ('<DeliveryRoute>
                            <DriverName>{sql:column("DeliveryDriver")}</DriverName>
                            {for $d
                            in /DeliveryList/Delivery
                            return $d/Address}
                            </DeliveryRoute>')
FROM DeliverySchedule
```

	(No column name)
1	<DeliveryRoute><DriverName>Silly Sally</DriverName><Address>6126 North Sixth Street, Rockhampton</Address><Ad...
2	<DeliveryRoute><DriverName>Big Johnny</DriverName><Address>444 North N Street, Rockhampton</Address><Addr...

Figure 7.37 Our XQuery statement now contains the **sql:column** function.

Our XML result stream contains data from the XML document and from the SQL Server table (JProCo.dbo.DeliverySchedule). The DriverName values from the DeliverySchedule table became the text value of the DriverName element.

```
<DeliveryRoute>
   <DriverName>Silly Sally</DriverName>
   <Address>6126 North Sixth Street, Rockhampton</Address>
   <Address>6445 Cashew Street, Rockhampton</Address>
</DeliveryRoute>
```

Figure 7.38 Our final XML result stream contains data from the XML document and from the SQL Server table, DeliverySchedule.

Lab 7.2: Binding SQL to XML

Lab Prep: Before you can begin the lab you must run the SQLInteropChapter7.2Setup.sql script. It is recommended that you view the lab video instructions found in Lab7.2_BindingSQLtoXML.wmv, available at *www.Joe2Pros.com.*

Skill Check 1: Add the DeliveryRoute field from the DeliverySchedule table as the first top element named <RouteNo>. When you click on the first record, your XML should resemble the figure you see here.

```
<DeliveryRoute>
  <RouteNo>3</RouteNo>
  <DriverName>Silly Sally</DriverName>
  <Address>6126 North Sixth Street, Rockhampton</Address>
  <Address>6445 Cashew Street, Rockhampton</Address>
</DeliveryRoute>
```

Figure 7.39 Skill Check 1 result.

Skill Check 2: Query the MusicHistory table at the /Music/Song/Title path and add the<genre> root tag with a Name attribute. Populate the attribute with the sql:column value from the MusicTypeName field.

```
<genre Name="Rock">
  <Title>Red, Red Wine</Title>
  <Title>Manic Monday</Title>
  <Title>Pretty Woman</Title>
</genre>
```

Figure 7.40 Skill Check 2 result.

Answer Code: The T-SQL code to this lab can be found in the downloadable files in a file named Lab7.2_BindingSQLtoXML.sql

Binding SQL to XML - Points to Ponder

1. The steps for joining three (or more) tables are the same as joining two tables. First – join all tables and confirm they are working properly using a "SELECT *" statement. Narrow down the SELECT list to include the specific fields you need only after all tables have been joined.

2. While table aliasing saves keystrokes on two-table joins, it greatly helps readability when joining three or more tables.

Chapter Glossary

Binding SQL to XML: referencing relational columns in your XML field is known as "binding" the relational column.
Binding XML to SQL: definition.
CROSS APPLY: definition.
nodes( ): definition.
value( ): definition.

Chapter Seven - Review Quiz

1.) You want to combine the results of a SQL Server table and XML into a single tabular result. What technique will allow you to bind these two sources of data?

O a. Cross Apply
O b. Inner Apply
O c. Inner Join
O d. Cross Join

2.) You are writing a query which returns data from a table in SQL Server. Some of the data is stored as relational data and some is stored in XML data type columns. Your query needs to return a relational result set that contains data from relational fields and attribute values from XML data type columns. Which **two methods** must you use to return all of them in a result set?

□ a. The value( ) method

□ b. The exist( ) method

□ c. The query( ) method

□ d. The nodes( ) method

3.) You can bind table data with XML data but can only display fields from one or the other in your field Select list.

O a. True
O b. False

4.) You have the following code.

```
SELECT SongDetails.value('@TitleID','int')
FROM MusicHistory
CROSS APPLY MusicDetails.nodes('/Music/Song')  AS _____
WHERE MusicTypeID = 3
```
Complete the code after the AS to produce a result set.

O a. AS SongTbl(SongInfo)
O b. AS SongInfo (SongTbl)
O c. AS SongTbl(SongInfo).value( )
O d. AS SongInfo (SongTbl).value( )

5.) Look at this XQuery statement below:

query('**<DeliveryRoute>**for $d in /DeliveryList/Delivery return $d/Address **</DeliveryRoute>**')

What is wrong with this code?

   O a. The root tag is missing
   O b. Slashes are facing the wrong way
   O c. Need curly braces before and after the <DeliveryRoute> element
   O d. Need curly braces inside the custom tags and around the XPath statements

6.) Look at this XQuery statement below:

('<root>**<DriverScore>**{ }**</DriverScore>**
{for $d in /root/Driver return $d/Total}</root>')
You want the DriveScore tag element value to pull from the Rating field of the dbo.CompanyDriver table. What code should you put in the curly braces between the DriverScore element tags?

   O a. sql:column("DeliveryDriver")
   O b. column:sql("DeliveryDriver")
   O c. sql:column("dbo.CompanyDriver")
   O d. column:sql("dbo.CompanyDriver")
   O e. sql:column("Rating")
   O f. column:sql("Rating")

Answer Key

1.) a   2.) a, d   3.) b   4.) a   5.) d   6.) e

Bug Catcher Game

To play the Bug Catcher game run the SQLInteropBugCatcherCh7.pps from the BugCatcher folder of the companion files. You can obtain these files from www.Joes2Pros.com or by ordering the Companion CD.

Chapter 8.   Creating .NET Applications

Anyone reading this book probably knows applications and programs are contructed using programming languages. The storyline of the film *The Matrix* relies heavily on this point – in the computing world every program, object, and cool app is comprised of thousands (sometimes millions) of lines of code. Even the "tools" we use to write code are all ultimately based on a seemingly infinite combination of 0's and 1's.

People often ask why we need to learn about .NET or C#, when our main goal is to become SQL Server experts and database developers. In short, the possibilities brought about by the .NET framework and SQL Server's groundbreaking changes introduced in the 2005 version are mammoth – we can't truly become *bona fide* SQL professionals without knowing something about their interaction.

Prior to 2005, using SQL Server in combination with other programming languages was daunting and tackled only by expert SQL Server developers, if at all. Thus, from a SQL Server perspective, we need to understand these new capabilities. As well, Microsoft's .NET innovation has been a quantum leap forward for the application development and programming world. The CLR (common language runtime) is core to the .NET initiative. Over the next three chapters, we will see the power of the CLR in action. This chapter will introduce us to managed code and familiarize us with the C# programming language. Subsequent chapters will expose us to SQL CLR and PowerShell.

We are familiar with writing scalar functions in T-SQL code which returns a single value. Most SQL Server functions will return their values from data in a table (e.g., sales totals) or from a simple calculation (like getting currency conversion amounts). But what if your scalar value needed to be the current stock price for the ticker symbol you pass in? How would you write T-SQL code to get values from the internet through a web service? This would be extremely difficult, if not impossible. However, this task could be easily accomplished by writing a small program in C#. This program could literally be comprised of just a few lines of code thanks to the web services classes which are built into .NET.

Small, easy-to-write C# applications can be imported and run in SQL Server as a function or stored procedure. This way SQL programming objects can now leverage the power of .NET without needing to add dozens of new keywords to T-SQL. C# code is needed to create an app, but SQL Server can work with that app using the T-SQL keywords you have already learned.

READER NOTE: *Please run the script SQLInteropChapter8.0Setup.sql in order to follow along with the examples in the first section of Chapter 8. All scripts mentioned in this chapter may be found at **www.Joes2Pros.com**.*

Introduction to C#

There are many programming languages like Java, C++ (pronounced "See Plus Plus"), and also assembly languages. In this chapter we will focus on the creation of .NET applications by writing .NET code. The .NET Applications we will create in this chapter will all use the C# ("See Sharp") language.

Begin by navigating to your Joes2Pros folders and confirm you find the C#Stuff folder and its contents (Figures 8.1 and 8.2).

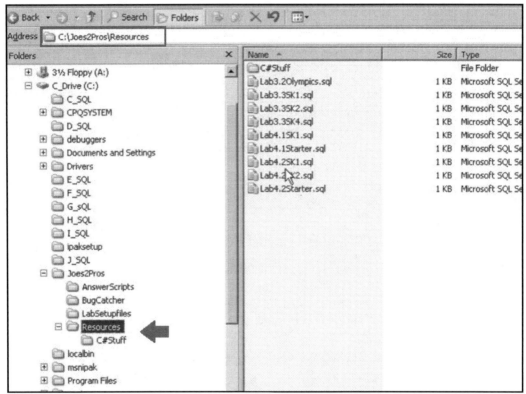

Figure 8.1 If you do not have this Resources folder, you can copy it from *Joes2Pros.com*.

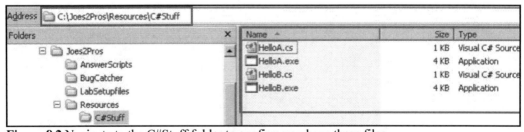

Figure 8.2 Navigate to the C#Stuff folder to confirm you have these files.

(Note: if you are unable to see the file extensions (.exe) and/or the filepath, you can use Tools > Folder Options > View in order to review your settings. Check the option "Display the full path in the title bar." Un-check the "Hide extension for known file types" option.)

Applications

Applications consist of many instructions that run on your computer. The application sends commands to the operating environmment. The code that goes into the creation of an application is known as **source code**.

Source Code

You can think of source code as the instructions that built the application, much like a blueprint creates a downtown skyscraper. The building's blueprint was executed via a construction process to create the actual building. The blueprint is not inside the building but was necessary to build the skyscraper. The source code is not inside of the application either, but it was used to help constuct (or compile) it into an application or **assembly**.

Observe that the two executable program files, HelloA.exe and HelloB.exe, are each 4 KB in size (see Figure 8.2). Double click on HelloA.exe to see the "Hello World" greeting (see Figure 8.3). Hit the Enter key in order to close or terminate this program. Repeat the process for the HelloB.exe program (see Figure 8.4).

Figure 8.3 Double-click to launch the HelloA.exe file.

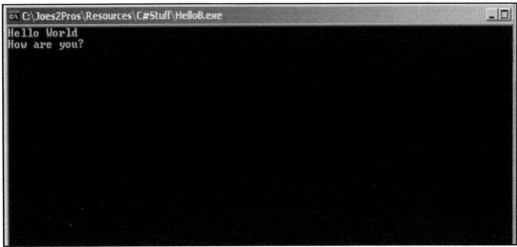

Figure 8.4 Repeat the process for HelloB.exe and hit Enter to close the window.

The instructions – or source code – of the HelloA and HelloB programs must be different, since they display different results. To view the source code for each program, you must view the code using an editor program. The most popular editor for C# code is Visual Studio, which we will use later in this chapter. Initially, we will use the simplest text editor (Notepad) to look at our source code. Simply right-click to open the HelloA.cs and HelloB.cs files with Notepad (see Figure 8.5).

Name	Size	Type
HelloA.cs	1 KB	Visual C# Source file
HelloA	4 KB	Application
H	1 KB	Visual C# Source file
H	4 KB	Application

cs is the C-Sharp code
(Source Code)

Figure 8.5 The files with the extension ".cs" contain the C# ("C Sharp") code.

The code inside the **static void Main( )** brackets (a.k.a., curly braces) is the source code which creates the HelloA program (see Figure 8.6). The WriteLine statement "Hello World" is the greeting we saw printed by the program (shown earlier in Figure 8.3), and the ReadLine statement is what caused the program to wait for us to hit Enter to close the program.

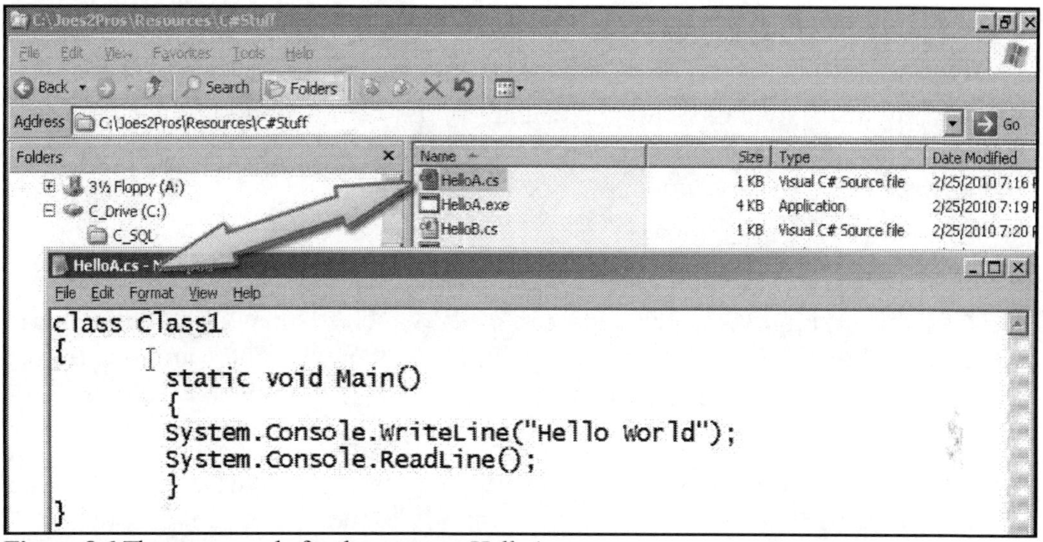

Figure 8.6 The source code for the program HelloA.exe.

The source code for the HelloB program is similar, but note that it includes an additional WriteLine statement which displays "How are you?"(see Figure 8.7).

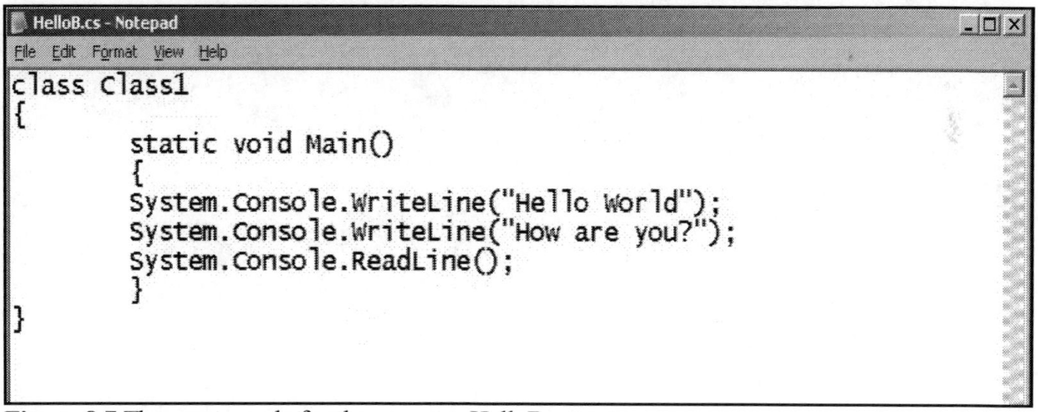

Figure 8.7 The source code for the program HelloB.exe.

Assemblies

An assembly is a deployable unit of .NET code. Sometimes an assembly is the application and sometimes it is a supporting part of the application. Think of your spell-checker in Microsoft Word. That is an assembly that does not run on its own but instead supports an application. If a new, improved spell-checker version is released, you can use it without having to change your Word application. All applications consist of one more more assemblies.

Writing C# Code

C# is really just a style of writing executable commands. It has a few of its own rules, such as, all statements must end with a semi-colon. That makes it easy to identify the end of a C# statement.

Creating Classes

All C# programming takes place inside a class (which is short for classification). Classes are like objects that hold all of your C# statements. The beginning of the class is marked by the class keyword and name and an { (an open curly brace). The end of the class is marked by a corresponding } (ending curly brace).

Let's open a new Notepad window where we will write the source code for a new HelloC program. This program will run similarly to the HelloA and HelloB programs (display a greeting message and then await for the user to hit Enter before closing).

We will keep our code simple by calling our class "Class1" and begin with an empty set of braces (see Figure 8.8).

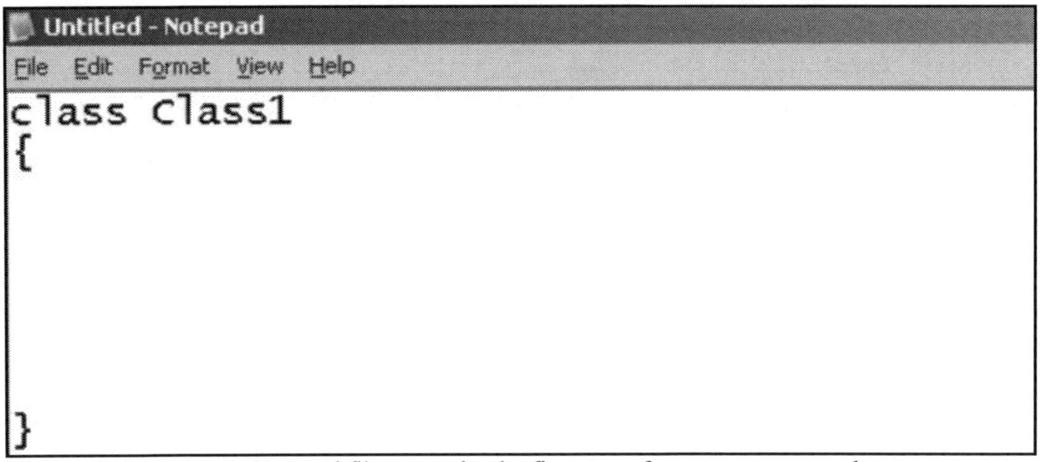

Figure 8.8 In an empty Notepad file, we write the first step of our new source code.

Creating Methods

Think of a method as an action like talking, running, or eating. Methods are the verbs of the programming world. You can easily spot methods, which include a set of parentheses ( ) at the end of the method name. If you are creating a method, you will define it by putting code inside a set of curly braces {} which appear after the parentheses.

You can name your method just about anything you want. If you name it Main (with a capital M), then that makes it the first method that will be executed when the application starts.

C# applications always start with the method name Main( ). Note that "static void Main" is C# speak for "Start here." Just like XQuery, everything in C# is case-sensitive.

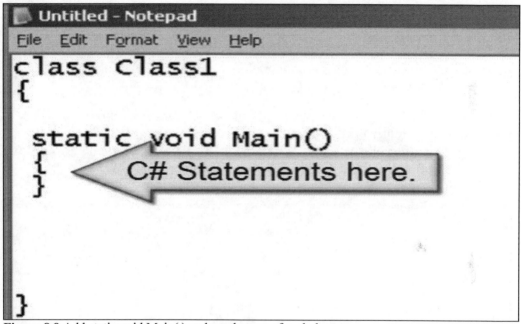

Figure 8.9 Add static void Main( ) and another set of curly braces.

Calling on Methods

Calling on methods looks a lot like creating methods, except you don't need to define what the method does – that was done previously and you are simply using the method. Because you don't need to define it, you also won't use curly braces when calling a method. Just put a semi-colon after the parentheses.

Pseudo code for creating a method:

MyMethod ( ) {statements defining the method appear inside the curly braces}

Pseudo code for calling a method:

MyMethod( );

One very important thing to note about methods is they perform an action on or for something. For example, if you had a method named Blink( ) you need to specify what should blink. If you want your clock to blink, you might write

Clock.Blink( ); as your statement. If you wanted the second hand of your clock to blink, you might say Clock.SecondHand.Blink( ); for that statement. Expect one or more objects (like clock or second hand) separated by dots, until you get to the object which should perform the actual action.

In programming languages (including .NET and C#), a common pattern is to name items or instructions beginning with general terms and getting progressively more specific until you get to the action. For example, if I told you to go on vacation in Tampa, the C# version of this instruction might look like this:

USA.Florida.Tampa.GoOnVacation( );

Now let's write our statements (shown below in Figure 8.10). Note that every statement in C# must end with a semi-colon.

Without the fourth line to pause the program and wait for the user to catch up, the program would rapidly open the Command Prompt window, flash the first three statements, and then close. The Console is the black box (Command Prompt) we saw earlier (in Figures 8.3 and 8.4). The ReadLine( ) command causes the program to standby and remain open until the user hits Enter.

```
class Class1
{
    static void Main()
    {
        System.Console.WriteLine("Hello World");
        System.Console.WriteLine("How are You?");
        System.Console.WriteLine("I am fine!");
        System.Console.ReadLine();
    }
}
```

These first three statements will write to your console window.

This fourth statement will wait until you hit "Enter".

Figure 8.10 The four commands contained in our HelloC program.

Our code is complete. Save the file as HelloA.cs in the C#Stuff folder.

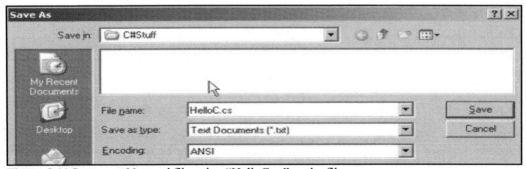

Figure 8.11 Save your Notepad file using "HelloC.cs" as the filename.

Compilers

Compilers are computer programs which turn source code into assemblies. An application is made up of one or more assemblies. In this lab, we will have a single-assembly application to keep things simple.

Just as a constuction team in Germany would probably have blueprints written in German, a compiler is language-specific. For example, to turn C# code into a C# assembly, you need a C# compiler.

Compiling C# Code

When you create your code, it's really just a text blueprint for an application. To turn your code into an application you must compile it. To turn C# code into a .NET application, you use the C# Compiler (CSC).

Mouseover the other .cs files in your C#Stuff folder and notice they are labeled "Visual C# Source file" (Figure 8.12). However your brand new HelloC.cs file isn't yet recognized by the system as a Visual C# Source file. At this point it is just a set of instructions. It won't become an executable file until you compile it.

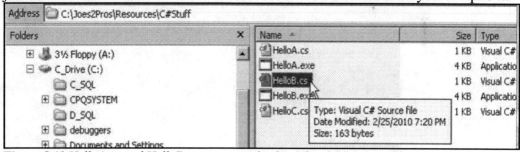

Figure 8.12 HelloA.cs and HelloB.cs are recognized as Visual C# Source files.

HelloA.cs and HelloB.cs are recognized as Visual C# Source files.

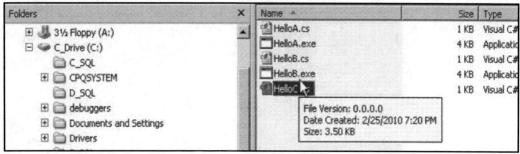

Figure 8.13 The HelloC.cs file won't be recognized as a Visual C# Source file until we compile it.

Our next goal will be to compile the HelloC.cs file and thereby create a HelloC.exe file.

Open a Command Prompt window. (In general, the steps are Start > Run > CMD > Enter. Your steps may vary slightly depending on the OS you are running.)

Follow the steps you see here to change the directory (cd\) to the Joes2Pros folder and point the Command Prompt to the C#Stuff folder (see Figure 8.14).

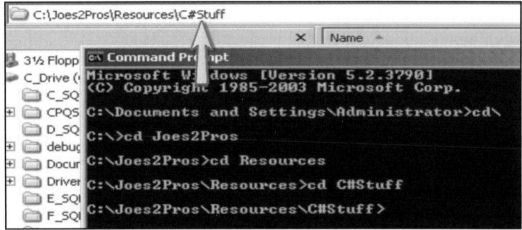

Figure 8.14 Follow these steps to point the Command Prompt to the C#Stuff folder.

```
c:\ Command Prompt

C:\Joes2Pros\Resources>cd C#Stuff

C:\Joes2Pros\Resources\C#Stuff>dir
 Volume in drive C is C_Drive
 Volume Serial Number is 8C5F-48AA

 Directory of C:\Joes2Pros\Resources\C#Stuff

02/25/2010  09:58 PM    <DIR>          .
02/25/2010  09:58 PM    <DIR>          ..
02/25/2010  07:16 PM               119 HelloA.cs
02/25/2010  07:19 PM             3,584 HelloA.exe
02/25/2010  07:20 PM               163 HelloB.cs
02/25/2010  07:20 PM             3,584 HelloB.exe
02/25/2010  09:58 PM               215 HelloC.cs
               5 File(s)          7,665 bytes
               2 Dir(s)     550,703,104 bytes free

C:\Joes2Pros\Resources\C#Stuff>csc HelloC.cs
Microsoft (R) Visual C# 2008 Compiler version 3.5.30729.1
for Microsoft (R) .NET Framework version 3.5
Copyright (C) Microsoft Corporation. All rights reserved.
```

Figure 8.15 Type this command (csc HelloC.cs) and hit Enter to compile the HelloC program.

Please note that if your C# Compiler (CSC) isn't set up correctly, then you will not get the expected result (shown in Figure 8.15). In order to compile items in the C#Stuff folder, your CSC must be set up to be globally accessible. If you get the error message *"error CS2001: Source file 'HelloC.cs' could not be found. Fatal error CS2008: No inputs specified."* or *"'CSC' is not recognized as an internal or external command, operable program or batch file."*, then please follow the steps in the Lab8CSC_Setup.wmv video to set up your compiler before proceeding. (That process is also detailed here in Figures 8.16 through 8.22.)

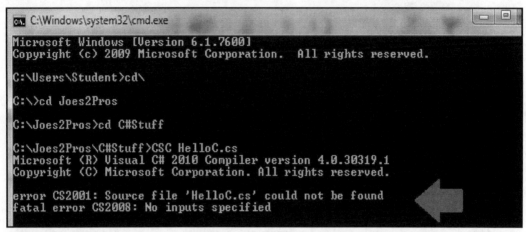

Figure 8.16 If your CSC isn't set up correctly, you may receive this error message.

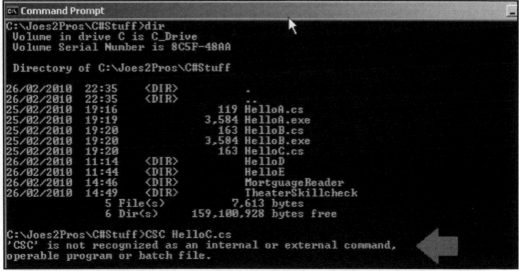

Figure 8.17 Another possible error message you will see, if your CSC isn't set up correctly.

From your Start menu, Search for "csc.exe"

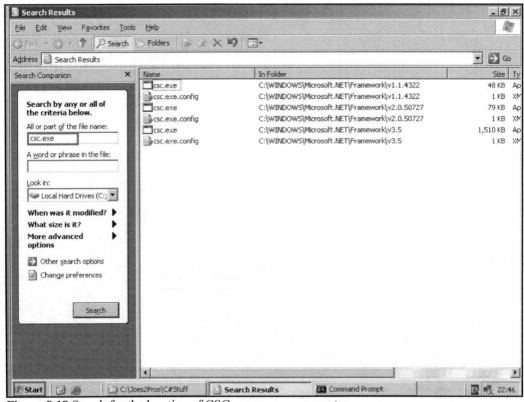

Figure 8.18 Search for the location of CSC.exe on your computer.

Your search may locate multiple C# compilers, as shown in Figure 8.18. If this is the case, simply choose the newest version. Right-click to view its properties.

Highlight and copy the path of the newest CSC.exe file.

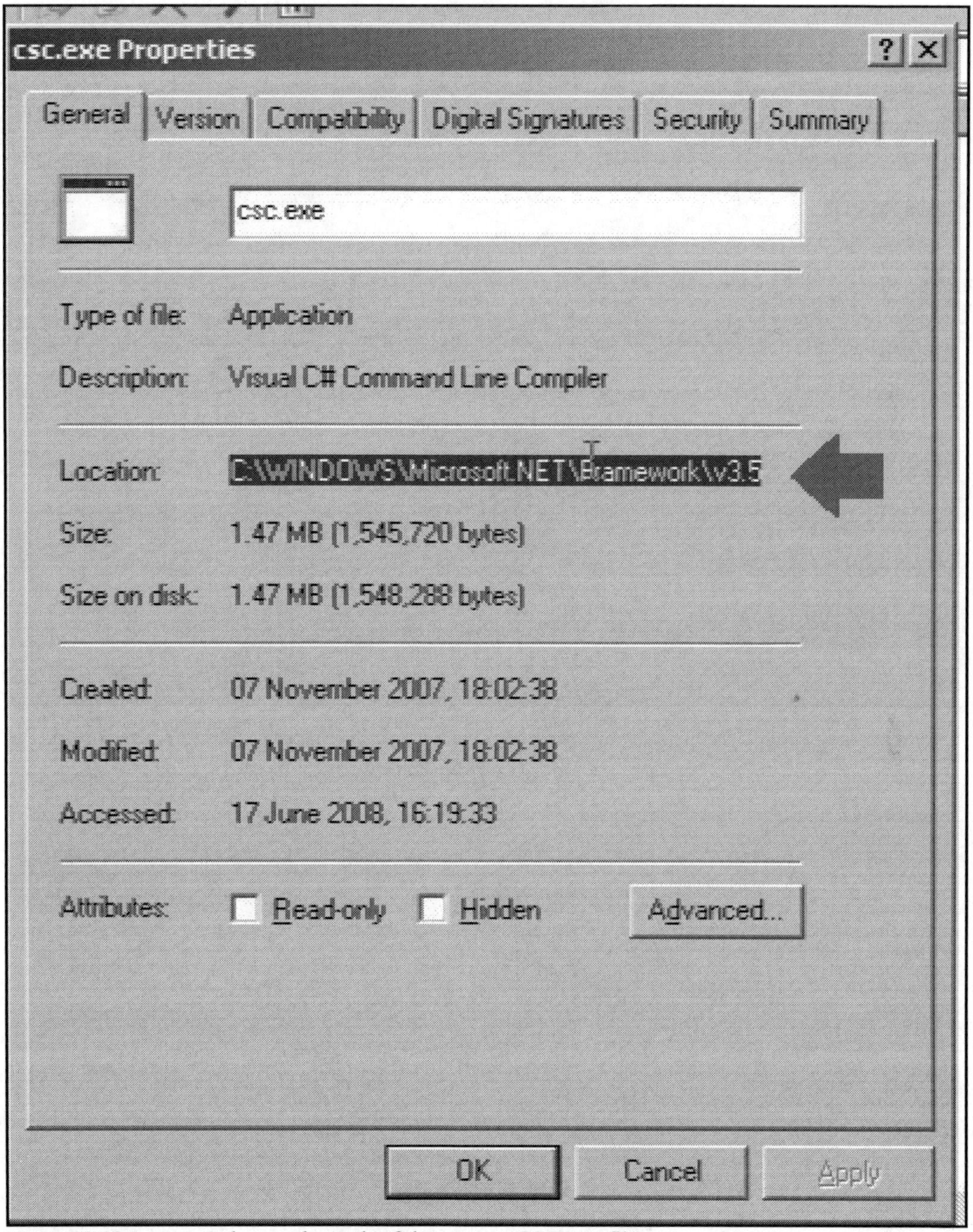

Figure 8.19 Locate and copy the path of the newest CSC.exe file.

Right-click "My Computer" > Properties > Advanced > Environment Variables.

In System Variables, click "New" (System Variables).

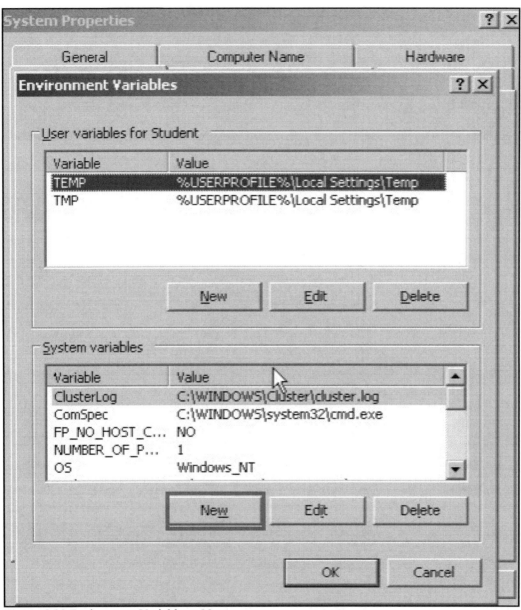

Figure 8.20 Environment Variables > New.

In the New System Variable dialog, type "Path" (for Variable name) and paste in the path of your CSC.exe file (for Variable value), then click OK. And click OK once more to close the Environment Variables dialog.

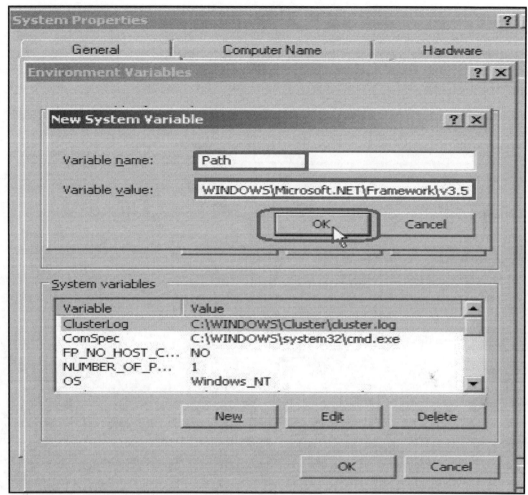

Figure 8.21 Variable name: "Path", Variable value: paste in the path of your CSC.exe file.

Close your original Command Prompt window, and open a new Command Prompt. Repeat the step to compile (originally shown in Figure 8.15).

Figure 8.22 Type this command (csc HelloC.cs) and hit Enter to compile the HelloC program.

247

Notice that we now see the compiled HelloC.exe file (see Figure 8.23).

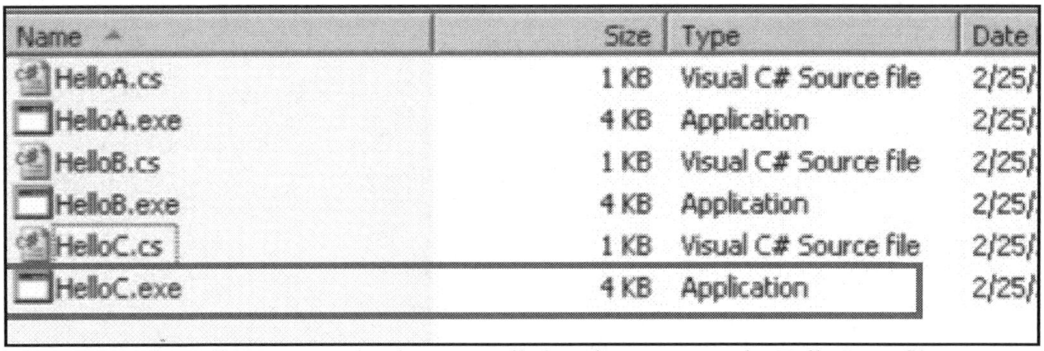

Name ▲	Size	Type	Date
HelloA.cs	1 KB	Visual C# Source file	2/25/
HelloA.exe	4 KB	Application	2/25/
HelloB.cs	1 KB	Visual C# Source file	2/25/
HelloB.exe	4 KB	Application	2/25/
HelloC.cs	1 KB	Visual C# Source file	2/25/
HelloC.exe	4 KB	Application	2/25/

Figure 8.23 The HelloC program has been compiled, and we now see the HelloC.exe file.

Running C# Code

To run your C# program, you can double-click the .exe file or type the application name in the command line and hit "run."

Double click the file to launch the program (see Figure 8.24).

Figure 8.24 Our HelloC program runs successfully.

Other C# Coding Considerations

If you find an error in your application, your first step will be to make an update to the source code. At that point are you done? Maybe you have days' worth of changes to make to your source code. When you are satisfied all the changes are in, then you can re-compile to create a new assembly. In the meantime, the assembly will remain the old assembly until you compile the changes.

Hit Enter to close the program. Let's return to the HelloC.cs file, right-click to open it with Notepad, and make a modification to our source code.

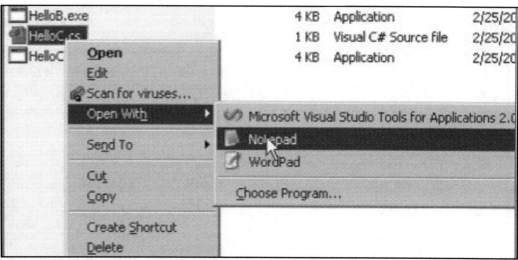

Figure 8.25 Right-click the HelloC.cs file and open it with Notepad.

Make a slight modification to the source code. Here we will add "Super" to the line "I am fine!" (see Figure 8.26). Then save and close the Notepad file.

```
HelloC.cs - Notepad
le  Edit  Format  View  Help
lass Class1


static void Main()
{
        System.Console.WriteLine("Hello world");
        System.Console.WriteLine("How are You?");
        System.Console.WriteLine("I am Super fine!");
        System.Console.ReadLine();
}
```

Figure 8.26 Modify your source code slightly.

Return to your C#Stuff folder and notice the updated timestamp on the HelloC.cs file you just modified, saved, and closed. However, notice the compiled program file (HelloC.exe) still has an earlier timestamp (see Figure 8.27). Your source code has been updated, but the program won't reflect this change until you recompile it.

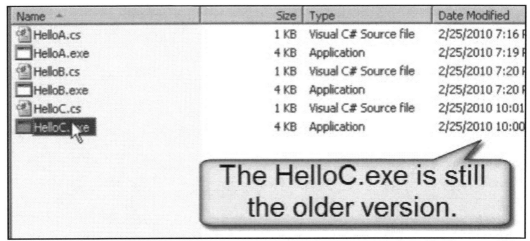

Figure 8.27 Your source code has been updated, but the program won't reflect this change until you recompile it.

Verify this by running the program (double-click the HelloC.exe file) and seeing that the old language is still there – your modification isn't yet showing. Hit Enter to close the program. Then recompile the program (repeat the step shown in Figure 8.22) by opening a Command Prompt, navigating to the C#Stuff directory, typing the command "csc HelloC.cs", and hitting Enter.

```
Command Prompt - CSC HelloC.cs
Microsoft Windows [Version 5.2.3790]
(C) Copyright 1985-2003 Microsoft Corp.

C:\Documents and Settings\Student>cd\

C:\>cd Joes2Pros

C:\Joes2Pros>cd C#Stuff

C:\Joes2Pros\C#Stuff>CSC HelloC.cs
Microsoft (R) Visual C# 2008 Compiler version 3.5.21022.8
for Microsoft (R) .NET Framework version 3.5
Copyright (C) Microsoft Corporation. All rights reserved.
```

Figure 8.28 Recompile the program by typing this command (csc HelloC.cs) and hitting Enter.

Launch the program again and verify that the new source code instructions are now reflected in your program result (see Figure 8.29).

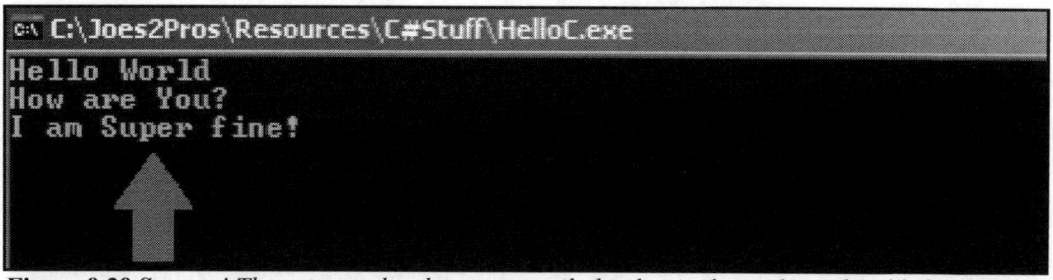

Figure 8.29 *Success! The program has been recompiled* and now shows the updated information.

As mentioned earlier, C# is case-sensitive. Therefore "Class" and "class" are NOT the same word as far as C# is concerned.

Keywords such as *class, static*, and *void* must always have lowercase lettering.

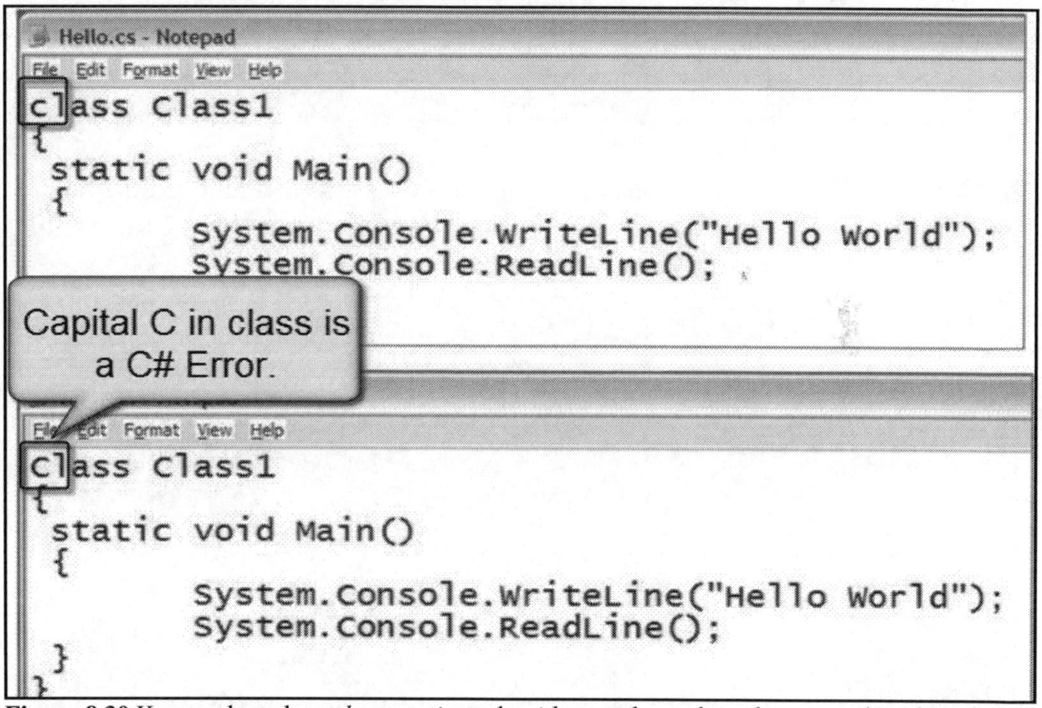

Figure 8.30 Keywords such as *class, static*, and *void* must always have lowercase lettering.

Return to the Notepad file containing your source code for HelloC.cs and change the first word "class" to "Class" (beginning with an uppercase letter) and save the file. When you attempt to recompile HelloC.cs, observe that just this small error causes the compile process to fail (see Figure 8.31).

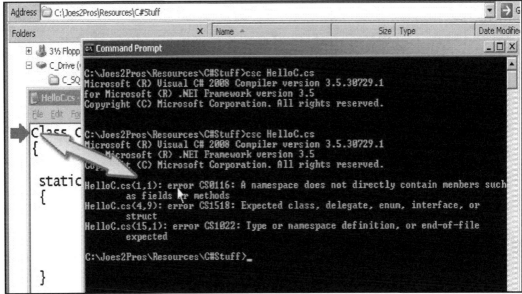

Figure 8.31 C# is case-sensitive. A single case mistake will cause an error.

Return once more to your source code file HelloC.cs and correct this error. Revert to "class" beginning with a lowercase "c" and save the file. Observe that your attempt to recompile HelloC.cs is successful.

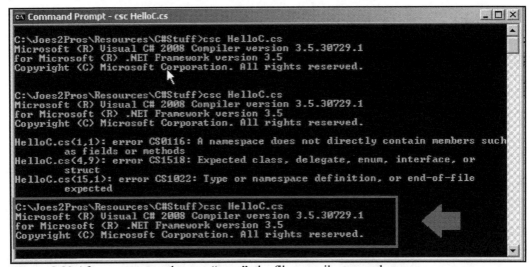

Figure 8.32 After you correct the case "error", the file compiles properly.

If you get any unusual errors when you attempt to compile or recompile, double checking your uppercasing and lowercasing should be your first step in troubleshooting.

Lab 8.1: Introduction To C#

Lab Prep: Before you can begin the lab you must have downloaded the companion CD available at *www.Joe2Pros.com* and setup the resources and C# folder on your C drive.

Skill Check 1: Create a SkillCheck1.cs file that displays 2 lines that say…

Make sure the program waits for the user to hit Enter.

Name ▲	Size	Type	Date
HelloA.cs	1 KB	Visual C# Source file	2/25
HelloA.exe	4 KB	Application	2/25
HelloB.cs	1 KB	Visual C# Source file	2/25/2010 7:20 P
HelloB.exe	4 KB	Application	2/25/2010 7:20 P
HelloC.cs	1 KB	Visual C# Source file	2/25/2010 10:28
HelloC.exe	4 KB	Application	2/25/2010 10:28
SkillCheck1.cs	1 KB	Visual C# Source file	2/25/2010 10:32
SkillCheck1.exe	4 KB	Application	2/25/2010 10:32

Figure 8.33 Skill Check 1 result.

Answer Code: The C# code to this lab can be found in the downloadable files in a file named Lab8.1_IntroToC#.sql

Introduction to C# - Points to Ponder

1. A class is a set of data or methods that can manipulate data.

2. All programming must be done inside of a class.

3. Main( ) is the starting point for a C# program.

4. All methods including Main( ) must be inside a class.

5. Write( ) and WriteLine( ) are methods of the Console and are used to display information to the console screen.

6. If an app is compiled successfully, an executable (.exe) will be generated.

Introduction to Visual Studio

Thus far we have used Notepad to build all of our code files. This works because the C# compiler (CSC) understands the code which we write in Notepad and save as ".cs" files. In other words, *C# understands Notepad.*

However, because it is a basic, no-frills text editor, Notepad cannot offer us any specialized support with our code syntax or construction. In other words, *Notepad doesn't understand C#.*

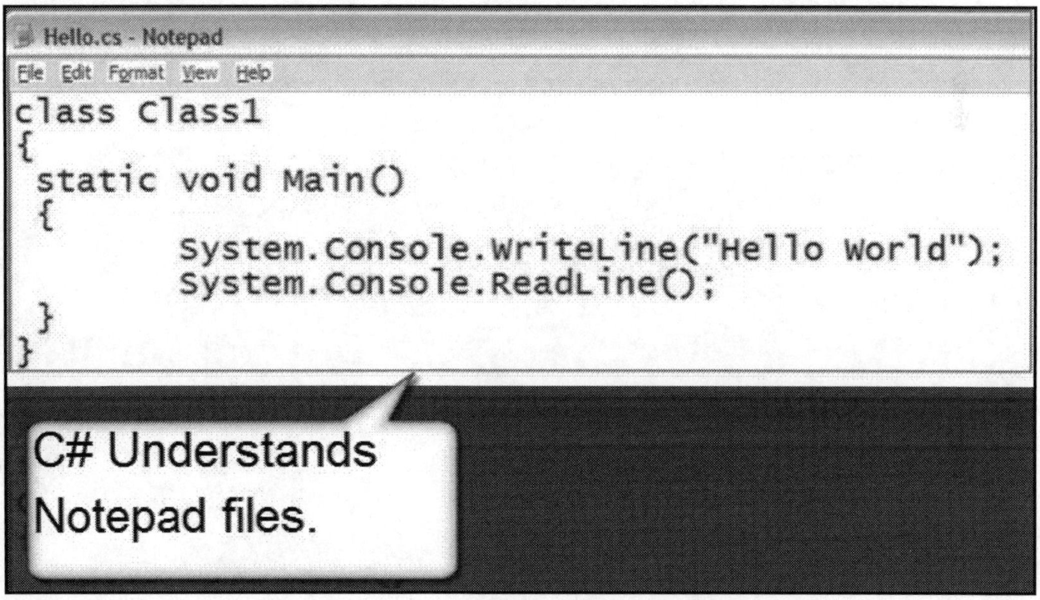

Figure 8.34 C# "understands" Notepad , but Notepad doesn't understand C#.

Pause for a moment to consider the specialized support we rely upon when writing T-SQL code in SSMS (Microsoft SQL Server Management Studio). We get keyword hints in the form of color-coding, IntelliSense to prompt us on spelling and syntax errors, auto-suggested dropdowns for available objects and functions, and extremely specific error messaging that helps pinpoint the cause and remedy for our mistakes.

Whether we're business people, students, or teachers, we can easily recognize the enormous benefit we receive from the program-specific support provided by SSMS. Next we will examine Microsoft Visual Studio and the specific support it provides for C# developers.

Integrated Development Environment (IDE)

Notepad has been included in every version of Windows (i.e., since 1985) and is a very handy, easy-to-use text editor program. So why do so many people pay for word processing programs, such as Microsoft Word, when they could simply use their Notepad utility to create documents and letters? MS Word really makes life easier by offering spelling, grammar, and formatting suggestions which save time and give your documents a professional look. You could say that MS Word is a *Development Environment* for writing documents.

We will create our next C# example as a project in Microsoft Visual Studio, instead of Notepad. Visual Studio is a programming environment, also referred to as an *integrated development environment (IDE)*.

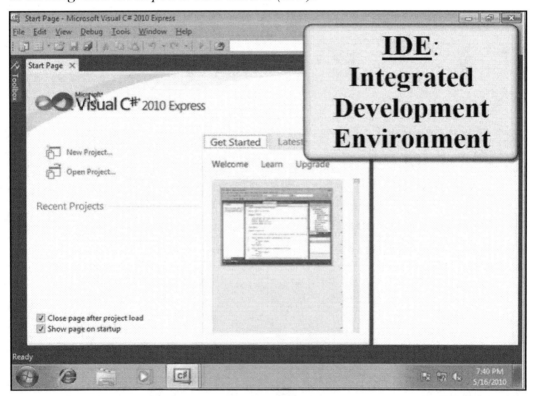

Figure 8.35 Visual Studio is an example of an integrated development environment (IDE).

Any version of MS Visual Studio (2008 or higher) or Visual C# (2008 or higher) will allow you to run the C# examples you find in this book.

C# is the most popular of the .NET languages.

At Joes2Pros.com, you can obtain a more detailed introduction to C# as a complimentary download (www.Joes2Pros.com/downloads/Intro_Chapter2.pdf). This document discusses Visual Studio and Visual C#. Microsoft offers "Express" versions (www.microsoft.com/express) of some of its software programs (e.g., SQL Server Express, Visual Studio Express, Visual C#, Visual Basic Express), which are limited, no-charge trial versions. While these generally contain fewer features than the full license or enterprise editions, they are a terrific way for students to learn and experience these programs hands-on.

Figure 8.36 Microsoft Express downloads page.

Creating a Project in Visual Studio

As you would for any application, launch Visual Studio or Visual C# from your Start Menu. Open a "New Project" from the File menu or by clicking the "New Project" icon on the Start Page.

Several templates are available. Choose "Console Application" and name your new project "HelloD" (see Figures 8.37 and 8.38).

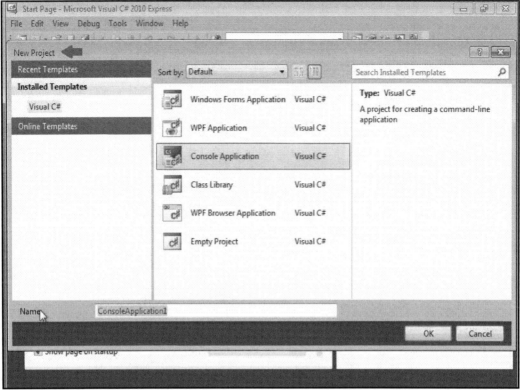

Figure 8.37 Open a New Project and choose the Console Application template.

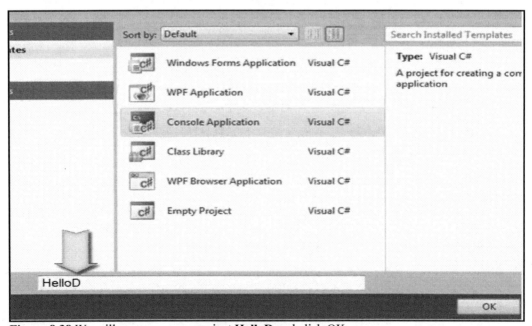

Figure 8.38 We will name our new project **HelloD** and click OK.

Notice the basic structure of a C# program has been created for us. The project name (HelloD) is visible in several places, and the static void Main( ) statement is ready for us to begin writing code (see Figure 8.39).

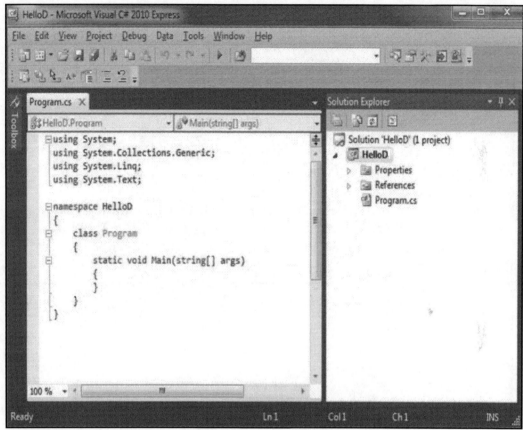

Figure 8.39 Visual Studio has created the basic structure of a C# program for us.

Next we want to save our project to a location by clicking File > Save HelloD As, which opens the Save Project dialog (see Figure 8.40). Click Browse to open Windows Explorer and navigate to your \Joes2Pros\C#Stuff folder.

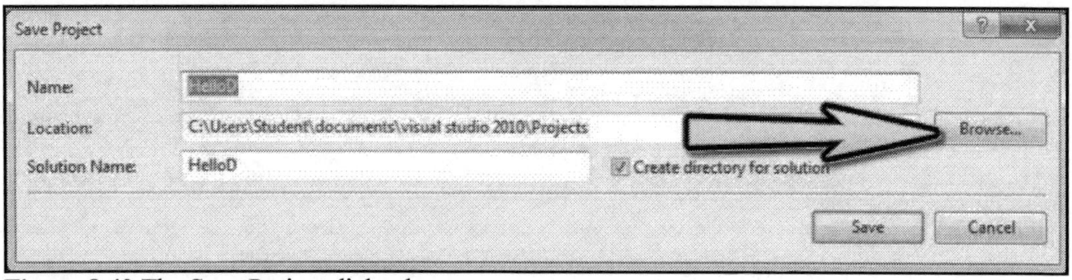

Figure 8.40 The Save Project dialog box.

Selecting the destination folder then returns you to the Save Project dialog. Uncheck the box "Create directory for solution" and click Save.

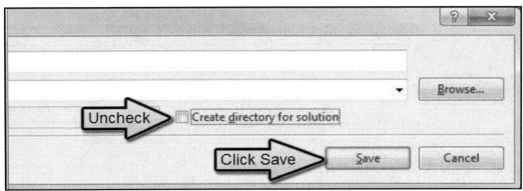

Figure 8.41 The final clicks needed to save our project in the C#Stuff folder.

Now that we have created and stored our new project, we are ready to write some code. Our work area resembles an earlier screen capture (Figure 8.39). If we close or minimize the Solution Explorer, that will give us more room to work in the Text Editor pane (shown below in Figure 8.42).

```
HelloD.Program                          Main(string[] args)
using System;
using System.Collections.Generic;
using System.Linq;
using System.Text;


namespace HelloD
{
    class Program
    {
        static void Main(string[] args)
        {

        }
    }
}
```

Figure 8.42 When you open a new VS project template, it is ready for you to begin writing code.

We will write HelloD as a very simple program using WriteLine and ReadLine statements. As we construct our code, we will observe the features of the Visual Studio IDE which assist us and make it easy to write good code.

IntelliSense

The two lines of our program will consist of one WriteLine statement and one ReadLine statement:

> System.Console.WriteLine("Hello D World");
> System.Console.ReadLine( );

Intellisense's *autocompletion* functionality provides useful suggestions for your code. As we begin typing "System" for our first WriteLine (Figure 8.43) statement, we see all valid possibilities we can use at this point in our code. (Scroll up and down the list and notice the the numerous possibilities!!) This list consists of each item's properly formatted name and an icon denoting the type of each item (e.g., a method, a program, a variable, etc.). An informational tag with a more verbose definition appears to the right of the list for the currently selected item.

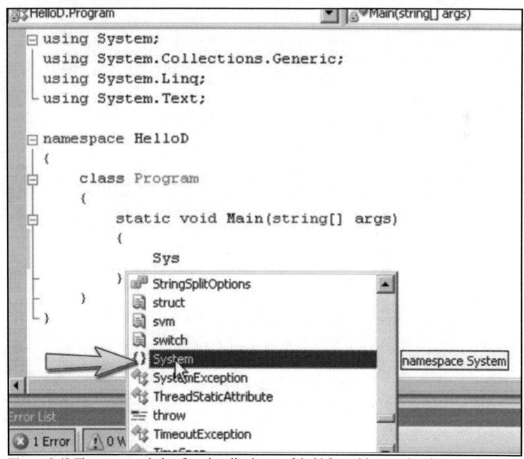

Figure 8.43 The autocompletion functionality is a useful aid for writing good code.

Notice the suggestion lists appear as we continue typing our first statement. This is similar to the suggestions we receive from the IntelliSense functionality included in SQL Server 2008.

Some advanced developers may find IntelliSense somewhat annoying (i.e., since some of them began their dev careers before IntelliSense was available). However,

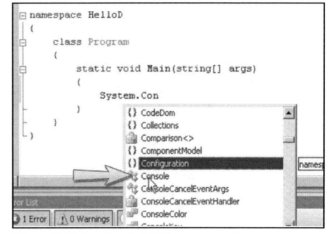

Figure 8.44 Another IntelliSense example.

autocompletion has been consistently included in Microsoft programming environments since Visual Basic 5.0 and IntelliSense has been further developed and enhanced thanks to the inception of the .NET framework. Unless we accidentally hit Tab or Enter as we code, IntelliSense isn't going to inadvertently add something unexpected to our code.

As you complete the first line of code, notice that autocomplete doesn't slow down your writing of the WriteLine statement.

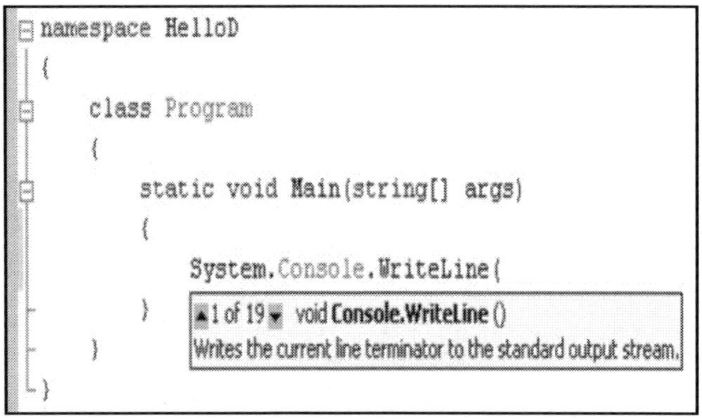

Figure 8.45 IntelliSense defines the WriteLine() method.

It provides suggestions which are useful if you would like input, but otherwise, it allows you to simply type your code unimpeded.

Error Detection

Just like we've seen in our SQL Server code, IntelliSense helps provide error detection support.

In the last section, we demonstrated that changing one lower case letter to an upper case in our source code constituted an error which prevented our program from compiling. Let's do the same with our HelloD code and observe the cues which IntelliSense provides (see Figure 8.46).

When we change "class" to "Class", red underlines immediately appear indicating an error in our code. An informational tag appears and pinpoints the location of the problematic syntax. While it doesn't say "hey, this should be a lowercase instead of an uppercase", we can see that the problem relates to "Class" (see Figures 8.46 and 8.47).

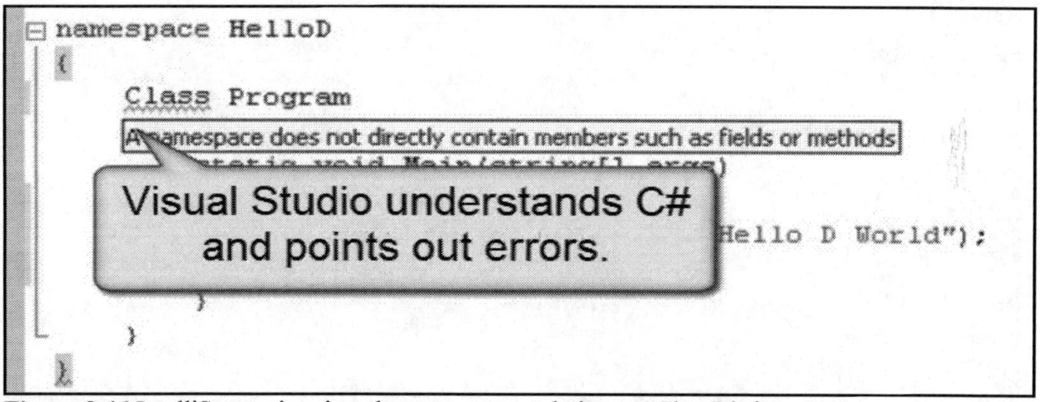

Figure 8.46 IntelliSense pinpoints that our syntax relating to "Class" is incorrect.

Our capitalization of "Class" is tricking IntelliSense into thinking it's a namespace, instead of the keyword "class" denoting the classification of our object as a program (see Figures 8.46 and 8.47).

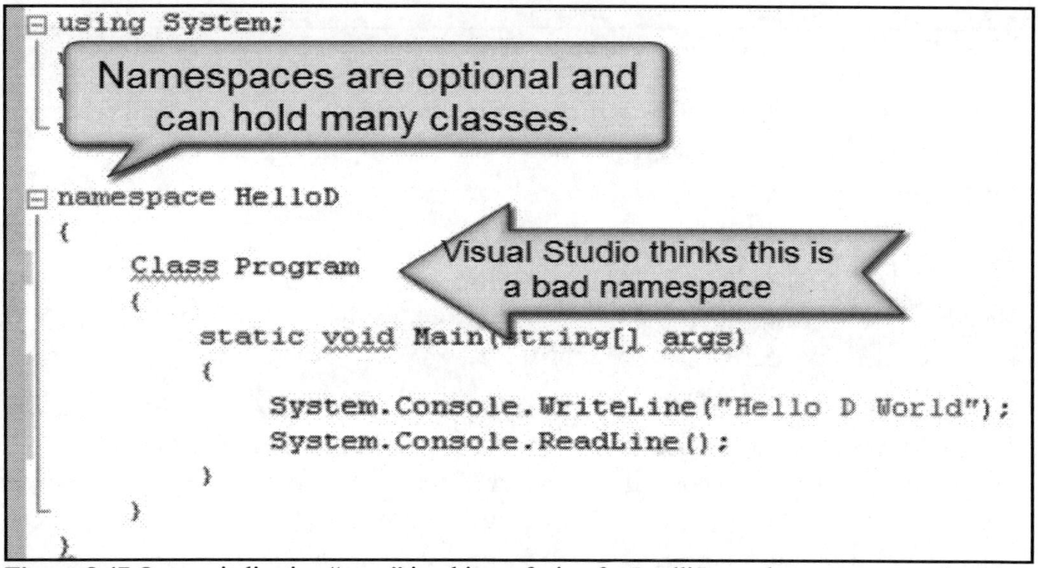

Figure 8.47 Our capitalization "error" is a bit confusing for IntelliSense, but we get enough cues to know that "Class" is likely causing the problem with our code.

Observe that when we revert "Class" to the appropriate syntax ("class"), the red underlines disappear. The color-coding scheme also reverts to normal (see Figure 8.48).

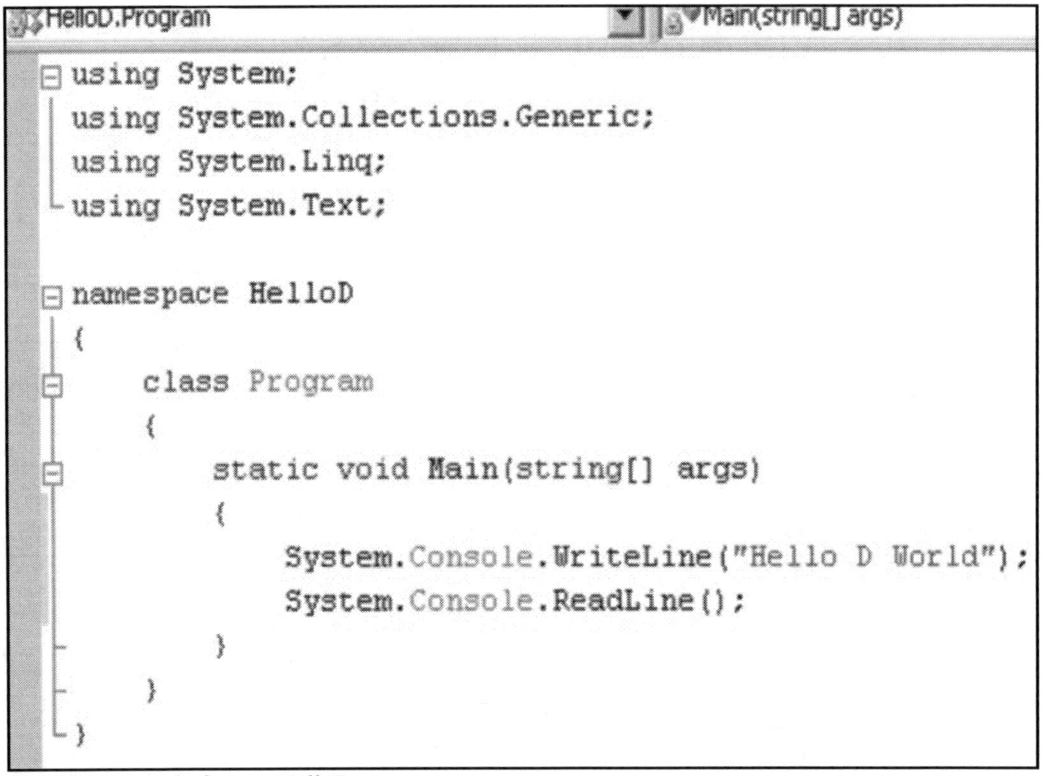

```
HelloD.Program                                    Main(string[] args)

using System;
using System.Collections.Generic;
using System.Linq;
using System.Text;


namespace HelloD
{
    class Program
    {
        static void Main(string[] args)
        {
            System.Console.WriteLine("Hello D World");
            System.Console.ReadLine();
        }
    }
}
```

Figure 8.48 Code for our HelloD program.

With our source code properly written, we're now ready to compile and run our program, HelloD. Once your code matches Figure 8.48, be sure to save your program.

Running and Testing Code

Recall our steps from the previous section which we used in order to compile source code and generate our program.

Since we wrote our code in Notepad, we had to save each text file (.txt) as a C# file (.cs). We then used a command line tool or program (in the "Console" or "Command Prompt") to compile our source code into an .exe file. Finally, we ran the program by launching (double-clicking) the .exe file. (These steps are summarized in Figure 8.49.)

Name ▲	Size	Type	Date Modified
HelloA.cs	1 KB	Visual C# Source file	25/02/2010 19:16
HelloA.exe	4 KB	Application	25/02/2010 19:19
HelloB.cs	1 KB	Visual C# Source file	25/02/2010 19:20
HelloB.exe	4 KB	Application	25/02/2010 19:20
HelloC.cs	1 KB	Visual C# Source file	25/02/2010 19:20
HelloC.exe	4 KB	Application	25/02/2010 19:20
HelloD		File Folder	26/02/2010 08:28

Steps to test your C# application
1.) Save CS file
2.) Compile CS file
3.) Run exe file

Figure 8.49 A summary of the steps we ran to transform our Notepad files into .exe program files.

With Visual Studio, the process to build, compile, and run your program is streamlined. In fact, Visual Studio presumes you will need to do this quickly ("on-the-fly") in order to efficiently run and test your code.

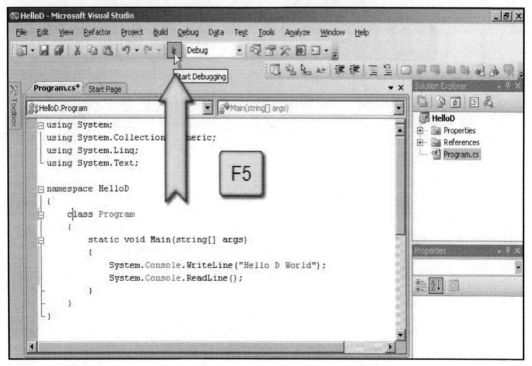

Figure 8.50 Hit the green "play" button or the F5 key to begin compiling.

Click the green control (sometimes called the "play" button) to compile and run your program (see Figure 8.50). Alternatively you can hit the F5 to compile and run, just the same as we do in the SQL Server setting.

Success! Visual Studio compiled and ran our program, and we see the Console (a.k.a, Command Prompt window) launched and displaying our greeting, "Hello D World" (see Figure 8.51).

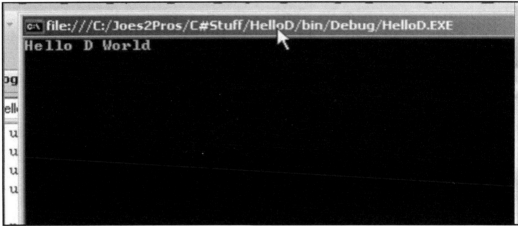

Figure 8.51 HelloD was compiled and now shows in Console.

Using Variables

Suppose we are asked to modify our greeting to print five times.

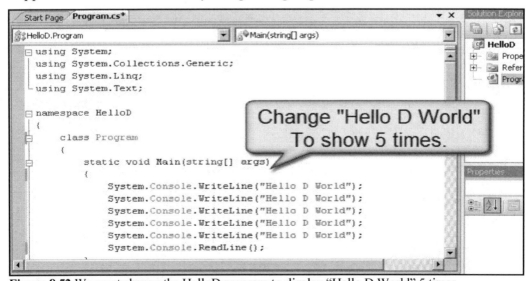

Figure 8.52 We must change the HelloD program to display "Hello D World" 5 times.

To accomplish this goal, we need to simply copy and add four more instances of our WriteLine code (as shown in Figure 8.52).

That was easy – when we run the program, we see the five instances of the "Hello D World" greeting displayed (see Figure 8.53).

Figure 8.53 The HelloD program now displays "Hello D World" 5 times.

The next request we receive is to change every instance of the "Hello D World" greeting to be "Hello DD World."

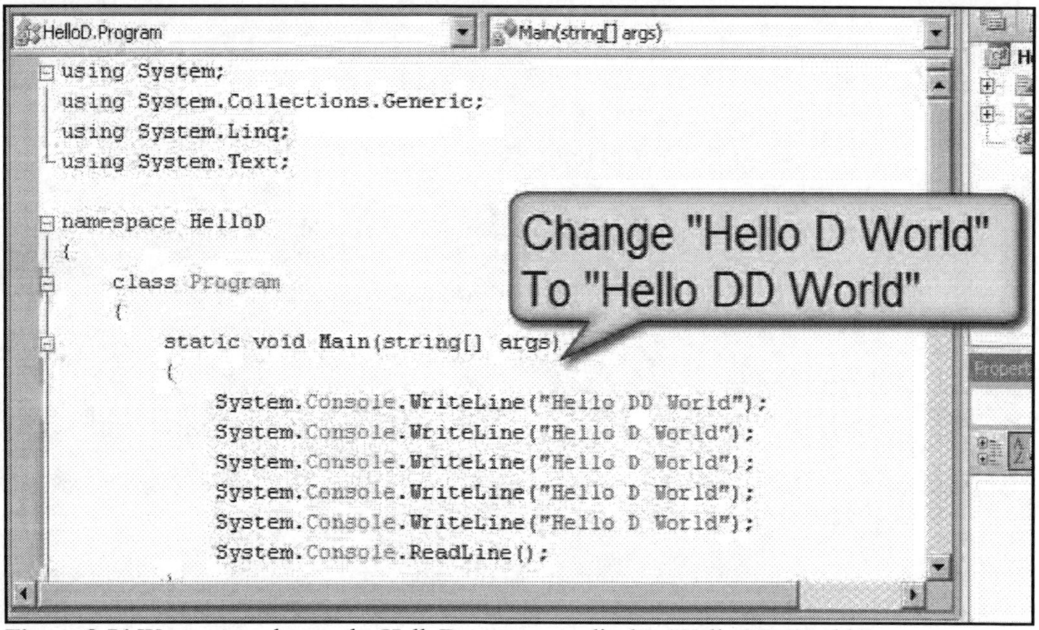

Figure 8.54 We want to change the HelloD program to display "Hello DD World."

With just five instances to change, it's fairly quick to just cut and paste the change into each line (see Figure 8.55).

```
HelloD.Program                          Main(string[] args)
using System;
using System.Collections.Generic;
using System.Linq;
using System.Text;

namespace HelloD
{
    class Program
    {
        static void Main(string[] args)
        {
            System.Console.WriteLine("Hello DD World");
            System.Console.WriteLine("Hello DD World");
            System.Console.WriteLine("Hello DD World");
            System.Console.WriteLine("Hello DD World");
            System.Console.WriteLine("Hello DD World");
            System.Console.ReadLine();
```

Figure 8.55 We've manually changed each "Hello D World" to say "Hello DD World."

When we re-run the program, we see the "Hello DD World" change has carried through and reflects properly in the program output (see Figure 8.56).

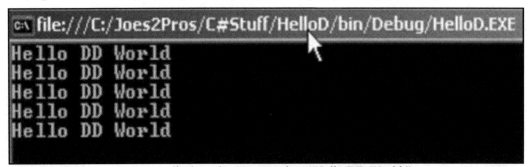

Figure 8.56 The program now displays the new greeting, "Hello DD World."

Our last two examples haven't been difficult – we manually made slight changes to five lines of code and quickly accomplished our goal. However, throughout the *Joes 2 Pros* series, we've seen that good coding practices include using smart, reusable code and eliminating the need to modify code manually.

To that end, let's introduce a variable into this code module, so that changes to this code may be made in a more automated fashion. Begin by adding a string variable named sMessage. We will set this variable equal to the string of the current greeting ("Hello DD World") (see Figure 8.57).

```
ss Program

  static void Main(string[] args)
  {
        string sMessage = "Hello DD World"
        System.Console.WriteLine("Hello DD World");
        System.Console.WriteLine("Hello DD World");
        System.Console.WriteLine("Hello DD World");
        System.Console.WriteLine("Hello DD World");
        System.Console.WriteLine("Hello DD World");
```

Figure 8.57 We have added a string variable and set it equal to the greeting, "Hello DD World."

Replacing the slogan or greeting in each line of code with the variable makes our code more robust, reusable, and allows changes to be made without ever needing to change the main body of our code block (see Figure 8.58).

```
class Program
{
      static void Main(string[] args)
      {
            string sMessage = "Hello DD World";
            System.Console.WriteLine(sMessage);
            System.Console.WriteLine(sMessage);
            System.Console.WriteLine(sMessage);
            System.Console.WriteLine(sMessage);
            System.Console.WriteLine(sMessage);
            System.Console.ReadLine();
      }
}
```

Figure 8.58 The variable sMessage now appears in each line of code.

When we rerun the program, we see the result is the same and matches the output before we replaced the variable (see Figure 8.56).

Figure 8.59 The output with the variable matches the prior result.

Suppose now we receive a request to change the greeting again. Management now wants it to be "Hello DeeDee World." Thanks to our work adding the variable, this change can be accomplished by assigning the new value ("Hello DeeDee World") to the variable and recompiling (see Figures 8.60 and 8.61).

```
class Program
{
    static void Main(string[] args)
    {
        string sMessage = "Hello DeeDee World";
        System.Console.WriteLine(sMessage);
        System.Console.WriteLine(sMessage);
        System.Console.WriteLine(sMessage);
        System.Console.WriteLine(sMessage);
        System.Console.WriteLine(sMessage);
        System.Console.ReadLine();
    }
}
```

Figure 8.60 Thanks to the variable, changing its value automatically updates each line of code.

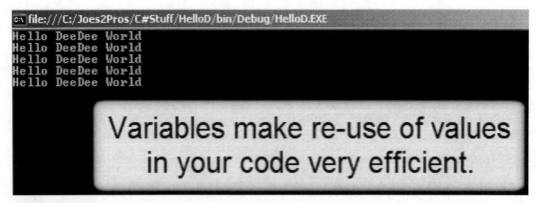

Figure 8.61 We rerun the program and see the variable has neatly updated each line of the output.

Project Files

Let's take a quick look at all of the assemblies we have created so far. As we know, an *assembly* is a deployable unit of .NET code.

The assemblies we created using Notepad in the last section are HelloA.exe, HelloB.exe, and HelloC.exe (see Figure 8.62).

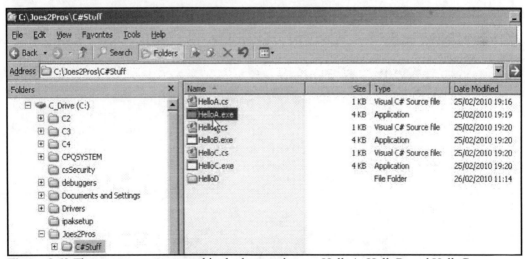

Figure 8.62 The programs we created in the last section are HelloA, HelloB, and HelloC.

The HelloD folder was created by Visual Studio to house all of the files for our project (as shown earlier in Figures 8.38-8.41). The .csproj and .sln files are the ones which manage the assembly (see Figure 8.63).

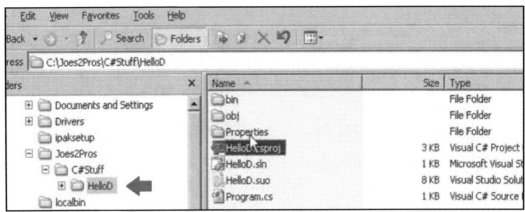

Figure 8.63 Visual Studio creates a folder to house all files for a project.

Where is the actual assembly (.exe file) stored? If we drill into the bin (short for "binary") folder and then into the Debug folder, we see the HelloD.exe file (see Figure 8.64).

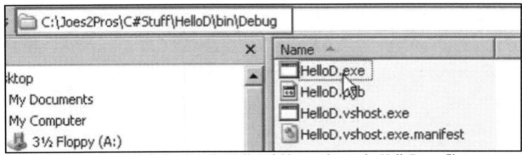

Figure 8.64 When we drill further into the HelloD folder, we locate the HelloD.exe file.

When we double-click the assembly file to launch the program from within the Debug folder, the program runs and displays the output (see Figure 8.65).

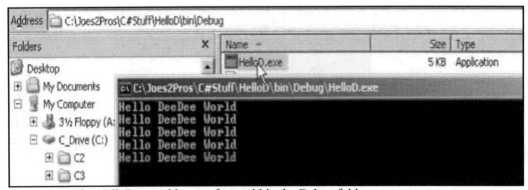

Figure 8.65 The HelloD assembly runs from within the Debug folder.

Note that the filepath for the assembly located in the Debug folder is the same filepath **[C:\Joes2Pros\C#Stuff\HelloD\bin\Debug\HelloD.exe]** we've seen each time we've run the HelloD program. If we refer back to each previous instance where we ran the HelloD program, we will see this same filepath displayed atop the Console window (see Figures 8.51, 8.53, 8.56, 8.59, and 8.61).

An executable (.exe) file is known as an **out of process assembly**. Out of process assemblies contain enough information to launch or run on their own.

Test this for yourself by removing the HelloD.exe file from the Debug folder and placing it on your desktop (see Figure 8.66). Close Windows Explorer and double-click the .exe file to run the program (see Figure 8.67).

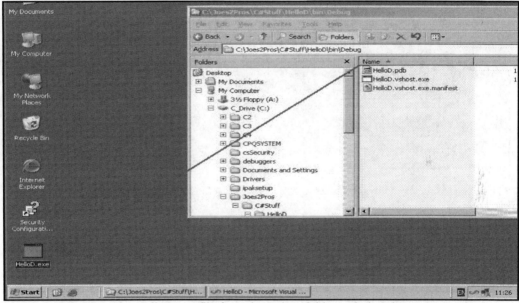

Figure 8.66 Remove the HelloD.exe file from the Debug folder and place it on your Desktop.

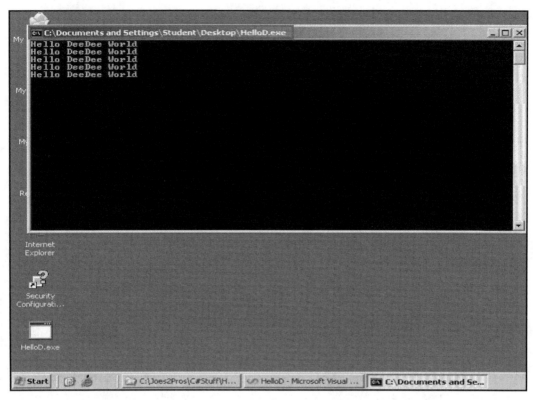

Figure 8.67 Close Windows Explorer and see that the HelloD program runs from your Desktop.

Lab 8.2: Introduction to Visual Studio

Lab Prep: Before you can begin the lab you must have downloaded the companion CD available at *www.Joe2Pros.com* and setup the resources and C# folder on your C drive.

Skill Check 1: Create a C# Project called HelloE that produces the following result (see Figure 8.68).

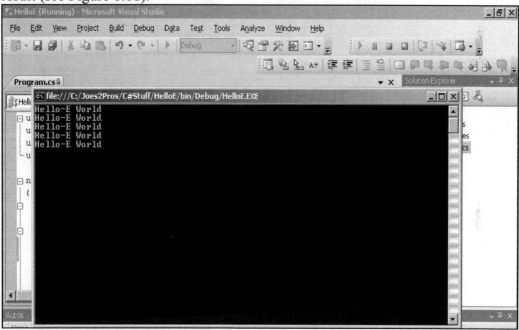

Figure 8.68 Your Skill Check 1 result.

Answer Code: The C# code to this lab can be found in the downloadable files in a file named Lab8.2_IntroToVisualStudio.sql

Introduction to Visual Studio - Points to Ponder

1. Visual Studio is an integrated development environment which helps you build and diagnose (test) applications.

2. Building C# applications in Visual Studio is known as programming in Visual C#.

3. An assembly whose extension ends in .exe is known as an "Out of Process" assembly.

4. You can create .NET assemblies in other .NET languages, such as Visual Basic, Visual J#, and Visual C++.

5. A deployable unit of .NET code is called an assembly.

Managed Code

You often hear .NET code referred to as **managed code**. There are many advantages offered by the managed code approach over traditional approaches. To appreciate these advantages, we first must have a basic understanding of prevalent application development practices prior to the introduction of the .NET framework. The two predecessor models we will consider can be categorized as **monolithic programming** and **modular programming.**

Monolithic Programming

In the **monolothic programming** model, each computer program was self-contained. It spoke directly to the computer architecture, and each application had to contain everything it needed to interface with the computer hardware. For example, if a game needed a "pow" sound, the developer would need to build a sound driver into the program.

This forced software programmers to become hardware experts, which tended to make development slow and expensive. It also meant that your application was tied to the current machine and CPU. Any upgrade in computer architecture meant that your application most likely wouldn't run on your upgraded machine – you would need to buy the version which would work on that type of computer.

Modular Programming

Since everyone reading this book is familiar with the Windows operating system (OS), that's an easy context in which to understand the concept of **modular programming**, which separated code into modular areas.

Rather than developing programs which needed to speak directly to the computer's architecture, software developers only needed to be concerned with writing applications that could speak to the Windows application programming interface (API). The OS handled the hardware interface, including device drivers and talking to the processor (CPU).

In our example of the sounds for a gaming program, the developer would be able to call on the API connected to the sound card and sound driver – no longer was there a need to code those into every individual application. All the games and applications you ran could call on the same sound card and driver. Software programmers could focus on applications and hardware experts could focus on supplying the operating system with the proper drivers.

.NET Programming

While modular programming spurred faster and less expensive development cycles and caused the software industry to boom in the 1990s, applications were still dependent upon a particular OS. Your apps could run on the Windows OS but not Linux or Mac.

The concept of .NET programming was announced in 2000 by Microsoft, who subsequently debuted the .NET framework in Visual Studio .NET in early 2002. The .NET framework introduces a layer between the application and the OS. Rather than speaking directly with the OS, the application only needs to speak with this new layer, called .NET runtime or CLR (for **c**ommon **l**anguage **r**untime) (see Figure 8.69).

.NET is an environment that runs other applications and a how-to list of what can be done in that environment. You can think of .NET as another form of modular programming that allows programmers to write code to be deployed to the .NET environment, which in turn runs on any OS (Windows, Linux, Mac, etc.). The CLR manages the calls from the .NET application to the binary of the operating system. Therefore .NET code is often referred to as "managed code."

The concept behind .NET is that code can be written once and then run anywhere. The OS no longer is responsible for running the application. As long as the .NET framework is installed on the system, then it doesn't matter whether the system is Mac, Linux, Windows, etc. -- if the .NET runtime is there, then the application will run.

Applications which run in the CLR are also called ".NET applications" and are written in a .NET programming language.

Currently C# is the most commonly used of all the .NET languages.

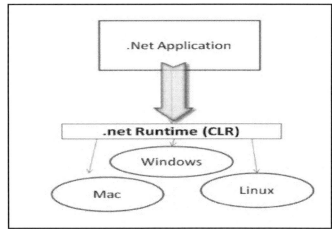

Figure 8.69 Code written in .NET talks to the CLR Applications speak only with the CLR, not the OS.

278

Working with Managed Code Projects

Let's create some managed code in the form of a Console application called MortgageReader. Since C# is one of the .NET programming languages, all of the C# programs we have written in this chapter are examples of managed code.

Open Visual Studio or Visual C#. Choose a "New Project", then choose the"Console Application" template. Enter "MortageReader" as the project name and click OK (see Figure 8.70).

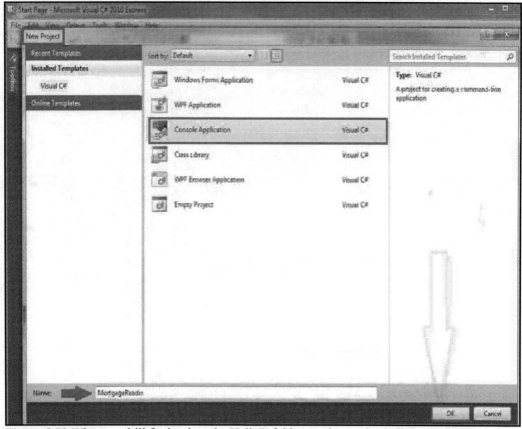

Figure 8.70 When we drill further into the HelloD folder, we locate the HelloD.exe file.

From the File menu, choose the "Save As" option to save this project in your desired location (C:\Joes2Pros\C#Stuff). Be sure to un-check the "Create directory for solution", and click OK.

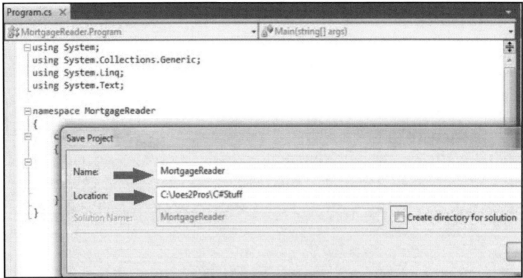

Figure 8.71 Save this project in the C#Stuff folder (C:\Joes2Pros\C#Stuff).

Add two WriteLine statements ("Starting App" and "App Finished") and a
ReadLine statement (see Figure 8.72).

```
Program.cs* ×
MortgageReader.Program                              Main(string[] args)

using System;
using System.Collections.Generic;
using System.Linq;
using System.Text;

namespace MortgageReader
{
    class Program
    {
        static void Main(string[] args)
        {
            System.Console.WriteLine("Starting App");

            System.Console.WriteLine("App Finished");
            System.Console.ReadLine();
        }
    }
}
```

Figure 8.72 Our program consists of two lines ("Starting App" and "App Finished").

280

Run the program (see Figure 8.73).

Figure 8.73 When we run the program, we see our two WriteLines, as expected.

Importing Namespaces

Notice the "using System;" statement at the beginning of our program. Repetition of "**System.**" below in our code block is redundant and unnecessary. The "using" keyword is the way C# imports namespaces to be implicitly used by all the other statements in the CS file.

```
MortgageReader.Program                          Main(string[] args)
    using System;
    using System.Collections.Generic;
    using System.Linq;
    using System.Text;

    namespace MortgageReader
    {
        class Program
        {
            static void Main(string[] args)
            {
                System.Console.WriteLine("Starting App");

                System.Console.WriteLine("App Finished");
                System.Console.ReadLine();
            }
        }
    }
```

Figure 8.74 The System. portion of these statements is unnecessary, since "using System;" imports the namespace.

Remove "**System.**" from each line of code contained within our Main statement (see Figure 8.75). The program will still run just fine.

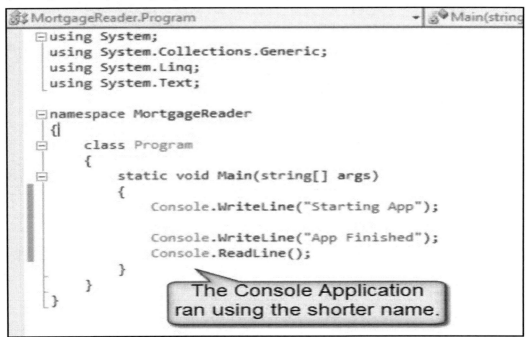

Figure 8.75 Remove "System." from each line in our program and re-run the program.

Try deleting the "**using System;**" statement and notice that the program will no longer run (see Figure 8.76).

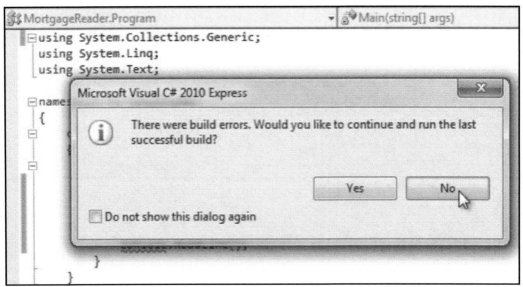

Figure 8.76 If you remove the "using System;" statement, the program will not run.

Working with Input/Output

Input/Output in .NET is called IO and is located in the System.IO namespace. This will allow you to read text from (or save it to) files on your computer.

In the Joes2Pros > Resources folder on your local drive, locate the MortgageRate file (see Figures 8.77 and 8.78).

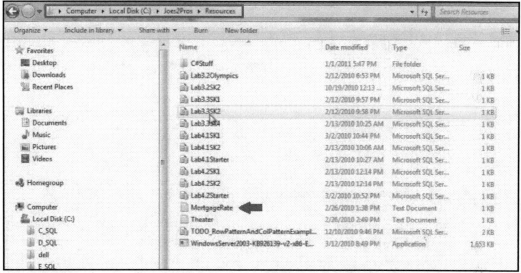

Figure 8.77 Navigate to the Joes2Pros Resources folder (C:\Joes2Pros\Resources).

Lab3.2SK2	10/19/2010 12:13 ...	Microsoft SQL Ser...
Lab3.3SK1	2/12/2010 9:57 PM	Microsoft SQL Ser...
Lab3.3SK2	2/12/2010 9:58 PM	Microsoft SQL Ser...
Lab3.3SK4	2/13/2010 10:25 AM	Microsoft SQL Ser...
Lab4.1SK1	3/2/2010 10:44 PM	Microsoft SQL Ser...
Lab4.1SK2	2/13/2010 10:06 AM	Microsoft SQL Ser...
Lab4.1Starter	2/13/2010 10:27 AM	Microsoft SQL Ser...
Lab4.2SK1	2/13/2010 12:14 PM	Microsoft SQL Ser...
Lab4.2SK2	2/13/2010 12:14 PM	Microsoft SQL Ser...
Lab4.2Starter	3/2/2010 10:52 PM	Microsoft SQL Ser...
MortgageRate	2/26/2010 1:38 PM	Text Document
Theater	2/26/2010 2:49 PM	Text Document
TODO_RowPatternAndColPatternExampl...	12/10/2010 9:46 PM	Microsoft SQL Ser...
WindowsServer2003-KB9..139-v2-x86-E...	3/12/2010 8:49 PM	Application

Figure 8.78 The MortgageRate.txt file is available at Joes2Pros.com if you don't already have it.

We want the three values from the MortgageRate text file to be displayed by our program (see Figure 8.79).

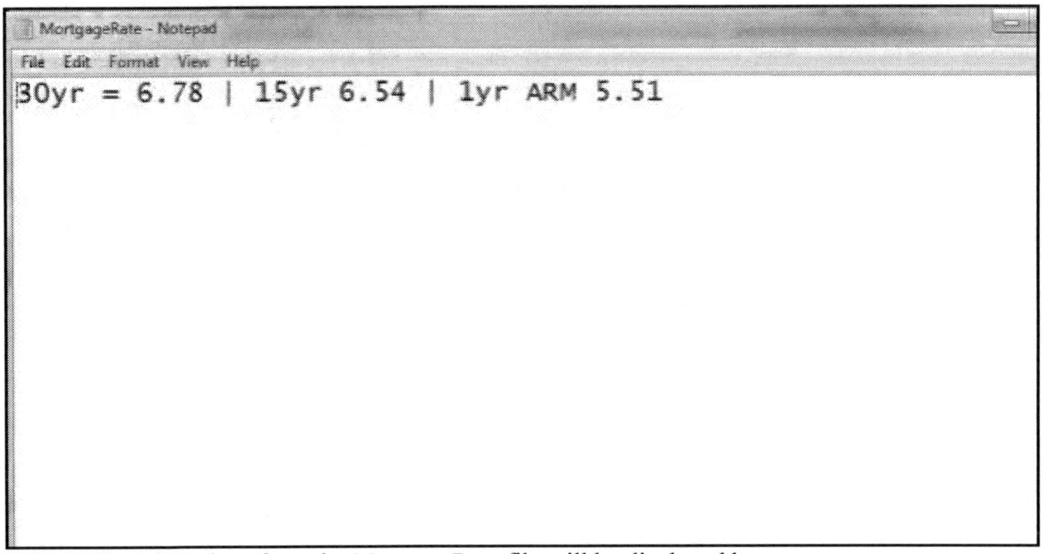

Figure 8.79 The values from the MortgageRate file will be displayed by our program.

Our code adding the MortgageRate data from the text file will appear between the Starting App and App Finished statements (see Figure 8.80).

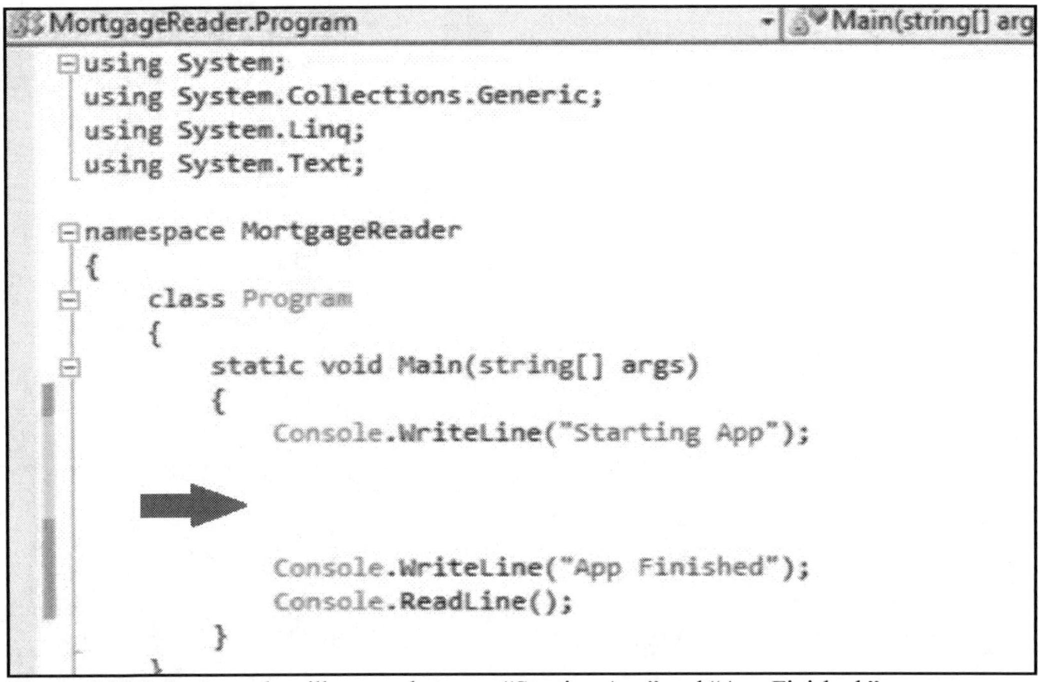

Figure 8.80 Our new code will appear between "Starting App" and "App Finished."

StreamReader will allow our program to read from the file (see Figure 8.81).

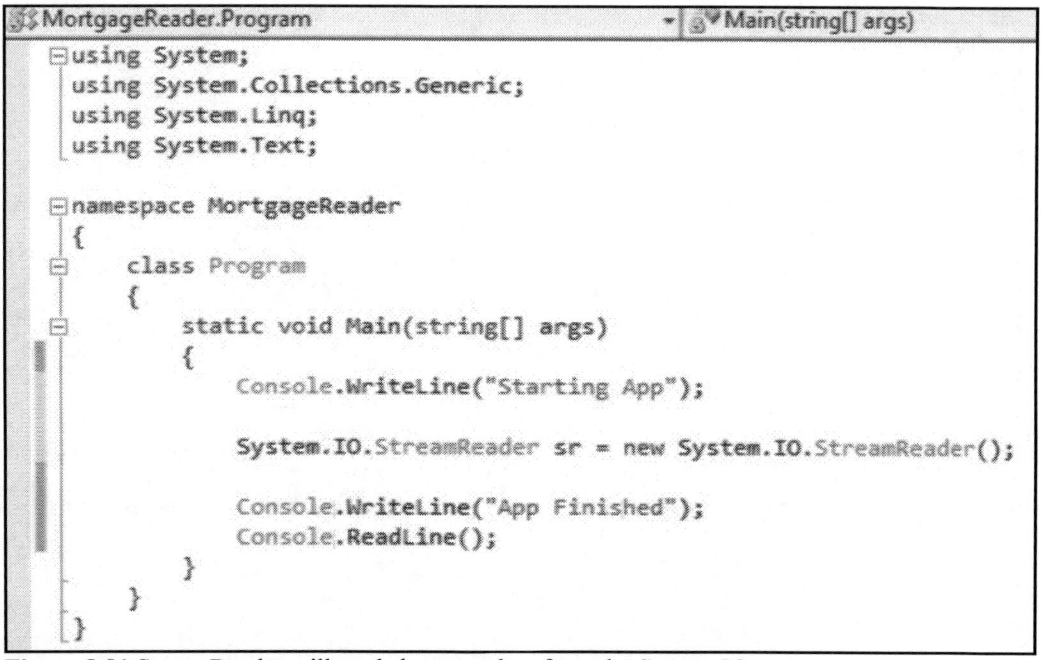

```
MortgageReader.Program                                    Main(string[] args)
using System;
using System.Collections.Generic;
using System.Linq;
using System.Text;

namespace MortgageReader
{
    class Program
    {
        static void Main(string[] args)
        {
            Console.WriteLine("Starting App");

            System.IO.StreamReader sr = new System.IO.StreamReader();

            Console.WriteLine("App Finished");
            Console.ReadLine();
        }
    }
}
```

Figure 8.81 StreamReader will read character data from the System.IO namespace.

We will import the **System.IO.** namespace at the beginning of our program.

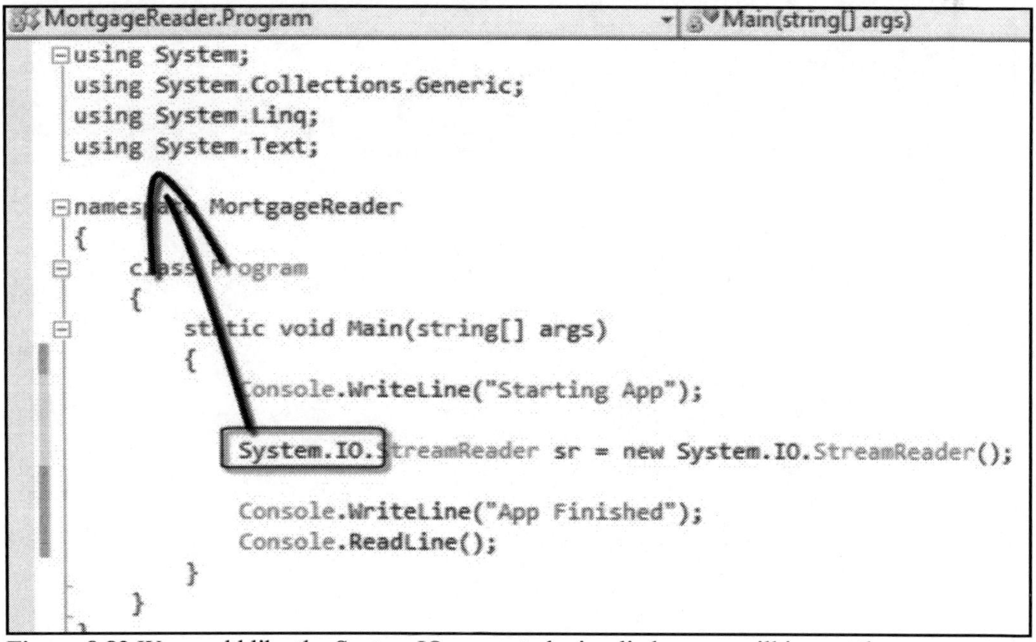

```
MortgageReader.Program                                    Main(string[] args)
using System;
using System.Collections.Generic;
using System.Linq;
using System.Text;

namespace MortgageReader
{
    class Program
    {
        static void Main(string[] args)
        {
            Console.WriteLine("Starting App");

            System.IO.StreamReader sr = new System.IO.StreamReader();

            Console.WriteLine("App Finished");
            Console.ReadLine();
        }
    }
}
```

Figure 8.82 We would like the System.IO. name to be implied, so we will import the namespace.

The **System.IO.** namespace has been imported and thus no longer needed in the main body of our program (see Figure 8.83).

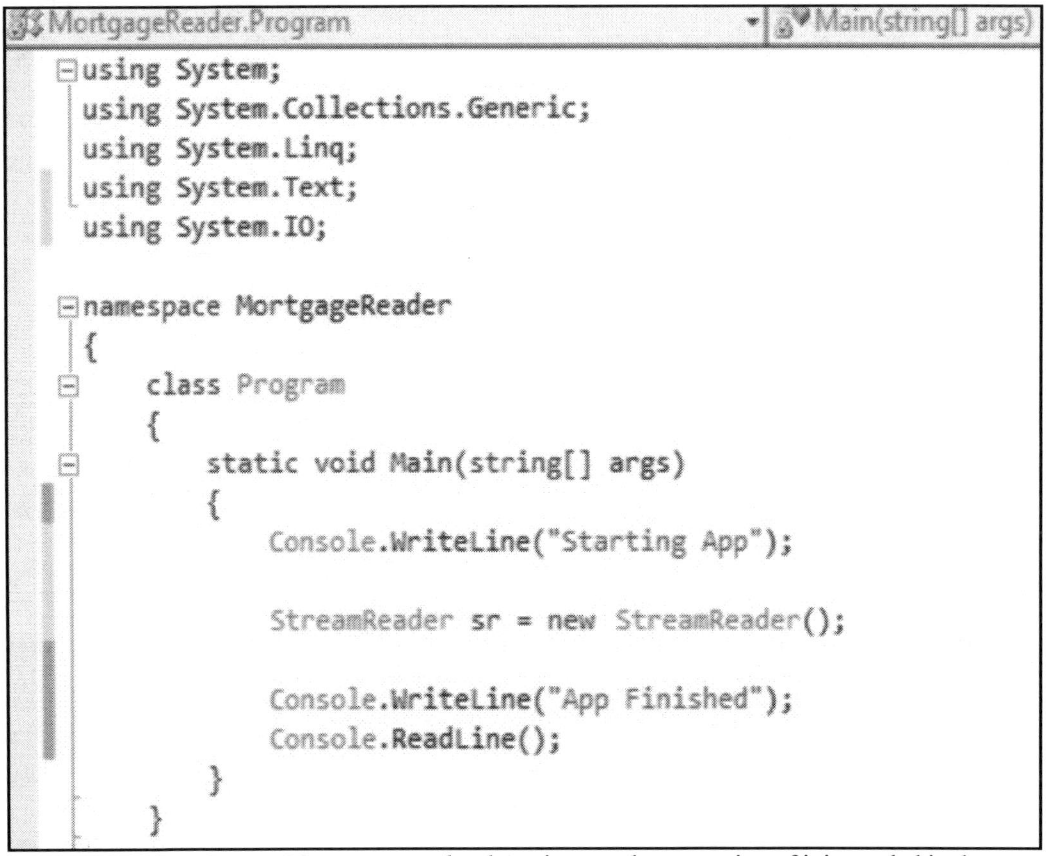

```
MortgageReader.Program                                  Main(string[] args)
    using System;
    using System.Collections.Generic;
    using System.Linq;
    using System.Text;
    using System.IO;

namespace MortgageReader
    {
        class Program
        {
            static void Main(string[] args)
            {
                Console.WriteLine("Starting App");

                StreamReader sr = new StreamReader();

                Console.WriteLine("App Finished");
                Console.ReadLine();
            }
        }
    }
```

Figure 8.83 Since System.IO. namespace has been imported, no mention of it is needed in the body of our program code.

Our next step will be to bring in the filepath of MortgageReader.txt, so that StreamReader may pull in the needed data from the text file. (See Figures 8.84 through 8.88.)

```
using System;
using System.Collections.Generic;
using System.Linq;
using System.Text;
using System.IO;

namespace MortgageReader
{
    class Program
    {
        static void Main(string[] args)
        {
            Console.WriteLine("Starting App");

            StreamReader sr = new StreamReader();

            Console.WriteLine("App    Filepath here.
            Console.ReadLine();
        }
    }
}
```

Figure 8.84 StreamReader needs the filepath for the MortgageReader file.

Copy the filepath from the Joes2Pros\Resources folder (see Figure 8.85).

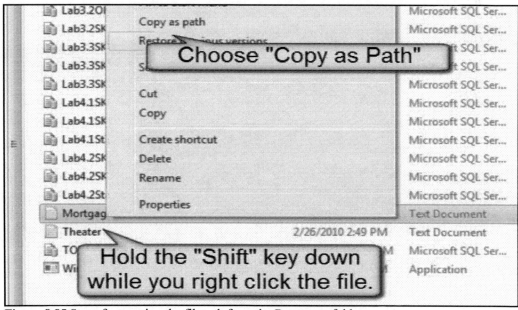

Figure 8.85 Steps for copying the filepath from the Resources folder.

Paste the filepath for the text file into the parentheses following StreamReader. Enclose the filepath in double quotes and precede it with an @ symbol.

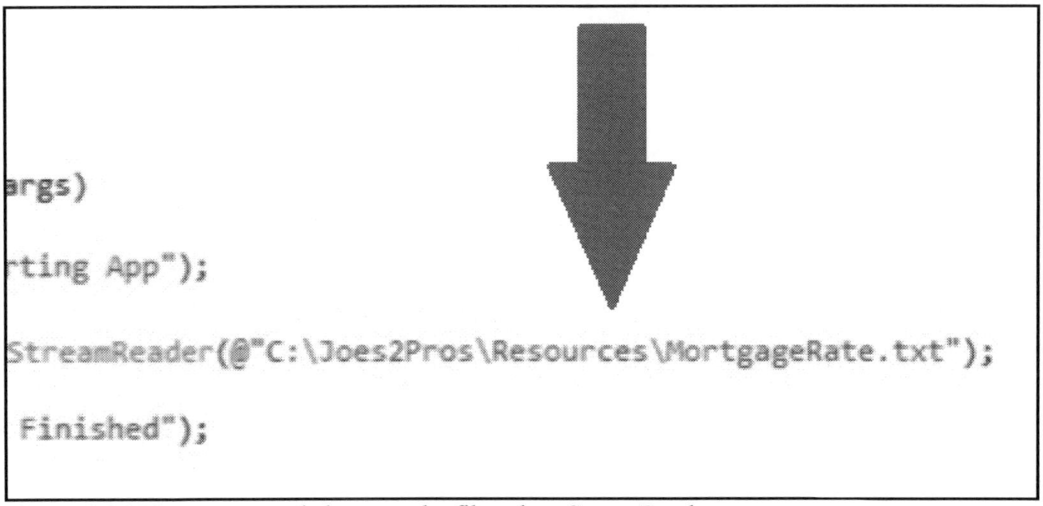

```
args)

rting App");

StreamReader(@"C:\Joes2Pros\Resources\MortgageRate.txt");

 Finished");
```

Figure 8.86 The syntax needed to pass the filepath to StreamReader.

```
MortgageReader.Program                                    Main(string[] args)
using System;
using System.Collections.Generic;
using System.Linq;
using System.Text;
using System.IO;

namespace MortgageReader
{
    class Program
    {
        static void Main(string[] args)
        {
            Console.WriteLine("Starting App");

            StreamReader sr = new StreamReader(@"C:\Joes2Pros\Resources\MortgageRate.txt");

            Console.WriteLine("App Finished");
            Console.ReadLine();
        }
    }
}
```

Figure 8.87 A full view of our current code, including the filepath syntax from Figure 8.86.

Next we want to capture the StreamReader into a string variable (named s2), so that we can display it to the Console (see Figure 8.88).

```
MortgageReader.Program                                          ▼  Main(string[] args)
using System;
using System.Collections.Generic;
using System.Linq;
using System.Text;
using System.IO;

namespace MortgageReader
{
    class Program
    {
        static void Main(string[] args)
        {
            Console.WriteLine("Starting App");

            StreamReader sr = new StreamReader(@"C:\Joes2Pros\Resources\MortgageRate.txt");
            string s2 = sr.ReadToEnd();
            Console.WriteLine(s2);

            Console.WriteLine("App Finished");
            Console.ReadLine();
        }
    }
}
```

Figure 8.88 The string variable will capture the output from StreamReader and display the contents of MortgageReader.txt to the Console.

Run the program (see Figure 8.89).

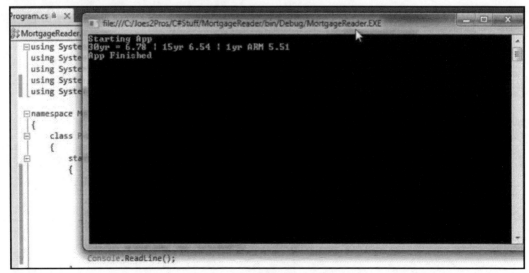

Figure 8.89 The final output of our program, MortgageReader, with the full filepath.

Notice this says "Starting App", then it give us our mortgage rates, then it says "App Finished."

Figure 8.90 A closeup of the output of our MortgageReader program

Lab 8.3: Managed Code

Lab Prep: Before you can begin the lab you must run the SQLInteropChapter8.3Setup.sql script. It is recommended that you view the lab video instructions found in Lab8.3_ManagedCode.wmv, available at *www.Joe2Pros.com.*

[CLASS NOTE: you do not need to run any setup script beyond SQLInteropChapter 7.0setup.sql]

Skill Check 1: Create a new C# Console project called TheaterSkillCheck that pulls out all of the information from the Theater.txt file. The first line of your application should WriteLine "What is good to see". The last line should pause with a ReadLine( ) statement. The middle should use a Stream Reader to pull out all contents of the Theater.txt file into a string and display that string to the Console.

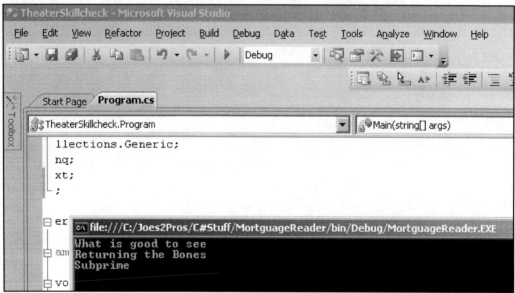

Figure 8.91 Skill Check 1 result.

Answer Code: The T-SQL code to this lab can be found in the downloadable files in a file named Lab8.3_ManagedCode.sql

Managed Code - Points to Ponder

1. An executable (.exe) file is known as an *"out of process" assembly.* Out of process assemblies contain enough information to launch or run on their own.

2. An assembly whose extension ends in .dll is known as an *"in process" assembly.*

3. DLL is short for **d**ynamic-**l**ink **l**ibrary.

4. Code that is managed in Microsoft's common language runtime (CLR) is called managed code.

5. Code that is managed by your Operating System is called unmanaged code.

6. You can create managed code using a .NET Framework language such as Visual Basic .NET or Visual C#.

7. Although you can write the same type of code using Transact-SQL, managed code does a better job of handling calculations and complex execution logic.

Chapter Glossary

Assembly: a deployable unit of .NET code.

C#: ("see sharp"), objected oriented programming language; can be used to build .NET applications and/or to interoperate with SQL Server.

C# Compiler: (CSC), compiler use for the C# language.

CLR: definition.

Compile: definition.

Executable: (.exe) definition. See *out of process assembly.*

IDE: (integrated development environment), a programming environment.

IntelliSense: definition.

Managed code: definition.

Modular programming: definition.

Monolithic programming: definition.

Namespace: definition.

.NET: definition.

Out of process assembly: an executable file (.exe).

Source code: definition.

static void Main( ): definition.

Visual Studio: definition.

Chapter Eight - Review Quiz

1.) What is the relationship between assemblies and applications?

  O a. An application can consist of many assemblies.

  O b. An assembly can consist of many applications.

2.) Which of the following will contain your source code?

  O a. Hello.exe

  O b. Hello.cs

3.) You have updated your source code but your assembly is still running the old code. What must you do to update your assembly to use the new source code?

  O a. Compile the EXE File to the assembly

  O b. Compile the CS file to the assembly

  O c. Reboot the computer.

4.) What is the name of the method that is always the starting method for a C# program?

  O a. Main( )

  O b. main( )

  O c. Start( )

  O d. start( )

5.) Which of the following statement about C# is true?

  O a. C# is case sensitive.

  O b. C# is case insensitive.

6.) What is Visual Studio?

  O a. A replacement language for C#

  O b. A program needed before you can install

  O c. A development environment for writing code

Chapter 8. Creating .NET Applications

7.) Using the following code.

        System.Console.WriteLine("Boo");

What is name of the method?

   O a. System
   O b. Console
   O c. WriteLine
   O d. Boo

8.) You have the following code below:

  System.Console.ReadLine( );

You want to refer to console by the short name below.

  Console.ReadLine( );

How would you do this?

   O a. Put 2 semi-colons at the end.
   O b. Import the System namespace.
   O c. Import the Console object.

Answer Key

1.) a   2.) b   3.) b   4.) a   5.) b   6.) c   7.) c   8.) b

Bug Catcher Game

To play the Bug Catcher game run the SQLInteropBugCatcherCh8.pps from the BugCatcher folder of the companion files. You can obtain these files from www.Joes2Pros.com or by ordering the Companion CD.

Chapter 9.   SQL CLR

.NET can run managed code because it has the CLR. If SQL Server wanted to run managed code in its own environment, it would need its own .NET runtime. The SQL CLR is the engine SQL Server uses to run .NET code. Not all types of .NET projects are useful in SQL Server, so we will need to know what the SQL CLR can and cannot run.

SQL has its own built-in CLR. The SQL CLR runs managed code for SQL Server.

We will also review security and permissions settings which must be addressed in order to use the SQL CLR. These include settings at the server, database, and object levels.

READER NOTE: *Please run the script SQLInteropChapter9.0Setup.sql in order to follow along with the examples in Chapter 9. All scripts mentioned in this chapter may be found at **www.Joes2Pros.com**.*

In-Process Assemblies

Until now we have used Visual Studio to create executable assemblies (with an "exe" extension). These serve as a nice introduction to programming because they run on their own and are not just a piece of a process. They are self-contained processes and run independently. If an assembly does not run on its own, but instead is one part of another process, then it's called an **in-process assembly**. You can recognize **in-process assemblies** by their "dll" extension.

Why would you create an assembly that can't run on its own? For the same reason you might buy a screwdriver: it's a tool that can never work by itself, but it can aid you and be one of the tools you use to accomplish a part of the work.

In the last chapter, we created an .exe file – in other words, we created an **out-of-process assembly.** Out-of-process assemblies are applications which you can invoke (i.e., which you can run), just as we were able to run our HelloD.exe program.

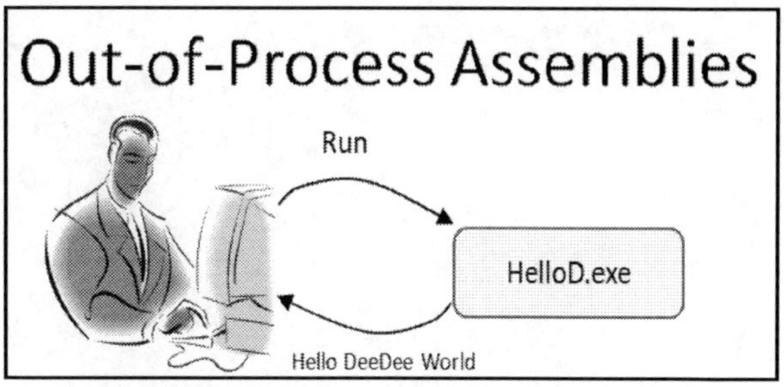

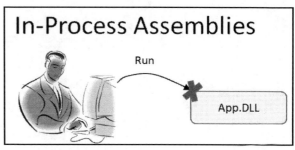

Figure 9.1 We can invoke (or run) the HelloD.exe app.

On the other hand, sometimes you will create an assembly for the sole purpose of providing information to another assembly which actually runs the application. These supporting applications are called **in-process assemblies**, which are programs you cannot run directly.

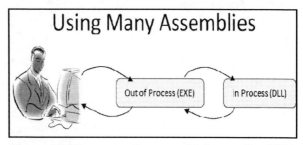

Figure 9.2 We cannot directly call (or run) a DLL app.

In this section, we will create a DLL module, which we cannot call directly. We will create an .exe app which will call on the DLL and receive information from it.

Using Many Assemblies

Figure 9.3 We can run the .exe, which can call a DLL.

297

Creating a Class Library (DLL)

Let's begin creating our in-process assembly. The steps will be similar to the new project we created in the last chapter (Figures 8.70-8.71), except that the project type will be a Class Library.

Launch Visual Studio and create a new project (File > New Project) named "UtilitiesLibrary." Then save your project in the C:\Joes2Pros\C#Stuff folder.

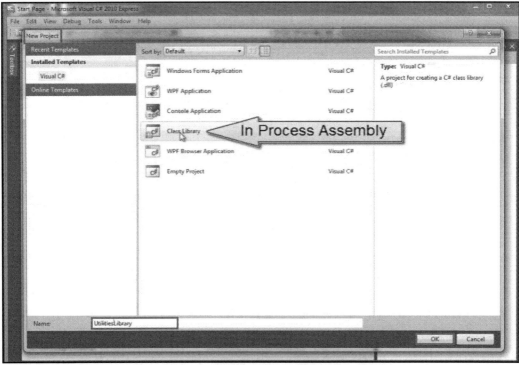

Figure 9.4 Create a new Class Library project named UtilitiesLibrary.

Immediately you will notice there is no Main( ) method. Unlike .exe assemblies, in-process assemblies don't initiate a program. They wait until they're called upon (see Figure 9.5).

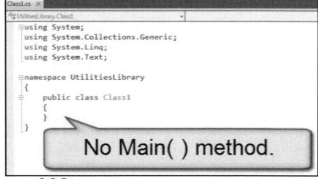

Figure 9.5 In-process assemblies have no Main( ) method.

Consuming an In-Process Assembly

Replace the general "Class1" with the more meaningful class name, "Methods." We are going to create a method which will return your OS version. (Initially we will accomplish this using a string value, and later we will have the program actually check our machine to detect the OS version and return that information to the calling app.)

Add the public static string with the method, GetOSVersion( ). Have your return statement initially display the message "I have a cool OS". End your code with the ; (semicolon) delimiter (see Figure 9.6). *Save your file before proceeding.*

```csharp
using System;
using System.Collections.Generic;
using System.Linq;
using System.Text;

namespace UtilitiesLibrary
{
    public class Methods
    {

        public static string GetOSVersion()
        {
            return "I have a cool OS";
        }

    }
}
```

Figure 9.6 Write the code for our first in-process assembly, UtilitiesLibrary.

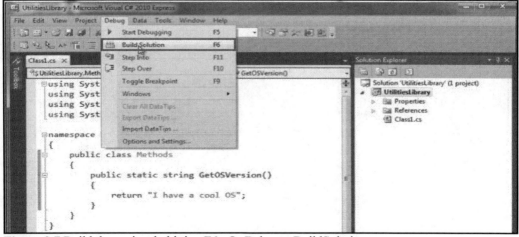

Figure 9.7 Build the project byhitting F6. Or Debug > BuildSolution.

Once you have successfully built the project without errors (either by hitting F6 or clicking BuildSolution, as shown in Figure 9.7), close out of the project. Our next step will be to create a brand new project that will consume UtilitiesLibrary.dll, the in-process assembly that we just built.

Launch Visual Studio and create a New Project, which you will name "GetOSAndCallDLL." The project type will be Console Application.

Be sure to click OK to create this project. Save it in the C:\Joes2Pros\C#Stuff folder before proceeding.

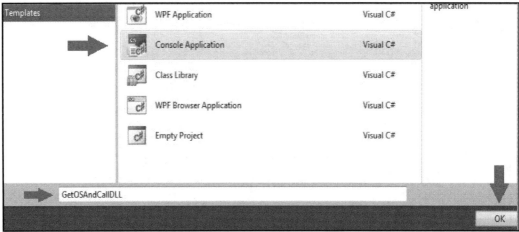

Figure 9.8 Since this is a Console Application, it will be an .exe (i.e., out-of-process assembly).

We know that the DLL we just created and the .exe we are about to create will need to work together (see Figure 9.9). Before writing any code in our calling application (GetOSAndCallDLL), we first need to detour to take a step which will allow our .exe to locate and reference our .dll file.

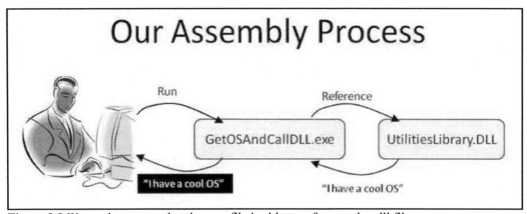

Figure 9.9 We need to ensure that the .exe file is able to reference the .dll file.

Adding a Reference

Navigate to the UtilitiesLibrary.dll file on your hard drive:

Open your Joes2Pros folder > C#Stuff > UtilitiesLibrary > bin > Release > UtilitiesLibrary.dll (please note that depending on your machine setup and Visual Studio version, your DLL may be located in the Debug folder).

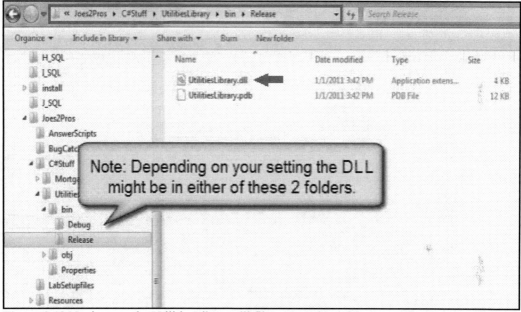

Figure 9.10 Navigate to the UtilitiesLibrary.dll file on your hard drive.

Let's return to our Console Application and add a reference to this DLL, so that our process can consume the information from the DLL. From within the project GetOSAndCallDLL, expand the References folder in the Solution Explorer.

Right-click to Add Reference (see Figure 9.11).

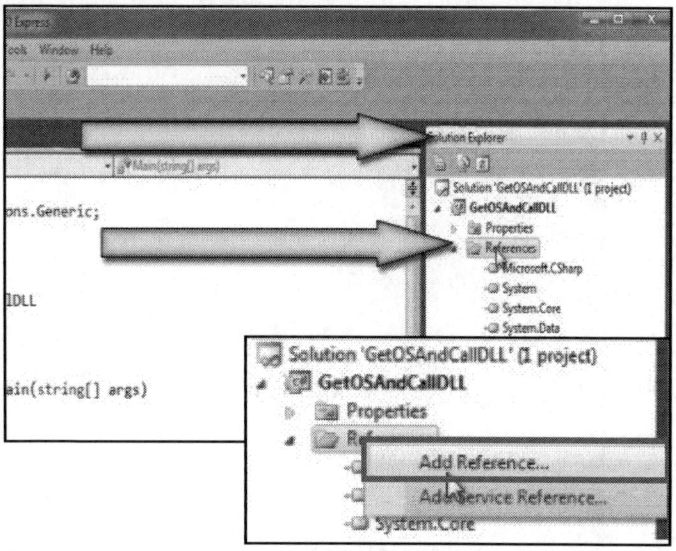

With the Add Reference

Figure 9.11 These steps will launch the Add Reference dialog.

dialog open, click the Browse tab and traverse the same path you used earlier (Figure 9.10) to locate the UtilitiesLibrary.dll file.

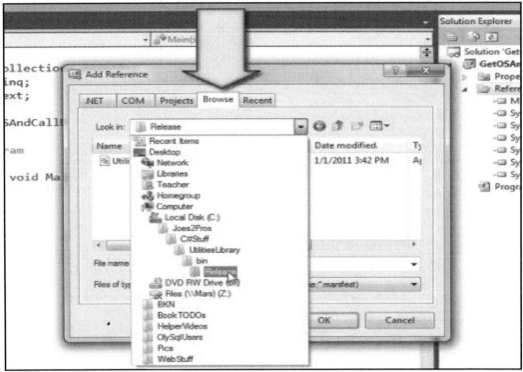

Figure 9.12 From within the Add Reference dialog, navigate to the UtilitiesLibrary.dll file.

Click OK when you locate the file. Notice it immediately appears in your Solution Explorer and is ready for use (see Figure 9.13).

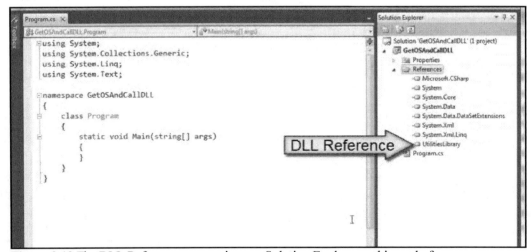

Figure 9.13 The DLL Reference appears in your Solution Explorer and is ready for use.

Using a Reference

With the reference to the DLL in place, we can now use it in our code. We will call it from the Main method (from Chap 8, recall that static void Main( ) is C#'s way of saying "begin here").

We know the goal of our assembly process (Figure 9.14) is to have the .exe file call the .dll file. Inside of our code block, we're going to have the Main( ) method consume the information from the DLL and show it to the Console. Thus, when we're done, the user will call the .exe (i.e., the out-of-process assembly) which will call the DLL (i.e., the in-process assembly). It will return the "I have a cool OS" back to the out-of-process assembly which will turn it into a Console Writeline (see Figure 9.15).

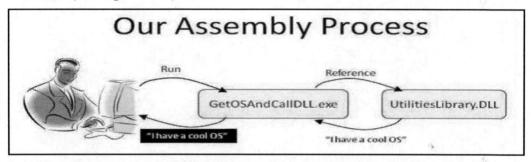

Figure 9.14 The goal of our assembly process (originally shown in Figure 9.9).

```csharp
Program.cs* ×
GetOSAndCallDLL.Program                          ▾  Main(string[] args)        ▾
 using System;
 using System.Collections.Generic;
 using System.Linq;
 using System.Text;

 namespace GetOSAndCallDLL
 {
     class Program
     {
         static void Main(string[] args)
         {
             string s = UtilitiesLibrary.Methods.GetOSVersion();
             Console.WriteLine(s);
             Console.ReadLine();
         }
     }
 }
```

Figure 9.15 Our code block inside of the .exe file which will call the .dll file.

Once your code is identical to Figure 9.15, save your file before proceeding. Using the same steps we took earlier to build our UtilitiesLibrary project, build the project by hitting F6 or Debug > BuildSolution. Then hit F5 or the green "Start Debugging" icon to compile (i.e. to run) the program (see Figure 9.16).

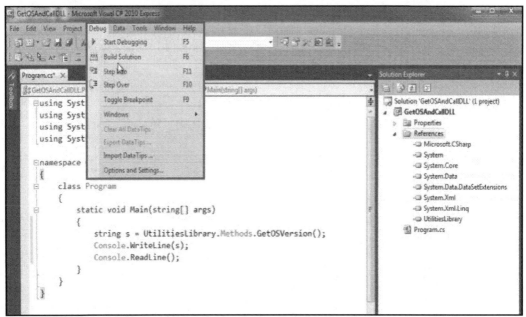

Figure 9.16 Hit F6 and F5 to build and compile the GetOSAndCallDLL.exe program.

The WriteLine outputs the message, "I have a cool OS" to the Console.

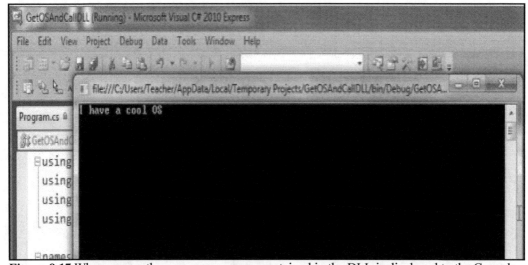

Figure 9.17 When we run the .exe, our message contained in the DLL is displayed to the Console.

Observe that the Console message displays the information contained in our DLL file. If we change the DLL, we can change exactly what the out-of-process assembly that consumes the DLL says. So let's close out of this project (GetOSAndCallDLL) and return to the DLL file. (BE SURE TO SAVE YOUR .EXE FILE LOCALLY, IF YOU HAVEN'T ALREADY DONE SO.)

Re-open your UtilitiesLibrary project:

Launch Visual Studio > Recent Projects > "UtilitiesLibrary"

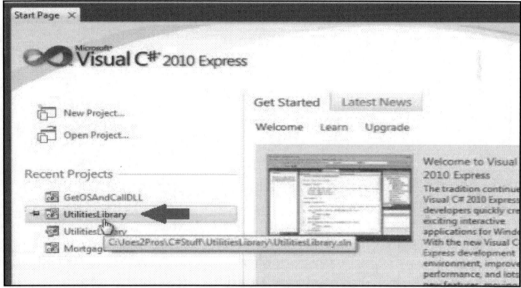

Figure 9.18 Return to the UtilitiesLibrary (DLL) project.

We are going to modify our "I have a cool OS" message (see Figure 9.19).

```
using System;
using System.Collections.Generic;
using System.Linq;
using System.Text;

namespace UtilitiesLibrary
{
    public class Methods
    {

        public static string GetOSVersion()
        {
            return "I have a cool OS";
        }

    }
}
```

Solution 'UtilitiesLibrary' (1 p
  UtilitiesLibrary
    Properties
    References
    Class1.cs

Figure 9.19 This is our current code. We will change this message (see Figure 9.20).

In place of "I have a cool OS", we will have the return command send the message string "Windows 7" (see Figure 9.20).

```
Class1.cs ×
UtilitiesLibrary.Methods                          GetOSVersion()
using System;
using System.Collections.Generic;
using System.Linq;
using System.Text;

namespace UtilitiesLibrary
{
    public class Methods
    {
        public static string GetOSVersion()
        {
            return "Windows 7";
        }
    }
}
```

Figure 9.20 We are changing our DLL message to "Windows 7."

Save this project. Build it. And then close it. Our next step will be to return to our .exe project (GetOSAndCallDLL). Without making a single change, our calling app will now run differently because of this change we just made to the DLL.

Figure 9.21 Return to the GetOSAndCallDLL (EXE) project.

Let's go ahead and execute this. Notice that the message now says "Windows 7."

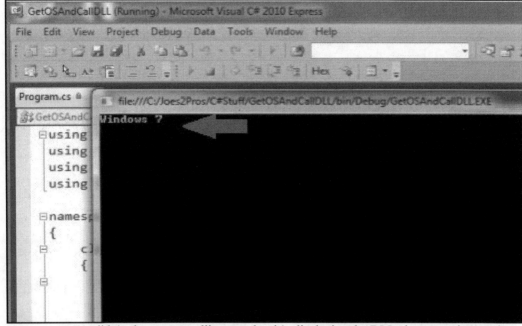

Figure 9.22 We didn't change our calling app, but it's displaying the DLL change we just made.

What's happening is that the string is set to this Reference's method, GetOSVersion( ). That's returning the string which says Windows 7.

Thus, the DLL is our in-process assembly that's helping to drive data that feeds the out-of-process asssembly.

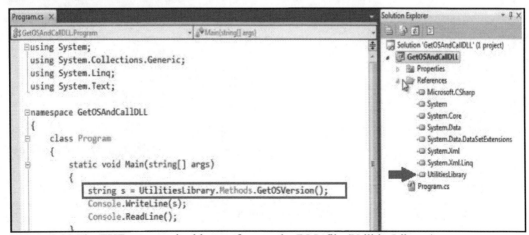

Figure 9.23 The EXE program is able to reference the DLL file (UtilitiesLibrary).

307

Updating Your In-Process Assembly

If you update your DLL, you need to make sure the .exe will use the new DLL file to get the new information. We will change the DLL from a hard-coded message to one that dynamically pulls out the true OS version.

Before we make the change, notice that our in-process assembly (in other words, the DLL file UtilitiesLibrary.dll) was last updated at about 3:46 pm.

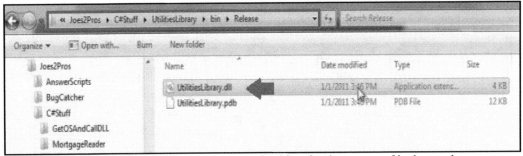

Figure 9.24 Before we modify the DLL, we are checking the timestamp of its last update.

It's now 3:47pm. We will make a change where the DLL will find your operating system version, and then it's going to dynamically return that info.

Start your Visual Studio and open up your UtilitiesLibrary project.

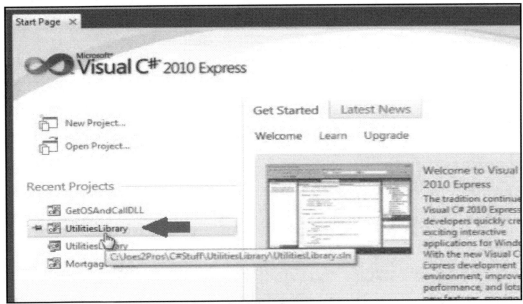

Figure 9.25 Return to the UtilitiesLibrary (DLL) project.

When we re-open the project, we see our code with the familiar Windows 7 messaging (see Figure 9.26).

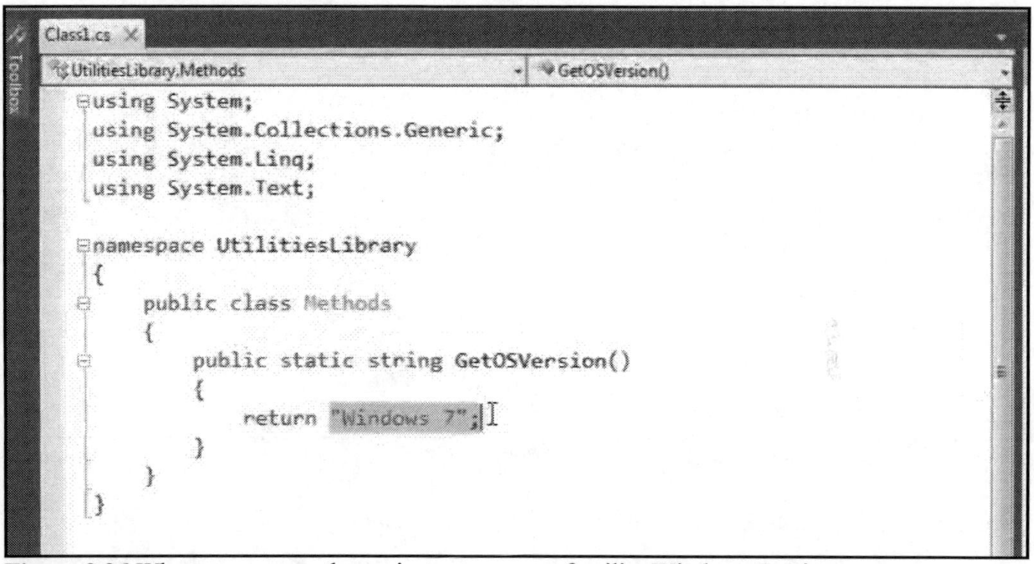

Figure 9.26 When we re-open the project, we see our familiar Windows 7 string message.

Replace the hardcoded message with this code:

System.Environment.OSVersion.ToString( );

Be sure to save your project, build it (F6 or BuildSolution), and close it.

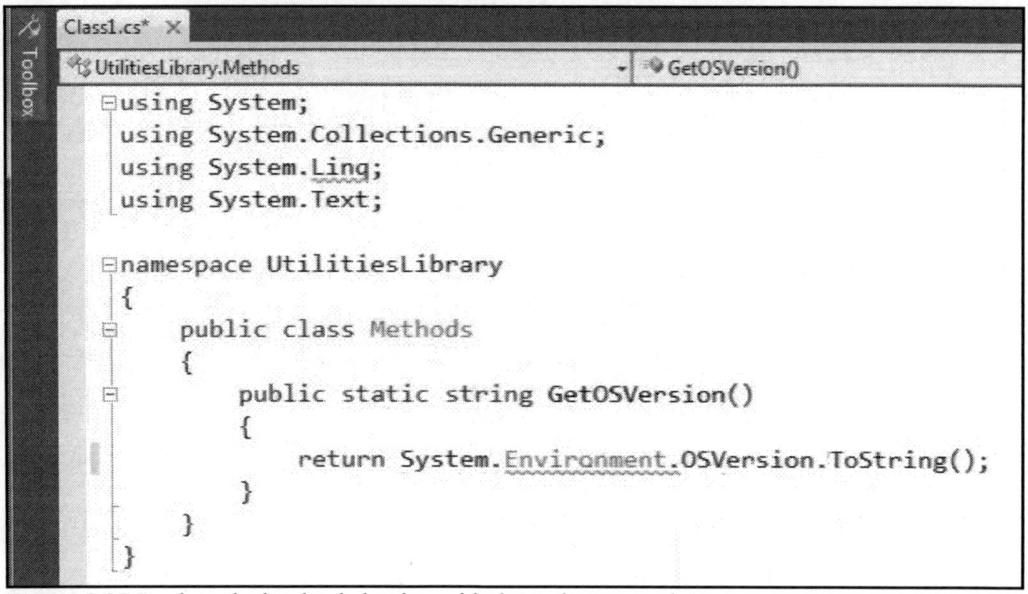

Figure 9.27 Replace the hardcoded string with the code you see here.

309

After we close the DLL project and re-check the directory, we see the new timestamp (3:47 PM) confirming that the DLL file has been updated.

This newer DLL has a new instruction set. So when you call on it now, it's going to return your actual operating system (OS) version.

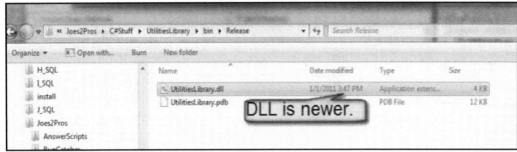

Figure 9.28 The revised DLL shows a later timestamp.

Return one last time to the GetOSAndCallDLL project (see Figure 9.29).

Figure 9.29 Return to the GetOSAndCallDLL (EXE) project.

We see our code is unchanged (it is the same as previously shown in Figure 9.23).

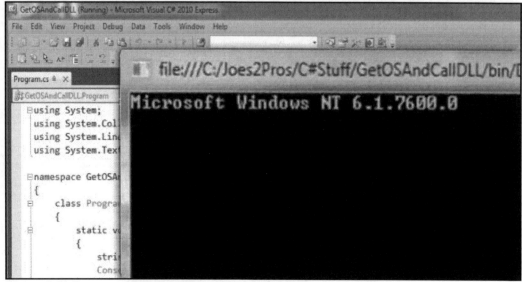

```
using System;
using System.Collections.Generic;
using System.Linq;
using System.Text;

namespace GetOSAndCallDLL
{
    class Program
    {
        static void Main(string[] args)
        {
            string s = UtilitiesLibrary.Methods.GetOSVersion();
            Console.WriteLine(s);
            Console.ReadLine();
        }
    }
}
```

Figure 9.30 Our code is unchanged.

Let's run the program. We didn't change the EXE, but it picked up on the change to our DLL. Our out-of-process assembly (EXE) is calling on our in-process assembly (DLL) and displaying my precise OS version (see Figure 9.31).

```
file:///C:/Joes2Pros/C#Stuff/GetOSAndCallDLL/bin/[
Microsoft Windows NT 6.1.7600.0
```

Figure 9.31 Our assembly process has achieved our goal.

Lab 9.1: In-Process Assemblies

Lab Prep: Before you can begin the lab you must run the SQLInteropChapter9.1Setup.sql script. *Please note there is no need to run this script if you already ran any script in Chapters 7-10.*

Skill Check 1: Add a new method to the in-process assembly called GetBookName which has the code you see below. Get the out-of-process assembly to capture the value of the GetBookName method of the DLL and show it to the Console.

```
public static string GetBookName()
{
    return "Joes 2 Pros Vol-5";
}
```

```
file:///C:/Joes2Pros/C#Stuff/GetOSAndCallDLL/bin/Debug/GetOSA
Microsoft Windows NT 5.2.3790 Service Pack 1
Joes 2 Pros Vol-5
```

Figure 9.32 Skill Check 1

Answer Code: The T-SQL code to this lab can be found in the downloadable files in a file named Lab9.1_InProcessAssemblies.sql.

In-Process Assemblies - Points to Ponder

1. An assembly whose extension ends in .dll is known as an in-process assembly.

2. DLL is short for **dynamic-link library**.

3. Code that is managed in Microsoft's common language runtime (CLR) is called managed code.

4. Code that is managed by your Operating System is called unmanaged code.

5. You can create managed code using a .NET Framework language, such as Visual Basic .NET or Visual C#.

6. Although you can write the same type of code using Transact-SQL, managed code does a better job of handling calculations and complex execution logic.

Managed Code in SQL Server

SQL Server has its own built-in CLR, which is the SQL CLR. SQL Server 2005 and 2008 are fully capable of running managed code.

SQL Server can only run in-process assemblies (e.g., DLL files). It will not run executable files.

Note: In order to perform the steps in this section, you must have first completed Lab 9.1.

Our first SQL CLR example will utilize the same DLL we just created with C# code (LibraryUtilities.dll). In fact, the demonstration in this section parallels the previous demonstration. Since the DLL has already been created, we will use SQL Server to perform the same tasks done by the executable (the out-of-process assembly GetOSAndCallDLL.exe) in the previous Visual Studio example.

Enabling the SQL CLR

You probably will need to enable the SQL CLR on your system (see Figure 9.33). For security reasons, SQL Server disables the CLR access by default.

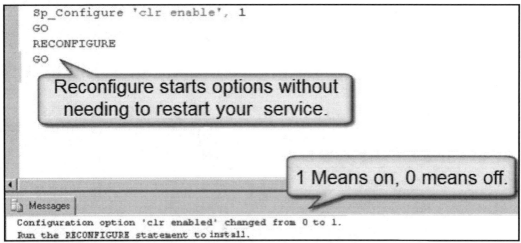

Figure 9.33 This code will enable the SQL CLR on your system.

Referencing a DLL (Dynamic-Link Library)

Recall we had to explicitly add a Reference to the DLL's filepath inside the EXE project file (shown earlier in Figures 9.10-9.13) in order for the executable to locate and reference the DLL.

SQL Server includes a similar step in order to communicate with a DLL. This is accomplished with a CREATE ASSEMBLY statement.

We would like to use the DLL created in the last section (UtilitiesLibrary.dll). This code (see Figure 9.34) will allow the DLL to access our SQL Server. Since it's the same file we used previously, you should recognize the same filepath we traversed earlier (as shown in Figures 9.10, 9.12, and 9.28).

```
CREATE ASSEMBLY JProCoUtilities
FROM 'C:\Joes2Pros\Resources\C#Stuff\UtilitiesLibrary\bin\Release\UtilitiesLibrary.dll'
WITH PERMISSION SET = SAFE
```

Figure 9.34 This code gives us the ability to have SQL Server communicate with the DLL .

We just read that the DLL has already been created and that in this section SQL Server will work with the DLL. This is true for most readers, and if you successfully ran the above CREATE ASSEMBLY statement, then you are able to proceed to the next step (see Figure 9.39 – the assembly figure).

However, readers who used Visual Studio 2010 to create their DLL may have gotten this error (see Figure 9.35) and will need to make one small adjustment before proceeding. At the time of this writing, SQL Server 2008 requires assemblies to be set to .NET Framework 3.5 in order to interact with them. VS2010 is built on .NET Framework 4.0. Follow the steps in Figures 9.36-9.37 in order to remedy this situation.

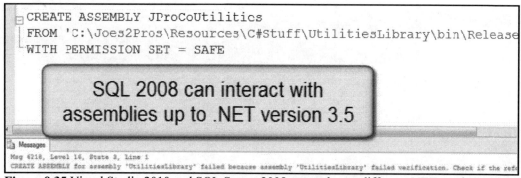

Figure 9.35 Visual Studio 2010 and SQL Server 2008 currently use different .NET versions.

Open the project file for this in-process assembly (e.g., DLL) in Visual Studio. In the Solution Explorer, right-click the project file and select Properties.

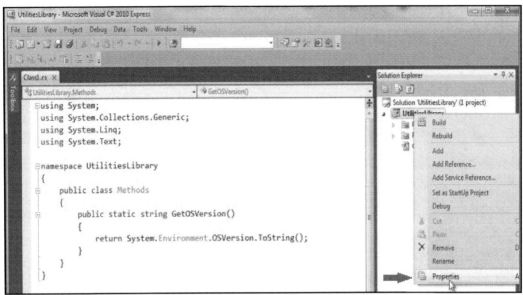

Figure 9.36 Open the project file for UtilitiesLibrary.dll and open its Properties.

On the Application tab, change the "Target framework" dropdown value from ".NET Framework 4" to ".NET Framework 3.5" (see Figure 9.37) and click "Yes" when the Target Framework Change message box opens and asks if you're sure you want to make this change. After this change, save and then build the solution (F6 or Debug > BuildSolution).

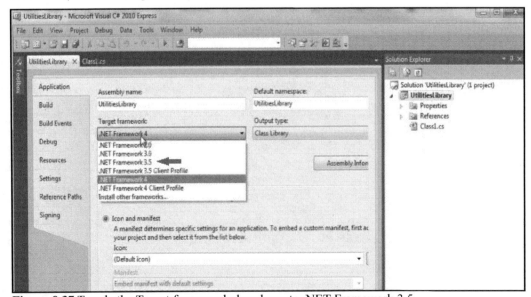

Figure 9.37 Toggle the Target framework dropdown to .NET Framework 3.5.

The CREATE ASSEMBLY code will now run successfully (see Figure 9.38).

Figure 9.38 All readers should now be able to create the JProCoUtilities assembly.

This query uses the PERMISSION_SET option. (PERMISSION_SET = SAFE) The next section of this chapter will address SQL permission levels with respect to external files (e.g., DLL files).

Using a DLL

The assembly we just created, JProCoUtilities, contains every class and method which is found in UtilitiesLibrary.dll (see Figure 9.39). Therefore, these now are all potentially available for our use in SQL Server.

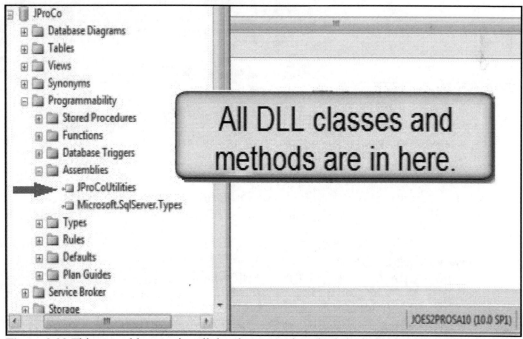

Figure 9.39 This assembly contains all the classses and methods included in UtilitiesLibrary.dll.

While we can't query or directly call on JProCoUtilities, we just need to create a programming object inside of SQL Server for each of the DLL's methods or functions which we want to use in SQL Server. Our CREATE FUNCTION or CREATE PROC statements will reference the assembly (AS EXTERNAL NAME JProCoUtilities…).

One method we created in UtilitiesLibrary.dll is GetOSVersion( ) (Figure 9.27).

We will create a function GetOSVersion( ) in SQL Server

(see Figure 9.41).

```
UtilitiesLibrary.Methods                    GetOSVersion()
using System;
using System.Collections.Generic;
using System.Ling;
using System.Text;

namespace UtilitiesLibrary
{
    public class Methods
    {
        public static string GetOSVersion()
        {
            return System.Environment.OSVersion.ToString();
        }
    }
}
```

Figure 9.40 We wrote this method using Visual C-Sharp.

Figure 9.41 We want to use the UtilitiesLibrary.dll's GetOSVersion( ) method in SQL Server.

Before we can write the query to create the GetOSVersion( ) function, we need to review a few points regarding the structure and terminology of the Visual C# code module which built GetOSVersion( ). Similar to the way we must specify the filepath (C:\Joes2Pros\Resources\C#Stuff\UtilitiesLibrary\bin\Release\UtilitiesLibrary.dll) in order to reference the DLL (as we saw in Figure 9.38), we also need to specify the fully qualified name to path to it within our SQL Assembly (JProCoUtilities):

- When referring to an assembly using the EXTERNAL NAME clause (as we will see later in Figure 9.43), we need to bear in mind that we are calling Visual C# and the fully qualified name is case-sensitive.

- If the .NET assembly does not have a namespace, then refer to it in SQL Server by *SQLAssemblyName.ClassName.FunctionName*.

- If the .NET assembly does have a namespace, then refer to it in SQL Server by *SQLAssemblyName.[Namespace.ClassName].FunctionName*.

Since our assembly in this case (UtilitiesLibrary.dll) has a namespace, our query will need to reflect *SQLAssemblyName.[Namespace.ClassName].FunctionName*.

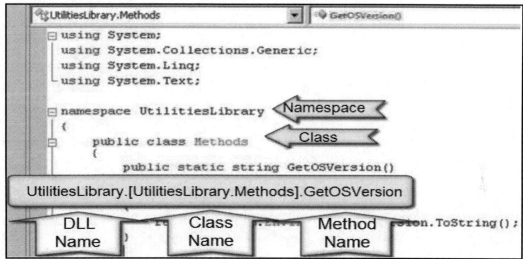

Figure 9.42 The structure and syntax of the C# code module which created UtilitiesLibrary.dll.

We have the fully qualified name of the method to include in the AS EXTERNAL NAME clause of our CREATE FUNCTION query (see Figure 9.43).

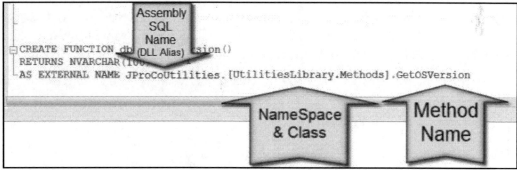

Figure 9.43 The fully-qualified name appears in our CREATE FUNCTION statement.

Run the code you see here (Figure 9.44) to create the function.

```
CREATE FUNCTION dbo.GetOSVersion()
RETURNS NVARCHAR(100)
AS EXTERNAL NAME JProCoUtilities.[UtilitiesLibrary.Methods].GetOSVersion
```

Messages
Command(s) completed successfully.

Figure 9.44 This code creates the function dbo.GetOSVersion( ).

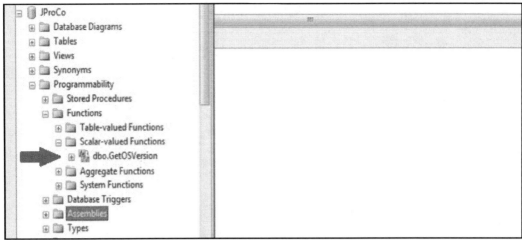

Figure 9.45 The location of the function dbo.GetOSVersion( ) in Object Explorer.

Executing Managed Code From T-SQL

Our final step will be to have the SQL CLR execute the managed code and receive some return information. We would like to have the SQL CLR repeat the demonstration from this chapter's first section and check our hard drive to obtain the name and version of the operating system (OS) we are running.

We just created the function GetOSVersion( ) as an object in the JProCo database. When we invoke this function in SQL Server, it achieves the same effect as when we ran the EXE in Visual Studio and called on the DLL.

Notice that this result is identical to our final result in the Visual Studio example (see Figure 9.31).

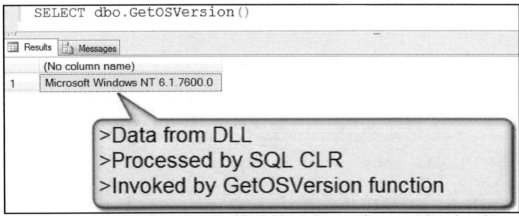

Figure 9.46 The SQL CLR inspects our local hard drive and returns the name and version of the OS which we are currently running. The SQL CLR has detected that we're running Windows 7 Pro (Version 6.1, Build 7600).

When we created the JProCoUtilities assembly, SQL Server embedded a copy of the DLL in the JProCo database. In fact, if we were to delete UtilitiesLibrary.dll from our hard drive, the SQL assembly (JProCoUtilities) would still run since it contains a copy of all of UtilitiesLibrary.dll's classes and methods.

The SQL CLR uses this copy of the DLL to accomplish the same work done by UtilitiesLibrary.dll. For example, it just inspected our local hard drive and returned the name and version of the OS

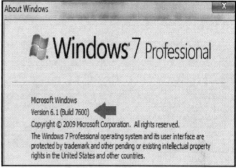

Figure 9.47 Windows Version 6.1.7600.0

which we are currently running.

Lab 9.2: Managed Code in SQL

Lab Prep: Before you can begin the lab you must run the SQLInteropChapter9.2Setup.sql script. *Please note there is no need to run this script if you already ran any script in Chapters 7-10.*

Skill Check 1: In JProCo Create the dbo.GetBookName( ) function from the GetbookName fuction of the DLL. Call on the SQL function. Your result should resemble the figure below.

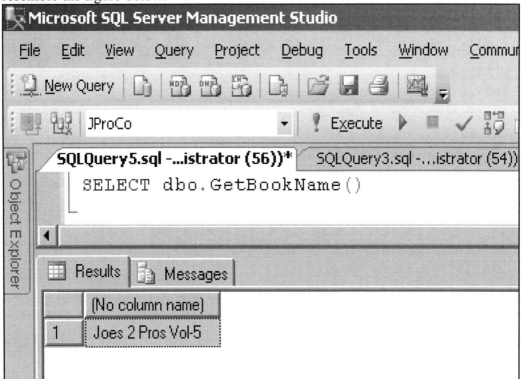

Figure 9.48 Skill Check 1 result.

Skill Check 2: Enable the SQL CLR in the dbBasic database.

Skill Check 3: Create an assembly named dbBasicsUtilities in the dbBasics db based on the in-process assembly C:\Joes2Pros\Resources\C#Stuff\UtilitiesLibrary\bin\Debug\UtilitiesLibrary.dll.

Skill Check 4: In dbBasics, create the dbo.GetBookName( ) function from the GetBookName function of the DLL. Call on the SQL function. Your result should resemble the figure below.

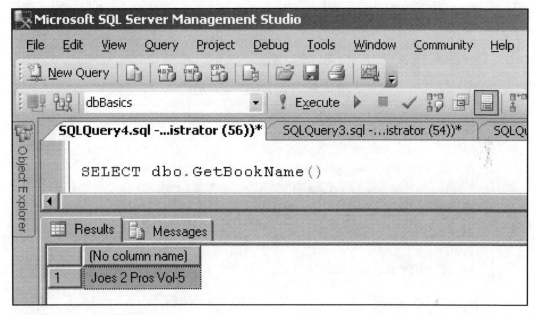

Figure 9.49 Skill Check 4 result.

Answer Code: The T-SQL code to this lab can be found in the downloadable files in a file named Lab9.2_ManagedCodeInSQL.sql

Managed Code in SQL - Points to Ponder

1. In SQL Server 2005 and 2008 you can use managed code and implement these assemblies as database objects.

2. SQL Server supports the use of in-process assemblies (DLL's) through the SQL CLR.

3. By default, SQL Server does not allow you to run managed code. To run managed code, enable the CLR by running sp_configure 'clr enable'.

4. Significant setting changes may require you to stop and restart the SQL Server service. (*Example:* sp_configure 'clr enable'). The RECONFIGURE keyword allows the setting to be implemented without a service stop and restart.

5. To enable CLR in SQL Server, you must have ALTER SETTINGS permissions at the server level (i.e., you must be a member of the sysadmin or serveradmin roles).

6. To use managed code within SQL Server 2005 or 2008, you must create a managed assembly, import it into the database, and configure its security options.

7. SQL Server can load "in-process" assemblies (DLL) but not "out-of-process" (EXE) assemblies.

8. Assemblies must consist of only one file because SQL Server 2005 and 2008 do not support multi-file assemblies.

9. Use managed code when:
   o You want to access the functionality of the .NET Framework.
   o The code performs complex logic that is CPU-intensive.
   o You want the code to run on the client side to leverage the processing power of the client computer rather than tax the server.

10. Use T-SQL when:
   o The code primarily accesses data and has little or no procedural logic.
   o The code can run on the server without impacting performance.

11. CPU functionality runs much faster in managed code versus the same task performed with T-SQL.

12. Intensive calculations run more efficiently in CLR stored procs than in T-SQL based stored procs.

13. When you refer to a .NET assembly from the EXTERNAL NAME clause, you must remember you are calling C# and the fully qualified name is case-sensitive.

14. If your .NET assembly does not have a namespace, then refer to it in SQL Server by *SQLAssemblyName.ClassName.FunctionName*.

15. If your .NET assembly does have a namespace then refer to it in SQL Server by *SQLAssemblyName.[Namespace.ClassName].FunctionName*.

16. If you have lightweight pooling enabled, you must first disable it before enabling CLR on your system.

Code Access Permissions

We often read or see television stories featuring people participating in "extreme sports", such as skydiving or bungee jumping. Being safety conscious, most people tend to avoid dangerous activities. Similarly, we know that SQL Server is an extremely security-conscious platform. The groundbreaking 2005 version of SQL Server made security a top priority and introduced a revolutionary security model.

One important way that SQL Server protects your data and your system is that it restricts its own access to files and programs which are external to SQL Server. Like nearly every networked platform and program in existence in the last two decades, SQL Server has been targeted by black-hats seeking to gain notoriety and wreak havoc. Prior to the 2005 version, it had been targeted by hackers who would attempt to control your system (and hopefully your network) by infiltrating SQL Server and using malicious code to compromise your data and spread viruses and worms.

In our last example, we saw that SQL Server will not access external files or programs without explicit permission having been set by someone with a very high level of access (e.g., a system admin). We also saw that the default setting for SQL CLR is OFF (see Figure 9.33) and we had to reconfigure our system in order to enable the CLR.

As a trusted enterprise platform and RDBMS, SQL Server is there to support your system – not dominate it or leave it vulnerable. This level of safety may limit some potential "cool tricks" which your users may occasionally want to try out with SQL Server. Just as the last two decades have taught us to be wary of "cool apps" or interesting links we receive via email, we recognize the tradeoff for us (and our users) not being able to do "cool tricks" on the fly involving SQL Server is well worth it.

As IT professionals, we recognize the importance of keeping data and systems safe and can appreciate the protection provided by SQL Server's robust security model. SQL Server's renowned security is big part of the success of SQL Server in the enterprise space. *(And that increased success and marketshare is no doubt why many of us are studying this series to gain or update our SQL skills!!)*

SQL Server provides an array of options so that system admins can judiciously modify code access permissions to accommodate necessary operations, such as using managed code.

Permission Call Stack

Being over 21, I have the permission to enter any bar or tavern I choose to. However, my young nephew does not have permssion to do that. If I tried to bring him along when I entered a bar and said, "He's with me," should they let in a child simply because I say so? No. Besides that it's just a bad idea to have a child in a bar, that would also jeopardize the bar owner (who is subject to tight regulations and could lose his license to serve liquor), as well as even jeopardize me (I could be cited for contributing to the delinquency of a minor).

However, I would be allowed to take him to an R-rated movie which he could not access on his own. There are places which children can access freely, places where children are permitted only if accompanied by an adult, and places where they are forbidden. There are also places where adults may not go unless accompanied by a child, such as the childrens reading area of the public library.

The case of the bar or tavern is an example of a full **permission call stack**. The bar said I could come in but disallowed my bringing a child along with me. The bar did a check of our permissions and said "no way."

In our demonstration, we will observe a scenario where SQL Server has access to a DLL file (UtilitiesLibrary.dll). SQL Server and the DLL work well together until SQL Server needs to access a file to which the DLL has permissions but SQL doesn't. We will see SQL Server throw an error and refuse to proceed until we change the permissions.

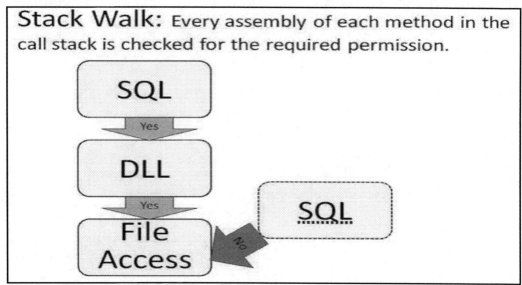

Figure 9.50 If SQL Server doesn't have direct access to a resource, it won't allow itself to access it under any circumstances. Think of SQL as a very stubborn and strict enforcer of the rules.

External Resources

SQL Server polices itself and won't allow itself to access any information or resource for which it doesn't have direct permissions. In our demonstration you will see SQL Server deny itself access to a file (MortgageRate.txt). The DLL (UtlilitiesLibrary.dll) has full access to be able to read this file, and SQL Server has access to the DLL. But when we ask SQL Server to run the process which involves reading the MortgageRate.txt file, it throws up a red flag and forces us to explicitly grant it permission to the text file before it will proceed.

SQL Server's preference is to access only SQL resources. There is rarely anything outside of SQL Server (such as files or folders) that your SQL Server needs to interact with. Therefore, such external resources are usually assumed to be off-limits. If SQL Server is interacting with other areas of your system, it is extremely cautious and assumes it may be being asked to this as part of a malicious attack. As SQL Admins, our safest practice is to adhere to this model and seek to restrict SQL Server's access to external resources as much as possible. (And to make sure that we trust those resources which we allow to connect to our pristine SQL Server environment.) In our demonstration, we will temporarily unrestrict SQL Server's permissions to access our hard drive and all of our files (PERMISSION_SET = UNSAFE) (Figures 9.58 and 9.62).

Recap of Assemblies in SQL

In order to examine code access permissions, we need to generate some changes to the managed code and resources which SQL Server and the SQL CLR are consuming.

Our existing SQL assembly, JProCoUtilities, currently contains two methods: dbo.GetOSVersion( ) and dbo.GetBookName( ).

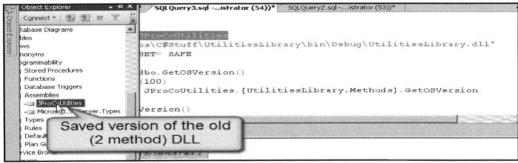

Figure 9.51 The embedded DLL (aliased JProCoUtilities) currently contains two methods.

We will update the DLL (i.e., the native Visual C# file) to add a third method, GetMortgageRates( ). We then must update the SQL assembly (JProCoUtilities) and create a new function dbo.GetRates( ).

The GetMortgageRates( ) method is based on the MortgageReader app we created in the last chapter (Figures 8.70-8.90). The new SQL Server function, dbo.GetRates( ), will similarly call on an assembly which will read a text file on our hard drive and return mortgage rate data. Since that will all be accomplished by the SQL CLR, we will be pressed at multiple points to ensure that we have granted SQL Server direct permissions to any needed files or environments to which it doesn't already have access.

Before we change anything, let's observe that the DLL's latest timestamp ("Date modified") shows 1/2/2011 at 6:00PM. After we modify this DLL, we will re-check the timestamp so that we may observe that the DLL file has been changed in Visual Studio.

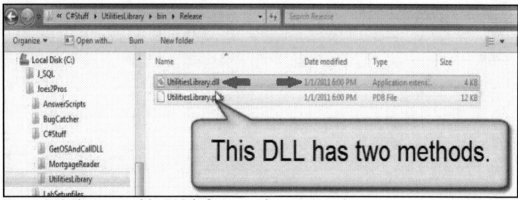

Figure 9.52 Timestamp of the DLL before more changes are made.

Let's also observe that the two VS methods currently contained in the DLL, GetOSVersion( ) and GetBookName( ), have no need to access files on the C drive.

Figure 9.53 Currently the UtilitiesLibrary.dll has no need to access files on the hard drive.

Open your UtilitiesLibrary project in Visual Studio and update it by adding the code shown here (Figure 9.54) for the GetMortgageRates( ) method. Be sure to also add the statement at the top ("using System.IO;"). After adding the code, save the file and Build Solution (F6) to ensure that it runs without errors.

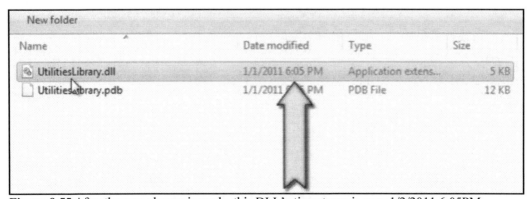

```csharp
using System;
using System.Collections.Generic;
using System.Linq;
using System.Text;
using System.IO;

namespace UtilitiesLibrary
{
    public class Methods
    {
        public static string GetOSVersion()
        {
            return System.Environment.OSVersion.ToString();
        }

        public static string GetBookName()
        {
            return "Joes 2 Pros Vol-5";
        }

        public static string GetMortgageRates()
        {
            StreamReader sr = new StreamReader(@"C:\Joes2Pros\Resources\MortgageRate.txt");
            string s = sr.ReadToEnd();
            return s;
        }
    }
}
```

Figure 9.54 Add this code to the UtilitiesLibrary.Methods code module.

Name	Date modified	Type	Size
UtilitiesLibrary.dll	1/1/2011 6:05 PM	Application extens..	5 KB
UtilitiesLibrary.pdb	1/1/2011 ... PM	PDB File	12 KB

Figure 9.55 After the new change is made, this DLL's timestamp is now 1/2/2011 6:05PM.

Revise your CREATE ASSEMBLY statement (from Figure 9.38) and rerun it as an ALTER ASSEMBLY in order to update the SQL assembly, JProCoUtilities.

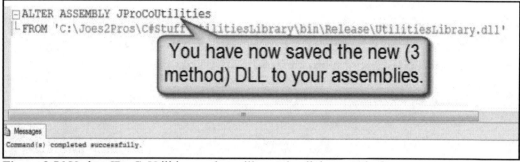

Figure 9.56 Update JProCoUtilities, so that will contain all three methods.

Now create the new function dbo.GetRates( ).

```
CREATE FUNCTION dbo.GetRates()
RETURNS NVARCHAR(100)
AS EXTERNAL NAME JProCoUtilities.[UtilitiesLibrary.Methods].GetMortgageRates
```

Messages

Command(s) completed successfully.

Figure 9.57 Create the new function dbo.GetRates( ).

Attempt to run the function and notice that SQL Server doesn't have permission to read files from your hard drive. This is the stack walk example described earlier (shown in Figure 9.50). SQL Server has access to the DLL but refuses to read a file on your hard drive without being granted these permissions.

The error message is verbose, but we see multiple mentions of System.Security.SecurityException, System.Security.CodeAccessSecurityEngine, and System.Security.CodeAccessPermission (see Figure 9.58).

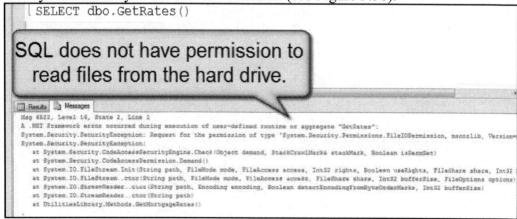

Figure 9.58 SQL Server doesn't have permission to read files from the hard drive.

331

Even if you set SQL's permissions to the most unrestricted level (UNSAFE - see Figure 9.59), SQL Server still won't allow itself permission to access the text file on your hard drive.

In order for a database to be authorized to set the UNSAFE permission level, the db must first be established as *trustworthy* across your entire system. This error message tells us we will first have to set JProCo's status to trustworthy.

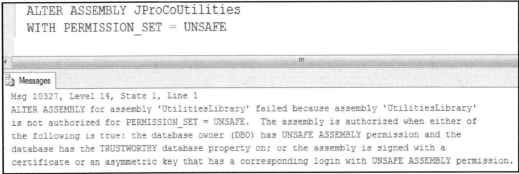

Figure 9.59 For a db to give itself more permissions than SQL Server, it must be trustworthy.

There are two ways we can locate a databases's trustworthy status. Use the query below to check the trustworthy status for JProCo (0 = OFF, 1 = ON).

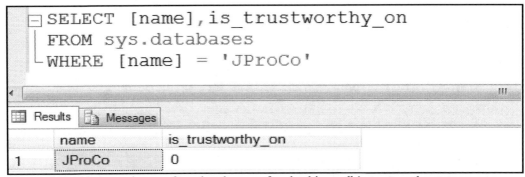

Figure 9.60 This query is one of two handy ways for checking a db's trustworthy status.

Run this ALTER DATABASE statement setting JProCo's trustworthy status to ON. (*Note:* if you are not a system admin, this code may not run properly.)

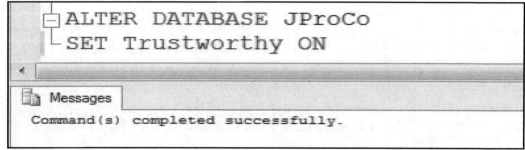

```
ALTER DATABASE JProCo
SET Trustworthy ON
```

Messages

Command(s) completed successfully.

Figure 9.61 This syntax will change the trustworthy status of a database.

Looking at a database's properties in Object Explorer Details is another handy tool for checking a database's trustworthy status. Navigate to the database in Object Explorer and click on it to highlight the db. Then choose Object Explorer Details from the View menu (see Figure 9.62).

Object Explorer Details

Search

. (SQL Server 10.0.2531 - MoreTechA6\Student)\Databases

Name	Policy Health State	Recovery Model	Compatibility Level	Collation	Owner
System Databases					
Database Snapshots					
dbBasics	Full	100	SQL_Latin1_General_CP1_CI_AS	MoreTechA6\Student
dbMovie	Full	100	SQL_Latin1_General_CP1_CI_AS	MoreTechA6\Student
dbSkillCheck	Full	100	SQL_Latin1_General_CP1_CI_AS	MoreTechA6\Student
dbTester	Full	100	SQL_Latin1_General_CP1_CI_AS	MoreTechA6\Student
JProCo	Full	100	SQL_Latin1_General_CP1_CI_AS	MoreTechA6\Student
RatisCo (Read-Only)	Full	100	SQL_Latin1_General_CP1_CI_AS	MoreTechA6\Student
TSQLTestDB	Full	100	SQL_Latin1_General_CP1_CI_AS	MoreTechA6\Student

JProCo

Date Created:	1/17/2011 3:19 PM	Mirroring Status:	None
ID:	7	Ownership Chaining:	False
Size (MB):	193.4375	Primary File Path:	C:\Program Files\Microsoft SQL Server\MSS...
Recovery Model:	Full	Read Only:	False
System Database:	False	ANSI NULL Enabled:	False
Compatibility Level:	100	ANSI Padding Enabled:	False
Data Space Used (KB):	1592	ANSI Warnings Enabled:	False
Collation:	SQL_Latin1_General_CP1_CI_AS	Arithabort Enabled:	False
Index Space Used (KB):	1432	Auto Close Enabled:	False
Owner:	MoreTechA6\Student	Auto Create Statistics Enabled:	True
Space Available (KB):	148888	Auto Shrink Enabled:	False
ANSI NULL Default:	False	Auto Update Statistics Enabled:	True
Case Sensitive:	False	Broker Enabled:	True
Default File Group:	PRIMARY	Full Text Enabled:	True
GUID:	5d183fdc-8c31-4762-8e73-3db65b14d886	Mirroring Enabled:	False
Mail Host:	False	Quoted Identifiers:	False
		Trustworthy Enabled:	True

Figure 9.62 Object Explorer Details is another handy way to check a db's trustworthy status.

Now you can run the ALTER ASSEMBLY statement:

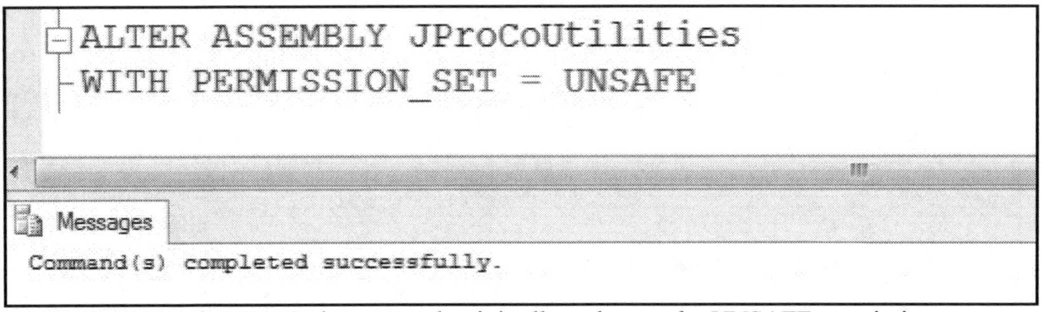

```
ALTER ASSEMBLY JProCoUtilities
WITH PERMISSION_SET = UNSAFE
```

Messages

Command(s) completed successfully.

Figure 9.63 Now that JProCo is trustworthy, it is allowed to set the UNSAFE permission.

And now you can successfully run the dbo.GetRates( ) function. In order to produce this result, the SQL CLR must actively access the MortgageRates.txt file on your hard drive (see Figure 9.64).

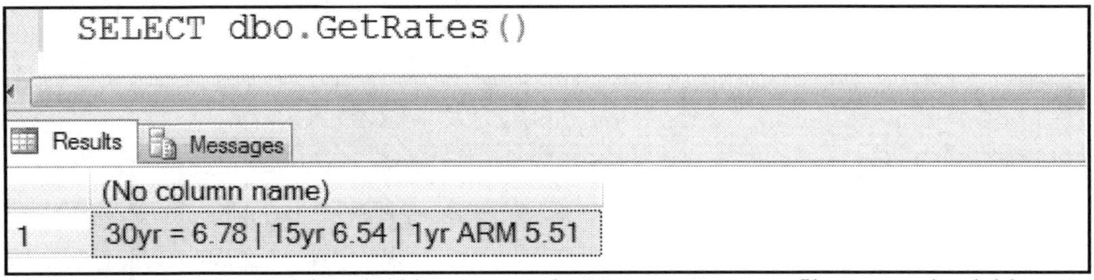

```
SELECT dbo.GetRates()
```

Results   Messages

	(No column name)
1	30yr = 6.78 | 15yr 6.54 | 1yr ARM 5.51

Figure 9.64 The SQL CLR is now able to access the MortgageRates.txt file on your hard drive.

Permission Set Safe

The SAFE level is most restrictive of the three Permission_Set levels (SAFE, EXTERNAL_ACCESS, UNSAFE). *Use the SAFE level wherever possible.* This level allows you to run managed code (as we saw in Figure 9.38), but it doesn't access any external system resources (e.g., files, registry files).

Permission Set Unsafe

This level essentially removes any restrictions and will allow SQL to do anything it is asked to do. This could leave your system open for attack since anyone accessing SQL Server can do anything to your entire system.

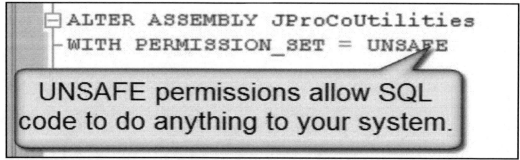

Figure 9.65 You should avoid using PERMISSION_SET = UNSAFE.

Permission Set External Access

It's very common for SQL Server to do some basic external access without having to change critical areas. For this common and relatively safe access of external resources, there is a permssions set called EXTERNAL_ACCESS. You must also set the database to trustworthy.

Since UNSAFE should only be used as a last resort, let's bring the access level down to a more prudent level (EXTERNAL_ACCESS) (see Figure 9.66). And then we must re-test the function to confirm whether it can still read the text file on the hard drive with the reduced permissions level.

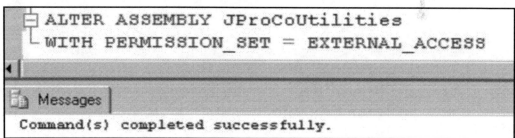

Figure 9.66 Reduce the SQL assembly's PERMISSION_SET to EXTERNAL_ACCESS.

Yes – when we rerun the dbo.GetRates( ) function, we see that it runs just fine with the reduced permissions level. We avoid the UNSAFE level and we still have all the functionality we need (see Figure 9.67).

```
SELECT dbo.GetRates()
```

	(No column name)
1	30yr = 6.78	15yr 6.54	1yr ARM 5.51

Figure 9.67 With EXTERNAL_ACCESS, the SQL CLR can access the file on our hard drive ok.

Note: Once you are done with this chapter and/or your practice work with the SQL CLR, it is recommended that you return your CLR enable status to the default of 0. In other words, disable the SQL CLR on your system.

```
sp_configure 'clr enable', 0
GO
RECONFIGURE
GO
```

Messages

```
Configuration option 'clr enabled' changed from 1 to 0.
Run the RECONFIGURE statement to install.
```

Figure 9.68 This code will disable the SQL CLR on your system.

The same sproc run without the the 0/1 parameter will simply check and tell you whether the CLR is currently enabled on your SQL Server.

```
sp_configure 'clr enable'
```

Results | Messages

	name	minimum	maximum	config_value	run_value
1	clr enabled	0	1	0	0

Figure 9.69 This result shows CLR integration is currently disabled (config_value=0).

```
sp_configure 'clr enable'
```

Results | Messages

	name	minimum	maximum	config_value	run_value
1	clr enabled	0	1	1	0

Figure 9.70 This result show CLR integration is currently enabled (config_value=1).

Lab 9.3: Code Access Permissions

Lab Prep: Before you can begin the lab you must run the SQLInteropChapter9.3Setup.sql script. *Please note there is no need to run this script if you already ran any script in Chapters 7-10.*

Skill Check 1: In dbBasics, update the dbBasicsUtilities assembly to use the new DLL. Create the GetRates( ) method from the [UtilitiesLibrary.Methods].GetMortgageRates method of the dll. Set the assembly to use the permission level which will allow it to access an external file on the hard drive. Have the scalar function return the values shown below (Figure 9.71).

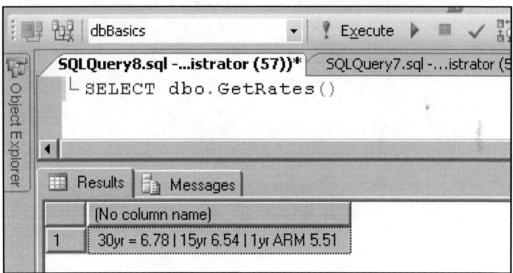

Figure 9.71 Skill Check 1 result.

Answer Code: The T-SQL code to this lab can be found in the downloadable files in a file named Lab9.3_CodeAccessPermissions.sql.

Code Access Permissions - Points to Ponder

1. To use managed code within SQL Server 2008 you must create a managed assembly, import the assembly into the database, and (depending on its privilege level) configure its security options.

2. The value of the PERMISSION_SET clause specifies the security level trust given to the assembly.

3. To import an assembly, use the CREATE ASSEMBLY statement.

4. To modify an assembly, use the ALTER ASSEMBLY statement.

5. To remove an assembly, use the DROP ASSEMBLY statement.

6. In SQL Server 2005 or 2008, to use managed code you must:
   o Create a managed assembly
   o Import the assembly it into the database.
   o Configure its security options (sometimes optional).
   o Create a database object (like a function or stored procedure) based on one of the methods.

7. There are three possible settings for PERMISSION_SET:
   o SAFE – the most restrictive (assemblies cannot access external systems like files, network, or registry).
   o EXTERNAL_ACCESS – code can run outside of SQL Server against other programs or entities such as the file system. The code has programming model and verifiability restrictions and cannot call unmanaged code. In order to execute managed code that will execute outside of SQL, you must use the ALTER DATABASE statement to set TRUSTWORTHY to ON.
   o UNSAFE – unrestricted. Does not have any access, programming model, or verifiability restrictions. The code has the ability to call unmanaged code. This permission is only for highly trusted code.

8. If an assembly requires the EXTERNAL_ACCESS or UNSAFE trust level you must grant the "EXTERNAL ACCESS ASSEMBLY" permission.

9. You can grant "EXTERNAL ACCESS ASSEMBLY" in one of two ways.
   o By using a certificate for the assembly's security context.

     o By making the database trustworthy and allowing all code assemblies that impersonate dbo to access external resources.

10.   The steps to make the database trustworthy and allow assemblies to impersonate dbo to access external resources are:

     o Grant the login for the dbo user EXTERNAL ACCESS ASSEMBLY.

     o Set the database's trustworthy property to ON:
ALTER *DatabaseName*
SET TRUSTWORTHY ON

Chapter Glossary

ALTER ASSEMBLY: definition.
Assembly: a deployable unit of .NET code.
C#: ("see sharp"), objected oriented programming language; can be used to build .NET applications and/or to interoperate with SQL Server.
C# Compiler: (CSC), compiler use for the C# language.
Class library: (.dll) definition; see also *in-process assembly*.
CLR: definition.
Compile: definition.
DLL: dynamic-link library.
Executable: (.exe) definition. See *out of process assembly*.
IDE: (integrated development environment), a programming environment.
In-process assembly: (.dll). definition.
IntelliSense: definition.
Managed code: Code that is managed in Microsoft's common language runtime.
Modular programming: definition.
Monolithic programming: definition.
Namespace: definition.
.NET: definition.
Out of process assembly: an executable file (.exe).
Permission call stack: definition.
PERMISSION_SET: definition.
SAFE: definition.
sp_configure: definition.
SQL CLR: the engine SQL Server uses to run .NET code.
static void Main( ): definition.
Trustworthy status: is_trustworthy_on (0 = OFF, 1 = ON).
Unmanaged code: code that is managed by your Operating System.
Visual Studio: definition.

Chapter Nine - Review Quiz

1.) You are creating a SQL Server database for a company. The company has a piece of .NET code that retrieves relevant information. You need to gather this information. What should you do?

  O a. Implement parameterized Transact-SQL queries in the application.

  O b. Implement Transact-SQL stored procedures in the database.

  O c. Implement CLR functions or stored procedures in the database.

  O d. Implement distributed web services.

2.) You want customers to see stock market reports that combine data that is retrieved from a DB with real-time investments information. You need to create the appropriate SQL objects that support the reports. What should you do?

  O a. Publish the data in the database as an XML web service by using the FOR XML AUTO clause.

  O b. Create a table to store the banking info for each customer. Create a trigger that fires when data is inserted into the table that joins with the data coming from the web Service.

  O c. Create a T-SQL stored procedure that uses a temporary table to store the banking information for each customer. Update the table with the values from the web service.

  O d. Have a developer create an assembly that calls the remote web service. Create a CLR function by using the assembly. Call the CLR function and combine the results with the banking info from the database.

3.) You have a CLR Assembly that contains a function that reads data from a spreadsheet and saves calculated results to a table in SQL Server 2005. You need to register the assembly with SQL Server 2008 by using the CREATE ASSEMBLY statement and the lowest privilege security that will work. Which permission set should you use?

  O a. DEFAULT

  O b. SAFE

  O c. EXTERNAL_ACCESS

  O d. UNSAFE

4.) You are creating a SQL Server 2008 database to handle a web-based application. The app will use a calculation-intensive operation such as calculating mortgage and fleet asset depreciation schedules. Of the answers below, which one will perform the calculations as quickly and efficiently as possible?

   O a. Implement parameterized stored views.

   O b. Implement T-SQL stored procedures in the database.

   O c. Implement CLR stored procedures in your database.

   O d. Implement a distributed web service.

Answer Key

1.) c   2.) d   3.) c   4.) c

Bug Catcher Game

To play the Bug Catcher game run the SQLInteropBugCatcherCh9.pps from the BugCatcher folder of the companion files. You can obtain these files from www.Joes2Pros.com or by ordering the Companion CD.

Chapter 10.   SQL PowerShell

The first time you hear the word "Shell", you might picture the hard protective shell that protects a turtle from predators. The only way to get to the turtle is via the very few openings present in the shell. The turtle tries to keep everyone out, but in the case of your operating system's Kernel many things should be allowed in, such as the "Ta-Da" sound when you score points in a game. The name shell originates from shells being an outer interface between the user and the internals of the operating system kernel. In fact any point and click you make sends a command for the shell to run which then accesses the kernel.

Ever since the early days of point and click in Microsoft Windows, there has been an accompanying command shell (like CMD.exe or Command.exe). If we have Windows, why do we still see and advantage to providing you with a shell? The answer is automation and reuse. If you want to set up 1000 computers just the same for a giant convention center and it took 20 clicks to get all the wallpaper, icons, and settings the way you wanted, what are the chances you could hire someone to do this and ensure that all the computer are precisely the same? (A human manually running a 20-click routine 1000 times is bound to make at least a few mistakes.) Those point and click commands could be made into shell commands which can run automatically as part of the machine startup.

Shells are useful and have been around as long as computers. SQL PowerShell is the newest shell framework, and this chapter will show some of its uses with SQL Server 2008.

One noteworthy feature of this chapter is that *none of the syntax is case-sensitive*. As SQL Server pros, we are accustomed to working in a case-insensitive environment. Thus, Chapters 1-9 of this book have been a departure from the rest of the series in that the XML and C# topics we covered were *case-sensitive*. In this chapter, we will see that SQL PowerShell and our command line utilities are all case-insensitive. (Note: some BCP command shortcuts are case sensitive, but we will not be using BCP in this chapter.)

READER NOTE: *Please run the script SQLInteropChapter10.0Setup.sql in order to follow along with the examples in Chapter 10. All scripts mentioned in this chapter may be found at **www.Joes2Pros.com**.*

The Windows Command Shell

The command shell is a computer program that reads lines of text entered by a user and interprets them for use in your operating system. This allows users to issue various commands in a very efficient but often a very manual way. Using the GUI makes running these commands very easy. Most times you can use either method to get your OS kernel to get the work done that you need. We will explore both of these ways of doing very similar tasks.

GUI Commands

We are all familiar with the use of a graphical user interface (GUI) such as Windows Explorer to navigate through the folders and files on our system. Windows Explorer is the GUI we utilize to interact with our operating system (OS) to perform tasks like locating or creating folder and subfolder items. We will perform a few basic tasks in Windows Explorer and then see how those same tasks can be accomplished by using a **command-line utility**.

Open your Joes2Pros folder and see the five folders currently present. We are going to create a sixth folder and name it FolderW (see Figure 10.1).

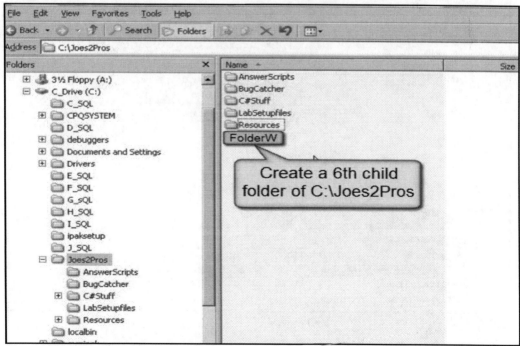

Figure 10.1 We will create a sixth folder beneath the C:\Joes2Pros folder.

Create the new folder File > New > Folder. Name the folder "FolderW."

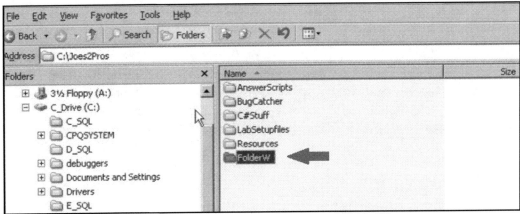

Figure 10.2 The sixth folder is now present and has been named FolderW.

Repeat the process to create three child folders (Jan, Feb, Mar) beneath FolderW.

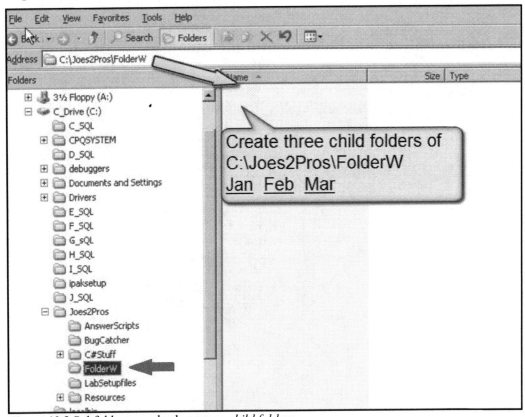

Figure 10.3 Subfolders are also known as *child folders*.

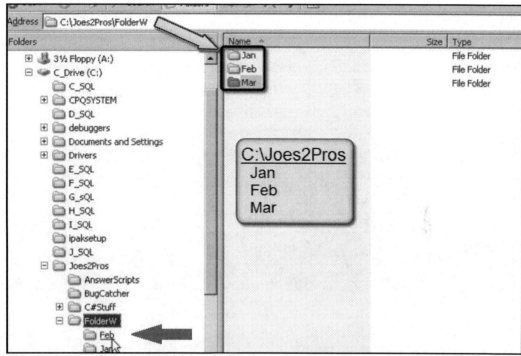

Figure 10.4 The three child folders are visible in the Windows Explorer tree and have been named Jan, Feb, and Mar, according to the specification we were given.

Create another folder under Joes2Pros named FolderC. FolderW contains the items we created in Windows Explorer. FolderC will contain the items which we will create using the Command Utility.

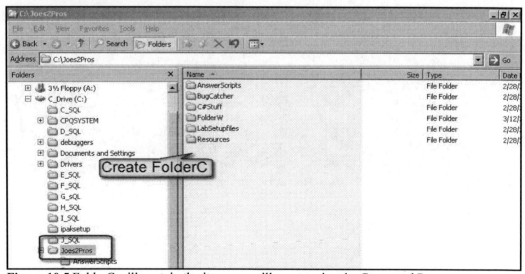

Figure 10.5 FolderC will contain the items we will create using the Command Prompt.

The Command Prompt

Recall that "directory" is a geek-speak word meaning folder. You will see this term used frequently in the syntax of the Command Prompt.

Open a Command Prompt by Start > cmd (enter this into the search box and hit Enter). The pre-Windows 7 syntax was Start > Run > cmd.

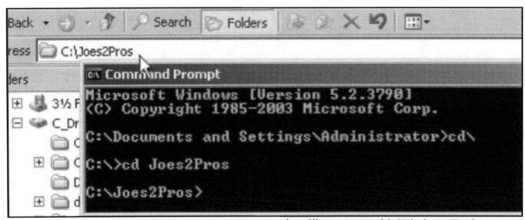

Figure 10.6 We used the Command Prompt in Chapter 8 to output Console Applications and in (*Beginning SQL Joes 2 Pros*) Volume 1 for BCP and sqlcmd..

We see the Initial Command prompt screen. We use the **cd** command to change the directory (i.e., the folder). The syntax **cd** will take us to the root directory of our C drive. In order to navigate to the Joes2Pros folder, use the **cd Joes2Pros** syntax and hit Enter (see Figure 10.7).

Figure 10.7 We can use CMD to traverse our system just like we can with Windows Explorer.

Our current position at **C:\Joes2Pros>** is the equivalent of being in the Joes2Pros folder in Windows Explorer. Notice the Windows Explorer filepath "C:\Joes2Pros" (shown in Figures 10.7).

When we put the focus on the C:\Joes2Pros folder, we see its contents displayed in the right hand side of Windows Explorer (see Figure 10.8).

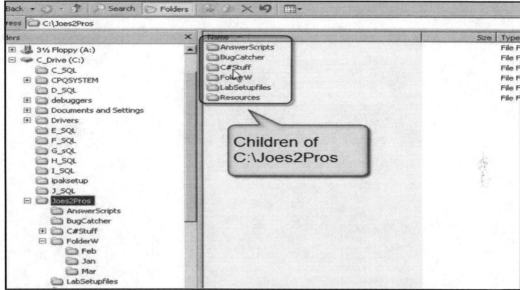

Figure 10.8 The Joes2Pros folder currently contains six child folders.

Our next goal is to display the contents of the Joes2Pros folder in CMD.

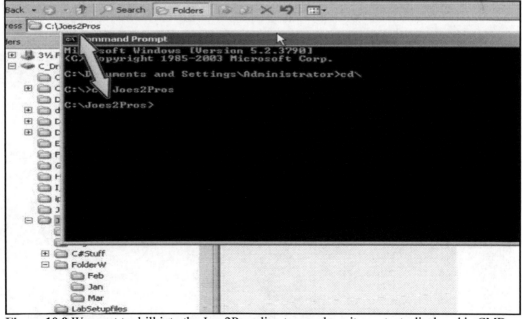

Figure 10.9 We want to drill into the Joes2Pros directory and see its contents displayed in CMD.

The **dir** command displays the contents and metadata for the Joes2Pros directory.

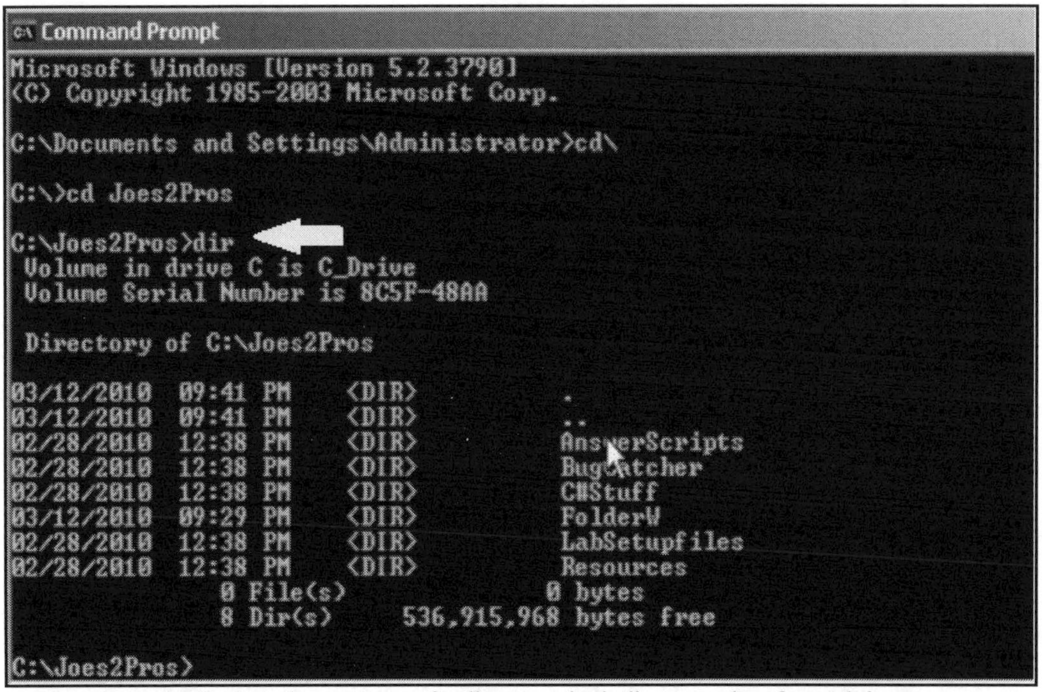

Figure 10.10 Dir displays the contents of a directory, including metadata for each item.

Test this on your own system and observe that the **dir** command displays all of the files and subfolders (including system folders) in each of your folders.

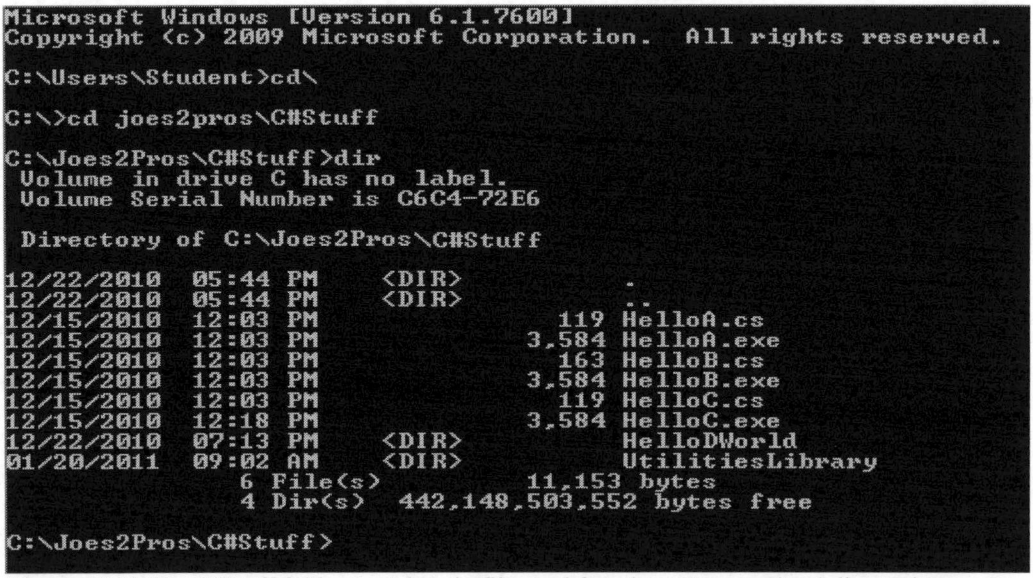

Figure 10.11 The C#Stuff folder contains six files and four (user + system) subdirectories.

Observe that the folders listed by the Command Prompt are the same which appear in the Windows Explorer interface.

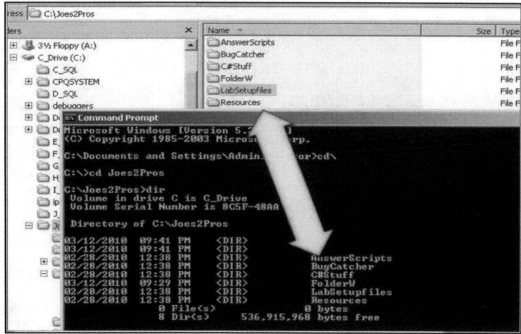

Figure 10.12 Dir displays the contents of a directory, including metadata for each item.

Use **md** ("**m**ake a new **d**irectory") to make a new folder called FolderC.

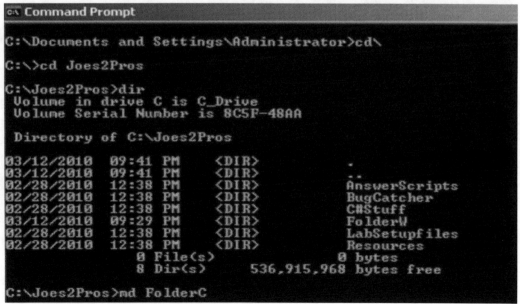

Figure 10.13 The md **command is used to** <u>m</u>ake new <u>d</u>irectories.

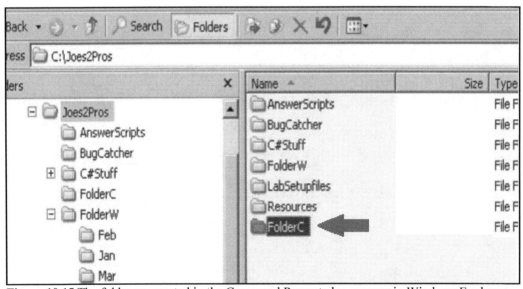

```
Command Prompt
02/28/2010  12:38 PM    <DIR>          Resources
                0 File(s)              0 bytes
                8 Dir(s)     536,915,968 bytes free

C:\Joes2Pros>md FolderC

C:\Joes2Pros>dir
 Volume in drive C is C_Drive
 Volume Serial Number is 8C5F-48AA

 Directory of C:\Joes2Pros

03/12/2010  09:43 PM    <DIR>          .
03/12/2010  09:43 PM    <DIR>          ..
02/28/2010  12:38 PM    <DIR>          AnswerScripts
02/28/2010  12:38 PM    <DIR>          BugCatcher
02/28/2010  12:38 PM    <DIR>          C#Stuff
03/12/2010  09:43 PM    <D              FolderC
03/12/2010  09:29 PM    <DIR>          FolderW
02/28/2010  12:38 PM    <DIR>          LabSetupfiles
02/28/2010  12:38 PM    <DIR>          Resources
                0 File(s)              0 bytes
                9 Dir(s)     536,915,968 bytes free

C:\Joes2Pros>
```

Figure 10.14 Rerun the **dir** command to see FolderC.

There are now seven folders showing, including FolderC, which we just created.

Figure 10.15 The folder we created in the Command Prompt also appears in Windows Explorer.

Our next goal will be to make a new folder inside of FolderC, except we will use the Command Prompt to create this subdirectory.

We first need to navigate to FolderC using the command **cd FolderC**.

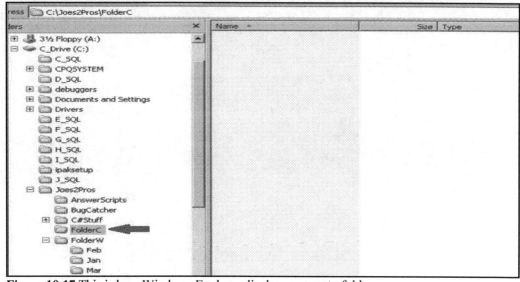

Figure 10.16 Navigate to FolderC using the command **cd FolderC.**

Before we create the new folder, let's confirm that FolderC is empty. Windows Explorer shows that FolderC is empty – no folders or files appear beneath it.

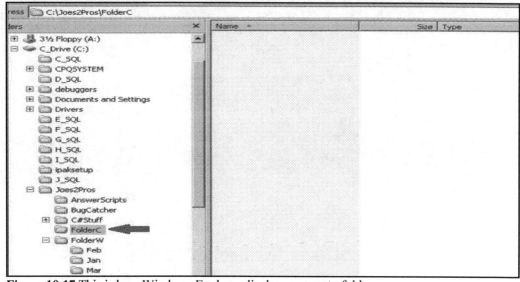

Figure 10.17 This is how Windows Explorer displays an empty folder.

When we run a **dir** command on FolderC, we see dots, which signify system folders. This is how an empty directory appears in CMD (see Figure 10.18).

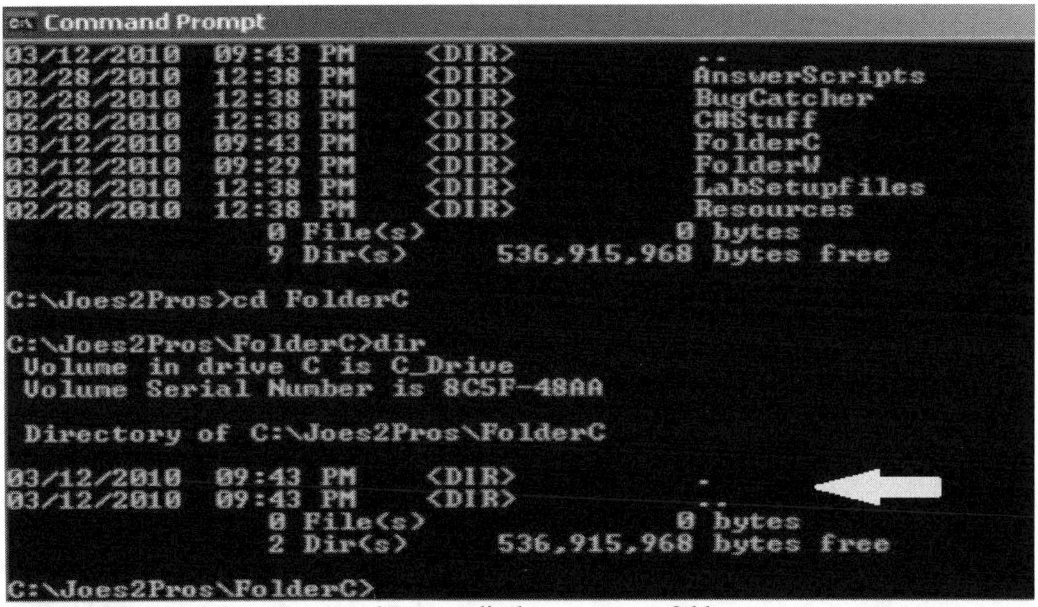

Figure 10.18 This is how Command Prompt displays an empty folder.

Now let's make the new folder and call it Apr (short for April - see Figure 10.19).

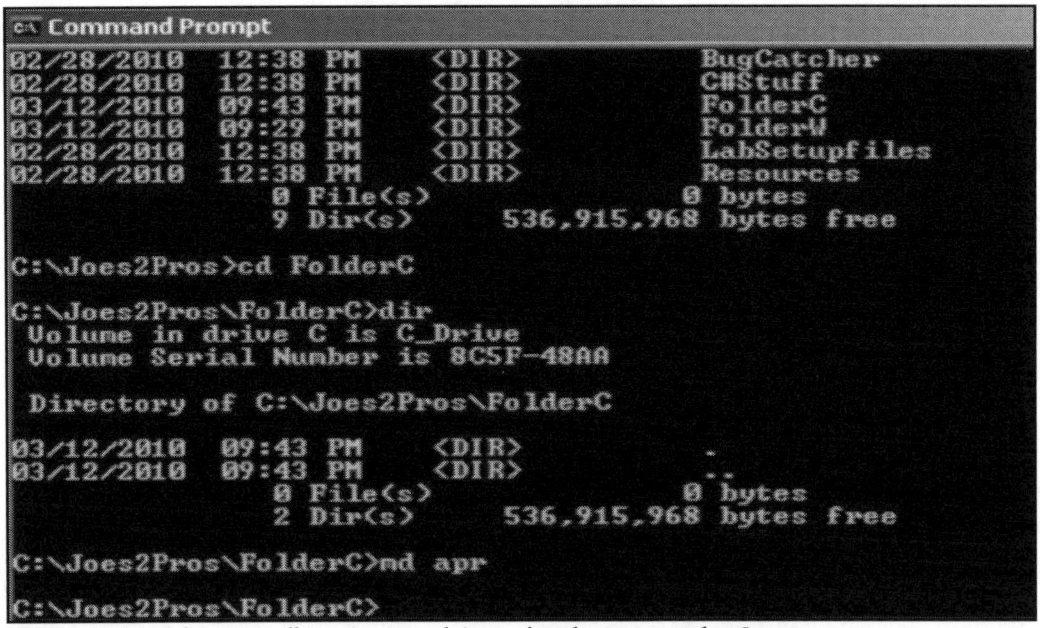

Figure 10.19 Make a new directory named Apr using the command **md apr**.

The new folder shows immediately in Windows Explorer

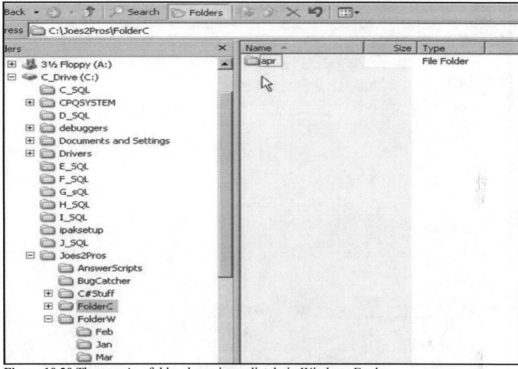

Figure 10.20 The new Apr folder shows immediately in Windows Explorer.

FolderC now has one child folder (apr). Let's make two more folders.

```
02/28/2010  12:38 PM    <DIR>          LabSetupfiles
02/28/2010  12:38 PM    <DIR>          Resources
              0 File(s)              0 bytes
              9 Dir(s)      536,915,968 bytes free

C:\Joes2Pros>cd FolderC

C:\Joes2Pros\FolderC>dir
 Volume in drive C is C_Drive
 Volume Serial Number is 8C5F-48AA

 Directory of C:\Joes2Pros\FolderC

03/12/2010  09:43 PM    <DIR>          .
03/12/2010  09:43 PM    <DIR>          ..
              0 File(s)              0 bytes
              2 Dir(s)      536,915,968 bytes free

C:\Joes2Pros\FolderC>md apr

C:\Joes2Pros\FolderC>md May

C:\Joes2Pros\FolderC>md Jun

C:\Joes2Pros\FolderC>
```

Figure 10.21 The commands **md May** and **md Jun** create two more child folders.

All three child folders appear beneath FolderC in Windows Explorer.

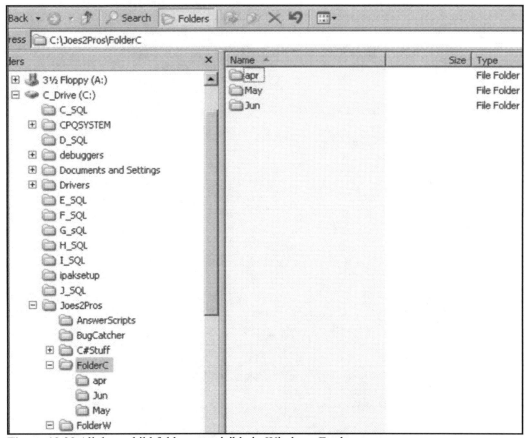

Figure 10.22 All three child folders are visible in Windows Explorer.

Notice that we accidentally created one of the child folders in lowercase (apr) rather than an intial cap (Apr). We can correct that mistake by renaming the folder. The **ren** command renames directories or files (see Figure 10.23).

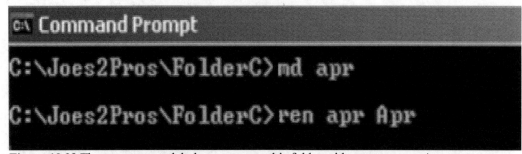

Figure 10.23 The **ren** command .helps us rename this folder with an uppercase A.

We now see all three child folders properly capitalized and appearing in the FolderC directory (see Figure 10.24).

Figure 10.24 All three child folders are now showing beneath FolderC.

Adding PowerShell to the Start Menu

Dropping CMD into your search box is a handy way to launch the Command Prompt each time you need it. For quicker access, you can add this program to your Start Menu.

Drop **cmd.exe** into your search box (Start > cmd.exe > Enter, as described earlier at Figure 10.6). Right-click on the program icon and choose "Open file location" (see Figure 10.25).

From the program's location on your hard drive, right-click the file and choose "Pin to Start Menu" (see Figure 10.26).

Figure 10.25 Right-click the icon and *Open file location.*

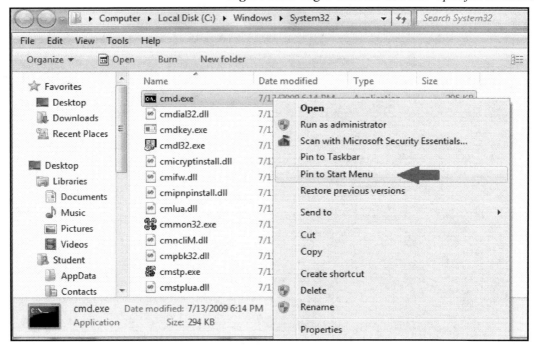

Figure 10.26 After the file location opens, right-click the program and choose *Pin to Start Menu.*

A shortcut to the program now appears in your Start Menu. You can access the Command Prompt in just two clicks.

Figure 10.27 A shortcut has been added to the Start Menu.

Later in this chapter we will work with SQL PowerShell. Similar to the Command Prompt, you can repeat this process to add a shortcut for SQL Server Powershell (SQLPS.exe) to your Start Menu.

Lab 10.1: Windows Command Shell

Lab Prep: Before you can begin the lab you must run the SQLInteropChapter10.1Setup.sql script. *Please note there is no need to run this script if you already ran any script in Chapters 7-10.*

Skill Check 1: Using the windows command shell create a folder under C:\Joes2Pros named FolderSK Under FolderSK make three child folders named Jul, Aug , Sep.

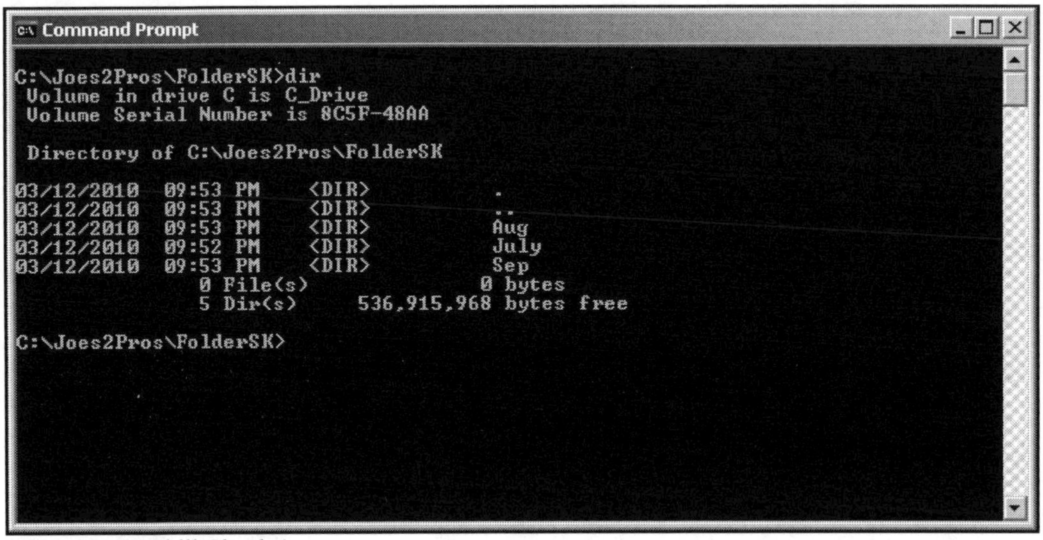

```
Command Prompt                                              _ □ ×

C:\Joes2Pros\FolderSK>dir
 Volume in drive C is C_Drive
 Volume Serial Number is 8C5F-48AA

 Directory of C:\Joes2Pros\FolderSK

03/12/2010  09:53 PM    <DIR>          .
03/12/2010  09:53 PM    <DIR>          ..
03/12/2010  09:53 PM    <DIR>          Aug
03/12/2010  09:52 PM    <DIR>          July
03/12/2010  09:53 PM    <DIR>          Sep
               0 File(s)              0 bytes
               5 Dir(s)     536,915,968 bytes free

C:\Joes2Pros\FolderSK>
```

Figure 10.28 Skill Check 1.

Answer Code: The T-SQL code to this lab can be found in the downloadable files in a file named Lab10.1_WindowsCommandShell.sql.

Windows Command Shell - Points to Ponder

1. A Shell is a computer program that reads lines of text entered by a user and interprets them for use by your operating system.

2. Every released version of Microsoft DOS and Microsoft Windows has a command-line interface tool. These are usually cmd.exe but in older systems like Window 95/98 are called COMMAND.

3. A Command Prompt is the command-line interpreter for most major operating systems.

4. The Command Prompt for all versions of windows since Window 2000 is cmd.exe.

5. cmd.exe is a native program for the Windows Kernel.

Navigating SQL PowerShell

PowerShell is Microsoft's automation framework and command-line shell built on top of the .NET Framework. This shell can carry out commands to the Kernel, as well as to any .Net application on your system.

SQL PowerShell is the shell that carries out the commands between SQL Server Management Studio (SSMS) and the SQL service. This means anything you can do in SSMS through the GUI can be automated in PowerShell, including navigating through your databases and their objects.

Soon all Microsoft applications running on the Windows platform will be PowerShell aware.

SQL Objects in Management Studio

Navigating in SQL Server's Object Explorer is a lot like using Windows Explorer to traverse the folders and files on your hard drive (see Figures 10.29 and 10.30).

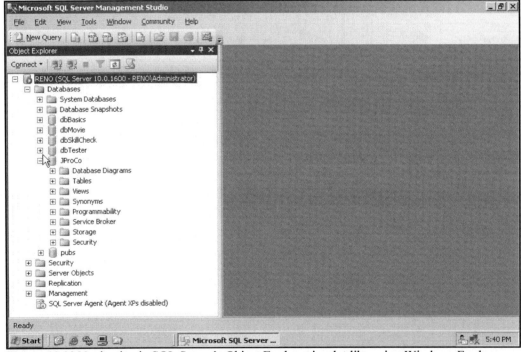

Figure 10.29 Navigating in SQL Server's Object Explorer is a lot like using Windows Explorer.

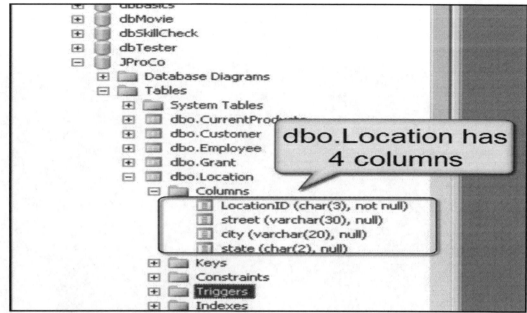

Figure 10.30 The Location table has 4 columns.

Another way of traversing SQL Server is with a command-line utility. However, you can't use the program cmd.exe to do this. The command shell called SQL PowerShell (sqlps.exe) is the program we need to work with our SQL Server items in a command line utility.

SQL Objects in PowerShell

There are two easy ways of launching your SQL PowerShell command-line utility. If you followed the steps to add sqlps.exe to your Start Menu (Figures 10.25-10.27), then Start > SQL Server PowerShell will launch it.

Another easy way is to open the Command Prompt and use the command sqlps (see Figure 10.31).

```
C:\WINDOWS\system32\cmd.exe - sqlps
Microsoft Windows [Version 5.2.3790]
(C) Copyright 1985-2003 Microsoft Corp.

C:\Documents and Settings\Administrator>cd SQL
The system cannot find the path specified.

C:\Documents and Settings\Administrator>sqlps
Microsoft SQL Server PowerShell
Version 10.0.1600.22
Microsoft Corp. All rights reserved.

PS SQLSERVER:\>
```

Figure 10.31 The SQLSERVER powershell..

Our familiar command, dir, has the same functionality in SQL PowerShell as it does in the Command Prompt. Run a **dir** to see what's available in SQLPS.

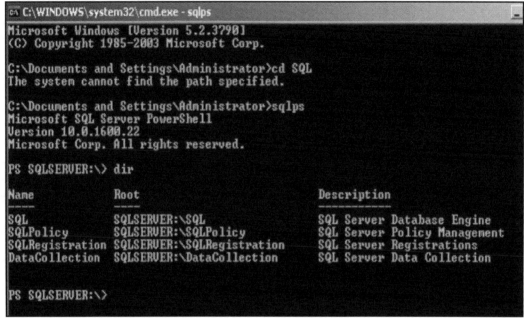

Figure 10.32 Run a **dir** command to see the available options at this level.

Since this series track deals with the SQL Server Database Engine, we will focus on this item. (*Note*: The other items shown here (Policy Management, Registrations, Data Collection) are topics of SQL Server Administration).

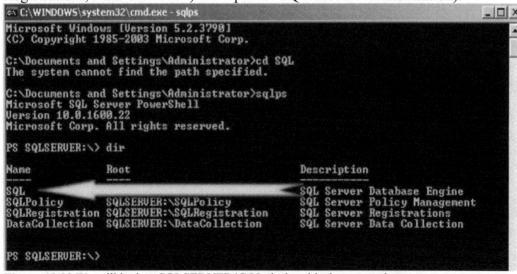

Figure 10.33 We will look at SQLSERVER:\SQL during this demonstration.

Choose the SQL Server Database Engine with **cd SQL**.

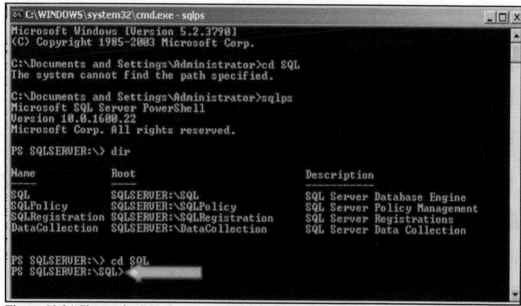

Figure 10.34 Choose the SQL Server Database Engine with **cd SQL**.

A **dir** command. Reno is my machine name. *The same shows in Object Explorer.*

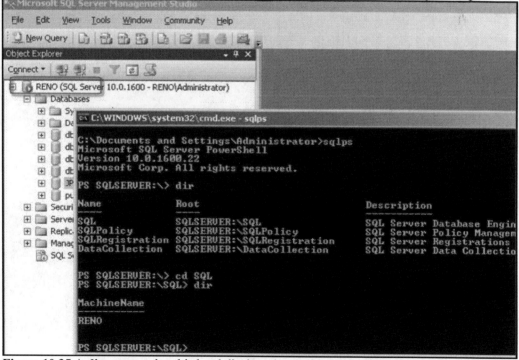

Figure 10.35 A **dir** command at this level displays the machine name, Reno.

Type a dir for Reno. It reveals that this is the default instance of SQL Server. *A server could have many instances of SQL Server installed on it.*

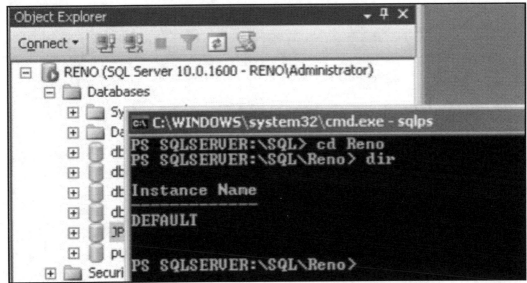

Figure 10.36 Reno is the default instance of SQL Server installed on this machine.

Let's change the default directory (**cd default**). Then run a **dir**.

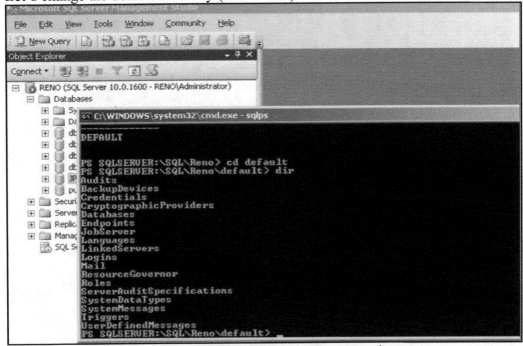

Figure 10.37 Run the command **cd default**. Then run the **dir** command.

From this list, let's choose to look at the Logins folder from within PowerShell.

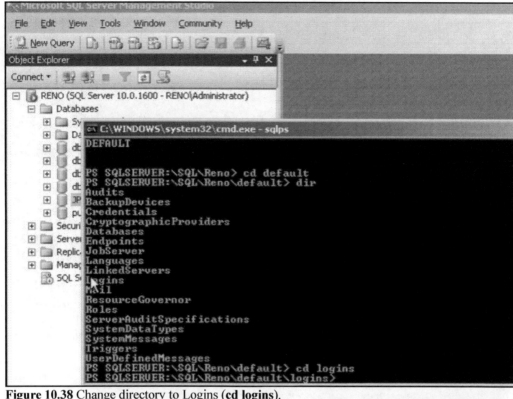

Figure 10.38 Change directory to Logins (**cd logins**).

Here we see the Object Explorer view of our current position (see Figure 10.39).

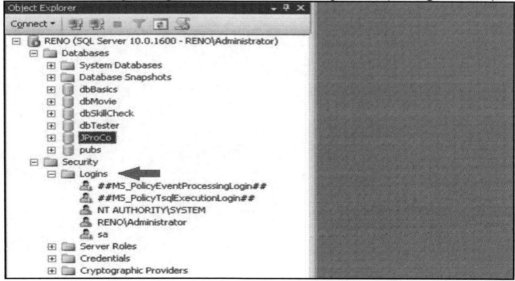

Figure 10.39 The Object Explorer view of our current position.

A dir command shows the same Logins list in SQLPS as in Object Explorer.

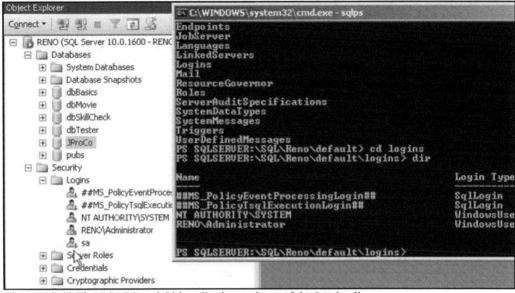

Figure 10.40 The SQLPS and Object Explorer views of the Logins list.

Let's traverse up a level with **cd..** (cd dot dot) With SQLPS the syntax is a bit different – you must include a space. ("**cd ..**" or cd space dot dot)

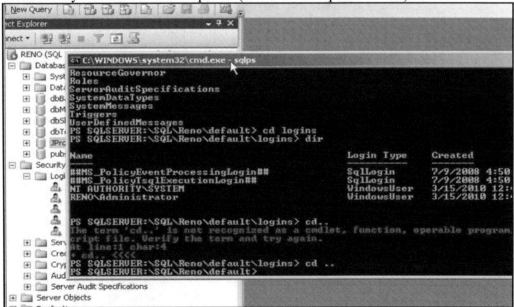

Figure 10.41 The command **cd ..** will take us up one level from our current position.

Before looking at the dir (directory contents) for this level, let's first clear the screen (**cls**) to give ourselves more room.

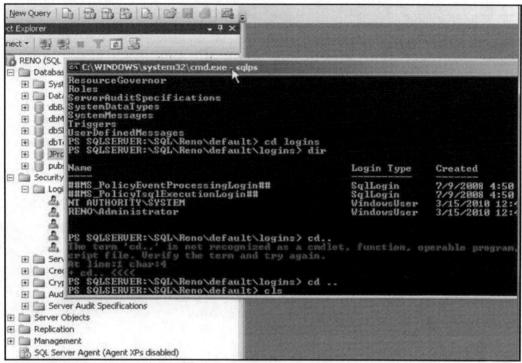

Figure 10.42 The command **cls** will <u>cl</u>ear our <u>s</u>creen.

The <u>dir</u>ectory contents of our default instance of SQL Server.

Figure 10.43 The directory contents at the level of our default instance of SQL Server.

Choose Databases (**cd Databases**).

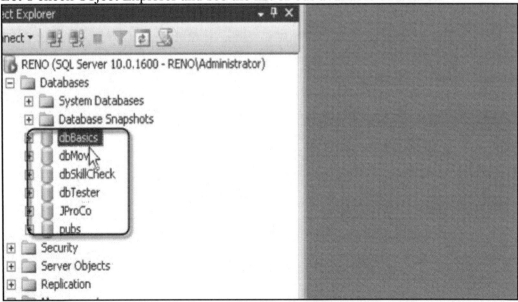

```
C:\WINDOWS\system32\cmd.exe - sqlps
PS SQLSERVER:\SQL\Reno\default> dir
Audits
BackupDevices
Credentials
CryptographicProviders
Databases
Endpoints
JobServer
Languages
LinkedServers
Logins
Mail
ResourceGovernor
Roles
ServerAuditSpecifications
SystemDataTypes
SystemMessages
Triggers
UserDefinedMessages
PS SQLSERVER:\SQL\Reno\default> cd Databases
PS SQLSERVER:\SQL\Reno\default\Databases>
```

Figure 10.44 cd Databases.

Let's check Object Explorer and see the list of our available databases.

Figure 10.45 Our current list of databases (Object Explorer view).

The SQLPS directory of databases includes the name and metadata for each current database. Let's drill in to look at JProCo and its contents (cd JProCo, dir).

```
C:\WINDOWS\system32\cmd.exe - sqlps
Triggers
UserDefinedMessages
PS SQLSERVER:\SQL\Reno\default> cd Databases
PS SQLSERVER:\SQL\Reno\default\Databases> dir

WARNING: column "Owner" does not fit into the display and was removed.

Name            Status      Recovery Model CompatLvl Collation
----            ------      -------------- --------- ---------
dbBasics        Normal      Full                 100 SQL_Latin1_
                                                     1_CP1_CI_AS
dbMovie         Normal      Full                 100 SQL_Latin1_
                                                     1_CP1_CI_AS
dbSkillCheck    Normal      Full                 100 SQL_Latin1_
                                                     1_CP1_CI_AS
dbTester        Normal      Full                 100 SQL_Latin1_
                                                     1_CP1_CI_AS
JProCo          Normal      Full                 100 SQL_Latin1_
                                                     1_CP1_CI_AS
pubs            Normal      Simple               100 SQL_Latin1_
                                                     1_CP1_CI_AS

PS SQLSERVER:\SQL\Reno\default\Databases> cd JProCo
PS SQLSERVER:\SQL\Reno\default\Databases\JProCo> dir
```

Figure 10.46 Our current list of databases (SQLPS view). Choose JProCo. Then dir.

The **dir**ectory of contents for the JProCo database is seen here (Figure 10.47).

```
C:\WINDOWS\system32\cmd.exe - sqlps
FileGroups
FullTextCatalogs
FullTextStopLists
LogFiles
PartitionFunctions
PartitionSchemes
PlanGuides
Roles
Rules
Schemas
ServiceBroker
StoredProcedures
SymmetricKeys
Synonyms
Tables
Triggers
UserDefinedAggregates
UserDefinedDataTypes
UserDefinedFunctions
UserDefinedTableTypes
UserDefinedTypes
Users
Views
XmlSchemaCollections
PS SQLSERVER:\SQL\Reno\default\Databases\JProCo>
```

Figure 10.47 The **dir**ectory of contents for the JProCo database.

Change directory to look at JProCo's tables.

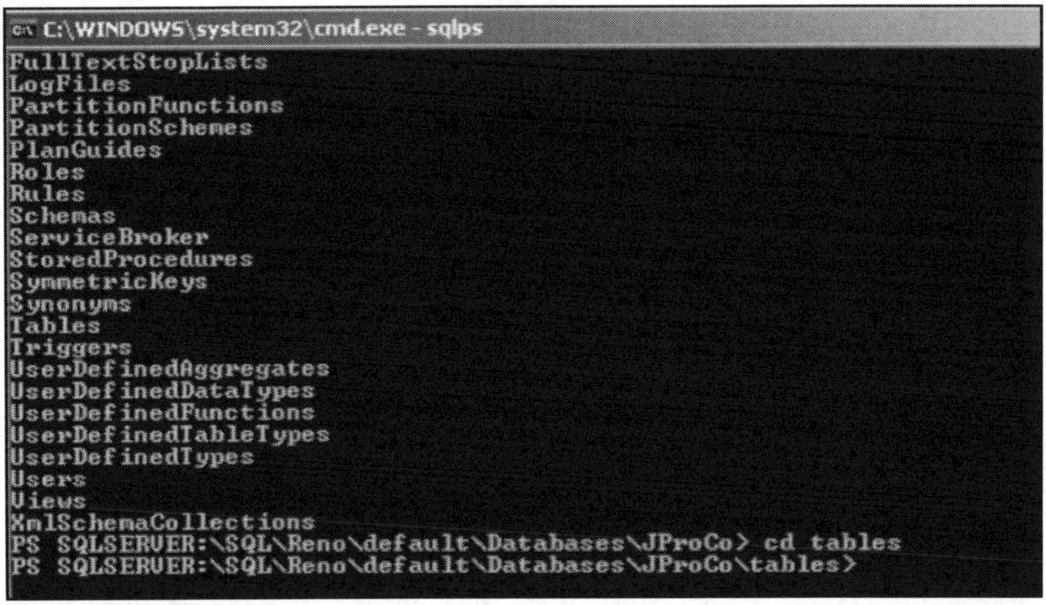

Figure 10.48 cd Tables.

We see the familiar JProCo tables. CurrentProducts, Customer, Employee, Grant, Location, and so forth.

Let's drill into the Location table (**cd dbo.location**).

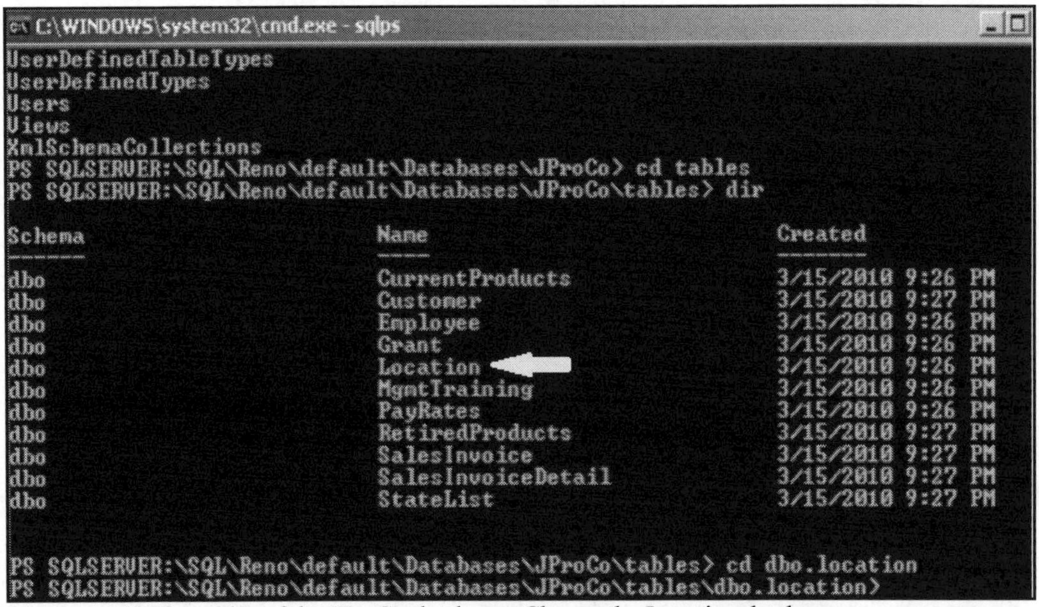

Figure 10.49 The tables of the JProCo database. Choose the Location database.

Directory view of the Location table. We are interested in looking at the Columns of the Location table.

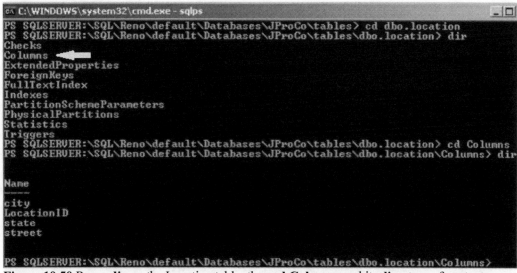

Figure 10.50 Run a **dir** on the Location table, then **cd Columns** and its <u>dir</u>ectory of contents.

Object Explorer shows the same column info (City, LocationID, state, street).

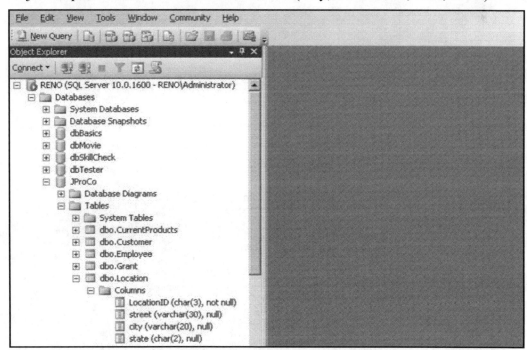

Figure 10.51 Notice that Object Explorer shows the same column info that we see in SQLPS.

Let's again traverse with the SQLPS and look at the Movie table in dbMovie. Here we see the six fields of the Movie table of the dbMovie database.

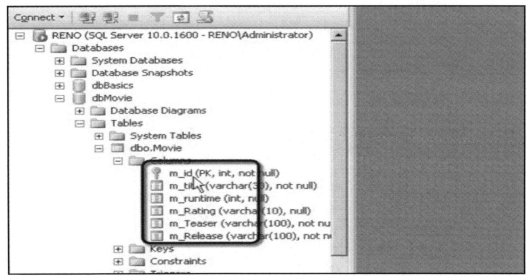

Figure 10.52 Our next demonstration will use some new tools to drill into the Movie table.

Before we move ahead to our Movie table example, we first need to see a few new commands and tools in SQL PowerShell (SQLPS).

PowerShell CmdLets

So far we have used only the typical DOS commands (e.g., dir, cd) to navigate within our SQL Server.

We now will look at some Cmdlets (pronounced command-lets) we find in SQL PowerShell. These use verb-noun pair combo (example: Get-ChildItem).

Notice that Get-ChildItem accomplishes the same result as the **dir** command.

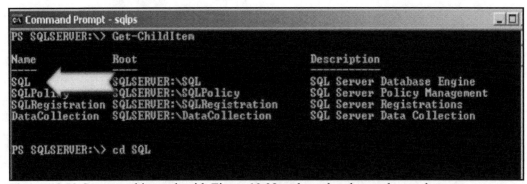

Figure 10.53 Compare this result with Figure 10.32 and see that the results are the same.

Notice that **set-location SQL** accomplishes the same as the command cd SQL (compare with Figure 10.34).

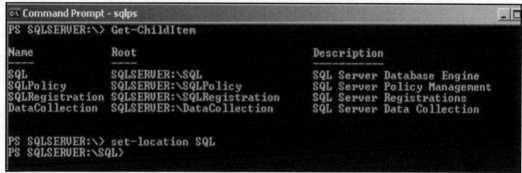

Figure 10.54 Compare this result with Figure 10.34 and see that the results are the same.

Notice that **Get-ChildItem** accomplishes the same as the DOS command **dir** (compare with Figure 10.35).

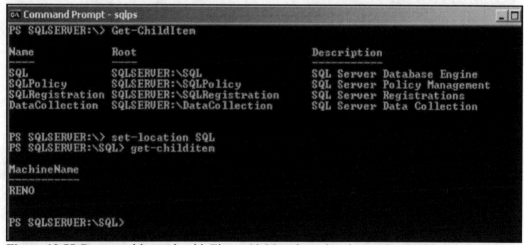

Figure 10.55 Compare this result with Figure 10.35 and see that the results are the same.

Get-ChildItem can be shortened to **gci** (see Figure 10.56).

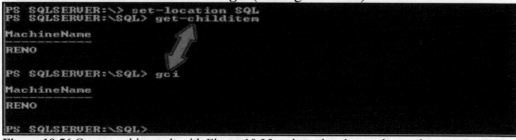

Figure 10.56 Compare this result with Figure 10.35 and see that the results are the same.

Notice that the cmdlets **set-location Reno** and **gci** accomplish the same result as cd Reno followed by the **dir** command (compare with Figure 10.36).

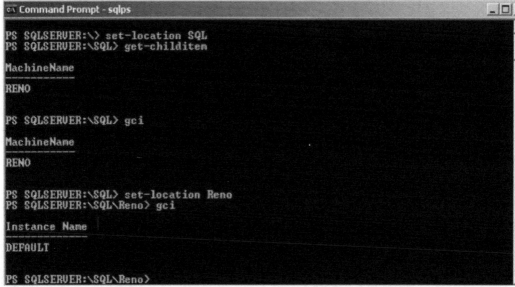

Figure 10.57 Compare this result with Figure 10.36 and see that the results are the same.

Now we will change the directory to that of our Default machine. Notice that the cmdlet **set-location** may be shortened to **sl**.

Figure 10.58 Set-Location may be abbreviated as **sl**.

Run **gci** to see the child items available in our Default instance of SQL Server.

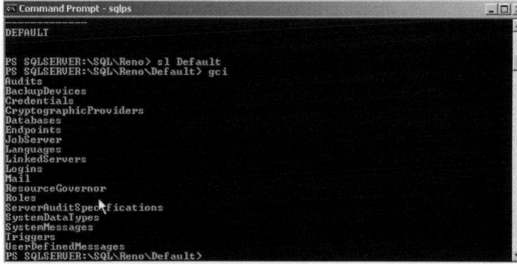

Figure 10.59 Compare this result **cd default** and **dir** (Figures 10.37 and 10.43).

Run **sl Databases** to drill into the Databases item.

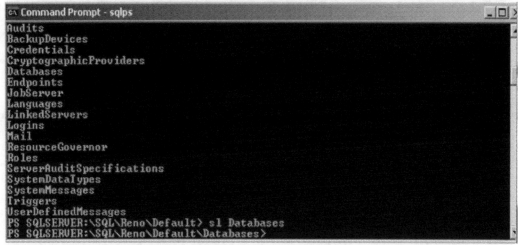

Figure 10.60 Compare this result **cd Databases** (Figure 10.44).

Run **gci** to see the child items available in Databases.

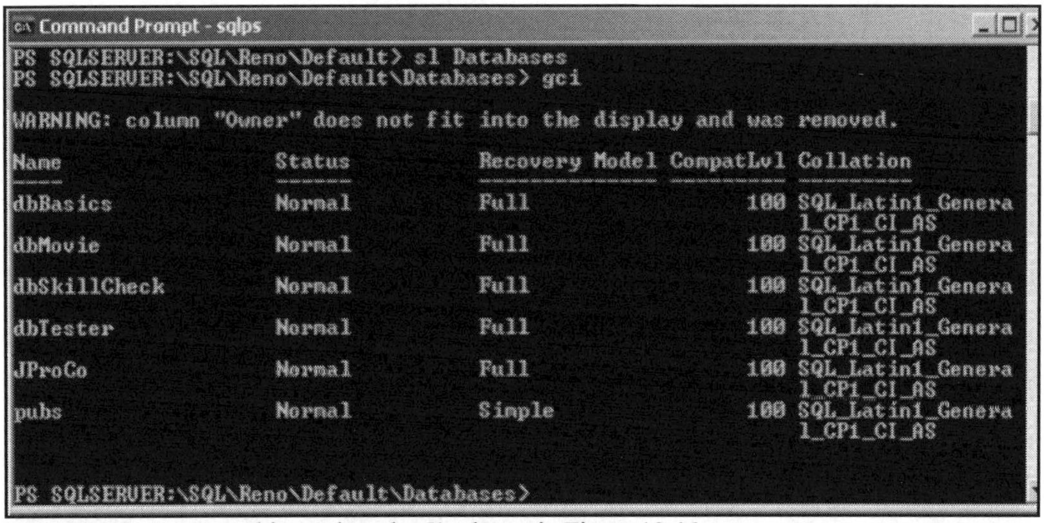

Figure 10.61 Compare this result to the **dir** shown in Figure 10.46.

Just like we used **cd ..** (cd space dot dot) to navigate up one level, **sl ..** (sl space dot dot) accomplishes the same in SQLPS.

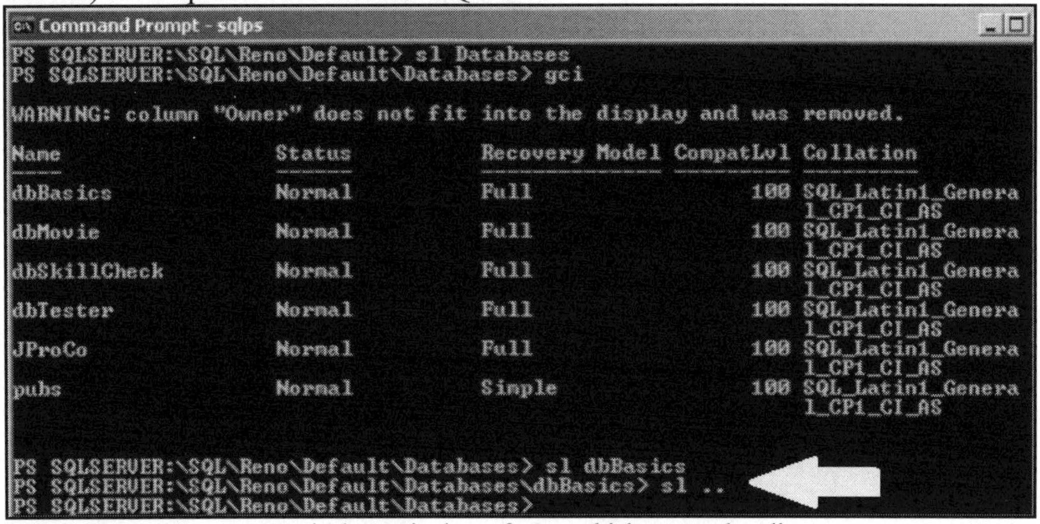

Figure 10.62 The syntax **sl ..** is the equivalent of **cd ..**, which we used earlier.

Now set-location to dbMovie (**sl dbMovie**). Then **gci** to see the various types of items available in the dbMovie database.

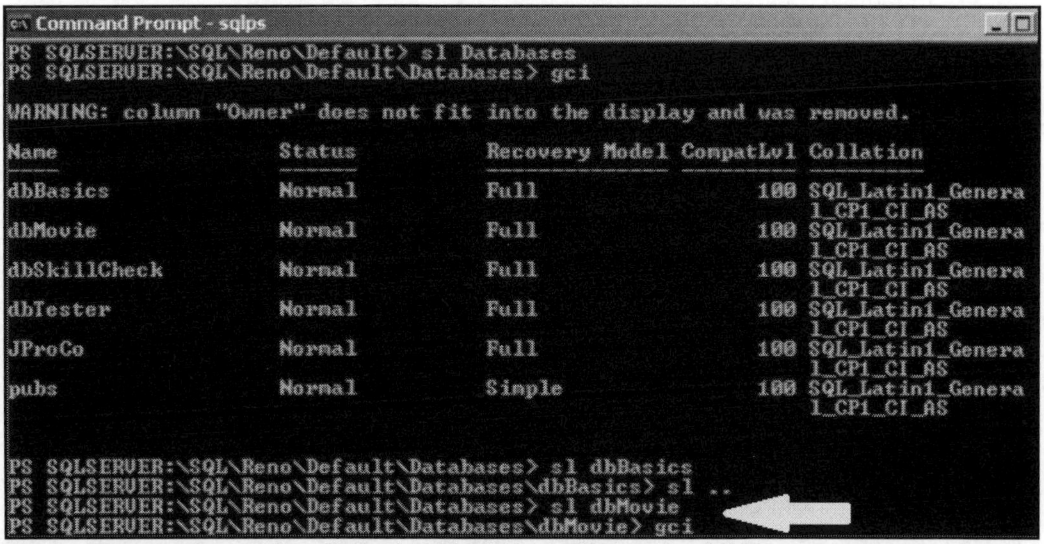

Figure 10.63 Navigate (**sl**) to dbMovie and drill in (**gci**) to see its child items.

We see the child items of dbMovie appear. We are interested in drilling into the tables (**sl Tables**).

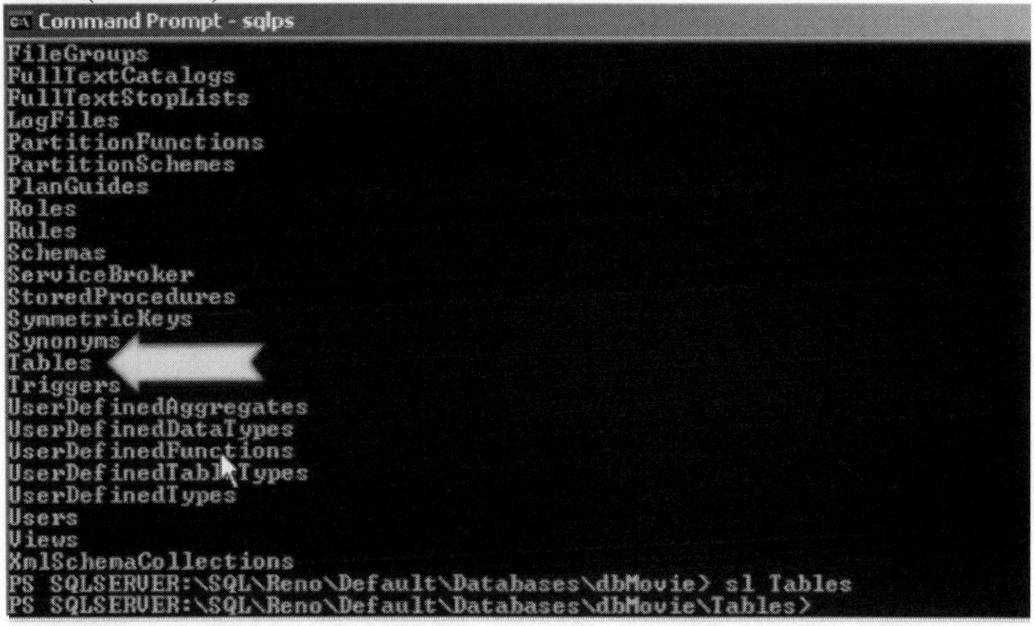

Figure 10.64 Navigate (**sl**) to the Tables.

Run **gci** to see the table(s) of dbMovie. Then navigate to the Movie table (**sl dbo.Movie**).

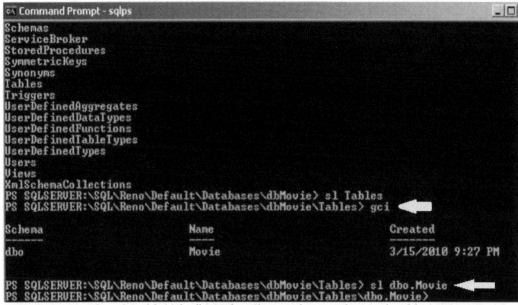

Figure 10.65 Look at the table(s) in dbMovie. Then navigate to the Movie table (**sl dbo.Movie**).

Run **gci** to see child items of the Movie table. Then navigate to the Columns (**sl Columns**) and run **gci** to see the child items of the Movie table's Columns folder.

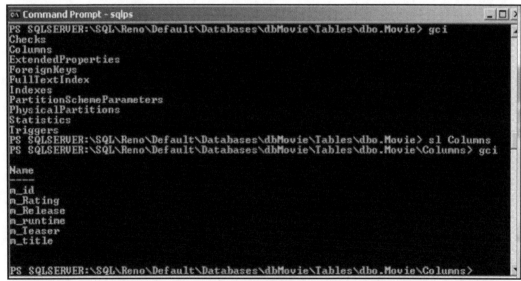

Figure 10.66 Look at the child items of the Movie table and of its Columns folder.

We see the six fields of the Movie table which we expected (and which we first saw in Figure 10.52). The Object Explorer view is in sync with the columns shown in SQL PowerShell (see Figure 10.67).

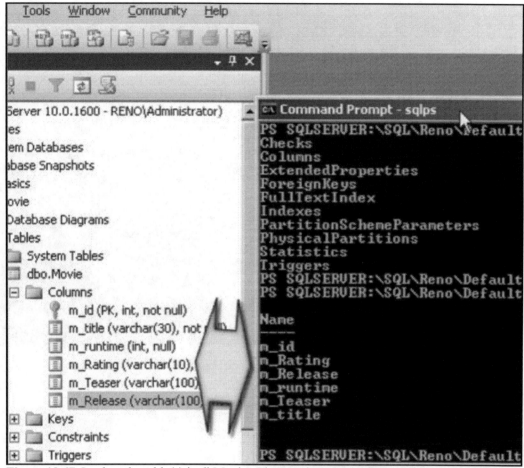

Figure 10.67 Look at the table(s) in dbMovie. Then navigate to the Movie table (**sl dbo.Movie**).

Lab 10.2: Navigating SQL PowerShell

Lab Prep: Before you can begin the lab you must run the SQLInteropChapter10.1Setup.sql script. *Please note there is no need to run this script if you already ran any script in Chapters 7-10.*

Skill Check 1: Use SQL PowerShell to find all the fields for the dbo.Activity table in the dbBasics database.

Figure 10.68 Skill Check 1.

Answer Code: The T-SQL code to this lab can be found in the downloadable files in a file named Lab10.2_NavigatingSQLPowerShell.sql.

Navigating SQL PowerShell - Points to Ponder

1. PowerShell goes beyond the cmd.exe shell that ships with windows.

2. PowerShell is Microsoft's automation framework and command-line shell built on top of the .NET Framework.

3. SQL PowerShell is a shell that carries out the commands between SQL Server Management Studio and the SQL service.

4. It's expected that all Microsoft applications running on the Windows platform will be PowerShell aware.

5. PowerShell can run most of the old shell commands like dir, cd, and cls but also has it own commands that appear as a verb-noun combination.

6. PowerShell is made up of a command line shell and its associated scripting language.

7. Windows PowerShell talks to and is integrated with the Microsoft .NET Framework.

8. Windows PowerShell 2.0 was released with Windows 7 and Windows Server 2008 R2. This was released to manufacturing in August 2009.

SQL PowerShell CmdLets

There are many SQL PowerShell cmdlets and a lot of very exciting things you can accomplish with SQL PowerShell. Our demonstration will focus on the **Invoke-Sqlcmd** cmdlet.

Suppose you want to open SQL PowerShell and have your location already set to the JProCo database.

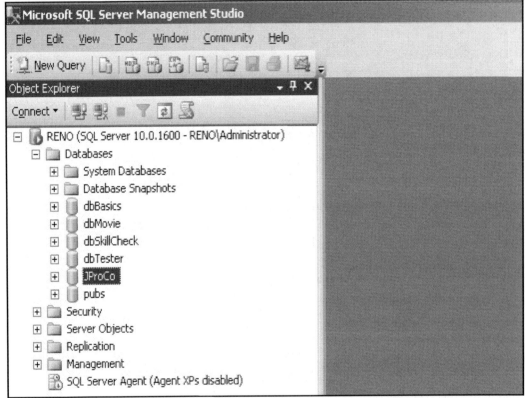

Figure 10.69 We want to be able to open SQL PowerShell directly to the JProCo context.

Rather than using the commands we saw in the last section and taking multiple hops to get to JProCo, we can simply right-click the JProCo icon in the Object Explorer and choose the Start PowerShell option (see Figure 10.70).

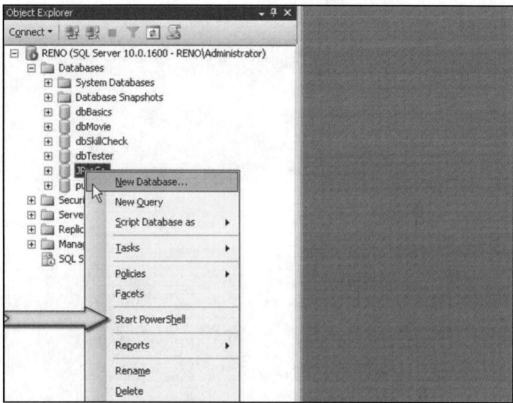

Figure 10.70 Right-click the JProCo db icon and choose **Start PowerShell**.

We've opened PowerShell and we immediately are pathed to JProCo.

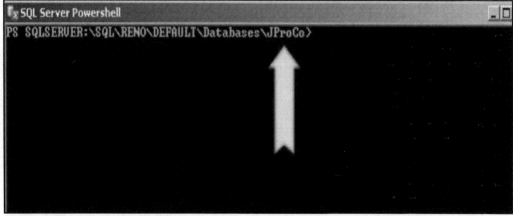

Figure 10.71 SQL PowerShell has opened directly to the JProCo context.

Let's get the child itens (**gci**) for JProCo. Results shown in Figure 10.73.

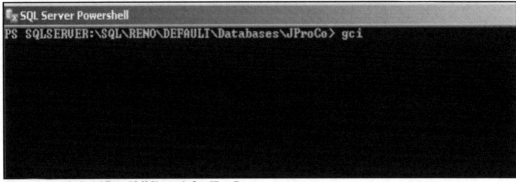

Figure 10.72 Gci (Get-ChildItems) for JProCo.

JProCo's child folders are shown here. Let's choose and drill into its Tables folder (**sl tables, gci**).

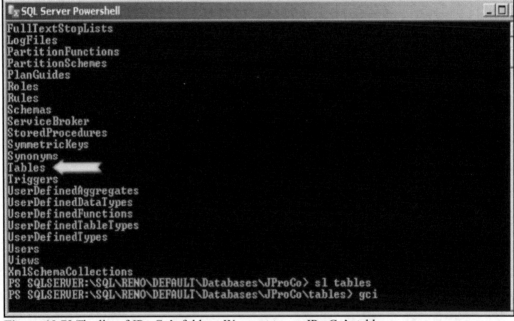

Figure 10.73 The list of JProCo's folders. We want to see JProCo's tables.

JProCo's Tables folder contains 11 tables (see Figure 10.74).

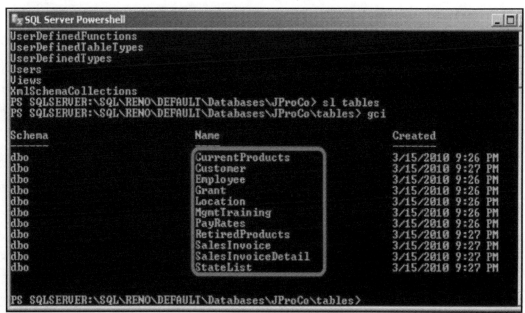

Figure 10.74 The 11 JProCo tables and some metadata is included in the Tables folder.

Let's go back up to the JProCo level and take another look at JProCo's child folders.

```
SQL Server Powershell                                          _ □
UserDefinedTableTypes
UserDefinedTypes
Users
Views
XmlSchemaCollections
PS SQLSERVER:\SQL\RENO\DEFAULT\Databases\JProCo> sl tables
PS SQLSERVER:\SQL\RENO\DEFAULT\Databases\JProCo\tables> gci

Schema                    Name                    Created

dbo                       CurrentProducts         3/15/2010 9:26 PM
dbo                       Customer                3/15/2010 9:27 PM
dbo                       Employee                3/15/2010 9:26 PM
dbo                       Grant                   3/15/2010 9:26 PM
dbo                       Location                3/15/2010 9:26 PM
dbo                       MgmtTraining            3/15/2010 9:26 PM
dbo                       PayRates                3/15/2010 9:26 PM
dbo                       RetiredProducts         3/15/2010 9:27 PM
dbo                       SalesInvoice            3/15/2010 9:27 PM
dbo                       SalesInvoiceDetail      3/15/2010 9:27 PM
dbo                       StateList               3/15/2010 9:27 PM


PS SQLSERVER:\SQL\RENO\DEFAULT\Databases\JProCo\tables> sl ..
PS SQLSERVER:\SQL\RENO\DEFAULT\Databases\JProCo> gci
```

Figure 10.75 The command **sl ..** (sl space dot dot) takes us back up to the JProCo level.

At this higher level, we no longer can see what the tables are.

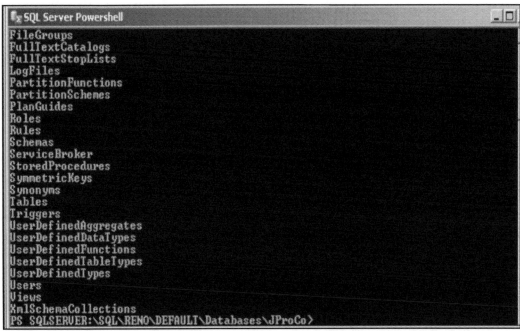

Figure 10.76 We are back at the JProCo level and can no longer see the table detail.

The command **gci Tables** will allow me to see the tables (i.e., get the child items of JProCo's Tables folder) without having to go down a level.

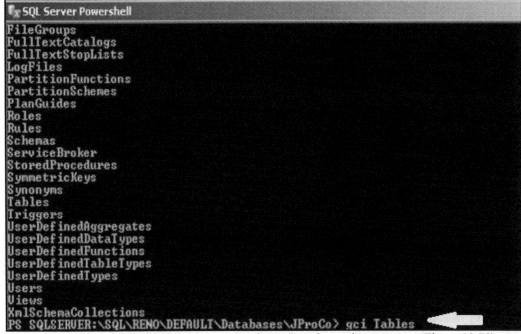

Figure 10.77 The command **gci Tables** appears here. (Results on the next page, Figure 10.78).

Without first going to that level, we can ask for the child items of the next object.

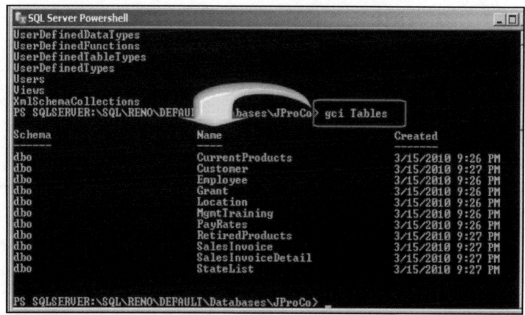

Figure 10.78 The command **gci Tables** shows us the 11 tables. Note that our context is still set to the JProCo level.

We've learned about several cmdlets already, such as **Set-Location** and **Get-ChildItem**. There are also specific cmdlets that are built into PowerShell and available if the machine you're working on has SQL Server 2008 installed.

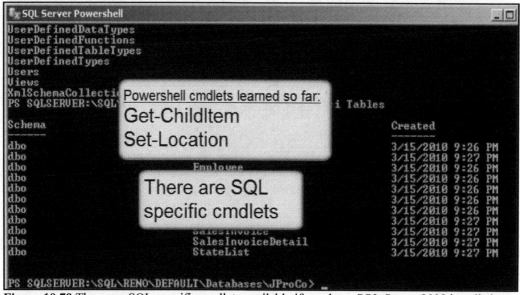

Figure 10.79 There are SQL-specific cmdlets available if you have SQL Server 2008 installed.

The SQL-specific cmdlet **Invoke-Sqlcmd** begins with this syntax. *Don't hit Enter yet – we need to add more code before we can run this statement.*

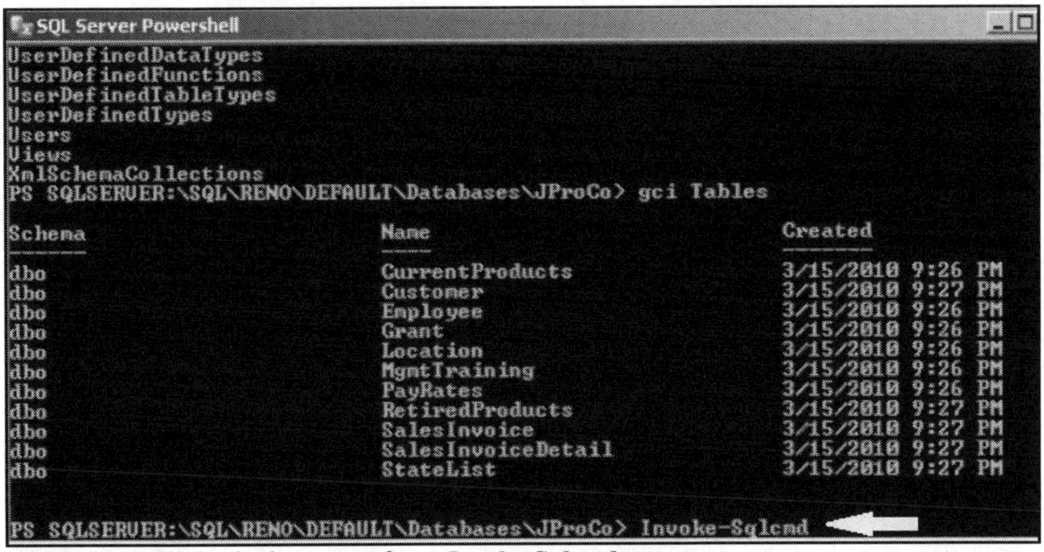

Figure 10.80 The beginning syntax for an **Invoke-Sqlcmd** statement.

We will also add the syntax to say that we want to run the query (SELECT * FROM Location). Hit Enter and see the result shown below (Figure 10.81).

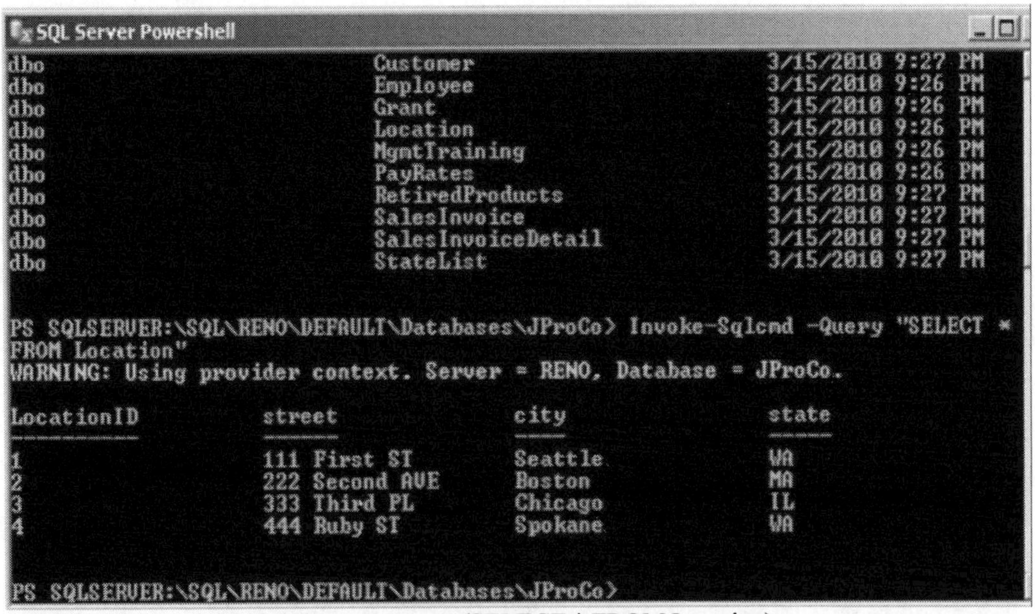

Figure 10.81 Invoke-Sqlcmd ran our query (SELECT * FROM Location).

Note that this works because we are in the JProCo db context. If we tried to run a query (SELECT * FROM Movie) from the JProCo context, it wouldn't work (see example of this in the next screenshot – Figure 10.82).

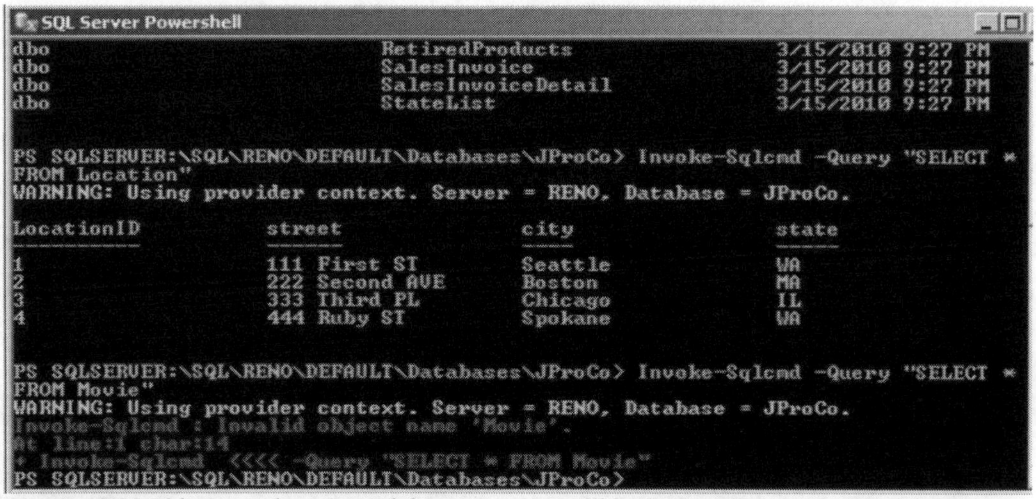

Figure 10.82 This query doesn't work because we're still in the JProCo context, not dbMovie.

Now from this point (Figure 10.82), if we wanted to, we could hit **sl ..** (sl space dot dot) to move up and then find the dbMovie context in order for this query to run properly.

However, this can be accomplished simply by adding one additional parameter in the Invoke-SQL command commandlet. The syntax is identical to the previous figure, except note the addition of **-Database "dbMovie"**.

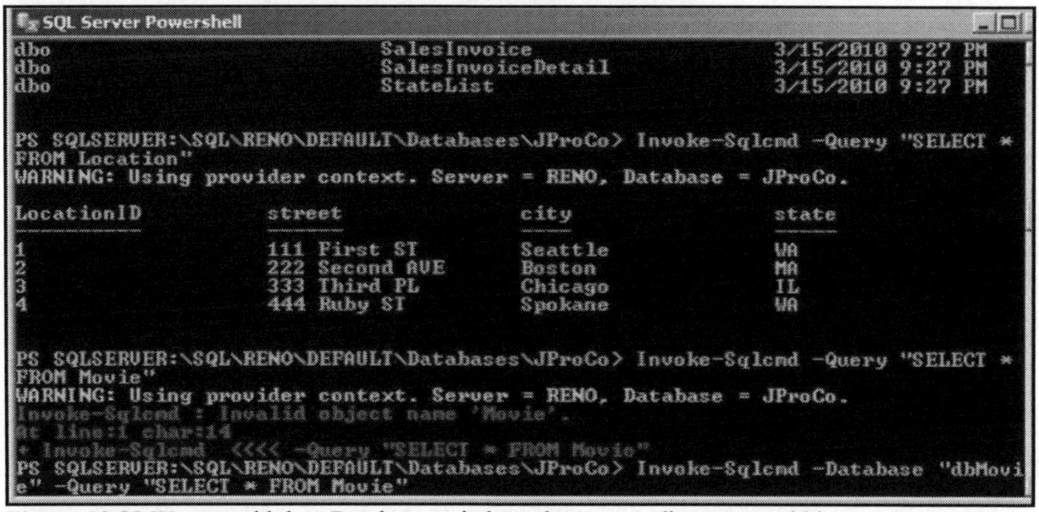

Figure 10.83 We can add the –Database switch to change our db context within our **Invoke-Sqlcmd** statement.

That worked! From within the context of the JProCo db, we were able to specify the Movie db context and successfully run a SELECT statement against the Movie table (statement in Figure 10.83, query result in Figure 10.84).

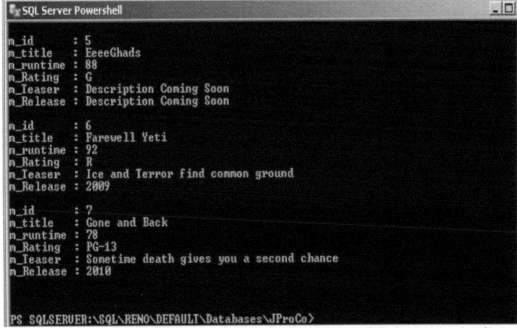

Figure 10.84 Our SELECT query against the Movie table ran successfully because our Invoke-Sqlcmd allows us to customize the db context within our query, even though our db context is still set to JProCo (as demonstrated by the last line of Figure 10.84).

Lab 10.3: SQL PowerShell CmdLets

Lab Prep: Before you can begin the lab you must run the SQLInteropChapter7.0Setup.sql script.

Skill Check 1: From your JProCo context in PowerShell, show all the records of the Grant table.

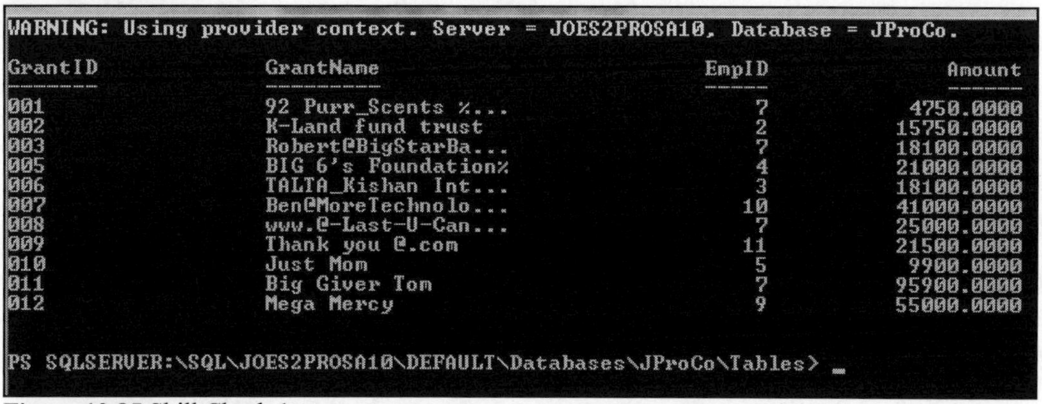

```
WARNING: Using provider context. Server = JOES2PROSA10. Database = JProCo.

GrantID          GrantName                    EmpID          Amount
-------          ---------                    -----          ------
001              92 Purr_Scents %...              7       4750.0000
002              K-Land fund trust                2      15750.0000
003              Robert@BigStarBa...              7      18100.0000
005              BIG 6's Foundation%              4      21000.0000
006              TALTA_Kishan Int...              3      18100.0000
007              Ben@MoreTechnolo...             10      41000.0000
008              www.@-Last-U-Can...              7      25000.0000
009              Thank you @.com                 11      21500.0000
010              Just Mom                         5       9900.0000
011              Big Giver Tom                    7      95900.0000
012              Mega Mercy                       9      55000.0000

PS SQLSERVER:\SQL\JOES2PROSA10\DEFAULT\Databases\JProCo\Tables> _
```

Figure 10.85 Skill Check 1.

Skill Check 2: While in the context of the dbBasics database (and no deeper than that) show all the table names of dbBasics.

```
Schema          Name                  Created
------          ----                  -------
dbo             Activity              1/22/2011 9:32 PM
dbo             Customer              1/22/2011 9:32 PM
dbo             Employee              1/22/2011 9:32 PM
dbo             FlatFileActivity      1/22/2011 9:32 PM
dbo             Location              1/22/2011 9:32 PM
dbo             Members               1/22/2011 9:32 PM
dbo             Military              1/22/2011 9:32 PM
dbo             PurchaseActivity      1/22/2011 9:32 PM
dbo             Shopping List         1/22/2011 9:32 PM
dbo             ShoppingList          1/22/2011 9:32 PM

PS SQLSERVER:\SQL\JOES2PROSA10\DEFAULT\Databases\dbBasics>
```

Figure 10.86 Skill Check 2.

Answer Code: The T-SQL code to this lab can be found in the downloadable files in a file named Lab10.3_SQLPowerShellCmdLets.sql.

SQL PowerShell CmdLets - Points to Ponder

1. Cmdlets are.NET classes that perform a particular operation.

2. Installing SQL in your system also install new PowerShell Cmdlets.

3. The most used SQL PowerShell CmdLet is Invoke-Sqlcmd cmdlet.

4. If a command is an executable file, PowerShell launches it in a separate process; if it is a cmdlet, it is executed in the PowerShell process.

SQL PowerShell – Bonus Troubleshooting Tip

SQL PowerShell is part of SQL Server 2008 and should appear once you've completed your SQL Server 2008 installation.

However, I have seen occasional instances where SQL PowerShell wasn't showing in the Command Window. (All other aspects of SQL Server were working well, but SQL PowerShell, BCP, and SQLCMD weren't showing.)

Since I've successfully remedied these cases by adding a new path to the program file (SQLPS.exe), I include the steps here to aid others who may encounter this situation. This is similar to the process shown in Chapter 8 (Figures 8.16 through 8.22) for setting up the C# Compiler (CSC.exe).

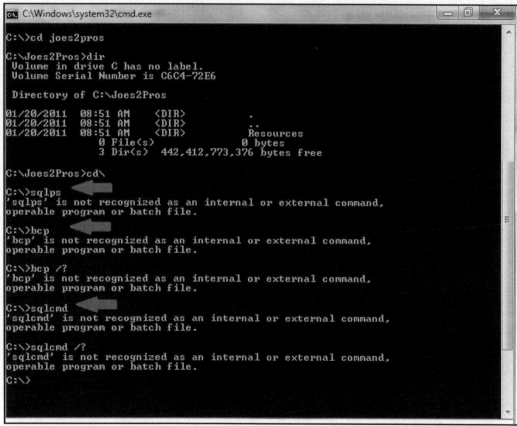

Figure 10.87 These messages indicate SQL PowerShell, BCP, and SQL CMD are not currently available to the Command Prompt.

From your Start menu, drop "SQLPS.exe" into the search box and hit enter.

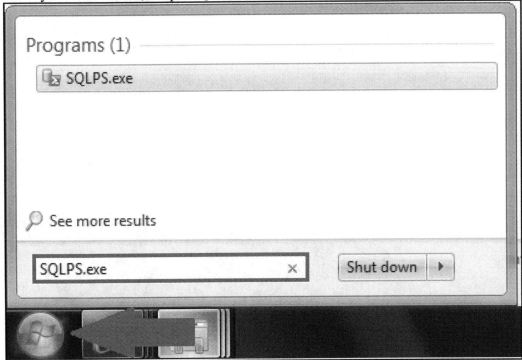

Figure 10.88 Search for the location of SQLPS.exe on your computer.

This search found four references to SQLPS.exe on my computer. Right click the one with "Program Files" in the file path.

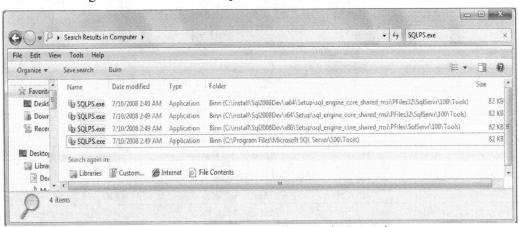

Figure 10.89 Right-click the result for the Program File to get its Properties.

Highlight and copy the filepath shown in "Location." My path is
C:\Program Files\Microsoft SQL Server\100\Tools\Binn (see Figure 10.90).

Keep track of this filepath (you will need it later). We first need to navigate to the
System Variables dialog (Figure 10.94) before we can paste it in.

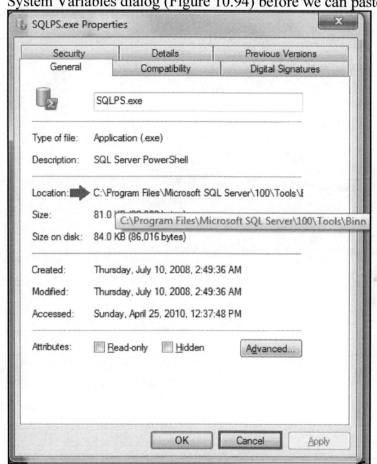

Figure 10.90 Locate and copy the path of the SQLPS.exe file.

Start > right-click Computer > Properties > click Advanced System Settings

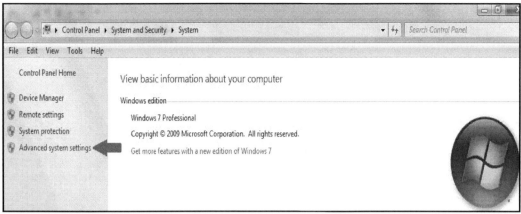

Figure 10.91 Start > right-click Computer > Properties > click Advanced System Settings.

Click Environment Variables

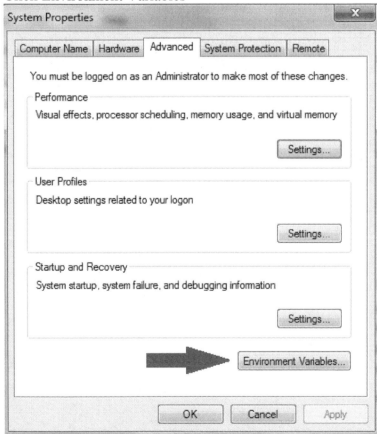

Figure 10.92 Click Environment Variables.

In "Sytem Variables", click New (Figure 10.93).

Variable name: Path
Variable value: C:\Program Files\Microsoft SQL Server\100\Tools\Binn

Click OK to close the dialog. Click OK again.

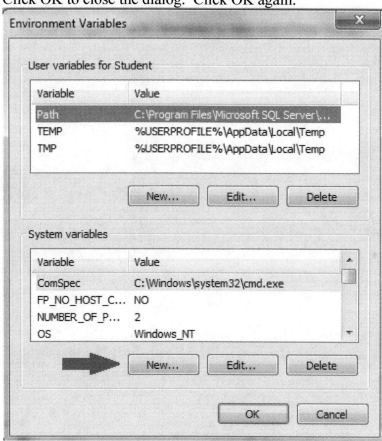

Figure 10.93 In "Sytem Variables", click New.

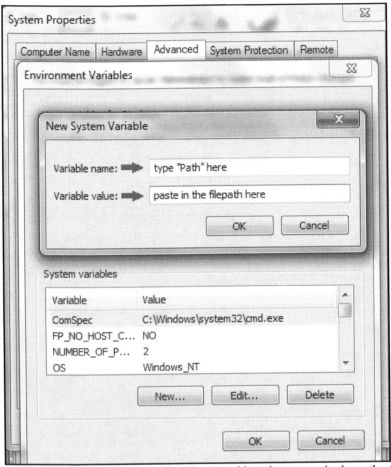

Figure 10.94 *Variable name:* "Path", *Variable value:* paste in the path of your SQLPS.exe file.

Open a new Command Prompt Window. The command SQLPS will now launch SQL Server PowerShell (see Figure 10.95).

```
C:\Windows\system32\cmd.exe - sqlps

Microsoft Windows [Version 6.1.7600]
Copyright (c) 2009 Microsoft Corporation.  All rights reserved.

C:\>sqlps
Microsoft SQL Server PowerShell
Version 10.0.1600.22
Microsoft Corp. All rights reserved.

PS SQLSERVER:\>
```

Figure 10.95 Type this command (sqlps) and hit Enter to launch SQL PowerShell.

Chapter Glossary

Cmdlet: "commandlet", .NET classes that perform a particular operation.
Command-line utility: definition.
Invoke-Sqlcmd: definition.
Kernel: definition.
PowerShell: definition.
SQL PowerShell: definition.

Chapter Ten - Review Quiz

1.) You have a table named Location. Using the SQL Server Windows PowerShell provider, you need to find all the columns in the table. Which cmdlet should you use?

O a.   Get-Item
O b.   Get-Location
O c.   Get-ChildItem
O d.   Get-ItemProperty
O e.   Invoke-sqlcmd

2.) You want to query all the records from the Employee table of JProCo. Which cmdlet should you use?

O a.   Get-Item
O b.   Get-Location
O c.   Get-ChildItem
O d.   Get-ItemProperty
O e.   Invoke-sqlcmd

3.) You want to see a list of all databases on your system listed in the sys.database catalog view. Which cmdlet should you use?

O a.   Get-Item
O b.   Get-Location
O c.   Get-ChildItem
O d.   Get-ItemProperty
O e.   Invoke-sqlcmd

4.) You SQL powershell is open to the following location.

`PS SQLSERVER:\SQL\JOES2PROSA10\DEFAULT\Databases\JProCo>`

You want to see a list of all the tables in JProCo. What command do you use?

O a.   Get-childitem
O b.   Get-childitem tables
O c.   Set-Location
O d.   Set-Location tables

Answer Key

1.) c   2.) e   3.) e   4.) b

Bug Catcher Game

To play the Bug Catcher game run the SQLInteropBugCatcherCh10.pps from the BugCatcher folder of the companion files. You can obtain these files from www.Joes2Pros.com or by ordering the Companion CD.

[THIS PAGE INTENTIONALLY LEFT BLANK.]

[THIS PAGE INTENTIONALLY LEFT BLANK.]

[THIS PAGE INTENTIONALLY LEFT BLANK.]

[THIS PAGE INTENTIONALLY LEFT BLANK.]

[THIS PAGE INTENTIONALLY LEFT BLANK.]

[THIS PAGE INTENTIONALLY LEFT BLANK.]

[THIS PAGE INTENTIONALLY LEFT BLANK.]

[THIS PAGE INTENTIONALLY LEFT BLANK.]

[THIS PAGE INTENTIONALLY LEFT BLANK.]

[THIS PAGE INTENTIONALLY LEFT BLANK.]

[THIS PAGE INTENTIONALLY LEFT BLANK.]

[THIS PAGE INTENTIONALLY LEFT BLANK.]

[THIS PAGE INTENTIONALLY LEFT BLANK.]

[THIS PAGE INTENTIONALLY LEFT BLANK.]

Index

K

Kernel, 342, 359, 360, 399
Keyword, 13

M

Managed code, 233, 277, 278, 279, 292, 296, 313, 314, 320, 324, 325, 326, 328, 334, 338
Metadata, 15, 16, 18, 19, 20, 24, 31, 48, 49, 100, 124, 145, 185, 348, 349, 369, 385
modify( ), 180, 188, 189, 190, 191, 195, 204, 205, 206
Modular programming, 277, 278
Monolithic programming, 293, 339

N

Nameless field, 80, 87, 88, 89, 90, 91, 92
Namespace, 263, 281, 283, 285, 286, 295, 318, 319, 325
next( ), 174
nodes( ), 180, 195, 211, 212, 214, 217, 230, 231

O

OpenXML Flags, 144
OpenXML function, 104, 105, 109, 113, 114, 115, 116, 117, 120, 123, 124, 125, 126, 129, 130, 135, 136, 137, 139, 141, 142, 143, 144, 145, 146, 174
Out of process assemblies, 273, 292, 293, 339

P

Path mode, 67, 68, 74, 75, 79, 91
Permission call stack, 327
PERMISSION_SET, 317, 328, 335, 338, 339
PowerShell, 1, 10, 233, 342, 355, 357, 360, 361, 362, 365, 372, 378, 380, 381, 382, 383, 387, 391, 392, 393, 398, 399, 400

Q

query( ), 159, 161, 173, 174, 180, 181, 182, 183, 184, 185, 187, 189, 195, 204, 205, 206, 213, 231

R

Raw mode, 34, 37, 39, 48

S

SAFE, 317, 334, 338, 339, 340
script, 8, 10, 13, 64, 77, 98, 111, 135, 142, 157, 171, 193, 203, 219, 229, 312, 322, 337, 358, 380
Shredding XML, 95, 96, 97, 128
Sorting Data, 64, 98, 135, 157, 193, 219, 253, 312, 358
Source code, 235, 236, 237, 238, 241, 248, 249, 250, 251, 252, 262, 264, 294
sp_configure, 324, 339
sp_XML_PrepareDocument, 103, 107, 108, 113, 124, 125, 127, 145
sp_XML_RemoveDocument, 119, 123, 124, 127, 145
SQL, 416
SQL CLR, 233, 296, 314, 320, 336
SQL PowerShell, 382, 393
static void Main( ), 236, 239, 259, 293, 303, 339
Stream, 20, 32, 33, 36, 43, 45, 46, 47, 48, 49, 50, 51, 52, 53, 54, 55, 56, 58, 59, 60, 63, 65, 66, 67, 68, 70, 71, 72, 74, 76, 77, 78, 79, 80, 83, 87, 88, 89, 90, 91, 92, 93, 94, 95, 99, 101, 127, 128, 148, 173, 175, 176, 177, 180, 186, 188, 208, 216, 228

ROOT, Root element, Rowpattern

ROOT, 35, 36, 40, 47, 48, 59, 60, 70, 79, 92, 93, 94
Root element, 27, 35, 40, 45, 46, 48, 49, 53, 55, 59, 60, 61, 68, 70, 79, 82, 85, 86, 101, 120, 160
Rowpattern, 105, 114, 124, 145

T

Text editor, 15, 236, 255, 256
text( ), 165, 166, 168, 172, 174, 181, 182, 185, 189, 190
Top level element, 27, 45, 46, 54, 57, 63, 68, 71, 75, 77, 78, 79, 81, 85, 86, 88, 89, 169
Trustworthy status, 332, 333
T-SQL, 46, 78, 89, 112, 122, 143, 157, 172, 195, 203, 219, 229, 253, 275, 291, 312, 323, 337, 358, 380, 391

U

Unmanaged code, 292, 313, 338

V

value( ), 180, 185, 195, 204, 205, 206, 211, 213, 214, 215, 230, 231

Visual Studio, 236, 255, 256, 257, 259, 260, 265, 266, 271, 272, 276, 278, 279, 293, 294, 297, 298, 300, 301, 305, 308, 314, 315, 320, 329, 330, 339

W

Well-formed XML, 35, 36, 40, 48, 49, 59, 61, 81, 82, 93, 95, 97, 149, 150, 151, 152, 156, 158, 212, 225

WITH clause, 106, 109, 113, 117, 132, 136, 145

X

XML, 1, 9, 10, 14, 15, 16, 17, 19, 20, 21, 24, 25, 26, 27, 28, 29, 30, 31, 32, 33, 34, 35, 36, 37, 39, 40, 43, 45, 46, 47, 48, 49, 50, 51, 52, 53, 54, 55, 56, 58, 59, 60, 62, 63, 64, 65, 66, 67, 68, 69, 70, 71, 72, 73, 74, 77, 78, 79, 80, 81, 83, 84, 85, 87, 88, 89, 90, 91, 92, 93, 94, 95, 96, 97, 98, 99, 100, 101, 102, 103, 104, 105, 106, 107, 108, 109, 111, 112, 113, 114, 115, 116, 117, 119, 120, 121, 122, 123, 124, 125, 126, 127, 128, 129, 130, 133, 136, 137, 138, 140, 141, 145, 148, 149, 150, 151, 152, 153, 154, 155, 156, 157, 158, 159, 160, 161, 162, 163, 164, 165, 166, 167, 168, 169, 170, 171, 172, 173, 174, 175, 176, 177, 179, 180, 181, 182, 183, 184, 185, 186, 187, 188, 190, 193, 195, 196, 197, 200, 204, 205, 206, 207, 208, 209, 210, 211, 212, 213, 215, 216, 217, 218, 219, 220, 221, 223, 224, 225, 226, 227, 228, 229, 230, 231, 340, 342

XML data type, 14, 125, 148, 149, 151, 152, 154, 158, 159, 173, 174, 176, 179, 180, 181, 188, 195, 204, 205, 206, 207, 208, 210, 231

XML fragment, 36, 48, 49, 149, 152, 158, 160, 164, 165, 166, 167, 172, 180, 181, 183, 184, 188, 200, 223, 224, 225

XQuery, 148, 159, 161, 165, 171, 172, 173, 174, 179, 180, 181, 182, 185, 187, 190, 191, 195, 196, 204, 208, 213, 214, 220, 223, 224, 225, 227, 228, 232, 239

XSINIL, 43, 44, 50

Made in the USA
Charleston, SC
06 July 2011